Women, Gender and Religious Cultures in Britain, 1800–1940

This volume is the first comprehensive overview of women, gender and religious change in modern Britain spanning from the evangelical revival of the early 1800s to interwar debates over women's roles and ministry.

This collection of pieces by key scholars combines cross-disciplinary insights from history, gender studies, theology, literature, religious studies, sexuality and postcolonial studies. The book takes a thematic approach, providing students and scholars with a clear, comprehensive and comparative examination of ten significant areas of cultural activity that both shaped, and were shaped by, women's religious beliefs and practices: family life, literary and theological discourses, philanthropic networks, sisterhoods and deaconess institutions, revivals and preaching ministry, missionary organisations, national and transnational political reform networks, sexual ideas and practices, feminist communities, and alternative spiritual traditions. Chapters survey the existing scholarship and identify new research trajectories. They are framed by an introduction and afterword that reflect on the implications of the resurging interest in religion and spirituality for gender and women's history. Together, the volume challenges widely-held truisms about the increasingly private and domesticated nature of faith, the feminisation of religion and the relationship between secularisation and modern life.

Including case studies, further reading lists and with a British rather than Anglo-centric approach, this is an ideal book for anyone interested in women's religious experiences across the nineteenth and twentieth centuries.

Sue Morgan is Reader in Women's and Gender History at the University of Chichester. Her publications include *Women, Religion and Feminism in Britain, 1750–1900* (2002) and *The Feminist History Reader* (2006).

Jacqueline deVries is Associate Professor of History and Women's Studies at Augsburg College in Minneapolis. She has published a number of essays on the intersections among religion, gender, feminism and war, and is co-author, with Cheri Register, of *Living Faith* (2007).

8·2010

Women, Gender and Religious Cultures in Britain, 1800–1940

Edited by
Sue Morgan and Jacqueline deVries

Routledge
Taylor & Francis Group

LONDON AND NEW YORK

First edition published 2010 by Routledge
2 Park Square, Milton Park, Abingdon, Oxon OX14 4RN

Simultaneously published in the USA and Canada by Routledge
270 Madison Ave, New York, NY 10016

Routledge is an imprint of the Taylor & Francis Group, an informa business

© 2010 Sue Morgan and Jacqueline deVries for selection and editorial
matter; individual chapters, the contributors

Typeset in Galliard by Taylor and Francis Books
Printed and bound in Great Britain by
CPI Antony Rowe, Chippenham, Wiltshire

British Library Cataloguing in Publication Data
A catalog record for this book is available from the British Library

Library of Congress Cataloging in Publication Data
Women, gender, and religious cultures in Britain, 1800-1940 / edited by
Sue Morgan and Jacqueline deVries. – 1st ed.
    p. cm.
  Includes bibliographical references and index.
  1. Women in Christianity–Great Britain–History–19th century. 2. Great
Britain–Church history–19th century. 3. Women in Christianity–Great
Britain–History–20th century. 4. Great Britain–Church history–20th
century. I. Morgan, Sue, 1957- II. Vries, Jacqueline de.
  BR759.W635 2010
  274.1′081082–dc22
                 2009045675

ISBN 10: 0-415-23115-9 (hbk)
ISBN 10: 0-415-23213-9 (pbk)
ISBN 10: 0-203-85185-4 (ebk)

ISBN 13: 978-0-415-23115-2 (hbk)
ISBN 13: 978-0-415-23213-5 (pbk)
ISBN 13: 978-0-203-85185-2 (ebk)

Contents

Notes on contributors

Jacqueline deVries (MA, PhD University of Illinois-Urbana Champaign) is Associate Professor of History and Women's Studies at Augsburg College in Minneapolis where she teaches modern European and comparative women's history. Her interest in the historical relationship between faith and feminism emerged while growing up in the conservative (Dutch) Christian Reformed Church during the second-wave feminist movement of the 1970s and 1980s. She first explored the historical relationships between religious ideas and feminist activism in her dissertation, and has since published a number of articles on the topic, including 'Transforming the Pulpit: Preaching and Prophecy in the British Women's Suffrage Movement', in Beverly Kienzle and Pamela Walker (eds) *Women Preachers and Prophets through Two Millennia of Christianity* (University of California Press, 1998); 'Rediscovering Christianity after the Postmodern Turn' in *Feminist Studies* (2006); 'Challenging Traditions: Denominational Feminism in Britain, 1910–20' in Karen Offen (ed.) *Globalizing Feminisms, 1789–1945* (Routledge, 2009), and a popular history *Living Faith*, co-authored with Cheri Register, which chronicles the diverse stories of Presbyterians in one influential congregation in the American Midwest (2007).

Joy Dixon is an associate professor of history at the University of British Columbia in Vancouver, Canada. Her first book, *Divine Feminine: Theosophy and Feminism in England* (Johns Hopkins University Press, 2001), explored the relationships between feminism and esoteric religions in the late nineteenth and early twentieth centuries. Her current project, tentatively titled *Sexual Heresies: Religion, Science, and Sexuality in Britain, 1870–1930*, explores the impact of the new sciences of sexuality and new understandings of sexual identity on religion and religious experience, from liberal modernism to the new orthodoxies of conservative Catholicism and evangelicalism. She is also writing a textbook – *Sexuality in Modern Europe* – which is an introduction to the history of sexuality in Europe from the mid-eighteenth to the late twentieth centuries. It traces the rise (and fall) of 'sexual identity' as both a historical phenomenon and a theoretical construct and will be published by the University of Toronto Press.

Carmen M. Mangion (MA, PhD London) is Honorary Research Fellow at Birkbeck College, University of London. Her research interests centre on the social and cultural history of nineteenth-century Britain, concentrating on the intersections of gender, religion and medical care. She has published several journal articles, chapters and book reviews on women, religion and medical care in nineteenth-century England and Wales and her book *Contested Identities: Catholic Women Religious in Nineteenth-century England and Wales* was published by Manchester University Press in 2008.

Julie Melnyk received her M.Phil. from Oxford University (English Literature 1789–1880), and her PhD in English from the University of Virginia. Now Associate Director of the Honors College and member of the English Department at the University of Missouri, she continues her research into nineteenth-century women's religious writing. In addition to producing numerous articles and scholarly presentations on this topic, she has edited two collections of original scholarly essays: *Women's Theology in 19th-Century Britain: Transfiguring the Faith of Their Fathers* (Garland, 1998) and, with Nanora Sweet, *Felicia Hemans: Reimagining Poetry in the 19th Century* (Palgrave, 2001). Her most recent book, *Victorian Religion: Faith and Life in Britain*, was published by Praeger in 2008.

Clare Midgley is Research Professor in History at Sheffield Hallam University, UK. Her contributions to feminist history and to the new imperial history include the monographs *Women Against Slavery* (Routledge, 1995), *Feminism and Empire* (Routledge, 2007) and the edited collection *Gender and Imperialism* (Manchester University Press, 1998). She has worked as co-editor of the journal *Gender and History* and been active in the Women's History Network in Britain and in collaborations with the Women's Library in London. She is currently working on a research project exploring the transoceanic network of reformers comprising Unitarians in Britain and America and members of the Brahmo Samaj, a Bengali religious and social reform movement. Covering the period between the 1820s and the 1920s, this project seeks to develop more nuanced understandings of cross-cultural interchanges on the 'woman question' in the age of empire.

Sue Morgan (MA, PhD Bristol) is Reader in Women's and Gender History at the University of Chichester where she teaches modern cultural history, specialising in religion and gender. Her interest in the histories of religion, gender and sexuality and the theoretical relations between them began when she was an undergraduate in the late 1980s. Since then she has published widely in the field, beginning with a study of the late-Victorian moral reformer Ellice Hopkins and the social purity movement. Her most recent publications include the edited collection *Women, Religion and Feminism in Britain, 1750–1900* (Palgrave Macmillan, 2002), *The Feminist History Reader* (Routledge, 2006), *Manifestos for History* (Routledge, 2007), co-edited with Keith Jenkins and Alun Munslow, and 'Theorising Feminist History: A Thirty Year Retrospective', *Women's History Review* Vol.18, No.3 (2009), pp.381–406. She is currently working on a book entitled *The Language of Love: Religion, Sex and Gender in Britain, 1880–1940*.

Susan Mumm has published in the areas of women's religious communities, the Victorian Church of England, and nineteenth-century purity movements. She is currently working on a history of the YWCA in the Commonwealth. She is Pro-Vice Chancellor of the College of Humanities and Social Sciences, Massey University, New Zealand.

Rhonda A. Semple is Assistant Professor in Modern British History at Saint Francis Xavier University in Nova Scotia, Canada. Originally a historian of secular empire, Dr Semple developed an interest in British missions while researching empire literature produced in and written about British India. Understanding the complex interplay between individual belief and institutional power in the British Empire continues to animate her research. After completing her PhD studies under Professor Andrew Porter at King's College London, she published *Missionary Women: Gender, Professionalism and the Victorian Idea of Christian Missions* (Boydell & Brewer, 2003) and has subsequently expanded her research to include the women in British Methodist mission work. Most recently she has focussed on the reception and adaption of belief cross-culturally, and the implications – both religious and secular – of institutional mission work for Indian communities. This work is funded by an SSHRC grant from the Government of Canada.

Pamela J. Walker is Professor of History at Carleton University in Ottawa, Canada. She is the author of *Pulling the Devil's Kingdom Down: The Salvation Army in Victorian Britain* (2001). Her current research considers the effect of transatlantic and imperial missionary efforts on Protestant and Jewish Britons. She is the director of Carleton's Centre for Initiatives in Education.

Sarah C. Williams (MA, D.Phil Oxon) was appointed to the position of Associate Professor of Church History at Regent College, Vancouver, Canada in 2005. A specialist in the field of nineteenth- and twentieth-century popular religion, she has written widely in this area, most notably *Religious Belief and Popular Culture* (Oxford University Press, 1999). Dr Williams' research interests lie in the relationship between religion and culture; political structures, ecclesial communities and theological ideas. She has sought to pioneer new approaches to historical methodology that break down the barriers between disciplines and work towards an integrated approach to modern religiosity. Her teaching reflects these interests. Dr Williams teaches history in the context of a graduate school of Christian theology. Before taking up this appointment she taught British and European political and cultural history from 1685 to the present day in the History Faculty at Oxford University.

Introduction

Sue Morgan and Jacqueline deVries

In what was probably his most well-known painting, 'Hope', first exhibited in 1886, the artist George Frederick Watts portrayed a blindfolded, barefoot girl sat crouched over the world clutching a broken lyre. That 'Hope' was represented by a female form was not surprising. Watts fervently believed, as did most of his contemporaries, that women were the spiritual salvation of an increasingly hostile and faithless world. The cultural familiarity of this highly romanticised image, with its gendered representation of a forlorn yet resolute belief in a greater metaphysical purpose, was part of the painting's appeal. Late-Victorian audiences and critics loved it. But this popular trope equating women with spiritual and redemptive powers exerted conflicting influences upon their lives and opportunities; it is to these debates that we now turn.

Historicising religion and gender

This volume examines the complex interplay between historical narratives of religion, gender and cultural change in Britain from the evangelical revival of the early nineteenth century to the interwar debates over women's ordination. It enters these debates at a decisive intellectual moment. The history of religion in Britain is currently undergoing something of a reformation, with scholarship on women and gender doing much to revivify the field. At a recent women's history conference at St Hilda's College, Oxford in 2009, for example, an entire strand of papers was devoted to 'Religion, Belief and Selfhood', something that would have been unimaginable in British feminist history circles thirty years ago. Early assessments of Christianity as responsible for a deceptively flattering, patriarchal construction of femininity that combined 'spiritual power with social impotence'[1] have given way to something of a 'religious turn' in gender history. Through denominational and institutional histories, biographical studies and literary representations, historians have begun to think in more nuanced and judicious ways about the influence of religion in the formation of women's private selves and public roles.[2]

Many reasons could be adduced for the resurgence of interest in religion and spirituality in the early twenty-first century. Unstable global religious politics, popular challenges to belief in God (think Richard Dawkins), and environmental concerns over the fall-out of the secular creeds of technology and consumerism – these are but a few of the cultural phenomena whose juxtaposition has proved volatile. Even history itself, it has been suggested, can function as a metaphysical fix, a 'prosthetic faith' for a humanity 'adrift from the agenda of divine salvation'.[3] Gender history may also have contributed to the interpretive shift towards religion. As a discipline, gender history has always been at the cutting edge of new theoretical innovations. By the late 1980s British women's history was diversifying from its socialist feminist origins into broader cultural and linguistic analyses of the multiple historical determinants at work in forging individual identities and relationships of power. In her classic 1986 article on gender as a useful category of historical analysis, Joan Scott identified western Christianity as a key site in the production of hegemonic constructions of gender.[4] The influence of cultural history, which attempts to comprehend the attitudes and values articulated by women and men as they sought to make sense of themselves and their conditions of existence, has also fuelled the renewed drive to historicise religious beliefs.[5]

Despite the 'religious turn' in gender and cultural history, historians of religion have by contrast produced little sustained research on women and gender. Church historian John Kent commented over twenty years ago that, as the 'most serious critical opposition' to modern Christian symbolism and theology, feminism would provide a re-animating perspective for the field.[6] But religious historians' unwillingness to discard class as a dominant analytical category has stultified the development of new approaches and debates. Callum Brown's *The Death of Christian Britain* (2001) stands alone for its thoroughgoing treatment of gender not merely as additional historical content but as part of a new explanatory framework of 'discursive Christianity'. Brown's work is not unproblematic, however. In his contention that 'women, rather than cities or social class, emerge as the principal source of explanation for patterns of religiosity',[7] he implies a lack of reciprocity between gender and class that contrasts directly with gender historians' insistence on the relational and mutually constitutive nature of all such categories. But in its recognition of religion as a qualitative rather than purely quantitative historical phenomenon, as an influential cultural discourse capable of shaping individual identities rather than merely church attendance, *The Death of Christian Britain* is an important methodological reference point in the social and cultural history of religion.

The assumption that women, to paraphrase Sarah Williams, were both the inheritors and makers of their own religious cultures underpins the content, theoretical approaches and structure of this volume.[8] Religious discourses were never passively received within religious institutions or in the wider culture; instead, they were constantly reinterpreted by women and invested with new meanings. As editors we began with a series of questions developed from our own engagements with gender history, cultural history and the history of religion: How did Britain's heterogeneous religious cultures shape women's beliefs and practices? In what ways did women create and develop their own diverse religious cultures? To what extent were women's faith and beliefs shaped by their gender, class, national identity, sexuality and denominational affiliation? And what were women's contributions to the making of modern British cultures of belief? In order to provide answers to these questions we eschewed a denominational or chronological approach in favour of a thematic and comparative one. The result is ten chapters that explore the diverse cultures in which women encountered, absorbed, influenced and organised religious faith, belief and practice: these include family life, literary and theological discourses, philanthropic networks, sisterhoods and deaconess institutions, revivals and preaching ministry, missionary organisations, national and transnational political reform networks, sexual ideas and practices, feminist communities, and alternative spiritual traditions.

Each author brought to the volume a common interest in gender studies combined with important cross-disciplinary insights from history, literature, sexuality, postcolonial studies, theology and religious studies. As editors we set contributors a demanding agenda: to survey the field, yet also make use of relevant individual and/or event-based case-studies for greater historical specificity; to be sensitive to a diversity of religious and denominational perspectives; to identify important intersections among gender, sexuality, class and region as well as confessional and religious loyalties; to emphasise a British rather than English perspective and delineate transnational border crossings where applicable. Authors were free to define 'religion' in whatever way they wished. Although references are made throughout to Jewish women and alternative spiritual traditions such as Theosophy and spiritualism, 'religion' is primarily, although not exclusively, interchangeable in this volume with Christianity, which was the dominant indigenous tradition of the period. The chapters do, however, evidence the fluidity of meanings contained within the term 'religion', and readers will find the term broken down into its constituent parts and functions. Our volume's contributors define religion variously as an intellectual belief system, a source of personal inspiration and private sustenance, an interior form of mystical experience, an influential cultural discourse, a platform for political action, and an institutional system of church and chapel structures. Finally, because studies of the historical convergence of religion and gender are still far from established, the collection aims not only to illustrate the emergent scholarship in these discrete areas, but also to identify gaps in the historiography and propose future research trajectories.

Heterogeneous cultures: chapter summaries

In her analysis of the powerful nineteenth-century 'thematic triumvirate' of religion, gender and family life, Sarah Williams argues that, as yet, historians have failed to move beyond a hegemonic preoccupation with evangelicalism and its emphasis on a highly feminised, domesticated piety. By adhering to the static tableau of middle-class family religion first articulated by Leonore Davidoff and Catherine Hall over twenty years ago, she argues, historians have replicated the same Victorian homilies on female moral superiority that demand our critical scrutiny, creating a picture that elides the social and spiritual diversity of popular family religion. Working-class religiosity, for example, often operated on the peripheries of Christian culture. Women and men combined church-based practices with folk myths and shared rituals that were often attributed a hallowed status. The syncretism of popular religious culture meant that family bibles often lay alongside lucky charms and protective amulets. To rethink modern domestic spirituality, Williams suggests alternative methodological approaches such as oral history and an exploration of material culture. Only in this way, she believes, will we fully appreciate the local, denominational and class-specific forms that religion took.

Julie Melnyk's chapter on women's writing also proposes a significant reconceptualisation, this time of mainstream definitions of theology. Excluded from the conventional theological mediums of the sermon and the academic treatise, women formulated their ideas on divine revelation, sin, the Church and the Holy Trinity through alternative genres such as novels, hymnody, poetry and magazine articles. Melnyk shows that women from Scottish Presbyterianism to Roman and Anglo-Catholicism were engaged in a comprehensive rethinking of dominant theological concepts. Some actively feminised the Godhead while others presented Christ as a perfect hypostatic union of male and female characteristics. Women's theological subcultures were sustained through 'para-ecclesiastical' organisations such as mothers' meetings, bible classes and journal readerships; the conservative gender ideologue Charlotte Yonge nurtured a female theological community for over forty years through her editorship of *The Monthly Packet* (1851–95). The impact of women's writings upon mainstream Christian thought awaits further research, but Melnyk's chapter illuminates the ways in which female theologians took seriously the notion that, as women, they had distinctive and important insights into the nature of God's relationship with humanity.

By the end of the nineteenth century philanthropy had become a highly visible, female-dominated culture. Susan Mumm's discussion of two rapidly developing organisations, the Girls' Friendly Society (GFS) and the Young Women's Christian Association (YWCA), shows that philanthropic cultures were saturated with operations of power not only between the benefactor and the beneficiary but between the female activists themselves. Controversies over recruitment methods, class and race dynamics and institutional hierarchies beset many societies, as did the search for the right balance between religious motivations and more secular desires to effect social and political change. Mumm argues that social historians' dominant antipathy towards religiously-oriented charities, despite their undeniable size and influence up until the mid-twentieth century, has resulted in a distorted view of the philanthropic relationship. Mutuality rather than social control, moral and social uplift rather than spiritual conversion, she argues, were often the defining characteristics. In addition, religiously-inspired female philanthropists effectively pioneered complex, not-for-profit organisations and gave women their earliest experiences of managing large-scale, international institutions.

Although small in number, Roman Catholic and Anglican sisterhoods loomed large in the nineteenth-century public imagination. Carmen Mangion explores the emergence of these often countercultural, all-female spaces where women's rejection of marriage and motherhood for a life of celibate devotion to God tested the cultural acceptability of the feminisation of religion. Convents, sisterhoods and to a lesser extent deaconess orders provided women with important opportunities to take up a recognised religious vocation which combined social ministry with spiritual leadership. Mangion shows that the awkward power relations among these three sororial cultures and their male religious hierarchies underwent a constant process of renegotiation well into the twentieth century. Whereas the Anglican Church was often obliged to tolerate the more autonomous, self-managed structures of the sisterhoods, deaconess institutions struggled for any formal ecclesiastical recognition and status. Yet despite persistent hostility, women continued to be attracted to the communal religious life. As Mangion reminds us, when women entered religious orders it was not out of a desire for personal freedom or independence but as part of a freely-made choice to accept self-imposed restrictions in the name of a higher calling.

The extent to which women could claim and enact spiritual authority is considered in Pamela Walker's chapter on women's preaching in the nineteenth-century. The fluidity of Protestant theologies of preaching and the significance of location and audience composition led to a series of unresolved debates on the role of female evangelists throughout the period. Revivalism, an influential site of ideas and practices for female oratory, according to Walker, capitalised on women's marginalised status and greater spiritual receptivity at moments of intense and extraordinary religious enthusiasm. Both the revival meeting and the séance, she argues, featured working-class women, whether Salvationists or spiritualists, acting as divine intermediaries controlling often highly transgressive cultural events. Through a comparative denominational analysis, Walker queries conventional periodisations that assume women's increasing marginalisation as religious sects became institutionalised. Methodist women, she points out, found ever-new ways to evangelise through breakaway sects, deaconess institutions and even emigration. But overarching theories about the nature of women's preaching and the timing of ordination are impossible without further comparative denomination studies that assess the influence of regional, class and imperial identities and power structures.

By the early twentieth century more women than men were working in the overseas mission-field. As both the wives of missionaries and single workers in their own right, women were seen as the embodiment of normative white femininity and potent vectors of British faith and civilisation throughout the empire. Rhonda Semple analyses the changing nature and parameters of mission cultures for women through the professionalisation of leading Anglican and Nonconformist missionary societies. Semple draws our attention to both the formal and informal modes of authority that enabled and delimited women's mission work, not least of which was their claim to racial privilege. In the mission-field, women undertook numerous teaching, hospital and social welfare activities but their mission to indigenous women could have ambivalent consequences, as in the British agitation over bride wealth. By the early twentieth century, despite greater emphasis upon vocational qualifications for women missionaries, she argues, the criteria for suitable female candidates remained centred on their ladylike and civilising qualities. As seen in Susan Mumm's chapter on philanthropy, a key debate among mission groups until well into the twentieth century was the extent to which the secular professions of education, medicine and social work should influence the shape and direction of religious evangelism.

The wider imperial, transatlantic and transnational dimensions of British women's religious activism are also considered in Clare Midgley's chapter on the religious underpinnings of various female reform movements in the long nineteenth century. She asks: In what ways did religious faith motivate women and give them the inner strength to question, criticise and defy worldly (male) authority? And how did it shape the particular discourses and methods of reform used and set gendered limits on its nature and scope? These are questions relevant to each chapter in the collection, but Midgley uses them to trace the transnational personal and structural networks of female reform in abolitionism, rescue work and anti-slavery. US and European connections not only provided British women with distinctive women-only organising methods, but also stimulated an important, often radicalising, cosmopolitan outlook, as in Quaker and Unitarian anti-slavery networks. Within the UK itself, Midgley observes, temperance was highly successful in recruiting working-class evangelical women in Wales and Scotland as well as Irish Catholic women. Her prosopographical analysis of leading individual reformers, including Elizabeth Fry, Josephine Butler, Mary Carpenter and Octavia Hill, illustrates the diverse relations between individual faith and social reform in the nineteenth century; however, as Midgley notes, the shift from religiously-oriented to more secular approaches to reform in the early 1900s has yet to be fully adumbrated.

In her chapter on women, religion and sexual cultures, Sue Morgan shows that modern sexual ideas were the product of a complex combination of the spiritual and the secular. Although largely neglected in histories of sexuality, churchwomen produced an influential, often radical, genre of sexual literature in the nineteenth and early twentieth centuries. Morgan traces a genealogy of religious women's activism and writing around sex in three main sections: the dominant heterosexual culture of marriage and reproduction including controversies around divorce, birth control and female sexual agency; women's anti-vice campaigns around prostitution, male sexuality and venereal disease; and, finally, the ways in which religion functioned as an important legitimation for dissident sexualities such as celibacy and same-sex desire. Religious discourses on sex were often problematic; while Christianity gave women a powerful language with which to challenge the sexual double standard, this was invariably contained within a conservative model of heterosexual relations. But, Morgan observes, it was precisely in their engagement with sexual morality that the churches were provided with the opportunity to demonstrate the relevance of faith to a rapidly modernising society.

Jacqueline deVries focuses on a central theme in the modern history of gender – the paradoxical relationship between feminism and religion. Aware of the ambiguous influence of religion on women's social status, nineteenth- and twentieth-century, British feminists simultaneously drew upon, reconfigured and rejected the religious cultures of which they formed a part. DeVries traces the major contours and turning-points of a historical relationship that, as yet, remains strikingly under-researched. Feminist political cultures were shaped by highly specific local and denominational contexts, from the relatively egalitarian theologies of the Quakers and Unitarians to the nationalist chapel cultures of Scottish and Welsh nonconformity. By the late nineteenth century freethinkers and New Women were disputing the morality of Christianity with its perpetuation of patriarchal values, yet they did not abandon religion *per se*, proffering instead alternative feminist spiritualities. Even the militant suffrage campaigns, deVries argues, appropriated religious forms, language and symbolism, and the major religious suffrage leagues established between 1909 and 1912 (Jewish, Anglican, Quaker, Free Church, Presbyterian and Scottish Leagues) are important testimony of the reciprocal relationship between religious and feminist cultures. Only by expanding our definitions of religion and feminism, and acknowledging the heterogeneity and reciprocity of these cultures, will historians be able to look beyond the theoretical limitations of the religion/feminist paradox.

By the early twentieth century secularisation was well under way in Britain. Denominational conflict had abated, new leisure pursuits distracted many away from Sunday morning services, and religious certainties dissolved in the face of such cataclysmic events as World War One. Or so the usual story goes. Joy Dixon's concluding chapter outlines radically new ways of thinking about secularisation that focus not on the conventional linear narrative of religious decline but rather on the dynamic relations between alternative forms of faith and the new sciences of evolutionary biology, comparative religions, sexology and psychology.

Modernity, argues Dixon, is a process shaped by continuous dialogues and multiple slippages between faith and doubt, masculine and feminine, the spiritual and the secular. Border crossings continually opened new possibilities. Spiritualist séances enabled young working-class female mediums to operate outside the boundaries of gendered and religious respectability; the feminist Frances Swiney combined Theosophy with eugenics in a religio-scientific discourse of human evolutionary progress; and Annie Besant's lifelong spiritual journey could be seen as metonymic of the new cultures of religious hybridity and spiritual eclecticism. For Dixon, the Victorian tropes of 'faith and doubt' are vastly inadequate for understanding the processes of modernisation and secularisation.

New challenges, new directions

Although not definitive, this collection attempts to map existing scholarship and propose new possibilities for enquiry. We aim to problematise familiar truisms, stimulate questions rather than provide answers and generate future, as yet unimagined, ways of thinking about religion and gender. One of the most stubborn historical narratives we aim to disrupt is the assumption that the privatisation and domestication of faith during the nineteenth century led to a 'feminisation of religion' and resulted in new roles and powers for women in religious contexts. This volume highlights instead the fictive and paradoxical nature of this claim. James Obelkevich's assertion that between 1750 and 1950 'religion retreated into the private sphere', losing 'the broad political and social significance it had had in previous centuries',[9] has long been a canonical position amongst social historians of religion, but, as Watts's image of 'Hope' reminds us, this narrative of religious change carries profoundly gendered implications. While promoted as the more 'spiritual' sex, women were excluded from virtually all positions of institutional religious authority. When women gradually made inroads into positions of religious leadership, Christianity was losing its hold on public life. Thus for Callum Brown it was the mass exodus of women from the Church in the 1960s, the decade of women's sexual and political liberation, that signalled Christianity's imminent demise. Brown's re-periodisation is provocative, but his assertion of women's 'guilt' is methodologically troublesome. As Joy Dixon asks in this volume, have Brown and other proponents of the 'feminisation of religion' thesis simply taken what was a Victorian cultural construction and naturalised it as a historical reality? In seeking to challenge the rather one-dimensional reading of women's spiritual agency embedded in the 'feminisation thesis', this book intimates new research agendas illustrating women's multiple and conflicting relations with religious institutions, ideas, and cultures.

And what are the implications of this for religious masculinity? As clergymen, theologians and ecclesiastical leaders, men were institutionally central to religion, yet they were also spiritually peripheral and frequently represented as the supposedly 'heathen' or 'secular' sex. Recent studies such as Timothy Larsen's *Crisis of Doubt* (2006) have complicated our understanding of these representations, as do several of the chapters in this volume. But our work here is exploratory. How do we find ways to write the history of religion and gender without allowing our analyses to revert back uncritically to the quintessentially Victorian binary of 'secular man' and 'spiritual woman'? Any full account of the gendering of women's spirituality will necessarily require greater attention to masculinity. Only in paying more attention to men's religious experiences *as men* will we be able to dismantle the clichéd historical binary of feminised piety and masculine doubt.

New chronological frameworks of secularisation are also generating debate. Once the province of primarily nineteenth-century historians, religion and spirituality are now drawing attention from twentieth-century specialists. New research mapping the complex relationships between religion and modernity has extended the main debates into the contemporary world, challenging conventional periodisations of modern British cultures of faith, unbelief, and secularisation. This collection contributes to that project in adopting the period 1800 to 1940 – for us as editors this represented a relatively coherent phase of faith-oriented British culture.

Given the more exploratory nature of the material available on the twentieth century, in contrast to the well-established historiography of the nineteenth, contributors were not expected to cover the complete time-frame in each chapter but simply to reflect consciously upon whatever choice of chronological parameters was most meaningful for their own analytical fields.

Rethinking the narrative turning-points in British religious history with a more finely tuned reperiodisation may have important implications for the history of gender itself. Although gender historians have long recognised that conventional chronologies do not reflect major shifts in women's lives they have been slow at reworking alternative schemas of their own. As the editors of a recent volume on gender and change have commented, cultural history's focus on the multiplicity and contingency of identity formation has led to synchronic rather than diachronic readings of the past and the tendency to neglect the all-important relationships between representation, materiality, causation and change.[10] Jeanne Boydston has similarly pointed out that by emphasising gender as a principally analytical, rather than historical, category, scholars have frequently invoked its significance in abstract and non-historically contingent ways, regardless of time, place and culture. The 'primaryness of gender in a given situation', she observes, 'should be one of our questions, rather than one of our assumptions'.[11] If women's historical agency and the relationship between 'religion and modernity' (a frequently invoked but relatively imprecise phrase) is to be understood in all its diverse forms, then a consideration of how both religion *and* gender have 'been constitutive rather than merely reflective of either continuity or change'[12] is vital. This volume points the way to just some of the new challenges and directions emerging in the history of women, gender and religion – it will be exciting to see the results.

Notes

1 Barbara Taylor, *Eve and the New Jerusalem: Socialism and Feminism in the Nineteenth Century* (London: Virago, 1983), p. 127.

2 See Jacqueline deVries, 'Rediscovering Christianity after the Postmodern Turn', *Feminist Studies* 31:1 (2005), pp. 135–55 and Frederick S. Roden, 'Gender and Religion in Recent Victorian Studies Publications', *Victorian Literature and Culture* (2003), pp. 393–403 for two useful review essays of the field.

3 Martin Davies, *Historics: Why History Dominates Contemporary Society* (London: Routledge, 2006), p. 122.

4 Joan Scott, 'Gender: A Useful Category of Historical Analysis', *American Historical Review* 91 (1986), pp. 1053–75.

5 For useful discussions of the theories and purposes of cultural history see Peter Burke, *What is Cultural History?* (London: Polity Press, 2004) and Anna Green, *Cultural History* (London: Palgrave Macmillan, 2008).

6 John Kent, *The Unacceptable Face: The Modern Church in the Eyes of the Historian* (London: SCM Press, 1987), p. 131.

7 Callum Brown, *The Death of Christian Britain: Understanding Secularisation 1800–2000* (London: Routledge, 2001), p. 9.

8 See Sarah C. Williams, 'Victorian Religion: A Matter of Class or Culture?', *Nineteenth Century Studies* 17 (2003), pp. 13–17.

9 James Obelkevich, 'Religion', in F.M.L. Thompson (ed.), *The Cambridge Social History of Modern England* (Cambridge: Cambridge University Press, 1990), p. 311.

10 Alexandra Shepherd and Garthine Walker, 'Gender and Change: Agency, Chronology and Periodisation', *Gender and History* Special Issue Vol. 20, No. 3 (2008).

11 Jeanne Boydston, 'Gender as a Question of Historical Analysis', in Shepherd and Walker, 'Gender and Change', p. 576.

12 Shepherd and Walker, 'Gender and Change', p. 457.

1   Is there a Bible in the house? Gender, religion and family culture

Sarah C. Williams

... but this is fixt
As are the roots of earth and base of all;
Man is for the field and woman for the hearth:
Man for the sword and for the needle her:
Man with the head and woman with the heart:
Man to command and woman to obey; All else confusion.[1]

Tennyson's evocative image of Victorian men and women at the heart of his poem *The Princess* (1847) is striking largely because of its familiarity. The poet is building on a well-crafted popular image of the mid-century woman. It is a domestic image of female faith and goodness dutifully rendered for the betterment of society and popularised quintessentially by the domestic ideologue Sarah Ellis. 'There is an honest pride which every true heart has a right to feel and England's pride should be in the inviolable sanctity of her household hearths. When these are deserted, the sentence of her degradation will be sealed.'[2] For Ellis the foundation of the nation's religious morality lies in the home under the guardianship of female piety. There is no question that gender, spirituality and the home form a powerful thematic triumvirate in her writings as they do in many nineteenth-century sermons, magazines, poems and literary depictions. It is this same thematic triumvirate which re-emerges in historical reconstructions of British culture from 1800 onwards.

It is ironic, therefore, given the close association between women, religion and the home in image and imagination, that these themes are rarely studied in an integrated scholarly manner. The study of modern religion, the study of gender, and the study of the family remain discrete and at times dichotomised areas of enquiry each with their own research methods, agendas and theoretical approaches. This scholarly disassociation has inhibited understanding of the complex interplay between these themes. Furthermore, it has left the thematic triumvirate operating as a powerful 'still life image'[3] which is largely assumed but unexplored, and reiterated but critically unqualified. This chapter traces the contours of these distinct scholarly debates as they have developed over the last three or four decades. Considering in turn the social history of religion, the history of gender, and the study of the modern family, it examines how differing methodologies, ideological concerns and scholarly agendas have tended to isolate the study of gender from that of religion and that of gender and religion from the familial context. In so doing this chapter seeks to highlight points of tension and points of resonance, suggesting possible bridges which could be built between historiographical fields to facilitate an integrated approach that can help bring the static picture to life.

Social history of religion

Historical interpretations of modern British religion have until recently neglected both women and gender as dimensions of enquiry. Such neglect is lamented by Gail Malmgreen in the first chapter of her important book *Religion in the Lives of English Women, 1760–1930* (1986). She points to the 'disappointing, though perhaps not surprising'[4] absence of women from the cornerstones of scholarship on modern British church history and the continued neglect of gender by the new generation of social historians who have relied on 'maddeningly uninformative'[5] sources. Malmgreen's work has done much to shift the conversation and to expand the range of religious history but the point still remains: two decades later her insights continue to be poignant and provocative. Social historians of religion have remained preoccupied with the association between religion and social class to the detriment of other themes. Subject matter has been delimited by the overriding concern to understand the relationship between institutional churches and the nature and composition of social groups. At the same time the methodological paradigms employed in the field are themselves derived from the presuppositions of social science, heavily imprinted by a view of societal structures in which class remains a primary category of analysis overshadowing more nuanced ways of reading the place of religion in British culture.

A brief sketch of the development of this research field illustrates all too plainly that this neglect has been not only topical but also methodological. Horace Mann, who administered the British Religious Census in 1851, set a powerful precedent in his preface when he categorised religious disposition on the basis of socio-economic group, concluding that the working classes were on the whole 'unconscious secularists'.[6] This category of religious affiliation, just like the relative 'religiosity' of the British middle classes, was established on the basis of 'households' with no attention paid to the variety and complexity of spiritual experience and expression *within* the home. For observers such as Mann, Henry Mayhew[7] and Charles Booth[7] the views of male heads of households were generally taken as reflective of the views of all those residing under one roof. The divergent material, social and cultural worlds of contemporary males and females make such neglect peculiarly problematic, as does the fact that women played a key role as conduits of belief and culture in the home. Echoes of these approaches continue to find their way into recent scholarship, dependent as it is on such sources. Late-twentieth- and early-twenty-first century historians, like nineteenth-century commentators, have continued to interpret the spiritual life of modern society by concentrating on the relationship between the churches and the working-class family as a hegemonic unit. E.R. Wickham, for instance, in his formative study, *Church and People in an Industrial City* (1957), took up the conclusions of the 1851 religious census, accepting uncritically the connections made by Horace Mann between urban home life, the working-class family and irreligion. K.S. Inglis,[9] Henry Pelling[10] and Standish Meacham[11] extended and reinforced this orthodox picture by highlighting the essentially middle-class character of the religion of the urban family, while Brian Harrison,[12] H.J. Dyos[13] and later Hugh McLeod[14] identified more specific aspects of church culture which militated against the involvement of different members of the working-class family in church life.

During the 1970s this orthodox position was given a theoretical underpinning in the form of the secularisation thesis. The arguments put forward by Wickham and Inglis were caught up in a wider social and theoretical schema in which religion was marginalised as part of the transformation of traditional agrarian communities into the modern associational state. Within this model, analytical priority was given to societal forces such as social class to explain variations in the functional role of religion over time. Religious beliefs, for example, were considered only in so far as they illustrated typical class attitudes or socially predetermined outlooks. The focus of scholarly attention became overarching structural factors determining the shape of religious behaviour within specific social groups. One has only to look at the work of Robert Currie, Alan Gilbert and Lee Horsley to see the development of this line of thinking in the writing of religious history.[15] It produced historiography in which middle-class 'church attendance' and working-class 'irreligion' were not only typified as communal characteristics of each social group but *explained* on the basis of major shifts in societal structures which had little if anything to do with the substance, form or character of the beliefs held by individual men, women and children.

The 1980s and 1990s, however, saw the development of a more nuanced revisionist approach to class and church-going. Many studies argued against the language of inevitability and determinism inherent within the secularisation thesis and others pointed to a much higher degree of working-class involvement in organised religion, softening the uniform charge of irreligion levelled at the class as a whole.[16] The use of statistical material on the occupational composition of churches and chapels strengthened this approach as did the insights gleaned for the later period from oral history.[17] These approaches have done much to nuance the picture of Victorian religion. And yet woven into the heart of the scholarship is a persistent analytical commitment to class as the principal organising factor adduced to account for variations in church connection. The content of religious belief remains a shadowy dimension which is frequently avoided because of its complexity. Moreover, although gender is now noticed as an important variable in patterns of religious observance, it often appears as little more than a statistical detail appended to wider accounts of church attendance.[18] At the same time the theory of secularisation continues to provide a linear scale against which quantitative measurements of religious change are assessed.[19] Trajectories of religious change have typically been determined on the basis of alterations in patterns of church attendance, weighted strongly in favour of changes in middle-class behaviour.

Belief, gender and the interrelationships between them have played very little part in shaping chronologies of religious change.

A primary explanation for the interpretative resilience of class as an explanatory category within the social history of religion is the methodology of social science itself and its definition of religion. Taking its model from the natural sciences, social science retains a distinction between the observer and the observed, directing attention beyond the meanings that have been produced historically by various cultures and that are embedded within their language, towards what are seen as external and objective class structures that language simply mirrors and reflects. Class is thus conceived as an external social referent that is foundational to the origin and cause of various systems of ideas including religion, sexuality and even the concept of family life. Grand narratives of secularisation have thus arisen in which social class plays a leading role in accounting for the inevitable decline of religion in the modern world. Moreover, for all its innovation of approach, much of the revisionism has continued to ask questions shaped within the same interpretive framework using the same methods and conceptualisation of the issues.[20] The upshot is that social historians of nineteenth- and early-twentieth-century religion have been slow to ask what other dimensions of cultural experience shaped the construction of religious identities beyond those of social class. As a result the complex relationship between spirituality, sexuality and religious belief has not been integrated into established historiographical frameworks.

History of gender

In stark contrast to the social history of religion, the question of identity has remained primary for historians of gender. The structural analysis of early women's history has been thoroughly reworked in recent years and a subtle picture has emerged of the many, various and at times conflicting ways in which male and female identities are constructed over time. Gender historians have begun to ask different and challenging questions about culture and identity. As Sue Morgan puts it, 'Gender history has shifted the debate away from a focus upon women to an examination of the interdependence and relational nature of female and male identities.'[21] With this shift in focus there has been a rapid development of sophisticated theoretical methods of cultural analysis incorporating and refining complex readings of texts. Indeed it is widely recognised that, in their intellectual innovation, feminist analyses now command the theoretical edge within the discipline of history.[22]

However, the irony is that until very recently feminist history has marginalised religion and spirituality as themes. The pervasive and lingering propensity among scholars to view religion as unremittingly patriarchal has much to answer for in this respect. When on occasion religion and gender have formed a dual focus there has been a strong tendency simply to append these themes as further categories to the basic methodological framework of understanding dictated by social history and dominated by social class. This is due in large part to the deep-seated association between the British feminist tradition and Marxist historiography.

E.P. Thompson's legacy has been formative as Catherine Hall recounts in her essay 'Feminism and Feminist History'.[23] The groundbreaking work of Davidoff and Hall, for example, set an influential pattern. At its core *Family Fortunes: Men and Women of the English Middle Class, 1780–1850* (1987) marries gender and class. Davidoff and Hall argue that delineations of gender and patterns of economic and social change operate together, such that consciousness of class 'always takes a gendered form'.[24] The book describes the emergence of the idea of separate male and female spheres as integral to the creation of the distinctive values of the English middle classes. From the late eighteenth century men and women of the provincial middle classes employed their evangelical beliefs to establish their own distinctive moral autonomy as a social group. As they elevated the primacy of the interior life of prayer and godliness, critiquing landed wealth as the only form of social legitimacy, they carved out a particular definition of domesticity which became foundational to middle-class identity by 1850. This convergence of evangelical discourse and middle-class socio-economic and cultural identity produced the ideal of home as a private sphere of piety, comfort and retreat woven around the person of wife and mother. By the mid-century the woman, as guardian of the spiritual welfare of her family, found herself confined within the private domestic sphere and excluded from the corrupting influence of the competitive public sphere of the male. Based on the model of separate spheres, this thesis has become the dominant paradigm for understanding nineteenth-century gender relations.

As with any pioneering work the thesis has been substantially critiqued.[25] Straightforward binary models of the separate spheres have been displaced by more nuanced accounts. Material has been worked and reworked as historians have shown the various and conflicted ways in which public and private were formulated and configured. Men and women are now shown as enmeshed in a matrix of circulating discourses, some of which competed with separate spheres, and some of which supplemented it.[26] Identities are now presented as mutable and multiple. Moreover, they are formed through an array and interplay of practices, habits and experiences.[27] But despite over a decade of revision the strong association established by Davidoff and Hall between religious identities, the construction of gender, and specific patterns of social structural change, has proved a difficult mould to break. When it comes to spirituality, historiographical orthodoxy has, thus far, won the day. Piety continues to be narrowly associated with the middle class and with particular models of public life, while a singular coherent respectable version of evangelicalism is seen as the glue which holds the static tableau of the Victorian family together.

Callum Brown's recent innovative and important work, *The Death of Christian Britain* (2001) continues, for instance, to exhibit many of these interpretive tendencies. It is Brown's ambition to topple the social-scientific method from its pre-eminent position, by incorporating analytical insights drawn from gender studies. From the outset Brown replaces a functional definition of religion with what he calls 'discursive Christianity'.[28] By this he means religiosity based on people's subscription to protocols of personal identity, which they derive from Christian expectations or discourses. Protocols are rituals or customs of behaviour, economic activity, dress, speech and so on that are collectively promoted as necessary for Christian identity. These are prescribed or implied in a discourse of Christian behaviour which can be heard by the historian in reported speech, oral testimony or autobiography. Individual and communal subscription to public discourse creates, Brown argues, a compelling religious culture which shapes the construction of social attitudes in society at large. What made Britain Christian, according to Brown, was the way in which a Christian discourse infused public culture and was adopted by men and women in forming their own highly gendered identities.

At the heart of this narrative Brown identifies particular encompassing definitions of masculinity and femininity. These separate gendered identities emerged after 1800 to constrain behaviour and shape overarching social configurations. Women were at the fulcrum of these ideals. It was their responsibility to instruct at the fireside, impress their families with Christian teaching, watch over the sanctity of the family and in this way reinforce the validity and centrality of evangelical sensibilities in society as a whole. 'Theirs was', as Brown puts it, 'a privileged and pivotal religiosity.'[29] This is a religiosity which is strikingly similar to that ascribed to the British middle class by Davidoff and Hall. Women were the pivot not only for individual moral reformation within the family but for the moral regeneration of the nation. Brown traces this feminised piety through an analysis of the obituary columns of religious magazines, concluding that female religiosity was relatively unproblematic for the evangelical. If women were by nature pious then their capacity to confer piety required their judicious separation from 'the world', an arena Brown interprets as synonymous with the public sphere.[30] Conversely, just as female piety was centrally located in the home, so masculinity was constructed in opposition to the stability, order and spirituality of the hearth. Indeed Brown argues that from 1800 to 1950 masculine identity was formed in antithesis to religiosity. He argues that within the evangelical and popular press, definitions of masculinity revolved around the susceptibility of the male to worldly temptations and his need of a mother or wife to rein in his wilfulness and avert his natural tendencies to undermine the family and society.

Brown's analysis puts weight on such discourse as the basis for establishing a new chronology of religious change. From the 1840s these two dimensions of gender and piety/impiety became what Brown calls 'mutually enslaved discursive constructions'.[31] So long as women's identities were formed by a particular brand of Christian discourse which shaped their self perception, formed their roles as custodians of the home, and fostered a trans-generational transmission of certain kinds of prescriptive moral values, then the 'nation's last puritan age'[32] was upheld. It was on this basis that Britain remained Christian until 1963 according to Brown. It is the timing of secularisation which is fundamentally questioned in his work rather than the narrative framework itself. Religious language replaces social class as the causal factor in a process of relentless decline. The echoes of Davidoff and Hall's approach sound loud and clear in Brown's analysis. And, through them, we hear the repetition of nineteenth-century prescriptive literature – the voice of Ellis and the refrains of Tennyson's poem. There is an ironic sense in which this argument, for all its innovation, actually reiterates Ellis's comment with which we began this chapter. When the sanctified hearths are deserted then the 'sentence of degradation will be sealed'.[33] According to Brown it was the 'swinging sixties' which brought about this 'degradation'. Since then, a formerly religious people have entirely forsaken organised Christian affiliation in a 'sudden plunge into a truly secular condition'.[34] What we find, therefore, is a revamped chronology of the secularisation narrative which, despite locating gender at the centre of its argument, replicates the same unexamined homilies as mid-Victorian writers.

Brown's approach is helpful in many respects. Crucially, it draws gender more firmly into the social history of modern Christianity and it recognises the compelling role of language in the formation of cultural identity. It also acknowledges the strength of Christianity as a central sustaining discourse within British culture well into the twentieth century. Furthermore, at a methodological level, language is helpfully centralised as an indispensable part of the final description of belief, not as some kind of superstructure that merely reflects the real changes taking place outside and beyond the text. At the same time, however, Brown's approach needs further refinement if it is to bring our 'still life image' alive. The vestiges of a class-based paradigm still persist. The Christian discourse that Brown talks about is little different from the middle-class sensibilities found in *Family Fortunes*. Moreover, this discourse is assumed to be both unitary and dominant. Brown's understanding of discursive Christianity, shaped as it is by an ideal type of highly gendered church-based evangelicalism (or Puritanism as he calls it from time to time), is applied as a singular definition of Christian discourse across a variety of social contexts. Brown's work is in danger, therefore, of replacing one meta-narrative based on models of social discipline and class control with another based on the imposition of discursive power as expressed through particular hegemonic ideals of masculinity and femininity.

When we look closely at religious cultures from the perspective of the home, far from finding a coherent core discourse arising from a single 'puritan' stance, we actually find a variety of religious idioms which intersect with but also extend beyond the stylised version of evangelical Christianity adopted by Brown. Evangelicalism on its own is an inadequate umbrella category to express the varieties of theological position, ecclesiological structure, religious disposition and denominational milieu which co-existed throughout this period and which together shaped the religious culture of the nation. Moreover, to deploy one singular Christian discourse about gender as encompassing and typical is at best to simplify and at worst to gravely misrepresent the diverse spectrum of ideas about gender, many of which were locally, denominationally, theologically, even occupationally specific. In addition, important religious discourses about gender and family life also lay outside and on the peripheries of Christianity. These 'folk narratives', as they are referred to in this chapter, or idioms of religious expression must be taken into account, as must denominational differences, because they continue to play a vital part in popular culture, offering parallel and competing notions of 'Christian Britain' throughout the period considered by Brown.[35] Individual families were sites in which a multiplicity of religious narratives were expressed. Some families, for instance, positioned themselves in relation to the supernatural through a discourse which remained partially independent of both the Church and of orthodoxy, and which deliberately subverted elements of the core narrative Brown describes. In these settings religious beliefs were legitimated by an appeal to authoritative familial or communal traditions which existed independently of any Christian narratives associated with evangelical Christianity. They reflected the 'way things were', or 'the way things had always been done'. 'Rightness' was conferred on present actions by extending to them the sanctity of time. In this way behaviour was constrained and dictated on the basis of tradition and folklore passed down orally from generation to generation. Folk myth could serve as a directive for moral action in the present because great-grandma did it that way and so did her mother before her. Deference to the customs of story-tellers who mediated and disseminated such traditions could act as the foundation of a family's sense of history, identity in the present, and continuity in the future. Moreover, story-telling remained a powerful determinant of female identity within the family, giving older women a heightened authority by virtue of their role as repositories of folk custom, medical lore and family tradition. Popular religion cannot simply be evaluated on the basis of the degree to which it conformed to church-based definitions of religiosity. For the participants themselves, folk customs, traditions and practices combined with the selective and conditional appropriation of church-based Christianity to provide a repertoire of overlapping and competing beliefs. Folk beliefs of this kind were not simply confined to the working class. *Cassell's Saturday Journal* ran an article in 1899 entitled 'Do you possess a mascot?' in which it argued that a mascot or charm was an essential possession in any family home.[36] Economy and good sense were appealed to in advertising the 'supernatural' values of these objects as 'investments women could make on behalf of their families'. Advertisements of such kinds targeted women of all social classes albeit in slightly different formats. 'Do you want to know what are the lucky days of the month, lucky numbers, colours or the Christian name of the person you are going to marry?'[37] said one advertisement. If so then the answer was to ensure that every home had either a copy of *The Dream Book* (1890) for the servant class or *Planets of the Month* or *Consult the Oracle* (1875) for the mistress. These were considered essential household items to be consulted regularly at times of decision or anxiety. Very little work has yet been done on folk practice and family traditions within middle-class homes but preliminary investigations suggest that popular religion was a dimension of belief in every area of society, existing on the edges and alongside distinctive denominational cultures. A pattern of occasional and conditional church attendance correlated with these kinds of beliefs. Families could retain a strong sense of identification with a local church, but this identification had very little to do with the denominational specifics of that church. Basic Christian teaching could, for instance, be considered important but the denominational distinctions made by Sunday school teachers, vicars, ministers or missioners were largely irrelevant to parents making decisions about which Sunday school to send their children to week by week.[38] Within such families the ideal of the Christian faith in a generic sense was upheld as important but the specifics were seen as subsidiary, if not irrelevant.

This kind of familial religious culture is in marked contrast to families which retained and reinforced strong habits of church attendance and strong denominational association. The two paradigms of association need to be explored in relation to one another. Mary Heimann has shown in her work on English Catholic devotion that the period from 1850 to 1914 saw a more strongly defined, prescribed and tightly cultivated Catholic culture in which observant members were more likely to view their faith in terms which distinguished them from non-Catholic families.[39] Such Catholic families must be viewed in the light of families studied in metropolitan Southwark who classified themselves first as Cockneys and second as Catholic and for whom a general 'Christian' training was seen as sufficient for all.[40]

Protestant nonconformist groups likewise fostered a higher degree of association between family and chapel culture in this period such that members' lives were in every detail constrained by the norms of their particular denominational association. William Kent describes in his autobiography *The Testament to a Victorian Youth* (1938) how the Methodist community in which he was raised operated as a 'whole sub-society'.[41] Kent's description of his strong Methodist upbringing in suburban Kennington depicts a family culture which revolved in every dimension around the local chapel community. The family socialised with other members of the community, used the same practices of prayer as others in the wider 'church family', meal times and customs were constrained by chapel conventions and the boundaries between home and chapel were further blurred through the practice of taking in successive lodgers from among the single male population of the church. The Methodist W.H. Lax also encapsulates this idea of parallel culture in his autobiography:

> There is in my opinion a distinction between the Methodist type of family life and all others. Just as Methodism presents its own form of evangelicalism among the churches so it has introduced to the world a specific type of family life.[42]

Lax goes on to describe a family life centred on prayer, Bible reading and weekly chapel attendance. Linda Wilson, in her study *Constrained by Zeal: Female Spirituality amongst Nonconformists 1825–1875* (2000), evokes a similar world of strong denominational allegiance among Particular Baptists, Congregationalists, Wesleyan Methodists and Primitive Methodists. Wilson explores the relative influence of familial and chapel culture as primary domains for the expression of women's spirituality. She concludes that denominational culture was the primary shaping force in constructing domestic ideals of femininity, norms of behaviour and customs of child rearing. Chapels functioned as extensions of the household for these women and it was in this environment that women learnt alongside men the theological meaning of Christianity and how to lead a Christian life expressed primarily in the home.

The ways in which denominational cultures shaped the specific details of family life are, therefore, important to consider, as are the differences which emerge within social groups over types of religious idiom and practice. When studying spiritual autobiographies from the late nineteenth century it is clear that a common outcome of 'religious conversion' was the *division* of families from local communities and *division* within families when some members insisted on traditional familial codes of religious conduct while 'converted' family members became increasingly associated with the particular cultures of nonconformist communities. This could lead to conflict, misunderstanding and the perceived withdrawal of the converted family or family member into an alternative support network beyond that of the kinship group. Joseph Gwyer, for example, describes in his autobiography *Sketches of the Life of Joseph Gwyer, Potato Salesman* (1877) how the social support received by his family shifted from local kin to Rye Lane Baptist church after he was baptised there as an adult in 1869. From this point onwards Gwyer begins to describe his church community as his family. In this way differing definitions of what constituted the 'true believer' could be as strong an indicator of identity as blood lines. Such converts were perceived to be separating themselves off from their local communities and entering another world which specifically and self-consciously cut across class, gender and communal lines.

Patterns of home life were deeply and directly implicated in these shifting religious allegiances. Indeed it was within the detailed fabric of family life that such distinctions were recognised and affirmed. 'Conversion' could, for instance, involve the home in a shift of culture, style, economy and behaviour. The description given of the conversion of one working man in the *British Workman Annual* of 1906 is telling in this respect:

> On the verge of the crowd hung a dark Irishman and seeing the anxious gaze I grasped his hand with the blunt enquiry whether all was well with his soul. Conversation followed and the stern man melted to tears. He was a Roman Catholic but had never had the claims of Christ put point blank in the manner of my question and the attic which served him for a home was squalid and wretched through the conduct of drunken parents and neglected children. But the Saviour's transforming power laid hold upon O'Connor's heart and reformed his life and renewed his home. Today in a clean and comfortable cottage he lives upon his frugal Dockers wage but his home is a credit to the district and he has proved how true it is that, 'Godliness is profitable unto all things'.[43]

The link between a penitent heart, a reformed life and a renewed home is a central part of late-nineteenth-century conversion narratives and this is so for men as well as for women. The home is described in terms of a tangible outworking of O'Connor's change of heart. The primary test of his conversion is his reliable breadwinning. Distinctions between 'converted homes' and 'unconverted' could be as subtle as who taught the children to pray at night. In families where church attendance was an irregular and occasional practice, mothers were the ones who taught their children to pray at night. But in families which strongly and immediately identified themselves with specific details of faith, and among whom church attendance was a regular habit and a central part of the weekly family routine, it tended to be fathers who taught their children to pray, who initiated prayer at family meal times and insisted on certain behaviour on Sundays.[44] In these environments the story-telling role of women gives way to the norms of congregational life as authoritative indicators of religious affiliation.

In this way communities were exposed to a range of familial allegiances and expressions of faith and members of households were exposed to a range of religious idioms, rather than to one type of gendered evangelicalism. Indeed, it was the combination of different religious discourses that constituted the most important criteria for distinguishing between different kinds of believing communities. A great deal more work needs to be done to unearth these subtle distinctions and the transmutations of orthodoxy which are apt to take place when faith is relocated round the kitchen table, in the bedroom and at the family hearth. Callum Brown's singular and coherent evangelical core does not do justice to the important varieties in the pattern and character of family culture arising from different kinds of denominational affiliation, nor does it account for the important role of popular religion in forming familial identities.

We are left, therefore, with a curious mixture in the historiography on gender and religion. On the one hand we have a methodological bias amongst social historians of religion, and on the other an ideological bias in gender history. The social history of religion in its preoccupation with social class has neglected other layers of associational, personal and communal identity. The history of gender has tended narrowly to associate religion with the institutional Church and with structural patterns of middle-class family life. Religious ideas, symbols and language have been excluded from wider discussions of cultural life. The isolation of these respective fields has resulted in both a static image of 'middle-class evangelical religion' and an equally static view of the relationship between religion and the formation of gender identities. This tendency is further reinforced when our third element of the thematic triumvirate is taken into consideration.

History of the family

The family has, until recently, appeared in the historiography as a relatively fixed point. G.M. Young in his *Portrait of an Age* (1936) described the family as an immovable structure at the heart of Victorian life; 'the stable fortified centre from which all advance takes place'.[45] This position has been reiterated with varying degrees of subtlety throughout the twentieth century. It is *structural* views of the family which have generally been imported into the writing of religious history. Social historians of religion have persisted in a methodological approach which identifies the family (along with the Church) with the formal institutional structures of society. They direct their efforts towards reconstructing the structural environment of family life and quantifying correlations with church attendance rather than towards understanding how the dynamics of family culture affected the construction of identities both spiritual and sexual.

The perpetuation of these definitions of family life within religious history has tended to insulate the sub-discipline from important and innovative developments within the field of family history. The last decade in particular has seen the family revisited, and the static image richly re-evaluated. Penny Kane, for example, in her study of Victorian families in nineteenth-century fiction, has done much to challenge the static image of the family as a category of social organisation in the period between 1840 and 1870.[46] High infant mortality rates, short life expectancy, the high proportion of children who did not grow up in the presence of two natural parents together constituted a highly fluid and unstable ideal. In addition to the inherent demographic, social and economic instability of nineteenth-century families, Kane also argues for what she calls 'a kind of psychic fluidity'.[47] She demonstrates how novels and plays from the seventeenth century onwards frequently concern foundlings, missing heirs and claimants, secret or fraudulent marriages and unwitting incestuous entanglements. Such themes take centre stage in the nineteenth century, suggesting a deep-seated cultural anxiety about the nature and stability of family life.

Karen Chase and Michael Levenson have further developed Kane's work, adding to the consideration of fictional images of the family a re-evaluation of the category of household as it was employed to count 'families' in the 1851 census.[48] They have examined the deliberate creation of *the household* as a category instead of family, interpreting it as an expedient measure on the part of the census officials to overlay contemporary anxiety over the vulnerability of the family with an artificial conceptual coherence. In their analysis, Chase and Levenson revisit the domestic ideologues. Sarah Ellis, for example, is recast as a shrewd professional, lucratively trading on the conventions of sentiment. The 1840s are reconfigured as a period of idealised domestic reaction to the failure of both the family and male/female relationships as seen in the Queen Caroline Affair and the trials of Caroline Norton in the 1830s. Thus the home emerges in recent historiography as a theatre where carefully crafted private images are projected for public consumption. Therefore, to see these mottoes of mid-century family life as stable is, as Chase and Levenson argue, 'to surrender to a mystification'.[49]

The emergent discipline of 'home history' has also done much to open the shadowy world of Victorian private life to historical inspection. Home history combines the study of objects and interiors using the methodologies of design history and a social historical perspective. Inga Bryden and Janet Floyd, for example, have looked again at the physical and material environment of the middle-class home as it was imagined in nineteenth-century domestic discourse.[50] They question the way in which scholars have read domestic ideology into their analysis of physical space and thus reiterated the image of the middle-class house as a highly structured, confined and enclosed space acting physically to reinforce the strict hierarchies of gendered power. They insist that the design, layout and material content of Victorian houses must be read as a complex, nuanced text suggesting a social geometry that cannot be reduced to a mere reflection of structures enacted outside the home.[51] Bryden and Floyd point to disparate forms, conflicting ideals and competing layers of domestic discourse within the material ordering of the household. Furthermore, they highlight the different uses of home, ranging from workplace to place of leisure as well as a context for charged encounters between classes and races. Relatives, lodgers, cooks, maids, nannies and footmen distort the 'still life image', crowding the picture and adding what Dickerson calls the 'density of meaning in the concept of keeping house'.[52]

In this way texture, subtlety and contradiction are now being injected into our understanding of the modern home and family. Yet this innovative work on the family has been carried out largely in isolation from ideas of religious belief and spirituality. This neglect is all the more striking given the large and growing literature on the consumption of mass-produced objects and their use in the decoration of public rooms in Victorian homes.[53] The sheer material presence of Christianity in every dimension of nineteenth-century culture renders this omission particularly problematic. As Mary Carpenter has pointed out in her unique and pioneering study *Imperial Bibles, Domestic Bodies* (2003) the religion of Victorian women 'was not simply Christian, nor even Protestant or Anglican Evangelical or dissenting; it was part of a burgeoning mass market of commercial religious publication and other religious goods'.[54]

John Tosh's work is an important and hopeful intervention in this respect. Tosh has reclaimed the home and family as an integral arena for the construction of masculine social identities and for the expression of religious faith in his book *A Man's Place: Masculinity and the Middle-Class Home in Victorian England* (1999). Drawing on innovations in the social history of the family, religion and gender, Tosh helpfully re-conceptualises domesticity as 'not just a pattern of residence or a web of obligations but a profound attachment, a state of mind as well as a physical orientation'.[55] This broader definition centred on ideas of interiority and human relatedness sheds light on the symbolic and representational character of family life in the Victorian period and moves the debate into an arena far beyond a mere structural reconstruction of the family. Tosh revisits the crowded Victorian interior as a display of male provision in the home. He shows the way in which masculine prowess was linked to vital material indicators of status, wealth and luxury. In this way, he argues, 'Home was a guide to man's wealth and a mirror of his moral character'.[56] Tosh's work calls into question the analytical distinctions between 'public male' and 'private female' spheres and demonstrates how establishing a household and a family, protecting his home and providing for his dependants was the means by which a man gained social recognition as an adult. Therefore, domesticity cannot be separated from work and male homosocial environments; each were dependent and interwoven with the other and it makes no sense to delineate the boundaries or dimensions of masculine experience. Tosh's sensitivity to the 'spiritualization of the household' and to the layering of faith, gender and family life is enormously helpful in providing models for future research.

Deborah Cohen's recent book *Household Gods: The British and Their Possessions* (2006) also picks up on the interrelated themes of the material culture of the home, gender and religion. Cohen traces the competing claims of God and Mammon in the middle-class home during the period 1830–1930. She argues that at every stage the relationship between families and their possessions was charged with moral and religious meaning. She establishes a trajectory of change in which the austerity of the early century gives way during the height of Victorian affluence (from the 1840s through to the 1870s) to a situation in which 'things themselves' were ascribed 'moral qualities'. This, she argues, allowed the Victorians to incorporate material acquisition with demonstrations of godliness in the act of furnishing a home.[57] Cohen's work, like Tosh's, provides an interesting example of the ways in which the methodological insights gleaned from the discipline of home history have much to offer the social and cultural history of religion in this period. Both historians rearticulate the language of acquisition in order to reveal the layers of motivation behind material accumulation in the family context. And both writers also pay careful attention to the different parts that men and women played in the furnishing of houses so as to trace the inter-related creation of gender. However, the focus of these studies has remained the middle-class home. Both Tosh and Cohen remain wedded to the social group most deeply implicated in British consumerism. In addition, the pattern of religious expression with which consumer activity is associated is generally defined by Cohen as 'evangelicalism'. Cohen confidently links the 'long road of home extravaganza' to 'the evangelical revival that swept the country in the late eighteenth and early nineteenth centuries'.[58] Even the period following the heyday of mid-Victorian evangelicalism, she argues, remained shaped by the presuppositions of evangelicalism which she defines variously as 'severe religion', or 'militant Christianity'.[59] Cohen relies heavily on Boyd Hilton's description of nineteenth-century evangelicalism[60] to suggest a relatively straightforward and stereotypical transition from the 'harsh evangelical doctrine of the atonement' in the period prior to 1860 to a more congenial 'Incarnationalism' ('a kindlier, gentler Christianity'[61] as Cohen calls it) which allowed later Victorian believers to forge a link between morality and household possessions. Once again we find evangelicalism being deployed as a hegemonic catch-all, assumed but ill-defined, into which all religious and moral expressions are conflated. Moreover, Cohen's work follows a chronology of change which assumes but nowhere problematises a straightforward linear decline of religious influence falling off steadily and persistently from the pinnacle of late-eighteenth-century revivalism. The echoes of Davidoff and Hall and traditional iterations of the secularisation thesis are heard again, this time as undercurrents in Cohen's work.

There is a great deal more that can be done using the approaches and methods of 'home history' to consider varieties of faith as expressed in the material culture of the home. This is so on a number of different levels. For example, it can provide a helpful window into the impact of different denominational allegiances on the routine and pattern of everyday life. Henry Mayhew, as he visited the homes of working-class Londoners in the 1850s, was impacted by the visual differences between Catholic and Protestant homes. The walls of Catholic homes were covered typically in 'hundreds of pieces of paper depicting saints' lives'. Protestant homes sported isolated mottoes such as 'God Bless this Home'.[62]

The display of images provides important indicators of the family/faith nexus, as can the particular details of the paraphernalia associated with family prayers. Mary Heimann puts great weight on vital distinctions between different versions and editions of Catholic prayer books, missals and catechisms.[63] Mapping possessions into wider patterns of family life is likely to be very instructive. The presence of Bibles not only as texts but also as material artefacts formed a vital part of the fabric of home life in the Victorian and Edwardian periods. Within many communities having a Bible on the table in the parlour, for instance, could link the private family with a wider communal identification with the Christian religion. It could also ensure the respectability of the family and the immediate link between family members whose baptisms and weddings were recorded on the front pages of the family Bible, and the local church in which the rites of passage were observed. Stan Hall, the son of a bus conductor, born near the Elephant and Castle in 1901, recalled in his reminiscence how

> It seemed the right thing to do to have a Bible on the table in one of the rooms, if you were fortunate to have more than one room. But it was hardly ever read although the larger it was the greater the impression of the holiness of the family.[64]

From the 1860s onwards District Visitors employed by the Charity Organisation Society (COS) were required to ask the following question when visiting a working-class home: *Is there a Bible in the house?* Layers of meaning are attached not only to the writing of the original COS questionnaire but also to the spatial and social setting in which the 'object' was sought, the question asked, and the answer given and recorded. Equally, Bibles were used to tell fortunes, to predict future marriage partners, even to cast spells. The story of the bullet in the Bible carried in the tunics of soldiers during the First World War was oft-repeated in family stories and taken to validate the special status of the Bible as a preventive charm against misfortune among family members and as a guarantee of well-being irrespective of the content of the text itself.[65] The meanings ascribed to objects could both reinforce and differ unexpectedly from conventional discourses of mainstream Christianity. How these Bibles were acquired, when, why and for whom; where these objects were kept and/or displayed are all interesting questions which can shed considerable light on the formation of gender roles and identities with regard to religious activities within the home. A fluid and complex relationship is revealed between people and things in which the tangible and symbolic force of religion is present.

Similarly, the study of popular folklore artefacts contained in folklore collections such as the Lovett Collection in the Cuming Museum in Southwark, or the rural folklore collections used by James Obelkevich in his study of South Lindsey,[66] are helpful in understanding the range and combination of religious practices expressed in the home. A wide range of objects were included in the decoration of homes with the specific purpose of averting ill fortune or attracting good luck to the home. Patchwork pin cushions sewn into the shape of a shoe were a common feature in working-class homes in the 1910s. The folklorist Edward Lovett describes the sale of such items in Camberwell.[67] They were attractive, colourful and designed to symbolise the prosperity attracted to the family as they journeyed down the path of life. Other small shoes were designed with the image of the Christian cross interwoven with the sun. These were likewise hung in the home for good fortune.[68] Small glass rolling pins were also a common feature in households in the London docks. These were given to sailors and filled with rum. When the rum was consumed they were filled with perfume, taken home and given to the woman of the house who hung them in the home for good luck.[69] In Catholic homes small sacred hearts were sewn of black silk, filled with Ash Wednesday ashes, and hung in the home as a potent protective guard against illness.[70]

Objects found in the home can also be considered alongside the practice of wearing mascots and amulets. Charms were sewn into the hems of garments or left in the pockets of coats for many years. They could be worn around the neck or pinned to the inside of tunics.[71] Women appear to have been responsible for the use of charms in home decoration whereas men carried charms more widely on their persons. Suburban dwellings in late Victorian and early Edwardian London also featured charms. Witch balls were suspended in front windows for decoration and to attract good fortune into the newly erected dwelling.[72] The use of witch balls was a revival of those found in late-eighteenth-century Bristol. They were marketed as 'ancient' and 'traditional' to build bridges between past and present allowing innovations to be accepted by incoming families within the framework of a familiar folk theodicy. These kinds of folk artefacts provided focal points for the coalescence of family traditions, communal memory, belief and gendered religious practice. Contextualising and resituating these objects can help us reconstruct patterns of belief and practice in the context of the home.

Conclusion

This chapter has surveyed three distinct but inter-related fields: the social history of religion, the history of gender and the history of the family. Each field has developed dramatically in the last three decades, injecting texture, complexity and energy into the 'still life image'. But, as we have seen, these areas of enquiry have yet to be fully integrated. The social history of religion has remained preoccupied topically and methodologically with social class to the detriment of other themes. Social historians of religion have remained isolated from the helpful theoretical debates taking place at the core of gender history. The vital and highly nuanced debates over social, sexual and political identities have by-passed many historians of religion leaving them asking interpretive questions shaped by traditional paradigms and reiterations of the secularisation thesis. Gender historians, on the other hand, for all their theoretical erudition, have tended to neglect religion and spirituality as a pervasive and formative influence on the construction of masculine and feminine identities. In addition, both gender historians and social historians of religion have remained wedded, in general, to structural ideas of the family and they have incorporated very few ideas from the rapidly developing arena of family history. The shifting, symbolic and theatrical character of the nineteenth-century family has been strongly re-emphasised of late. Binary oppositions based on models of separate public/private spheres have been fundamentally challenged in this arena. Home history and the study of material artefacts have played an important role in this. However, these new directions have emerged largely in isolation from religious themes, ideas and considerations.

The recent work of Callum Brown has built an important and valuable bridge between the first two areas of scholarship. By drawing on the insights and analytical approaches of gender studies, Brown has done much to fuse gendered identities with nineteenth- and twentieth-century religious discourse. Moreover, Brown has helped us reacclimatise ourselves to the possibility that Christianity remained a primary conduit of British cultural identity right through into the second half of the twentieth century. But even in Brown's innovative and integrative work the 'still life image' persists. The pious woman remains at the hearth, upholding the morality of the nation with a singular, albeit highly gendered, evangelical discourse which remains firmly bound to middle-class, church-based religious sensibilities. We still need to inject variety and dynamism into this image. Evangelicalism alone is an inadequate discursive catch-all. We need to develop greater sensitivity to the denominational differences which subtly but crucially distinguish the micro-cultures of affiliated families. Furthermore, we need to set specific denominational overtones, customs and atmospheres alongside equally significant popular religious idioms which lay outside and on the peripheries of Christianity. Such narratives of belief fractured homes, families and social groups and at times overwhelmed other categories of identity and created sharp distinctions between 'nominal' and 'converted' family members. We need to recognise the range of religious idioms operating within as well as between families and social groups. It was the detailed combination of different discourses within the culture of the home which formed the basis for defining different types of believing community.

John Tosh's work also represents another important bridge between the different dimensions of the thematic triumvirate. Tosh's work draws not only on gender history and the social history of religion but also establishes a three-dimensional paradigm by engaging carefully with the new insights offered by home history. There is much that can be done to extend Tosh's work further and to broaden the range of such analysis beyond the evangelical community and beyond the middle class. The study of popular artefacts, as discussed in this chapter, provides one possible example. Artefacts challenge the reduction of religious belief to formal institutional observance and they locate the focus of enquiry onto the home itself. Often, objects such as family Bibles operate as symbols around which the beliefs of family members coalesce. Family stories frequently surround the origins and preservation of such objects while the placing, use and definition of an object's role within the family form important indictors of gender roles. Oral history in particular offers exciting opportunities for the exploration of these themes in the twentieth century allowing us to capture and centralise narrated belief alongside enacted belief in the form of religious behaviour, and embodied belief in terms of devotional and/or popular practice in the home. It is the centralisation of belief in its diverse and multiple forms that will best help integrate the thematic triumvirate of gender, religion and the family.

Further reading

Callum Brown, *The Death of Christian Britain* (London: Routledge, 2001).

Inga Bryden and Janet Floyd, *Domestic Space: Reading the Nineteenth Century Interior* (Manchester: Manchester University Press, 1999).

Mary W. Carpenter, *Imperial Bibles, Domestic Bodies: Women, Sexuality and Religion in the Victorian Market* (Athens: Ohio University Press, 2003).

Karen Chase and Michael Levenson, *The Spectacle of Intimacy: A Public Life of the Victorian Family* (Princeton, NJ: Princeton University Press, 2000).

Nancy Christie, *Households of Faith: Family, Gender and Community in Canada 1760–1969* (Montreal & Kingston: McGill-Queen's University Press, 2002).

Deborah Cohen, *Household Gods: The British and Their Possessions* (New Haven: Yale University Press, 2006).

Penny Kane, *Victorian Families in Fact and Fiction* (New York: St Martin's Press, 1995).

Hugh McLeod, *Piety and Poverty* (New York: Holmes & Meier, 1996).

Elizabeth Roberts, *A Woman's Place: An Oral History of Working-Class Women 1890–1940* (Oxford: Blackwell, 1984).

John Tosh, *A Man's Place: Masculinity and the Middle-Class Home in Victorian England* (New Haven and London: Yale University Press, 1999).

Sarah C. Williams, *Religious Belief and Popular Culture: Southwark c.1880–1939* (Oxford: Oxford University Press, 1999).

Linda Wilson, *Constrained by Zeal: Female Spirituality amongst Nonconformists 1825–1875* (Carlisle: Paternoster Press, 2000).

Notes

1 Alfred Tennyson, *The Princess* (London: E. Moxen, 1847), 5.435–41.

2 Sarah Ellis, *The Young Ladies' Reader* (1845), p. 17.

3 Ellis uses the phrase 'still life' to describe the opening scene of her story *Hearts and Homes* (1859). The scene depicts a husband and wife sitting at the hearth. The husband is reading while his wife is bent low over her needlework, 'plying her needle with great industry'. The character of the scene is 'as nearly resembling what is called by painters "still-life" as any could well be'.

4 Gail Malmgreen (ed.), *Religion in the Lives of English Women, 1760–1930* (London: Croom Helm, 1986), p. 1–2.

5 Ibid., pp. 1–2.

6 Horace Mann, *Census of Great Britain, 1851: Religious Worship in England and Wales* (London: G. Routledge and Co., 1854), p. 93.

7 Henry Mayhew, *London Labour and the London Poor*, 3 vols ([S.I]: Woodfall, 1851).

8 Charles Booth, *Life and Labour* (London: Macmillan and Co., 1902), 'Religious Influences', i–vii.

 9 K. S. Inglis, *Churches and the Working Classes in Victorian England* (London: Routledge & Kegan Paul, 1963).

10 Henry Pelling, 'Religion and the Nineteenth-Century British Working Class', *Past and Present* 27 (April, 1964), pp. 128–33.

11 Standish Meacham, 'The Church in the Victorian City', *Victorian Studies* 11 (1967–68), pp. 359–78.

12 Brian Harrison, 'Religion and Recreation in Nineteenth-Century England', *Past and Present* 38 (December, 1967), pp. 98–125.

13 H. J. Dyos, 'The Slums in Victorian London', *Victorian Studies* 11 (1967–68), pp. 5–40.

14 Hugh McLeod, *Class and Religion in the Late Victorian City* (London: Croom Helm, 1974).

15 Robert Currie, Alan Gilbert and Lee Horsley, *Churches and Churchgoers: Patterns of Church Growth in the British Isles since 1700* (Oxford: Clarendon Press, 1977).

16 Jeffrey Cox, *The English Churches in a Secular Society* (Oxford: Oxford University Press, 1982), Mark Smith, *Religion in Industrial Society: Oldham and Saddleworth 1740–1865* (Oxford: Clarendon Press, 1995) and Hugh McLeod, *Piety and Poverty* (New York: Holmes & Meier, 1996).

17 Sarah C. Williams, *Religious Belief and Popular Culture: Southwark c.1880–1939* (Oxford: Oxford University Press, 1999).

18 See the argument made by Patrick Joyce in his introduction to P. Joyce (ed.), *Class* (Oxford: Oxford University Press, 1995), pp. 3–16, ii.

19 See, for example, the reiteration of the secularisation thesis in S. Bruce, *Religion in the Modern World: From Cathedrals to Cults* (Oxford: Oxford University Press, 1996).

20 See Sarah C. Williams, 'Victorian Religion: A Matter of Class or Culture?' *Nineteenth Century Studies* 17 (2003), pp. 12–19.

21 Sue Morgan (ed.), *The Feminist History Reader* (London and New York: Routledge, 2006), p. 4.

22 Ann-Louise Shapiro, 'History and Feminist Theory; or Talking back to the Beadle', Shapiro (ed.), *Feminist Revision History* (New Brunswick, NJ: Rutgers University Press,1994).

23 Catherine Hall, 'Feminism and Feminist History' in C. Hall, *White, Male and Middle Class: Explorations in Feminism and History* (Cambridge: Polity Press, 1992), pp. 1–40.

24 Leonore Davidoff and Catherine Hall, *Family Fortunes: Men and Women of the English Middle Class 1780–1850* (Chicago: University of Chicago Press, 1987), p. 13.

25 See, in particular, Amanda Vickery, 'Golden Age to Separate Spheres? A Review of the Categories and Chronology of English Women's History', *Historical Journal* 36 (1993), pp. 383–414.

26 Eleanor Gordon and Gwyneth Nair, *Public Lives: Women, Family and Society in Victorian Britain* (New Haven and London: Yale University Press, 2003), p. 2.

27 Gordon and Nair, *Public Lives*, pp. 2–3.

28 Callum Brown, *The Death of Christian Britain* (London and New York: Routledge, 2001), p. 12.

29 Ibid, p. 59.

30 Ibid, p. 61.

31 Ibid, p. 68.

32 Ibid, p. 9.

33 Sarah Ellis, *The Young Ladies' Reader* (1845), p. 17.

34 Brown, *Death of Christian Britain*, p. 1.

35 Sarah C. Williams, *Religious Belief and Popular Culture: Southwark c.1880–1939* (Oxford: Oxford University Press, 1999).

36 *Cassell's Saturday Journal* 5 Oct. 1899, p. 85.

37 Lovett, 'The Belief in Charms', *Folklore* 28 (1917), pp. 99–100.

38 The Essex Oral History Archive, Interview 331, 23.

39 Mary Heimann, *Catholic Devotion in Victorian England* (Oxford: Oxford University Press, 1995).

40 Williams, *Religious Belief and Popular Culture*, pp. 139–43.

41 William Kent, *The Testament to a Victorian Youth* (1938), p. 23.

42 W. H. Lax, *Lax and His Book: An Autobiography* (1937), p. 54.

43 *The British Workman Annual*, LI (1906), p. 39.

44 See Williams, *Religious Belief and Popular Culture*, pp. 126–63 and I. Bradley, *The Call to Seriousness* (New York: Macmillan, 1976), pp. 20–22. Bradley argues that in Anglican evangelical homes the habit of family prayer reinforced paternal authority in the home.

45 G. M. Young, *Victorian England: Portrait of an Age* (1936), p. 153.

46 Penny Kane, *Victorian Families in Fact and Fiction* (New York: St Martin's Press, 1995).

47 Kane, *Victorian Families*, p. 11.

48 Karen Chase and Michael Levenson, *The Spectacle of Intimacy: A Public Life of the Victorian Family* (Princeton, NJ: Princeton University Press, 2000).

49 Ibid., p. 6.

50 Inga Bryden and Janet Floyd, *Domestic Space: Reading the Nineteenth Century Interior* (Manchester: Manchester University Press, 1999).

51 Bryden and Floyd, *Domestic Space*, p. 7.

52 V. Dickerson, *Keeping the Victorian House* (New York: Garland Pub., 1995), p. xxi.

53 See, for example, Elizabeth Kowaleski-Wallace, *Consuming Subjects: Women, Shopping and Business in the 18th Century* (New York: Columbia University Press, 1997).

54 Mary W. Carpenter, *Imperial Bibles, Domestic Bodies: Women, Sexuality and Religion in the Victorian Market* (Athens: Ohio University Press, 2003), p.xvi.

55 John Tosh, *A Man's Place: Masculinity and the Middle-Class Home in Victorian England* (New Haven and London: Yale University Press, 1999), p. 4.

56 Tosh, *A Man's Place*, p. 24.

57 Deborah Cohen, *Household Gods: The British and Their Possessions* (New Haven: Yale University Press, 2006), p. xi.

58 Cohen, *Household Gods*, p. x.

59 Cohen, *Household Gods*, p. 30.

60 Boyd Hilton, *The Age of Atonement: The Influence of Evangelicalism on Social and Economic Thought, 1785–1865* (Oxford: Clarendon Press, 1991).

61 Cohen, *Household Gods*, p. 63.

62 Robert Roberts, *The Classic Slum: Salford Life in the First Quarter of the Century* (Manchester: Manchester University Press, 1971), p. 53.

63 Heimann, *Catholic Devotion*, pp. 137–74.

64 A. S. Hall, 'Reminiscences' (1988), p. 24. Held at Southwark Local Studies Library.

65 Williams, *Religious Belief and Popular Culture*, pp. 66–67.

66 James Obelkevich, *Religion and Rural Society in South Lindsey 1825–1875* (Oxford: Clarendon Press, 1976).

67 Edward Lovett, 'Amulets and Coster Barrows in London, Rome and Naples', *Folklore* 20 (1909), pp. 70–71.

68 Lovett, 'Amulets', p. 173.

69 Williams, *Religious Belief and Popular Culture*, p. 65.

70 Edward Lovett, 'English, Charms, Amulets and Mascots', *Croydon Guardian* 17 Dec. 1910.
71 Williams, *Religious Belief and Popular Culture*, pp. 54–86.
72 Edward Lovett, 'Old-fashioned Witchballs in Modern House Decoration', *Daily Mail*, 29 Dec. 1926.

2 Women, writing and the creation of theological cultures

Julie Melnyk

As late as the 1980s, most historians would have greeted the idea of nineteenth-century women's theological cultures with skepticism. Until at least the last decade of the nineteenth century, theology was gendered masculine, and, with few exceptions, women were denied access to the major theological genres: the sermon and the academic treatise. For most feminist historians, women's exclusion from theological discourse provided yet another example of the silencing of women's voices by a powerful patriarchal institution.

This skepticism resulted in part from a restricted idea of what constitutes theology. It is true that virtually no women of the nineteenth century participated in systematic or academic theology – and any woman attempting to contribute so overtly would be met with strong opposition. But to construe theology so narrowly obscures the full range of theological ideas operating within a culture and sometimes the origins of ideas later incorporated into academic theology. There is a broader understanding of theology that includes all thinking, speaking, and writing about God: it is in this sense that the nineteenth-century Unitarian divine Ezra S. Gannett claimed in 1849 that 'Every man has a theology of his own' – and pointedly chooses to use as his example not a man but a 'poor woman … who must work all the day to earn bread for her children.'[1]

In this larger sense, women participated actively in nineteenth-century theological discourse: they wrote and published works that wrestled with many of the central questions of Christian theology, including the nature of God and the Trinity, the nature of Christ, and the relation of God to creation, both natural and human. But they wrote in genres not traditionally associated with theology: devotional books, periodical articles, hymns, poetry, novels.

In the last two decades, many scholars working in different fields have begun to recognise the contributions of individual women writers to nineteenth-century theology. The work of some of these scholars appears in *Women's Theology in Nineteenth-Century Britain* (Garland, 1998). Other notable contributions include Christine L. Krueger, *The Reader's Repentance* (University of Chicago, 1992); Ruth Y. Jenkins, *Reclaiming Myths of Power* (Bucknell, 1995); and, more recently, Christiana de Groot and Marion Ann Taylor (eds), *Recovering Nineteenth-Century Women Interpreters of the Bible* (Society of Biblical Literature, 2007). Most work on nineteenth-century women's theology, however, has focussed on the ideas of particular individuals, with much attention given to canonical writers such as Christina Rossetti and Elizabeth Barrett Browning, and to social reformers including Josephine Butler and Florence Nightingale.[2]

These individual thinkers were influenced by and contributed to cultures – or, more precisely, subcultures – of women's theological thought: that is, they shared distinctive 'values, symbols, interpretations, and perspectives' within the realm of theology.[3] These subcultures were created and sustained through para-ecclesiastical organisations – mothers' meetings, missions support societies, and charitable and philanthropic groups, as well as through the medium of print in literary works, devotional books, and magazines. In this chapter I explore women's theological subcultures by examining their contributions to the discussion of three major theological issues: the sources and interpretation of divine revelation, the nature of Christ, and God's relationship to humanity. I focus here primarily on subcultures that developed from within dominant theological cultures. Because of their visibility and intrinsic interest, radical examples of women's theological cultures have often attracted the attention of feminist historians.[4] While studies of these marginalised sects can illuminate important aspects of nineteenth-century culture, their immediate influence generally remained limited. It was the subcultures within dominant traditions that affected the largest number of women and had the most lasting effect on mainstream theology.

The circulation of women's theologies and the production of theological cultures

Where did Christian women in the nineteenth century encounter theological ideas? Few, of course, read academic theology, but theological thinking reached them in a variety of forms. Within the formal worship service in the local church or chapel theological ideas came largely through the sermon, almost always given by male clergy. Women congregants, however, did not passively absorb theological teaching. To a limited extent, especially in urban areas, women could choose which church or chapel to attend and the theological position of the minister was an important factor in their choice. Even when such choices were limited or nonexistent, evidence from letters, religious fiction and the stories of parochial controversies suggests that congregants actively discussed and debated sermon contents.[5]

In formal worship services, women's theological ideas often appeared in hymns. Starting in the eighteenth century, women hymnwriters made important contributions to English hymnody, and they inevitably reshaped and reinterpreted theological ideas from their traditions even as they disseminated those ideas to both men and women in a uniquely powerful way.[6]

Women also encountered theological ideas in para-ecclesiastical religious and charitable organisations, often ones led by or dominated by women. In many dissenting sects, women led Sunday or weeknight Bible classes for girls, interpreting Scripture in an all-female context. In Roman Catholic girls' schools, nuns living in all-female communities passed on their own theological ideas to the girls entrusted

to their care.[7] Other groups, including mothers' unions and philanthropic organisations, while not specifically dedicated to the study of Christian texts and ideas,
provided a forum for the exchange of ideas and the development of a distinctive
subculture.[8] Many of these communities of women formed in the context of pre-
existing theological traditions and benefitted from established denominational
cultures and networks.

Face-to-face interactions like these provided access to theological ideas for
women of all classes. Religious women of the middle class, however, could also
access theology through print. They read books of sermons (particularly favoured
as Sunday reading); these were almost exclusively written by men, but readers had
a wider choice of preachers and theological positions than Sunday services offered.
Even more influential, perhaps, were devotional books, which were designed to be
read daily over a considerable period of time. Many of these works were written by
women (including, famously, Christina Rossetti), and they were an important
medium for the dissemination of women's theological thought, influencing their
readers' ideas about the nature of God, the meaning of revelation, and their own
identities as Christian women.[9]

Women readers also encountered theology in other genres, including magazine
articles, novels, and poetry, and many of these encounters were mediated by religious periodicals. Denominational magazines proliferated in the mid-nineteenth
century: there, mostly male and often clerical contributors wrote about the issues
of the day, including theological controversies. But more specialised religious
periodicals, generally edited by women, catered specifically to girls or women, and
proved to be powerful tools for creating community and disseminating a particular
theological culture.[10] Moreover, these magazines often contained book reviews,
alerting readers to literary and devotional works that reinforced this culture.

In the early part of the century, *The Christian Lady's Magazine* (1834–46),
edited by Charlotte Elizabeth Tonna, defined for its subscribers a theological culture which was strongly evangelical, controversial, and intellectual. Priced at one
shilling per issue it was aimed at a middle-class audience but it departed significantly from the usual content of ladies' magazines, notably in the inclusion of
Hebrew lessons, but also in its political and theological engagement. Tonna's
regular editorial column, called 'Politics' from 1834 to 1836 and 'The Protestant'
from 1837 to 1846, included discussions of political economy and factory legislation and also theology.[11] The articles, letters, book reviews, and even the literary
contributions, many of them by women, engaged with theological issues, including traditional questions about the nature of God and God's relation to human
beings, matters of dispute between evangelicals and Roman or Anglo-Catholics,
and intellectual challenges to traditional Christianity from geology to German
Higher Criticism.

A markedly different evangelical theological culture was developed and disseminated in the second half of the century through *The Christian World Magazine*, edited by Emma Jane Worboise (1866–87). Less intellectual than Tonna's
publication and reasonably priced at half a shilling,[12] *The Christian World Magazine* aimed to supplant secular, middle-brow monthlies. Its title did not define its

readership as exclusively female, but the inclusion of household tips, recipes, and a children's story indicates that its primary audience was Christian wives and mothers. (These domestic features, occupying only a page or two of each eighty-page issue, disappeared gradually over the first ten years.) The rest of the content included 'light' features on botany, health, and 'The Domestic Life of the Poets', but also poetry, serialised fiction, articles on national and religious politics and explicitly religious content, which often engaged theological issues. The tone of this magazine was evangelical and broad, appealing to a wide audience including dissenters and Anglican evangelicals.[13]

Anglo-Catholic women's periodicals also helped establish and sustain women's theological cultures. From 1851 to 1895 Charlotte M. Yonge edited one of the most influential of these, *The Monthly Packet of Evening Readings for Younger Members of the English Church*. Originally designed for middle-class and upper-class Anglican girls and priced at one shilling, in the end it reached a larger audience of women, dropping the word 'Younger' from its title in 1880. Although its content remained more conservative than its evangelical rivals, Yonge selected work on theological topics such as sin and punishment, the incarnation, and the meaning of the Eucharist, included reading suggestions, and nurtured her many female contributors, sustaining a women's theological community over more than forty years.[14]

The formation of these subcultures arose from the belief that women *as women* had something unique to bring to thinking about God, whether as a result of their intrinsic nature or their social position. In the nineteenth century, this belief was underwritten by ideological assumptions about women's nature which encouraged women's exclusion from the 'corruptions' of public life and exalted their superior spiritual sensitivity and capacity for self-sacrificial love.[15] This gender ideology also promoted the foundation of separate organisations and publications for women where these cultures could thrive.

Denominational affiliation and theological subcultures

Women's theological cultures formed subcultures within the context of larger theological cultures dominated by men. For some religious women, the foundational theology might be determined by circumstances of birth or family allegiance, but others exercised a significant degree of choice regarding their theological starting-point. Because of the intense religious conflict that characterised British Christianity over the period, middle-class women had ready access to competing ideas about revelatory epistemology, the nature of Christ, and the relationship of God to existing social institutions. This contact with a variety of theological traditions which increased as the century progressed and religious publishing expanded, encouraged women to develop new ideas and emphases that came to characterise their thinking about God.

In Scotland, the dominant theological tradition was Presbyterianism but doctrinal and institutional factors limited women's participation in its Calvinist theology. Emphasising the centrality of the family, Calvinism endorsed a 'highly patriarchal model of domestic life',[16] underwritten by its interpretation of the Old Testament, confining women to their subordinate roles within the household. The writings of one of their founders, John Knox, author of 'A Monstrous Regiment of Women' (1558), helped to enshrine misogynistic doctrine within the denomination. Moreover, Calvinist theologies of predestination often encouraged self-distrust and conformity to social expectations, as each woman struggled to confirm her sense of membership in the 'elect'. Presbyterian institutions also limited women's participation, barring women in Scotland not only from the ordained ministry until the 1960s, but also from lay positions as elders. Elders wielded considerable power within Presbyterianism, exercising a form of official discipline within each community which discouraged deviation from strict conformity and subjected even the potentially liberatory doctrine of vocation to strong institutional control. As a result, compared with English women of the same period, Scottish Presbyterian women seem to have contributed comparatively little to their dominant traditions of theological thought. Nevertheless, Lesley Orr MacDonald's work on Scottish Presbyterian women from 1830 to 1930 suggests that more research into Presbyterian women's theology could prove fruitful, including work on the writings of Scottish missionary women and on Scottish women's religious periodicals.[17]

In nineteenth-century England and Wales, the most important theological parties can be broadly characterised as Evangelical, Anglo-Catholic, and liberal, with Roman Catholicism as an increasingly influential minority tradition. Anglo-Catholics were all Anglicans, but evangelical and liberal theologies crossed denominational boundaries, including dissenters as well as members of the Church of England. These theological traditions provided the framework for the growth of women's theological cultures, influencing, and sometimes limiting, its extent and direction.

Most influential early in the century was evangelical theology, which directed the thinking of Low-Church Anglicans, Methodists, Baptists, and Congregationalists. Evangelical theology stressed the 'priesthood of the believer', that is, the ability of the individual Christian to interpret God's revelation for himself or herself and to carry on a relationship with God without the intervention of clergy. Evangelicals also saw charity and reform work as central to their religious lives, and they believed that the experiential knowledge gained through this Christian living could be as valuable as academic theology. The de-emphasis on clerical authority and endorsement of experiential knowledge proved especially beneficial for nineteenth-century women excluded from clerical roles but active in religious life. Evangelicals stressed the supreme authority of Scripture as the source of God's revelation to human beings, which made biblical interpretation the central theological activity. Finally, their Christology emphasised the atonement, Christ's sacrificial death, which made redemption accessible for all, regardless of gender.[18]

In its encouragement of women's participation in religious thought and action, evangelical theological culture set the tone for the other influential religious movements of the century. Victorian Methodism, in particular, inherited eighteenth-century traditions that encouraged women's leadership in cottage meetings and even women's preaching, but all groups shared a sense of urgency in the need for evangelism that promoted the fullest use of all human resources, male and female. Often, however, gender ideology limited the venues for women's participation and encouraged the formation of separate women's cultures within para-ecclesiastical groups such as Sunday schools, Bible studies, and charitable and mission organisations.

Victorian Anglo-Catholic theology originated in Oxford in the 1830s and gained influence rapidly. This theology re-emphasised the Roman Catholic element in Anglican thought. Anglo-Catholics elevated clerical authority, casting clergymen as direct heirs of the Apostles and reintroducing many Roman Catholic practices, including veneration of the Virgin Mary, the celebration of Saints' Days, and religious communities. In addition, they revived an interest in direct revelation through mystical experience. While both the incarnation and the atonement of Christ were important to all mainstream Christian groups, Anglo-Catholics placed particular emphasis on the Incarnation, the Word becoming flesh, which was re-enacted in the Eucharist, the fundamental rite of their worship.[19]

Anglo-Catholic women faced significant barriers when participating in theological thought, including the authority of the all-male clergy; the emphasis on education, especially in classical languages; and the higher-class profile of Anglo-Catholics, which meant that many women faced restrictions not merely from their gender but also their class position. The revival of religious communities and mysticism, together with a de-emphasis on women's biological role, however, offered opportunities for theological participation and for the formation of a separate women's theological culture.[20]

Of the three major theological traditions, liberal theology, as promulgated by the Unitarians and the Anglican Broad Church, had perhaps the least influence on women's religious thought until late in the century, at least when measured by the number of adherents.[21] Unitarians agreed in denying the doctrine of the Trinity and the divinity of Christ, but generally de-emphasised theology in favor of ethics and social engagement and encouraged a wide tolerance of theological dissent, to the point that apologists were at pains to argue that a Unitarian theology existed.[22] The Broad Church, too, encouraged tolerance for a wide range of theological views within the Church of England and, though they did not deny Christ's divinity, were prepared to countenance the denial of the doctrine of the atonement, the existence of Hell, and even the plenary inspiration of the Bible. Liberal traditions promoted a religion of rationality, minimising emotional and mystical elements and welcoming intellectual discoveries in textual criticism and science. They generally de-emphasised separate-spheres ideology in favor of a view that men and women were fundamentally similar, though women's inadequate education meant, in practice, that they were intellectually inferior. While these traditions still excluded women from the clergy, they often welcomed the contributions of a few educated women to theological thought: Harriet Martineau and Anna Letitia Barbauld, for instance, contributed theological articles to the Unitarian magazine, the *Monthly Repository*. Exceptional women thus participated in mainstream liberal theological discourse rather than establishing a separate, feminised subculture. During most of the nineteenth century, however, women's participation was hampered by particular features of the tradition: liberal theology relied on fields of knowledge, including advanced hermeneutics, from which almost all women were excluded and its conclusions were intensely controversial, which discouraged many women from publicly espousing them. Moreover, the Broad Church became identified in mid-century with 'muscular Christianity', an overtly masculine movement which reacted against the identification of religion primarily with 'feminine characteristics'.[23]

None the less, women in other theological cultures sometimes adopted liberal theology's emphases: some, like Worboise, embraced a widening of doctrinal tolerance; others used its more historical, contextualised reading of the Bible as a way of re-interpreting problematic or oppressive scriptural passages. Ultimately, the freedom of thought within the liberal tradition led some women like Martineau and Barbara Leigh Bodichon to abandon any form of orthodox religious belief.

Although not a dominant tradition, Roman Catholicism experienced a renaissance in nineteenth-century Britain and its influence increased substantially. Despite the growing Catholic population, the expansion of civil rights and the re-establishment of the Catholic hierarchy in 1850, prejudice against Catholics persisted: Catholic women were doubly marginalised in British society, as women and as members of a mistrusted religious minority. Moreover, within their own strongly clerical and hierarchical tradition there were few outlets for their theological ideas. Women's religious communities, however, provided a place where women's theological subcultures could thrive and most theological writing by Roman Catholic women in the period was published for use only within these communities. Carmen Mangion explores in this volume how the theological ideas and spiritual emphases of the founders of religious institutions were promulgated and preserved within their communities, with each institution constituting its own theological subculture. Although the number of professed sisters remained small, these theological subcultures exercised influence not only on the women directly associated with the communities, but also on generations of pupils taught in their schools.

From the roots of Britain's mainstream theological traditions sprang a variety of women's theological cultures, each sustained by particular institutions and enlightened by women's thought and religious experience. In each tradition, women confronted patriarchal structures which had excluded women's contributions. But whatever their doctrinal foundations, they all sought to find an alternative to a strongly masculinised image of God, incorporate women into the theological debate on God's relationship to humanity and re-examine the sources and authority of divine revelation, which had long been the province of men.

God's revelation

The epistemological question as to how we obtain our knowledge of God has always been central to Christian theology. Nineteenth-century women across the denominations addressed questions about sources of religious knowledge and wrestled to define the extent to which women could have independent access to that knowledge.

Most Victorian Christians agreed that the Bible was a primary source of divine knowledge, though there was less agreement about how and by whom the Bible should be interpreted. Nineteenth-century women, in particular, wanted to interpret the patriarchal texts in light of their own knowledge and experience. Within the evangelical traditions, the doctrine of the priesthood of the believer guaranteed women's right to interpret the Scripture (with the guidance of the Holy Spirit). Anglo-Catholics might impose the reservation that the Church itself had the final say in interpretation, but literate laypeople were still encouraged to engage with the Bible, and, in one genre or another, many published their interpretations.

Women's scriptural exegesis appears frequently in many different genres. It pervades religious novels: sometimes in a homiletic narratorial voice, other times filtered through admirable characters. Exegesis also appears frequently in poetry and hymns, sometimes in periodical articles, and almost always in devotional works. While every exegetical act by a woman was an assertion of religious authority, many instances of Scriptural interpretation in women's writing were casual or uncontroversial, reinforcing socially-endorsed moral behavior or attitudes. Others, however, bore directly on theological issues, including the nature of God and of revelation, and these, in turn, helped delineate the parameters of both women's and mainstream theological cultures under development in the nineteenth century.

Evangelical women writers tended to adhere to a more literal reading of Scripture, and their exegesis often followed fairly conventional lines. Given the internal tensions within the Bible, however, the choice of which texts to emphasise and explicate often produced unconventional results: for instance, in her defense of women's preaching, Catherine Booth, co-founder of the Salvation Army, insisted on a literal (and liberatory) interpretation of Galatians 3:28:

> 'There is neither Jew nor Greek, ... there is neither male nor female, for ye are all one in Christ Jesus' (Gal. 3:28). If this passage does not teach that in the privileges, duties, and responsibilities of Christ's Kingdom, all differences of nation, caste, and sex are abolished, we should like to know what it does teach, and wherefore it was written (see also 1 Cor. 7:22).[24]

In addition, the evangelical embrace of the Old Testament allowed for a substantial admixture of the prophetic tradition, as in the case of Josephine Butler, whose reading of the Bible led her to an image of God as advocate and liberator of the oppressed.

The Anglo-Catholic tradition, however, encouraged a less literal reading of the Bible, allowing for historical contextualisation and poetic language, which gave women interpreting the Bible considerable latitude, and this freedom increased through the century as the Higher Criticism began to influence ordinary Christians.

This freedom was particularly valuable to women writers dealing with misogynist elements of the Bible, including the legacy of Eve. Interpretations of Eve's sin and punishment by High Church poets Elizabeth Rundle Charles (*Sketches of the Women of Christendom*) and Christina Rossetti (*Letter and Spirit*) both de-emphasise Eve's unique responsibility for the Fall, seeing her as understandably deceived rather than fatally weak, and as the source of redemption as well as of sin.[25] By vindicating Eve, these women sought to remove obstacles to women's religious authority.

Some repressive injunctions could be difficult to overcome. St Paul, for example, repeatedly used the creation story and Eve's transgression to justify men's supremacy[26] and, in 1 Timothy 2:11–14, to relegate women to 'silence' and 'subjection':

> Let the woman learn in silence with all subjection. But I suffer not a woman to teach, nor to usurp authority over the man, but to be in silence. For Adam was first formed, then Eve. And Adam was not deceived, but the woman being deceived was in the transgression.

In response, some women, such as Josephine Butler, interpreted these passages contextually: in her view, St Paul applied 'the essential teaching of her Master to the accidents of the time and society in which he lived',[27] so that they do not carry authority beyond that society. Others countered them with other Pauline passages, such as Galatians 3:27–29: 'There is neither Jew nor Greek, there is neither bond nor free, there is neither male nor female: for ye are all one in Christ Jesus.' By citing and interpreting this passage as universal and authoritative, women writers harnessed the Scripture as support for their own religious and theological activity, as illustrated in the passage from the *Christian Lady's Magazine* quoted below.[28]

Some women exegetes in High Church traditions used their interpretive freedom to emphasise feminine elements in the Godhead, particularly through their treatment of the Holy Spirit. In their writings on Whitsuntide, celebrating the advent of the Holy Spirit at Pentecost, both Harriet Auber and Elizabeth Rundle Charles feminise the Holy Spirit through their exegesis. In Auber's Whitsuntide hymn, 'Our Blest Redeemer, Ere He Breathed', she initially emphasises the power of the Holy Spirit:

> He came in tongues of living flame,
> To teach, convince, subdue;
> All-powerful as the wind He came,
> As viewless too.

But Auber also feminises the Holy Spirit as a maternal 'dove' with 'sheltering wings'; like an ideal Victorian woman, the Spirit works through 'sweet influence', acting as mother to the Christian community with a gentle voice that 'checks each fault, that calms each fear/And speaks of Heaven'. Auber thus links this feminised Spirit with the full spiritual and cultural power of God while affirming a highly conventional construction of femininity. Elizabeth Rundle Charles, in *By the Coming of the Holy Ghost: Thoughts for Whitsuntide* (1888), identifies the creative force of God in Genesis, often interpreted as the Holy Spirit, with the Bride of Revelation. As Marion Ann Taylor points out, Charles uses biblical interpretation to represent the creative work of God's Spirit as fundamentally feminine:

> 'As a hen gathereth (Matt 23:37).' The love of the mother as well as of the father is appealed to in unveiling the love of God. 'As one whom his mother comforteth (Isa 66:13).' Here it is used with reference to the material world. And how beautiful and tender the symbol is! the whole world, as it were loved into life! ... The image is one, not of a momentary flash of creative power, but of the continuous brooding of creative life-giving love. Not as a maker ... but as a mother-bird, patiently watching the first throbs of life, and quickening them into movement, is the Creation represented.[29]

The exegeses of Auber and Charles revise the patriarchal God by emphasising the feminine characteristics of the Spirit.

Scripture was not the only source of divine revelation for Anglo-Catholics. Other sources included church tradition, which of course compelled women to accept men as intermediaries of knowledge but also provided a mystical tradition which allowed women greater scope for reimagining the relationship between God and human beings. Christina Rossetti, for example, revived the imagery of Christ as Bridegroom and the Soul as Bride, portraying the feminine figure as the paradigm of Christian experience and providing the mystic with direct knowledge of God as Love. In addition, the sacramentalism of Anglo-Catholic doctrine provided for the possibility of discovering God's revelation in ordinary life: just as the ordinary bread and wine of the Eucharist became for Anglo-Catholics the body and blood of Christ Himself, so ordinary actions and objects of everyday life took on almost mystical spiritual significance. This kind of sacramentalism, combined with the poetic interpretation of Scripture, encouraged the development of a remarkable tradition of High Church poetry.[30] In *Letter and Spirit*, Rossetti expresses in prose this sacramental vision:

> We should exercise that far higher privilege which appertains to Christians, of having 'the mind of Christ'; and then the two worlds, visible and invisible, will become familiar to us even as they were to Him; and on occasion sparrow and lily will recall God's providence, seed His Word, earthly bread the Bread of Heaven, a plough the danger of drawing back; to fill a basin and take a towel will preach a sermon on self-abasement; boat, fishing-net, flock or fold of sheep, each will convey an allusion; wind, water, fire, the sun, a star, a vine, a door, a lamb, will shadow forth mysteries.[31]

Through this sacramental vision, women and men approached theological knowledge on equal terms, both living God's reality as they attempted to put it into language, language often metaphorical and symbolic rather than literal.

Christ and women's theological cultures

In confronting the problem of the patriarchal Father-God, women of all main-stream denominations turned to the second person of the Trinity. With his selfless love and self-sacrifice, Christ seemed to embody 'feminine' characteristics against the 'masculine' authority and righteous anger of the Father. Evangelical women through the eighteenth and nineteenth centuries participated in the development and promulgation of a feminised image of Christ, one that emphasised his role as loving and suffering Saviour.[32] Women's identification with the feminised Christ could be used to claim for women a spiritual superiority and a measure of religious authority, as in this 1842 *Christian Lady's Magazine* article:

> 'In Christ Jesus there is neither male nor female': both are accountable crea-tures … and both, if they enter heaven at all, must enter 'through much tri-bulation'. But if it be so, that natural sorrow, when sanctified by divine grace, becomes instrumental in perfecting the heirs of glory; then we may reasonably look for the most frequent exemplification of Christian character in that sex which has to bear the largest burden of natural grief … the sorrows of the woman are 'greatly multiplied' [33]

For women, however, this kind of identification with Christ was double-edged: even as it gave them a claim to more religious and even social authority it linked that authority inextricably with suffering. Nevertheless, evangelical women pro-moted this feminine image of Christ: a loving, suffering, self-sacrificing, feminised Saviour.

While some Anglo-Catholic women also identified with Christ as a suffering Saviour, others developed an alternative image of Christ with its own implications for women's religious participation. They focussed not on the atonement but on the incarnation, Christ as the earthly embodiment of God's love, and its re-enactment in the Eucharist. High Church women such as Felicia Skene, a novelist and social reformer concerned with the rescue of fallen women, saw the imitation of Christ required of every Christian as a call to embody on earth God's compassion through service to others.[34] Sometimes women writers linked this call to service with a theology of action, emphasising that theological insight could be gained through acts of compassion. Within the Anglo-Catholic tradition, the revival of women's religious communities, almost all of which were active rather than con-templative, not only provided an opportunity for women to live a life of service to God and others, but also a place where this theology of action could flourish.[35]

These theological cultures with their differing Christologies had an influence on each other and on mainstream religious discourse: the feminised image of Christ became arguably the dominant Victorian paradigm, and the theology of action based on the imitation of Christ grew in importance throughout the late nine-teenth and early twentieth centuries.[36] Beyond orthodox Christianity, women also developed heretical Christologies, less pervasive but more radical than their main-stream counterparts, which introduced the idea of a fully female Christ.

Separate-spheres ideology, with its distinction between 'masculine' and 'feminine' virtues, presented Christians with the following puzzle: did Christ represent the perfection of all human virtue or only masculine virtue? The mainstream response was the feminisation of Christ, the claim that he embodied feminine and masculine virtues. Some groups, however, saw a need for a female Christ to complement the male Saviour. The Shakers found their female Christ in founder Ann Lee (1736–84), the Southcottians in Joanna Southcott (1750–1814). In her theological work *Suggestions for Thought* (1860), Florence Nightingale also considers the possibility of woman as Saviour:

> The next Christ will perhaps be a female Christ. But do we see one woman who looks like a female Christ? Or even like 'the messenger before' her 'face', to go before her and prepare the hearts and minds for her?[37]

Nightingale came to see herself as a female Saviour, repeatedly linking events in her life to the life of Christ and interpreting her suffering in Christ-like fashion. As Sue Zemka and Ruth Y. Jenkins emphasise, however, the Christ with whom Nightingale identifies is an unorthodox figure: fully human rather than divine, dying with his work unfinished and without a resurrection. But her theology remained largely unique to her: *Suggestions for Thought* was privately printed and circulated within a small group, so her unique Christology never reached a broad public.

Josephine Butler, however, has a better claim as founder of a female theological subculture. Her theological ideas emerged in the context of her public campaign against the Contagious Diseases Acts (CDA) in Britain and similar legislation in Europe and India. Women's social position and unique suffering became a central focus for her theological thinking as well as her explicitly political activity. The organisation she founded in 1869, the Ladies' National Association for the Repeal of the Contagious Diseases Act which grew to over 1,400 members, helped spread her ideas about women and God. In her widely-read pamphlets and books, she promoted a collective identification of women with Christ; she saw the female Saviour not as an extraordinary individual but as a community of women united in one cause. She repeatedly compared the sufferings of women, particularly working women and prostitutes, to those of Christ, and saw women as united in a salvific and revolutionary mission to institute God's kingdom on earth.[38] While many saw women's suffering as Christ-like, Butler extended this to unite women together as a communal Christ with the powers of redemption. Her distinctive Christology thus created a subculture with powerful practical consequences. Her theological ideas influenced not only women in the Ladies' National but also thousands of others in Britain and abroad who read her pamphlets and heard her speeches.[39] That the women she rallied and organised to combat the CDAs did not disband after their repeal but rather continued to work to realise that vision of the 'Redeemer's Kingdom', testifies to the sense of salvific mission they derived from Butler's theology.

God's relation to Woman

In traditional theological discussions of God's relation to Man, the use of the 'universal masculine' disguised the fact that, until the twentieth century, Christian discourse almost always represented God as dealing differently with women than with men. For nineteenth-century religious women, God's relation to women became a central theological question.

Evidence about how God relates to women was derived from a variety of sources. Some conservative thinkers regarded their own contemporary social arrangements as providentially determined, which led them to conclude that restrictive social roles for women enjoyed divine warrant and provided evidence of God's will for women.[40] More reform-minded Christians, however, wanted to challenge elements of the status quo as radically out of keeping with God's will. Thus many women writers denied that women's current position reflected God's will for women in society.

Explicit biblical injunctions about women, such as those in Paul's epistles, provided another source of evidence. Christian scripture, however, offers few explicit discussions of God's relation to Woman, so most women writers turned to another powerful source of evidence: extrapolation from God's dealings with individual women. Articles and books concerning women of the Bible were written and eagerly read by women in all theological traditions, but they were most powerful among evangelically-inclined women who held a higher view of the authority of the Bible.

Some of the most influential treatments of women of the Bible appeared in women's evangelical magazines. *The Christian Lady's Magazine* (*CLM*) and *The Christian World Magazine* (*CWM*) both published long-running series of articles on female characters from the Bible. The *CLM* published a 'Female Biography of Scripture' by 'Lydia' and the *CWM* produced reprints of articles by Harriet Beecher Stowe first published in America in the *Christian Union*, which Worboise retitled, improbably, 'Portraits of the Patriarchs', perhaps as a deliberate masking of its controversial content, perhaps as a way of signalling the creation of a new tradition of Patriarchs.

Both series cite the usual Old Testament examples, such as Esther and Deborah, though Lydia also tackles obscure figures such as 'Manoah's Wife' and 'The Wise Woman of Tekoah'. While Lydia is more cautious in her generalisations, both authors clearly wish to use these figures to reach conclusions about God's relations to women and to establish precedents for women's public utterance and leadership. The story of the prophetess Deborah (Judges 4–5) provides striking examples of women transgressing the boundaries of the private sphere by producing inspired public poetry and assuming leadership roles in government and in military action. Interpretations of Deborah's story indicate the direction taken by many of these treatments of biblical women. For example, Lydia's 1841 article on Deborah begins, as is typical of such religious revisionings of women's roles, with qualifications and hedges, stating the principle underlying women's separate sphere before presenting an example which seems to breach it:

The sentence of subjection originally pronounced upon the woman, as being first in the transgression, and the tempter of man, is not repealed by the gospel. Woman is still made inferior to man, as he is to the Lord. 'The head of the woman is the man, and the head of every man is Christ.' Silence, subjection, obedience; attention to household duties; to the care of the sick, to the education of children; ... these are the chief duties enjoined upon Christian women in the pages of the New Testament.[41]

In contrast, Lydia uses the story of Deborah to combat the generalisations of the Pauline epistles:

But though, as a general rule, the sphere of woman leads her far from the strife and shew of life, and bids her rather to retire and submit, than to come forward and act; yet the voice of nature and revelation alike sanction those occasional instances, in which she has emerged from obscurity to enact the part of a ruler or a patriot; or to bow the hearts of all by strains of eloquence and passion ... And the voice of inspiration sanctions this peculiar employment of extraordinary gifts.[42]

While Lydia here emphasises the 'occasional', 'peculiar', and 'extraordinary' nature of Deborah, she also invokes this case almost as legal precedent. She is even more explicit about the use of Deborah (and other biblical women) as examples for her nineteenth-century readers to follow: 'what woman, professing the quiet, unobtrusive character of a female disciple of Christ, would not have shrunk from the exercise of such endowments, had not the example of the holy women of old shewn how such gifts may be lawfully exercised'.[43] Christine Krueger in *The Reader's Repentance* analyses how Tonna's treatment of Deborah is used to vindicate her own public speech,[44] but here the *CLM* extends the possibility of special calling to the larger community of readers as well.

Stowe's later series in the *CWM* is bolder about the use of Deborah as a model, reflecting religious women's growing confidence about the justification of their public work. She portrays the woman-judge as natural outgrowth of Mosaic law: 'We are not surprised at the familiar manner in which it is announced as a thing quite in the natural order that the chief magistrate of the Jewish nation ... was a woman divinely ordained and gifted.'[45] Stowe emphasises not the special gift, but the ordinariness of women's leadership and its foundations in the system inaugurated by God. Jael's deception and murder of Sisera, from which Tonna distances herself, is here represented as a feminist act of communal self-defense: when Deborah praises Jael, Stowe comments: 'Deborah saw in the tyrant thus overthrown the ravisher and brutal tyrant of helpless women, and she extolled the spirit by which Jael had entrapped the ferocious beast whom her woman's weakness could not otherwise have subdued ... it is a woman driven to the last extreme of indignation at outrages practised on her sex that thus rejoices.'[46]

Lydia and Stowe treat Deborah as a model for women's participation in public action – political and even military leadership – and in public discourse, particularly poetry. Both authors explicitly link Deborah's story with Hannah and the Virgin Mary, suggesting a long tradition of religious women's poetry. Here, again, the *CLM* focuses on the exercise of extraordinary gifts, whereas Stowe represents this tradition of women's poetry as an outgrowth of egalitarian theocracy: 'We shall see, as we follow down the line of history, that women of this lofty poetic inspiration were the natural product of the Jewish laws and institutions. They grew out of them as certain flowers grow out of certain soils.'[47] Stowe reinforces her point by the multiplication of examples: in other articles she analyses Sarah, Hagar, Rebekah, Leah and Rachel, Miriam, Jephthah's daughter, Delilah, Hannah, Ruth, Judith, and Esther. She also extends her lesson beyond the 'patriarchs' to the women of the New Testament in 'The Church of the Master': 'Prophetesses and holy women, inspired by God, had always held an important place in its history, and it was in full accord with the national sense of propriety that women should hold a conspicuous place in the new society of Jesus.'[48]

Extensions of the tradition of typological exegesis, in which biblical characters could be interpreted as 'types' fulfilled in the lives of later believers,[49] allowed these women writers to use scriptural narratives as paradigms of God's attitudes towards women and their religious and even political work. However, while Lydia's interpretation of Deborah condones the public participation of a few chosen women, she still seems to relegate most women to 'silence, subjection, obedience' even as she invites each reader to consider herself to be a possible exception to the rule. In contrast, Stowe's interpretation extends the right to equality and public participation to all women as part of a liberatory Judeo-Christian tradition.

While evangelically-influenced women's theology insisted on the continuity of biblical teaching from the Old to the New Testament, women working in Anglo-Catholic traditions stressed the *discontinuity* between the old and the new dispensation, the time before and after the foundation of the Church, which made Old Testament female figures less readily available as role models. While they regarded the Bible as a source of revealed truth, they also held that the Church was a further, and to some extent a higher, authority, determining the proper interpretation of Scripture. Their collections about biblical women, such as Elizabeth Rundle Charles's book of poetry, *The Women of the Gospels* (1867), often focus exclusively on women of the New Testament.

Given the revival of Roman Catholic traditions and their focus on the incarnation, the most obvious Anglo-Catholic female paradigm is the Virgin Mary, whose reputation was revived in the nineteenth century.[50] In England, many Roman Catholic religious institutions centered their spiritual lives on the veneration of Mary, but the figure of the Virgin was a fraught one for nineteenth-century Anglo-Catholics.[51] High Church Anglicans were constantly accused of Romanising the English Church and one of the main points of contention was the veneration of Mary. So while Anglo-Catholic women writers invoked Mary, they often emphasised the meek, mild, and maternal Mary of Protestantism rather than the powerful feminine symbol of Roman Catholic tradition. For example, when in *Women of the Gospels* Elizabeth Rundle Charles turns in her fourth poem on Mary to her heavenly coronation, she celebrates Mary, but repeatedly attempts to deny her special status:

> Thou shalt be crown'd, O mother blest,
> Our hearts behold thee crown'd e'en now;
> The crown of motherhood, earth's best,
> O'ershadowing thy maiden brow.

Charles identifies the crown with motherhood itself, an honour Mary shares with many women. The following stanza praises Mary as 'First Singer of the Church', for her song of praise, the Magnificat (Luke 1:46–55), which was included in the Anglican Evening Service: nineteenth-century women writers often invoked Mary as religious poet rather than mother, using her as a model for women's religious utterance. The fourth and fifth stanzas, however, again emphasise Mary's humility and assimilate her into a larger community of Christian souls: 'Thou shalt be crown'd, but not a queen'; instead Mary shares the common triumph of redeemed Christian souls:

> Thou shalt be crown'd, but not alone,
> No lonely pomp shall weigh thee down,
> Crown'd with the myriads round His throne
> And casting at His feet thy crown.[52]

Charles's poem reduces Mary's authority and thus her usefulness as a paradigm of women's religious power, but it also reduces the distance between the Mother of God and the ordinary Christian woman, making God's dealings with Mary relevant to the question of his dealings with women in general.

New Testament women other than the Virgin Mary provided exemplars of God's relations with women that were used by writers from different theological cultures in different ways. The story of Mary and Martha of Bethany, related in Luke 10:38–42, was a particular site of contention that reveals differences in evangelical and Anglo-Catholic theological cultures. Although writers from both traditions celebrated Jesus's defence of Mary and her desire to participate in the intellectual and spiritual life he represented – 'Mary has chosen the better part, which will not be taken away from her' – many evangelicals were at pains to defend Martha's domestic work as worthwhile. In the most thoughtful of these defenses, the anonymous author of 'Far Above Rubies' (1870) interprets the story of Mary and Martha as a new vision of womanhood which integrates the material and spiritual without privileging either: 'Practical yet intellectual, strong yet tender, broad yet devout, many-sided in apprehension of gifts and graces.'[53] In contrast, the High Church tradition tended to identify Mary's choice of 'the better part' with a contemplative, celibate life, as Christina Rossetti does in *Letter and Spirit* (1883). In Anglo-Catholic women writers' interpretation of this story God offered women two different vocations: one as a married woman, serving the material needs of a family and one as a celibate woman, devoted entirely to spiritual enlightenment and worship.

This Anglo-Catholic focus on the contemplative life was enhanced by the focus on another source of exemplars of God's dealings with women: the tradition of female saints. These include New Testament figures (St Mary Magdalene, St Anne) as well as figures throughout Church history. Elizabeth Rundle Charles, among others, worked diligently to recover the lives of women saints in *Sketches of the Women of Christendom* (1880) and *Martyrs and Saints of the First Twelve Centuries* (1887). Among the women saints celebrated in the Anglican calendar, almost all post-biblical saints are virgin martyrs with the exception of the English saint Etheldreda, 'Queen, Virgin, and Abbess'. Her embrace of a monastic life underlines the importance of the celibate woman among Anglo-Catholics as well as the new opportunities their homosocial religious communities offered women. This calling of saints to celibate service challenged ideas that all women were 'called' to serve the family. In the latter part of the century evangelical women also found inspiration in female saints: Josephine Butler wrote admiringly of God's work through Catherine of Siena[54] and Emma Jane Worboise included stories of saints' lives in *The Christian World Magazine*.

Crucial to all these stories, biblical or hagiographical, is the idea of vocation and of God's calling an individual woman to fulfil a particular role. But these stories were invariably interpreted as carrying larger lessons about women's roles and abilities and their place in God's plan.

Changes in theology and women's theological cultures

The nineteenth century was a period of unsettlement and rapid change, and women's theological cultures both responded to changes in religious thought and institutions and helped to determine the direction of those changes. Historians sometimes conceptualise the changes under way in the nineteenth century in terms of 'feminisation'.[55] By the end of the century in Britain, women outnumbered men as church attenders and church workers in nearly every denomination. Despite the conservative force of all-male clergy, these women, with their ideas and preferences often shaped by their participation in female theological subcultures, influenced – or 'feminised' – the larger denominational culture: their influence helped alter, among other things, the culture's perception of Christ, its views of women's spirituality and vocation and the forms of its social engagement.

While often endorsing a separate 'woman's mission', nineteenth-century women's theological endeavours made bold claims about its nature and extent. Even as women's participation and leadership in public philanthropic work expanded, religious women writers continued to press for even more opportunities to fulfil God's will. They endorsed exclusively religious vocations for women, encouraging social acceptance of Anglican and Roman Catholic sisterhoods and deaconess organisations in Anglican and Presbyterian churches, for example. By 1877, an evangelical writer in *The Christian World Magazine* even argued that women's ministry included all public service up to and including work as clergy, doctors, lawyers, and members of Parliament.[56]

The focus of women's theological writing also shifted over the course of the century. During the 1830s and 1840s, sectarian conflict dominated, as evangelical and Tractarian apologists argued their positions and dissenters struggled with the Established Church for recognition of their civil and religious rights. In this period, women writers were often regarded by leading men in their camps as reservists called into action for crucial theological battles. After 1860, while doctrinal differences persisted, attention shifted to more urgent issues: secularisation and religious doubt and the unmet spiritual and physical needs of an industrial, urban society. In response, women's theological writing focused more attention on doctrines uniting Christians across denominations and calling for social action.

Despite the widening sphere of women's religious work and thought, by the end of the century mainstream churches, which had once offered women socially acceptable forms of public participation unavailable in secular society, now competed more directly with the wider world. As women gained entry into leadership positions in other professions, religious service remained restricted by gender, and the clergy remained an all-male preserve. The way forward for women lay in abandoning an ideology of difference in favour of a more egalitarian feminism. Liberal theology, with its emphasis on rationality and its roots in the Enlightenment, fostered this form of feminism. For this reason, women from the liberal theological tradition more often took the lead in political feminism in the early twentieth century. Some women writers contributed directly to liberal theological debates, publishing in mainstream journals such as the *Nineteenth Century*,[57] rather than the female periodical press. Other women found opportunities in the secular world that more conservative religious traditions denied them, opportunities to assume positions of leadership and to push for radical social transformation. As the nineteenth century ended, mainstream women's theological cultures lost much of their cultural influence and their centrality in women's religious lives.

Nevertheless, nineteenth-century women's theological cultures contributed to modern feminism in important ways. Although women from these cultures, with their ties to separate-spheres ideology and patriarchal texts, were left ill-equipped to deal with many of the economic and political issues central to modern feminism, they took from those cultures an emphasis on social change to bring society into line with God's will. They were able to apply their reconceptualised images of Christ and Christianity to critiques of patriarchal institutions. And within these subcultures, women were encouraged to organise and to participate actively in bringing about social change, representing it as 'vocation', 'mission' or 'ministry'.

Nineteenth-century women's theology also left its mark on British Christianity. Its image of Christ as loving, selfless and nurturing is still dominant in many churches, sustained in part by the hymns written by Victorian women. Their emphasis on a theology of action has been widely influential in the twentieth century as has their promotion of liberatory aspects of Christianity. Finally, these women's theological cultures form an important part of the tradition of women's theology, still practiced today, that takes seriously the idea that women *as* women – whether as a result of biology or gendered experience – have distinctive insights into the divine to contribute to thinking about God and God's relation to the world.

Further reading

Christiana de Groot and Marion Ann Taylor (eds), *Recovering Nineteenth-Century Women Interpreters of the Bible* (Society of Biblical Literature, 2007).

Ruth Y. Jenkins, *Reclaiming Myths of Power: Women Writers and the Victorian Spiritual Crisis* (Lewisburg, PA: Bucknell University Press, 1995).

Christine Krueger, *The Reader's Repentance: Women Preachers and Nineteenth-Century Social Discourse* (Chicago and London: University of Chicago Press, 1992).

Julie Melnyk (ed.), *Women's Theology in Nineteenth-Century Britain: Transfiguring the Faith of Their Fathers* (New York and London: Garland Publishing, 1998).

Sue Zemka, *Victorian Testaments: The Bible, Christology, and Literary Authority in Early-Nineteenth-Century British Culture* (Stanford: Stanford University Press, 1997).

Notes

1 Ezra S. Gannett, 'The Nature and Importance of our Theology', *Monthly Repository* 4th Series 12:1 (1849), pp. 107–30, here p. 109.

2 See also Linda M. Lewis, *Elizabeth Barrett Browning's Spiritual Progress: Face to Face with God* (Columbia: University of Missouri Press, 1998); Diane d'Amico, *Christina Rossetti: Faith, Gender, and Time* (Baton Rouge: Louisiana State University Press, 1999); Dinah Roe, *Christina Rossetti's Faithful Imagination: The Devotional Poetry and Prose* (London: Palgrave Macmillan, 2007); Sue Zemka, *Victorian Testaments: The Bible, Christology, and Literary Authority in Early-Nineteenth-Century British Culture* (Stanford: Stanford UP, 1997); Nancy Boyd, *Three Victorian Women Who Changed Their World* (Oxford: OUP, 1982); Helen Mathers, 'Evangelicalism and Feminism. Josephine Butler, 1828–1906' in Sue Morgan (ed.), *Women, Religion and Feminism in Britain, 1750–1900* (London: Palgrave Macmillan, 2002), pp. 123–37; Jenny Daggers and Diana Neal (eds), *Sex, Gender, and Religion: Josephine Butler Revisited* (New York: Peter Lang, 2006).

3 From a definition of 'culture' in J. A. Banks and C. A. McGee, *Multicultural Education* (Needham Heights, MA: Allyn & Bacon, 1989).

4 These radical women's subcultures include the Southcottians, Shakerism, Spiritualism, and Theosophy. See especially Catherine Wessinger (ed.), *Women's Leadership in Marginal Religions* (Urbana: University of Illinois Press, 1993); Frances Brown, *Joanna Southcott: The Woman Clothed with the Sun* (Cambridge: Lutterworth, 2002); Susan Juster, *Doomsayers: Anglo-American Prophecy in the Age of Revolution* (Philadelphia: University of Pennsylvania Press, 2003); Jean M. Humez, *Mother's First-Born Daughters: Early Shaker Writings on Women and Religion* (Bloomington: Indiana UP, 1993); Alex Owen, *The Darkened Room* (London: Virago, 1989); Joy Dixon, *Divine Feminine: Theosophy and Feminism in England* (Baltimore: Johns Hopkins University Press, 2001); and two articles in Pat Holden's *Women's Religious Experience* (London: Croom Helm, 1983): Vieda Skultans, 'Mediums, Controls, and Eminent Men' (pp. 15–26) and Diana Burfield, 'Theosophy and Feminism' (pp. 27–56).

5 Such discussions are mentioned briefly in letters and memoirs, but in *Overdale* (London: James Clarke, 1869), Emma Jane Worboise provides a striking fictional example in which women at the circulating library debate the theology of their vicar's sermon (pp. 262–69).

6 Hymns were considered so pedagogically powerful that denominations regularly 'corrected' the theology of hymns to be included in their hymnals.

7 Carmen M. Mangion, *Contested Identities: Catholic Women Religious in Nineteenth-Century England and Wales* (Manchester: Manchester University Press, 2008), p. 87.

8 According to Frank Prochaska, these meetings generally involved a 'religious address, often in the form of a commentary on a tract or passage from scripture, which resembled a sermon'. See Prochaska, 'A Mothers Country: Mothers' Meetings and Family Welfare in Britain, 1850–1950', *History* 74 (1989), pp. 379–99, here p. 385.

9 See, among many others, Christina Rossetti, *Called to be Saints* (1881), *Time Flies* (1885), *The Face of the Deep* (1892); Harriet Martineau, *Devotional Exercises for the Use of Young Persons* (1823); Caroline Fry, *Daily Readings* (1835); Sarah Mary Campbell, *My Daily Text Book* (1878); Charlotte Bickersteth Wheeler, *Chimes from By-gone Years: Thoughts for Daily Reading* (1878); Elizabeth M. Sewell, *Private Devotions for Young Persons* (1881).

10 For more detail, see my article 'Women's Theology and the British Periodical Press', in Linda Woodhead (ed.), *Reinventing Religion* (Aldershot: Ashgate, 2001), pp. 191–97.

11 For further analysis of these editorials, see Monica Correa Fryckstedt, 'Charlotte Elizabeth Tonna and *The Christian Lady's Magazine*', *Victorian Periodicals Review* 14 (Summer 1981), pp. 42–51.

12 At half a shilling (6d) an issue, *The Christian World Magazine* was half the price of secular monthlies such as *Blackwood's*, *Fraser's* and *Cornhill*, and within the budget of most middle-class families.

13 Circulation figures are difficult to establish for these religious women's periodicals. The best evidence of good circulation figures derives from their longevity: 31 years for *The Christian World Magazine*, 48 years for *The Monthly Packet*. The *CWM*'s parent publication *The Christian World* claimed a circulation of 100,000 in 1867 [Marianne Farningham, *A Working Woman's Life* (James Clarke, 1907)], and a Special Note to Readers in an 1871 issue of *CWM* apologises for selling out repeatedly in January, despite having four printings done (p. 160).

14 June Sturrock, 'Establishing Identity: Editorial Correspondence from the Early Years of *The Monthly Packet*', *Victorian Periodicals Review* 39:3 (2006), pp. 266–79.

15 See Sarah Williams' essay in this volume.

16 See Lesley Orr MacDonald, *A Unique and Glorious Mission: Women and Presbyterianism in Scotland 1830–1930* (Edinburgh: John Donald, 2000).

17 Nevertheless, MacDonald argues in *A Unique and Glorious Mission* that, from 1830 to 1930, Scottish Presbyterianism became increasingly 'feminised': influenced by evangelicalism and by the example of women's work in English churches and chapels, Presbyterian churches began to offer more opportunities for women's participation, though they continued to lag decades behind denominations in England (*passim*; see esp. Chap. 2).

18 D.W. Bebbington, *Evangelicalism in Modern Britain* (London: Unwin Hyman, 1989); Kenneth Hylson-Smith, *Evangelicals in the Church of England, 1734–1984* (Edinburgh: T&T Clark, 1988); Elisabeth Jay, *The Religion of the Heart* (Oxford: OUP, 1979).

19 See John Shelton Reed, *Glorious Battle: The Cultural Politics of Victorian Anglo-Catholicism*; (Nashville: Vanderbilt University Press, 1996), C. Brad Faught, *The Oxford Movement* (University Park: Pennsylvania State University Press, 2004).

20 See J. Shelton Reed, '"A Female Movement": The Feminization of Nineteenth-Century Anglo-Catholicism', *Anglican and Episcopal History* 57 (June 1988), pp. 199–238.

21 This tradition has, however, received much attention from feminist historians attracted by its progressive social agenda. See, among others, Kathryn Gleadle, *The Early Feminists: Radical Unitarians and the Emergence of the Women's Rights Movement, 1831–5* (New York: St Martin's Press, 1995); Ruth Watts, *Gender, Power and the Unitarians in England, 1760–1860* (New York: Longman, 1998).

22 See, for example, Ezra S. Gannett, 'The Nature and Importance of our Theology', *Monthly Repository* 4th Series 12:1 (1849), pp. 107–30. See also Gleadle, *The Early Feminists*.

23 See Tod E. Jones, *The Broad Church* (Lanham, Md.: Lexington Books, 2003).

24 Catherine Booth, *Female Ministry, or Woman's Right to Preach the Gospel* (London: Morgan & Chase, 1959), p. 19.

25 Congregationalist Elizabeth Barrett Browning famously re-interpreted the story of Eve as Greek tragedy in *A Drama of Exile* (1844), casting Eve as both sinner and saviour.

26 See I Corinthians 11:3, 8–9.

27 Butler, *Prophets and Prophetesses* (1898), quoted in Eileen Janes Yeo, 'Protestant Feminists and Catholic Saints in Victorian Britain' in Yeo (ed.), *Radical Femininity* (Manchester University Press, 1998), pp. 127–48; here, p. 136.

28 See also Josephine Butler's account of Catherine of Siena's vocational vision [*Catherine of Siena*, 3rd edn (London: Marshall, 1894), p. 46]. Barbara Bodichon quotes this passage at the beginning of *Women and Work* (London: Bosworth & Harrison, 1857), title page.

29 Marion Ann Taylor, 'Elizabeth Rundle Charles: Translating the Letter of Scripture Into Life', in *Recovering Women Interpreters*, pp. 149–63, here p. 159.

30 G.B. Tennyson, *Victorian Devotional Poetry* (Cambridge, MA: Harvard University Press, 1981).

31 Christina Rossetti, *Letter and Spirit* (London: SPCK, 1882), pp. 131–32.

32 For more on the development and uses of the feminised Christ, see my article '"Mighty Victims": Women Writers and the Feminised Christ', *Victorian Literature and Culture* 31:1 (March 2003), pp. 131–57.

33 'Lydia', 'Female Biography of Scripture: Manoah's Wife', *Christian Lady's Magazine* 17 (1842), pp. 503ff.

34 Suzanne Rickard, 'Victorian Women with Causes: Writing, Religion and Action', in Morgan (ed.), *Women, Religion and Feminism in Britain, 1750–1900*, pp. 139–57.

35 See Susan Mumm, *Stolen Daughters, Virgin Mothers: Anglican Sisterhoods in Victorian Britain* (London: Leicester UP, 1999); Brian Heeney, *The Women's Movement in the Church of England 1850–1930* (Oxford: Clarendon Press, 1988); Michael Hill, *The Religious Order: A Study of Virtuoso Religion and its Legitimation in the Nineteenth-century Church of England* (London: Heinemann, 1973); A.M. Allchin, *The Silent Rebellion: Anglican Religious Communities 1845–1900* (London: SCM Press, 1958).

36 Although many factors encouraged the growing influence of the feminised Christ and the theology of action on the religious mainstream, women's writings played a significant role. In particular, women's novels and hymns developed and popularised the feminised image of Christ, while women's participation in the discourse of charity and missions promoted a theology of action.

37 Florence Nightingale, *Cassandra and Suggestions for Thought*, Mary Poovey (ed.) (New York: New York University Press, 1992), p. 53.

38 See Josephine Butler, *The Hour Before the Dawn* (London: Trübner, 1876), and the analysis in Boyd, *Three Women*, p. 91.

39 Sue Morgan analyses Ellice Hopkins's identification of Christ with prostitutes in her social purity writings in *A Passion for Purity: Ellice Hopkins and the Politics of Gender in the Late-Victorian Church* (University of Bristol, 1999).

40 This view pervades the conduct books of Sarah Stickney Ellis, including *Woman's Mission* (1839), in which the ideal woman is described as 'Content with the sphere of usefulness assigned her by nature and nature's God' (66) – that is, the domestic role of the middle-class Englishwoman.

41 'Lydia', 'Female Biography of Scripture: Deborah', *CLM* 16 (1841), pp. 337–49, here, p. 337.

42 'Lydia', 'Deborah', p. 338.
43 'Lydia', 'Deborah', p. 349.
44 Tonna, pp. 125–56.
45 Stowe, 'Deborah', p. 413.
46 Stowe, 'Deborah', pp. 415, 417.
47 Stowe, 'Deborah', p. 418.
48 Stowe, 'The Church of the Master', *CWM* 10 (1874), p. 234.
49 See George Landow, *Victorian Types, Victorian Shadows: Biblical Typology in Victorian Literature, Art, and Thought* (New York: Routledge & Kegan Paul, 1980), esp. pp. 50–51.
50 See, among others, Marina Warner, *Alone of All Her Sex* (New York: Vintage, 1983); Carol Engelhardt Herringer, *Victorians and the Virgin Mary* (Manchester: Manchester University Press, 2008).
51 See also Carol Engelhardt, 'The Paradigmatic Angel in the House: The Virgin Mary and Victorian Anglicans', in Anne Hogan and Andrew Bradstock (eds), *Women of Faith in Victorian Culture* (London: Macmillan, 1998), pp. 159–71. More secular writers, however, could make powerful use of the Madonna figure: see Kimberley VanEsveld Adams, *Our Lady of Victorian Feminism* (Athens: Ohio University Press, 2001).
52 Elizabeth Rundle Charles, *The Women of the Gospels, The Three Wakings, and Other Poems* (New York: Dodd, 1867), pp. 24–25.
53 'Far Above Rubies', *CWM* 6 (1870), p. 305.
54 See Diana Neal, 'Josephine Butler: Flirting with the Catholic Other', in Daggers and Neal (eds), *Sex, Gender and Religion*, pp. 155–71, and Eileen Janes Yeo, 'Protestant Feminists and Catholic Saints in Victorian Britain' in Yeo (ed.), *Radical Femininity*, pp. 127–48.
55 See, for example, Barbara Welter, 'The Feminization of American Religion: 1800–860', in Mary S. Hartman and Lois Banner (eds), *Clio's Consciousness Raised: New Perspectives on the History of Women* (New York: Harper & Row, 1974), pp. 137–57; MacDonald, *A Unique and Glorious Mission*.
56 A.B., 'Woman's Public Work: Its Scope and Limits', *CWM* 13 (August 1877), pp. 626–34.
57 Thanks to Jacqueline deVries for drawing my attention to these articles, as well as for invaluable comments on earlier drafts of this paper.

3   Women and philanthropic cultures

Susan Mumm

In 1915 the writer and social campaigner Edith Picton-Turbervill, reflecting on the war work of the Young Women's Christian Association (YWCA), declared: 'In the YWCA's huts there is a magnificent spiritual work going on, because the workers themselves are spiritualising every secular thing with which they come in contact. They are making a common meal sacramental; they are making a wooden hut a house of God and a gate of heaven.'[1]

This observation highlights a theme that dominated most women's organised philanthropy in the nineteenth and twentieth centuries, that while the bulk of philanthropic work was concerned with the immediate material needs of its clientele, it was motivated by religious belief and teaching. Most of the charities that women were involved in before World War II were religiously oriented, but relatively few were actively conversionist in purpose. Far more common was a focus on the amelioration of the conditions of the poor. Throughout the nineteenth century and into the twentieth, religiously organised philanthropy remained overwhelmingly popular.[2] Contemporary estimates suggested that as many as 500,000 women were active in British charities alone by the 1890s, 'rapidly making benevolence into a feminized enclave of social life'.[3] For every woman who joined a reform group in order to campaign zealously for radical social change, far more were attracted to groups who effected incremental, modest changes through the pursuit of limited and religiously-bounded goals. Modest change and moral uplift became far more central to women's philanthropy than saving souls or transforming the social order.

Chronicling the enormous number of religious charities with which women were involved is a task beyond the capacities of any single historian.[4] What we know of these organisations arises from a patchwork of existing research that has focused mainly on individual groups and societies of varying size and importance. In examinations of the range of organisations built and developed by women, issues of survival and predisposition skew the available literature. The Whiggish tendency of the historical profession more generally has created a bias towards the more successful organisations and, especially in the history of social policy, in tracing the origins and development of those secular groups that later led to state provision of welfare services. Many histories of social work commence their account with a brief survey of societies such as the Charity Organisation Society founded in Britain in 1869 before moving on to the development of social work as an arm of state provision.[5] In the same way, histories of medical charities and voluntary (charitably-supported) hospitals are normally concluded with their merger into the National Health Service on its establishment in the 1940s. This methodological dominance of 'survival bias' means that it is difficult to recover information about smaller or short-lived charities. Local groups often composed of only a handful of women who took up a particular cause and then relinquished it when difficulties arose or conflicting obligations overcame their energy have left few traces. Yet many charities operated like this. Hence we know very little of the Norwich and Bungay Ladies' Bible Mission, the Richmond Street Child-bed Linen Provision Society, and even less of the Blue Lamp Mission (a midnight mission that attempted to rescue streetwalkers) or the Guild of the Poor Brave Things, founded to aid the disabled.[6] Others were never sufficiently well established to merit even a distinctive name, being simply mentioned in passing as the 'splendid work' of an individual or a small group. Those philanthropic organisations that survived invariably did so from their support of a broader cause that attracted more adherents, sympathisers with deeper pockets, a stronger initial band of workers, better co-ordination, goals that successfully balanced vision with feasibility, and the ability to attract a second generation of activists.

The historiography of women's philanthropy

Early histories of general charities portrayed these organisations as founded by great men doing noble deeds with the assistance of humble, unnamed and mostly female helpers.[7] When the first writing on women's charities appeared, these accounts typically adhered to the 'noble women' vein mined by hagiographers of figures such as Florence Nightingale. Growing in popularity from the 1860s, these uncritical, flattering character sketches depicted the lives and deeds of a small handful of selected 'women worthies'.[8] Social commentators and publicists emphasised the social utility of women's philanthropic work, downplaying its religious motivations whenever the group involved did not fit comfortably into mainstream Protestantism. First-wave feminists seized on the philanthropic activities of women – religious and secular (although few fell explicitly into that second category) – as a way of documenting women's wider social contributions and further evidence of women's suitability for citizenship. Indeed, alongside feminists who advocated a doctrine of equal rights, the emphasis upon women's presumed innate nobility, selflessness and moral and social motherhood was a major strand of feminist thought that drew heavily upon the example of women's philanthropic activity. Despite this, the reputation of charitable Victorian women suffered from that broader discrediting of Victorian virtues in this period. Lytton Strachey's depreciation of motives set a fashion for a sneering dismissal of charitable work, with his jibes at the work of Florence Nightingale, Cardinal Manning, Dr Arnold and General Gordon.[9] As noted previously, the rise of the welfare state focused historians' attention largely on secular charities and thus religiously-oriented charities were neglected even further.

When women's history emerged in the 1970s, scholarship on philanthropic women displayed a schizophrenic tendency. On the one hand, much was made of the significant contributions women had made to the field of social and moral reform. Frank Prochaska's groundbreaking study *Women and Philanthropy in Nineteenth Century England* (1980) has remained unchallenged in its methodology and approach with most historians content to assume that the vast number of as yet unresearched women's charities will simply fit neatly into his schema of contributors (with a social motivation) and workers (driven by religious beliefs).[10] Overall, historians have shown greater interest in liberal radical groups, however poorly organised or short-lived, than in the larger but more conservative societies, because they have regarded them as significant contributors to wider long-term cultural change. In this Stracheyan-like approach, socially conservative charities have been badly neglected by social and women's historians; all too often, it has been assumed that religiously-based charities were of this type.[11] Scant attention has also been paid to women's charitable work performed under religious auspices, not because it was performed by women but because it was religious. In the face of growing evidence to the contrary, the assumption that little originality, courage or creative thinking was present in religious philanthropic work has persisted.[12]

Contemporary feminist historical approaches to women's philanthropy have evinced two main approaches. Some, such as Maria Luddy and Anne Boylan, have viewed philanthropy as yet another neglected area of female-specific work and historical agency.[13] Others such as Ruth Roach Pierson have critiqued charitable activism as fostering woman-on-woman oppression, focusing their analyses on the class-based and racial differences between the servers and the served.[14] Both of these approaches suffer from a tendency to take the organisations' own rhetorical devices too literally. The sentimentalised language of the period overheated easily when combined with an intention to persuade the reader to act or to donate. We learn as much – if not more – about an organisation's real priorities from its budget allocations than we do from the proclamations of its leadership. A number of historians have sought out women-dominated charities like the Girls' Friendly Society (GFS) or the YWCA, partly because of their intrinsic interest and importance and partly because their existence refutes the assumption that all religiously-motivated charities were dominated by a male clerical class. Much remains to be learned of the nature of female leadership, however, within nineteenth-century organisations.

Almost all philanthropy of the period was organised around denominational affiliation, although some of the groups were, or at least claimed to be, non-denominational.[15] Some societies were so narrowly pitched within a specific religious context that it is hard to identify them as anything other than forms of sectarian coercion or bribery. Groups such as the Islington Mission, that refused aid to those who did not attend the favoured place of worship, or those that provided assistance only to those who claimed conversion, or shelters for the homeless that refused to give houseroom to anyone who hung non-religious pictures on their walls, are examples of this.[16] However, overt financial or economic rewards for conversion were seldom officially sanctioned. Others restricted charity to the deserving of their local congregation, neighbourhood or religious denomination. The Church of England Waifs and Strays Society, for example, assisted children only after a certificate of Anglican christening was produced, although this may have been less out of sectarian bias than from the need to avoid accusations of 'poaching' from other denominations. Other organisations, such as those founded to clothe Africans so mocked by Dickens, set goals that were almost grotesque in their narrowness, with aims profoundly unsympathetic to a modern mindset.[17] Some groups, such as the Society for the Suppression of Mendacity, were so hard-hearted in their treatment of the poor that they appear more as agencies of humiliation than charity. The much-maligned Charity Organisation Society was unpopular even in its own time largely due to its emphasis on 'scientific philanthropy'[18] and has been only partially rehabilitated by historical research.[19] Few historians have analysed the numerous 'bread and blankets' associations that had no aims beyond the immediate relief of the local poor, or the hundreds of groups that supplied childbed linen to poor mothers. It is tempting for the historian to pick and choose, to make moral judgments and to focus on organisations more congenial to contemporary views. But this raises critical issues of representativeness and typicality. More research on the unsympathetic, the routine, on those societies for the suppression of various pleasures is badly needed if we are to better understand the social function of these groups in the wider cultural context out of which they operated.

One key and shared element of charitable activity was the sense of purpose it provided to its participants. Women's writing in the period makes it clear that a longing for meaning and a sense of purpose that transcended the everyday, propelled many into the ranks of philanthropy.[20] The question of what that work meant to the women involved and how it helps us to better comprehend female philanthropic cultures – for both benefactor and beneficiary – is central to the remainder of this chapter.

The YWCA and the GFS

Organisations to assist vulnerable women and girls dominated women's philanthropy in the second half of the nineteenth century. The following discussion examines two of the largest in terms of membership and international expansion. The YWCA started as two independent organisations with the same name (both formed in 1855), in direct imitation of the Young Men's Christian Association established in 1845. Emma Robarts' YWCA was founded as a nationwide prayer union intended to alleviate the sense of spiritual isolation suffered by many women who were unable to find sympathy or understanding from their families or in their workplaces. The second YWCA, formed by Mary Jane Kinnaird, was established in response to a social rather than spiritual need, the provision of respectable accommodation for young working women in London. Kinnaird's YWCA was founded initially as a result of the need to house nurses travelling to the Crimea with Florence Nightingale. After the two YWCAs merged in 1877, non-denominational national schemes of provision for young women developed rapidly along with a growing network of international branches. The international body (World's YWCA) remained true to its name, even in countries where Christianity was a minority religion such as in India. The work was centred in local YWCA buildings, offering lunchrooms, classroom facilities, recreation rooms and often residential accommodation as well. What distinguished the YWCA was a relatively rapid shift in the early decades of the twentieth century from a religious and moral orientation to that of a more secular, socially and ethically focused organisation. This shift took place as a result of the influence of a new generation of leadership influenced by social gospel ideas, often as the result of practical experience with working women, in the teeth of determined resistance by some senior members of the organisation.

Second only in size and importance to the YWCA was the Girls' Friendly Society (GFS) whose origins, constituency and trajectory were very different. The GFS was founded by Mary Townsend, the wife of a wealthy banker, in 1875. Townsend intended the group to focus on the moral and social elevation of domestic servants and she designed a charity which aimed to provide friendship and social and moral support across class lines to young girls living in service away from their families. The GFS expanded quickly, achieving a membership of over 150,000 in England and Wales by 1901 and reaching a peak of 200,000 just before World War One. Although repeated attempts were made to broaden the membership it never successfully attracted members beyond the servant occupational sector. The GFS operated a sexual purity rule which rendered some girls ineligible for membership, at least in theory, although there is little evidence that this was a major deterrent.[21]

What were the attractions of the GFS? Membership dues were low, events were considered enjoyable and, for many girls, it was the only acceptable escape from the employer's house aside from church attendance and the weekly half holiday. Furthermore, the GFS sponsored many branches in smaller towns which meant that it could be genuinely local. Girls and their mentors (who were usually upper- and middle-class Anglican women of the neighbourhood) met on a weekly basis in church halls, private homes, or the local rectory and considerable social pressure was placed on mistresses by the elite 'lady members' to encourage their servants to join and to attend meetings. The narrowness of the GFS membership base arguably contributed to a contemporary public impression that YWCA members were more aspirational than their GFS counterparts and some girls 'graduated' from the GFS to the YWCA which was considered higher status. The majority of philanthropic 'ladies' had servant employees, thus the lady associates of the GFS worked among a class of woman with whom they already had an established dynamic. This may well have created a clearer institutional hierarchy than that of the YWCA where employer/employee lines would have been less established by social custom and practice.[22]

The GFS was firmly Anglican and became an important international society in a number of Commonwealth countries as well as in Britain. In certain colonies, such as Canada and New Zealand, it competed with the YWCA as a provider of first-destination residential and employment support for emigrant girls and women. In this capacity both agencies were capable of attracting substantial colonial government support seen as part of wider recruitment drives to attract suitable newcomers to the country. In Britain, the GFS remained more stable in focus and mission than the YWCA and could be regarded as a relatively static organisation which failed to adapt to women's modernising lives in the early twentieth century. After World War One it shrank relative to the fifty per cent decline in the live-in servant population while the YWCA expanded, albeit mostly beyond the United Kingdom.

Both the YWCA and the GFS offered a range of classes and social events for their memberships, although the YWCA's activities were far wider and better-resourced due to its larger size and broader appeal to potential benefactors. There is a tendency on the part of historians to assume that 'low' pleasures such as the tavern and the penny gaffe were more enjoyable for young women than gymnastic classes or the tea parties to which members could bring suitors or other young men. Some of it arises from the presentist assumption that middle-class philanthropic involvement was invariably oppressive and distasteful to its recipients. Young working women, however, were unlikely to pay weekly membership fees to be browbeaten, patronised or bored. Some of it is due to historians' continued disinclination to differentiate sufficiently between the various strata of the working classes and their aspirations. By contrast, nineteenth-century commentators emphasised the fine gradation of working-class life and opinions and celebrated working-class diversity.[23] The YWCA appears to have laid greater stress on the importance of an intelligent female membership, capable of taking care of itself in ordinary situations and of developing their own tastes and leisure preferences. After all, these young women worked in shops, factories, and across the service sector; relatively few were domestic servants living in their employers' homes.

Neither the YWCA nor the GFS were rescue organisations, but protection of girls and young women was an important goal of their missions. Many Victorian philanthropic societies had as their central or subsidiary aim the safeguarding of girls from the temptations of urban life, the dangers of seduction and tarnished reputations, and the subsequent hindering of social advancement. However, the temptations of the city were not only sexual. Idleness and lack of ambition were also considered undesirable and liable to strip the character of its moral strength. Unsupervised and unstructured leisure time according to female philanthropists could all too easily be spent in gossip, in shopping for inexpensive finery, in rowdy interplay with boys and girls of their own class, at dubious entertainments or just slumbered away in idleness. Petty theft was an ever-present temptation in some workplaces. All of these qualities were seen as undesirable and formed a central part of religious philanthropic warnings.[24]

The desire to protect young women could have negative effects, as in its emphasis on keeping girls off the street (both literally and figuratively) and its portrayal of the street as a site of danger. However, the discourse of female protection took on increasingly positive aspects during the later Victorian period as women philanthropists began to realise that young girls craved sociability and pleasure just as they and their own daughters did. Hence the focus in the YWCA in particular, but to some extent in the GFS as well, shifted from keeping girls in their employers' homes to offering safe and enjoyable places of constructive recreation. Club-rooms and lunch-rooms were considered as essential to the daily functioning of a YWCA branch, for example, as was a weekly prayer meeting. Needless to say, the former were invariably far better attended. These organisations also constantly navigated the boundaries of appropriate social and sexual behaviour. No charity wanted to have a reputation as a haven for 'bad' girls, so delineating the threshold criteria for admissibility became an important issue.[25] The handful of women charity workers unable to accept a demarcation between 'pure' and 'impure' girls often left organisations with particular purity rules such as the GFS to work on their own, so important an issue was this to them. Those wishing to work with girls or women with negative sexual reputations were thus often forced out of mainstream charity work into independent ministries or into the handful of rescue charities.[26]

The female membership of the GFS and the YWCA were not destitute. These organisations attracted girls and young women who worked as seamstresses or domestic servants often living away from their families. They would have been poor, but often with small savings accounts and the belief that good behaviour and wise choices might improve their position in life, if only modestly. Both societies also emphasised self-restraint as the key to upward mobility. The restraint of temper, it was argued, kept a young woman from throwing up her position in a moment of frustration or rage; restraint from immediate gratification meant that she might not run the risk of pregnancy or squander her earnings on drink or excessive finery; and restraint of demeanour prepared young women for promotion at work. As Wendy Gamber has argued, 'At its most expansive, self-control meant something more like self-determination. It offered a radical faith in the possibility of individual transformation, of realizing the secular promise of free will.'[27] Self-restraint as advocated and enabled by these organisations encouraged young women to save small sums, to plan for a better future and to see the classes and activities they participated in as beneficial to their aspirations as well as providing recreational and social opportunities.

A step beyond the domestic: women activists and the function of philanthropy

The literary historian Dorice Williams Elliott has raised the important question of why charity came to be seen as the natural extension of the domestic sphere for women, the first step out of the house.[28] After all, the ideology of protection for middle-class women worked against charitable activity, at least in those forms involving direct contact with the poor. Philanthropy allowed 'ladies' to become involved with dirt, depravity, pain and suffering with limited insulation from the sordid aspects of poverty and disadvantage. The Judeo-Christian tradition argued that relief of the poor was a religious duty but also taught that this might be fulfilled through almsgiving rather than direct personal action. Why then did so many women see direct involvement rather than monetary donations as such an important duty? I would argue that the compulsion to charitable activity for nineteenth-century women revolved around the concept of caretaking; women's 'natural' care-giving, pity and compassion, it was argued, would protect them from any moral or social contamination they confronted in the gritty realities of their work. More 'genteel' forms of philanthropy – such as those encompassed by the YWCA – exposed philanthropic women to a different but equally distressing set of working women's realities: sexual harassment in the workplace, unfair wages, arbitrary dismissal, over-work and socially sanctioned discrimination on almost every imaginable basis including age, religion, race and ethnicity, and, of course, sex. The amount of unrealised potential among less privileged women clearly snapped many charitable ladies out of their complacency concerning the fundamental justice of the society in which they lived.

Not surprisingly, then, charitable work could lead women into political activism. Some found that the contact philanthropy provided with poverty or wasted potential motivated them to move into more overtly political work as in Josephine Butler's transition from workhouse visiting to leadership of the movement to repeal the Contagious Diseases Acts. Because women's political activism is more fully chronicled than their philanthropic endeavour, historical records provide numerous examples of women who began in philanthropy and then became politicised by it – the trajectory followed by Edith Picton-Turbervill, many suffragettes and, possibly most famously, Beatrice Webb.[29] However, while charity work may have been a catalyst for more radical political activism for some, little is known about why and how these shifts in emphasis occurred. Some became frustrated with philanthropy's limited aims and there is evidence to show that not all women charity workers were social conservatives. As activists 'burned out', many rechannelled their energies into politics, thereafter maintaining fluid career paths between politics and charitable work. The fiery Sarah Grand, for example, moved from her notoriety as an author who attacked the sexual double standard through various suffragette activities to good works in the Home Counties. Her public career culminated as the Mayoress of Bath.[30] It is an oversimplification therefore to claim simply that charity work radicalised its workers, or that political disillusionment led people to philanthropic activity. The historical reality is messier, with many women maintaining a foot in both camps.

Radical political positions were rare among women philanthropists, however, except for the far-from-universal support for suffragism. Female philanthropists, largely content to work within the dominant social structures of their context, confined themselves to mainstream parties and showed little interest in the political process other than as a means for passing desired social legislation. The YWCA campaigned for changes to labour laws, for example, while the GFS aligned itself with the campaign to raise the age of sexual consent.[31] Nevertheless, the boundaries between charitable and political activism remain opaque; it is difficult for the historian to discern where philanthropy ended and more radical activism began. Some found philanthropic involvement caused their beliefs to shift towards a more liberal world view.[32] Others saw charity as the bedrock of maintaining the established social order, a safety valve that ameliorated poverty without bringing society's fundamental structures into question. Many major philanthropic donors of the nineteenth century such as the Carnegies adopted variants of this approach, which is sometimes called constructive philanthropy.[33] Emily Kinnaird and Mary Morehead of the YWCA were similarly convinced that they were creating a better world and working towards a more just society.

Inevitably, conflicts arose around women's roles and relationships to other social classes, observes Dorice Williams Elliott. She argues, with Norris Pope, that philanthropy offered a 'sphere of independent labour most accessible to ambitious women'.[34] By the mid-nineteenth century the general social consensus backed Hannah More's dictum that charity was the occupation of a lady. Christian teaching stressed the need for everyone to labour at their divinely-appointed tasks. It was important to the working out of God's plan for the world for every believer to be occupied with good works. 'Works' could be an episodic concept in a way that the modern understanding of 'work', as something disciplined in time-bounded regularity, is not.[35] The regularised work practices of the modern bureaucratised charity would have seemed very unfamiliar to Victorian and Edwardian women of the middle and upper classes. Their philanthropic toil came in bursts: intense activity linked to a cause or project, followed by a period of rest. This employment pattern, never enjoyed by industrial workers, seemed natural to the wives and daughters of politicians, financiers and the clergy. The demands of the social season or expectations of regular family travel abroad reinforced the cyclical nature of their philanthropic activity. For the women of this class, philanthropic works were a lifestyle choice dictated by a sense of duty or the call of conscience, not an economic necessity.

Rectifying disorder in the social laws

Many women-oriented charitable groups emerged from a desire to correct deficiencies in the disordered working of the social laws around them. Charities arose to rescue 'fallen women', to provide bread or medical care or to urge servants to self-educate and to enjoy organised leisure pursuits without educating them beyond their station (such as the Metropolitan Association for Befriending Young Servants). Others provided shelter for orphans, such as the Church of England Waifs and Strays Society.[36] Diana Kendall has described these efforts as a form of corrective social conservatism.[37] They did not intend to change the world out of a conviction that it was unjust but instead focused on rectifying social and moral imperfections that had developed within a broadly acceptable system. Implicit in many annual Victorian charity reports is an evolutionary argument in favour of benevolence. These suggest that while 'survival of the fittest' may have explained the overall dominance of the upper classes, limited intervention through charity prevented structural flaws from improperly disadvantaging those who had demonstrated general moral fitness through good behaviour, aspirations to respectability, and steady, if lowly, employment.[38]

Margaret Preston has gone so far as to claim that the eradication of sin among the poor was the goal of most nineteenth-century philanthropic organisations.[39]

I would argue, however, that while most charities maintained religious orientations, the picture is more complicated than Preston suggests. The YWCA, for example, displayed an emphasis on civil Christianity rather than on original sin. While the conversionist orientation of conservative religious activists may have targeted the reduction of sinful behaviour, no one seriously argued that the YWCA's members were in some way deeply depraved.[40] Instead, they were depicted by the Association's leadership as examples of ordinary girls of their class subjected to all the temptations and weaknesses connected with limited education, dull work and few family resources to support them. Pragmatic moral and social uplift was the emphasis of YWCA modernisers and generally dominant in the organisational ethos of all major women's charities of the period under scrutiny.

Religious identities

Christian religious teaching provided both the motivation for philanthropy and also created some of the problems that charities encountered. Women's philanthropic groups found the establishment and patrolling of boundaries defined by religion extremely troublesome. Virtuoso religion set very high standards, excluding those who failed to meet its requirements and focusing mainly on the further development of those who did.[41] An example of this is the GFS's 1879 decision to exclude girls living chaste lives from membership if they had had previous sexual experience, even if this fell short of the loss of virginity. This orientation came into sharp conflict with that of other charitable women who saw their work as social outreach and who were determined to include all but the flagrantly disreputable. The question of philanthropy's core purpose (whether conversion or assistance) tore the YWCA apart in the early twentieth century. One section of the association insisted on stringent religious tests for leaders (and to some extent, for the membership), while the bulk of the charity evolved into a more theologically modernist, socially-oriented organisation open to all women regardless of religious belief. YWCA loyalists reserved their fiercest attacks and their deepest animosity for their YWCA opponents when debating whether or not the conservatives or the modernists 'owned' the association's values. 'Are we a Christian or a catering organization?' asked conservatives during World War One, after the Association had greatly expanded its work among the troops in France and war workers at home. Those who saw their purpose as saving the souls of members eventually seceded in 1919 to form a rival society, the Christian Organisation of Women and Girls (CAWG).[42]

Although the YWCA traditionalists were fighting a losing battle, their adamant resistance to social and theological change convinced them that the Association had adopted methods 'which are notoriously of the world' and which suggested that the outward growth of the YWCA masked an internal spiritual decline. The material growth of the Association had resulted in 'beautiful buildings and many earthly comforts' but also in 'worldly methods which we deplore in these buildings', 'methods which are dangerous to the souls of those whom they hope to reach'.[43] What *were* these dangerous methods? Traditionalists argued that the

YWCA should attract girls only through 'bright, pure, innocent, home-making recreations' and that smoking, dancing, cards and theatre-going would open the floodgates to moral peril. While such moral opposition was doomed to failure the evangelical traditionalists had rightly identified a genuine shift in the orientation of the leadership. The YWCA's mission had moved from an emphasis in the 1860s on personal salvation to a commitment to Christian social reform by 1900. Religion did not cease to be important in the YWCA or any other woman's philanthropic organisation in the period under consideration but the theological emphases changed significantly.

The increasingly powerful social gospel influence within the twentieth-century YWCA focused attention on the social problems of the age and the challenges faced by their members. Yet even in this regard, the YWCA exhibited liberalism not radicalism. Social problems tackled by them included inadequate housing for single women, poor rates of pay, limited job opportunities, occupationally-compromised health, limits to educational opportunities and industrial conditions.[44] All of these were refracted through a modernist understanding of the teachings of Christ centred on justice, compassion and the importance of this life rather than the next. In essence, the YWCA's liberal philanthropic leaders saw the Sermon on the Mount as teaching the core values of Christianity which were focused not merely on personal salvation but also on compassion and meeting social injustice in all its forms. The duty of all women was to assist in moving society to a point where justice and mercy became the experience of all. The dominant, if tacit, religious orientation was incarnational rather than conversion-based. Neither the YWCA nor the GFS focused on rescue or repentance as did the midnight meetings of the mid-Victorian period and charities aimed at 'fallen women'. Neither were they concerned with workhouse conditions or the financial relief of the urban poor as were the 'slummers' and district visitors.[45] They focused instead on the instilling of religious influence and general uplift, aiming to 'improve the poor but not change them'.[46] While some historians have depicted this as an expression of social conservatism which insisted that everyone remained in the social stratum into which they were born, it could be argued that their philosophy of self-restraint also created an emphasis on uplift and improvement. Girls and young women could be socially, intellectually, physically and morally elevated, but the total transformation of personality accompanying conversion was rarely required or expected.

Power and charity

Although we may be able to discern something of the attitudes of the benefactors of charity, it is a more difficult task to determine the views of the beneficiaries. Any consideration of philanthropic work is saturated with questions of power, both explicit and concealed. Women who gave money or time to good works exercised power relative to their social standing, economic affluence and organisational expertise. They may have enjoyed other forms of power as well, including control over how less-fortunately-situated women lived and the choices they were able to make. Given our contemporary discomfort with such exercises of power and our concern with the moral implications of social control, this is an area of research where many condemnations of charity arise.

There is an assumption that people dedicated to good causes today are well-intentioned individuals, whether or not we agree with the particular social changes being championed. As historians, we should not assume that women in the past were unaware of the implications and ambiguities of their charitable work. Nor should we presuppose that all religiously-based philanthropy of the past was anti-change or devoted to shoring up (directly or indirectly) the existing social formation. Religion was far more than a conservative social force. Power dynamics certainly existed in any charitable transaction and cannot be dismissed, but the overall relationship was far more complex and far more reciprocal than has been previously realised. As more research is undertaken, patterns of mutual influence within the philanthropic relationship may appear. As Lawrence Friedman observes, 'connectedness or civic-minded reciprocity with others was generally a far stronger quality than self-help individualism ... workers often learned from and were changed by those they sought to help'.[47]

We need more complex ways, therefore, of thinking about the benefits and drawbacks of the philanthropic relationship. For philanthropic benefactors, the work broadened their horizons, gave them serious responsibilities beyond the home and operated as a form of unpaid but culturally valued work. To what extent, however, were women philanthropists oblivious to the deleterious effects of their charitable actions? How can we be sure that they lacked so utterly in self-awareness and insensitivity, as the received model of philanthropy assumes?[48] Such an assessment renders the recipients of charity into either passive victims of inappropriate assistance or grasping, hypocritical opportunists who seized whatever was available to them despite being aware of the oppressiveness of the relationship. Such readings are too simplistic, monochromatic and over-generalised. More likely is a narrative that moves from such extremes to the middle of the philanthropic spectrum where a combination of good intentions, egotism, guilt, insensitivity, devotion, opportunism, a sense of obligation, opportunities for broadening social networks and a wide range of cross-class relationships would be operating simultaneously in a complex web of interpersonal and institutional transactions. Lawrence Friedman emphasises philanthropists' capacity for self-criticism, claiming that mutuality should never be underestimated: '[R]eformers often discovered that ... they were imposing on themselves the same requirements of piety, control, and self-determination that they required of the less fortunate. Reform changed the reformer as it changed circumstances for the "needy" recipient.'[49] I would argue, however, that the discernible mix of empowerment and identification in this relationship was even messier and more motivationally complicated than the concept of mutuality suggests.[50]

The cohort of women who founded these charities and led their fund-raising efforts were pioneers in the development of women's non-profit businesses. The organisation of growth in new charities like the YWCA and the GFS presented a very different set of challenges for women philanthropists than simply maintaining pre-existing, relatively stable institutions. Such wide-ranging and ambitious work demanded the development of an internal bureaucracy to administer it. Formal incorporation allowed charities to hold property, conduct business as an entity, enjoy legal rights to make contracts, borrow money, or mortgage property. As a result, strategies and practices constantly evolved. The records of the GFS and the YWCA, two of the fastest-growing organisations in the late nineteenth century, reveal constant experimentation with management and programming. Services offered to women were centralised, decentralised and recentralised; regions and functions enjoyed very different levels of autonomy; financial cross-subsidisation was adopted, abandoned, and readopted as societies responded to internal growth and external pressures. Women charitable leaders were senior executives with responsibility for large and complex institutions whose business was charity and whose staff were an uneasy mix of hundreds of voluntary and salaried workers.

Leadership for these charities came from appropriate denominational backgrounds. There were no Catholics on the board of the YWCA, for example, founded as it was by women from a mixture of Protestant denominations. Funding, however, was drawn from across the religious spectrum. Philanthropic generosity crossed religious and gender lines, less so class lines, although there were strenuous efforts to get working-class members to contribute and to develop habits of generosity and donation within the limits of self-help and prudence.[51] Both the YWCA and the GFS required membership fees, but are still classifiable as philanthropic organisations because fees formed only a tiny percentage of their operating costs.

It is often claimed that charitable work infantilised and subordinated its recipients.[52] This perspective is over-influenced by Dickens' blinkered lady philanthropists, just as Sarah Gamp has loomed disproportionately (and somewhat unrepresentatively) over the history of nursing reform. Recipients of charity were not powerless. Even if all else failed them, they retained the power to refuse, or to remove themselves from the charitable relationship. After all it was remarkably easy, particularly in urban areas, to avoid being assisted if one did not want to be. Evidence suggests that hatred of the workhouse was more extreme than dislike of philanthropy, which was less disruptive to the life and sense of individualism of the recipient.[53] Furthermore, since Christian churches promoted charity so thoroughly, nineteenth-century recipients may have found these private forms of philanthropy more acceptable than state support. Modern psychology identifies the ability to accept help from others as one of the defining characteristics of a mature personality; this prompts the question as to whether or not the acceptance of assistance in the past was always such a thoroughly demeaning experience.

Another way of considering the philanthropic relationship is through the theme of 'waste' following the approach developed by Carolyn Steedman.[54] The avoidance of waste (and the strategic display of profligate waste in a higher social and economic echelon) was a central theme of Victorian culture, thus waste-avoidance was likely to resonate with women. Similar to good housekeepers who abhorred waste, lady philanthropists arguably saw their work as a major defence against the charge that their own lives were being wasted. Working girls could waste, too, but in different ways: they could waste time and money, squander their health through poor rest and diet and throw away their reputation through unseemly flirtation. The socially conservative approach of the GFS and its emphasis on making better servants rather than promoting social advancement did not encourage a concern over the waste of the abilities of their members. As an organisation more aspirational and more focused on career development, however, the YWCA exhibited a greater preoccupation with the concept of waste in all its diverse forms. In this model, women's religious charity could be viewed as a form of socio-economic frugality, protecting deserving girls and women from being wasted by a social system as likely to drag them down as lift them up.

Women joined, managed and staffed a vast range of charities in the nineteenth and twentieth centuries. They did so from a mixture of motives both personally and socially determined. Religious faith, a desire to find meaning in work and compassion for those who had limited opportunities combined to motivate many to commit themselves to charitable benevolence. The relative privilege of female philanthropists influenced their thinking on social issues whilst simultaneously reshaping their own identities through causes they believed to be greater than themselves. Recipients of philanthropy responded in ways as individual and varied as the charitable givers' own motivations. In the large associations aimed at working girls and women, we find a charitable worldview simultaneously in transition and at the same time firmly fixed in traditional models. In order to develop a richer and more nuanced understanding of these countless and largely uncounted transactions, historians need to attend to the large number of ordinary, even mundane, charities that sheltered beneath the umbrella of Christian teaching and attempted to meet or ameliorate almost every imaginable human need.

Acknowledgments

The author would like to acknowledge the financial support of the Social Sciences and Humanities Research Council of Canada. The research underpinning this chapter would not have been possible without its assistance.

Further reading

Lawrence J. Friedman and Mark D. McGarvie (eds), *Charity, Philanthropy and Civility in American History* (Cambridge: Cambridge University Press, 2003).

Bernard Harris, *The Origins of the British Welfare State: Social Welfare in England and Wales, 1800–1945* (London: Palgrave, 2004).

Frank K. Prochaska, *Women and Philanthropy in Nineteenth Century England* (Oxford: Clarendon, 1980).

Notes

1 Edith Picton-Turbervill, 'Introduction' in J. Kennedy Maclean and T. Wilkinson Riddle, *The Second Picture of the War* (London: Marshall Brothers [c.1919]), p. 38. Picton-Turbervill (1872–1960) was a Labour Party Member of Parliament,

a YWCA worker, the first woman to preach from an Anglican pulpit, a peace activist and a campaigner against child labour in Indo-China.

2 Even today, if one examines charitable organisations on a global basis, purely secular agencies are outnumbered by religiously oriented agencies.

3 Seth Koven, *Slumming: Sexual and Social Politics in Victorian London* (Princeton: Princeton University Press, 2004), p. 7.

4 Charity and philanthropy are terms that are often used interchangeably. Philanthropy was traditionally distinguished from charity by its emphasis on the need for the organisation of benevolence, whereas traditional charity involved direct assistance from a known giver to a known recipient, preferably in a face-to-face transaction.

5 For example, F. Honigsbaum, 'The Evolution of the NHS', *British Medical Journal* (Oct 3 1990) vol. 301, pp. 694–99; Dennis T. Haynes and Barbara W. White, 'Will the "Real" Social Work Please Stand Up? A Call to Stand for Professional Unity', *Social Work* 44 (1999).

6 The Blue Lamp Mission was based in Pultney Street; references to it can be found in the Lambeth Palace Archives and in the Charles Booth online archive; the Guild of the Poor Brave Things was founded by Grace Kimmins (1871–1954) in London when she was 'Sister Grace' in the West London Mission in 1894; it emphasised the importance of play in developing the skills of the physically disabled (Seth Koven), entry for Kimmins, *Oxford Dictionary of National Biography* (OUP, 2004); for local Ladies' Bible Societies see William Canton, *A History of the British and Foreign Bible Society*, 2 vols (Charleston: BiblioLife, 2008).

7 For example, the biographies of Thomas Coram, founder of the Foundling Hospital. John Brownlow, *The History and Design of the Foundling Hospital, with a Memoir of the Founder* (London: Jacques, 1851, reprinted 1881).

8 See, for example, Jennie Chappell, *Four Noble Women and Their Work* (1898) and Charles Stewart Loch, *Charity and Social Life* (London: Macmillan, 1910).

9 In each case, Strachey, employing his brilliant satiric gifts, twisted the facts of a life of achievement to suggest that the work was self-serving, driven by inner demons, or pointless, and that impure motivation somehow cancelled real and durable accomplishments.

10 Prochaska's otherwise excellent study overemphasises rescue organisations and neglects the uplift and improvement groups.

11 Bernard Harris, *The Origins of the British Welfare State: Social Welfare in England and Wales, 1800–1945* (London: Palgrave, 2004), pp. 60–64.

12 See, for example, Pat Starkey, '"Temporary" relief for specially recommended or selected deserving persons: the mission of the House of Charity, Soho, 1846–1917', *Urban History* 35, 1 (2008), pp. 98–99, 114–15.

13 Anne Boylan, 'Women in Groups: an analysis of women's benevolent organisations in New York and Boston, 1797–1840', *Journal of American History* 71 (1984), pp. 497–523. Boylan divides women's philanthropy into benevolent, reformist, and feminist. Luddy sees Irish female philanthropy as reflecting only the first two elements: Maria Luddy, *Women and Philanthropy in Nineteenth-Century Ireland* (Cambridge: Cambridge University Press, 1995), p.5; see also Prochaska, vii.

14 Mike W. Martin, *Virtuous Giving: Philanthropy, Voluntary Service and Caring* (Bloomington: Indiana University Press, 1994), pp. 110–12; Colin Jones, 'Some Recent Trends in the History of Charity', *Charity, Self-interest and Welfare in the English Past* (Guildford: UCL Press, 1996), pp. 51–64; Ruth Roach Pierson et al., *Canadian Women's Issues: Bold Visions* (Toronto: Lorimer, 1995), pp. 189–90.

15 Because this essay deals with two charities whose range focused on the United Kingdom, Canada, Australia, and New Zealand, its focus is on Christian charities, as all of these countries were overwhelmingly Christian in the period before World War One.

16 For example, the Hastings Ladies Association for Schools in the East in Association with the Church of England, or the 'souperism' of assistance during the Irish famine that demanded conversion in exchange for aid. Starkey mentions that the House of Charity did not permit non-devotional wall adornment (p. 105).

17 F. David Roberts, *The Social Conscience of the Early Victorians* (Stanford: Stanford University Press, 2002), pp. 245–46.

18 The following admiring extract is taken from Octavia Hill's 1883 account of how the COS dealt with applicants for 'daily relief'; it describes an elaborate exercise in bureaucratisation and delay. 'The names are taken down, and one of the blank forms used by the Charity Organisation Society … is filled up with the account given by the applicant of himself and his circumstances. The form will then contain a statement of the names and ages, occupation, and earnings of every member of the applicant's family, his present and his previous address, the parish relief he receives (if any), the name of the club or benefit society to which he belongs (if there be such), the particular help he asks for, and the ground of the application. The form is immediately forwarded to the Charity Organisation Society, who thoroughly investigate the information it contains by means of a paid officer. It is returned with its statements either verified or contradicted, and now shows, in addition to what it contained before, the report of the relieving officer, that of the minister of any denomination with which the applicant is connected, and his character as given by his previous landlord and other references. On the day when the application is first made, and the Charity Organisation Society apprised of it, a postcard or other message is sent to the visitor of the street or court where the applicant resides. This informs her of the application, and also that she is expected to send in on the ensuing Friday any information regarding the case which she may already have, or may learn from a visit paid during the week' (Octavia Hill, *Homes of the London Poor*, 1883, accessed at http://www.victorianlondon.org/publications/homesofthelondonpoor-4.htm).

19 Michael J. D. Roberts, 'Charity Disestablished? The Origins of the Charity Organisation Society Revisited, 1868–71', *Journal of Ecclesiastical History* 2003 54 (1), 40–61; Jane Lewis, 'The Boundary Between Voluntary and Statutory Social Service in the Late Nineteenth and Early Twentieth Centuries', *Historical Journal* 1996 39 (1), 155–77; Robert Humphreys, *Sin, Organized Charity and the Poor Law in Victorian England* (New York: St Martin's Press, 1995).

20 Florence Nightingale wrote movingly of the desire for work in *Suggestions for Thought for Searchers after Truth* (London: Spottiswoode, 1860), and it is the theme of Anna Jameson's *Sisters of Charity, Catholic and Protestant, Abroad and at Home* (London: Longmans, 1855).

21 Early writers on the GFS, such as Brian Harrison, over-emphasise the purity element. Brian Harrison, 'For Church, Queen and Family: The Girls' Friendly Society 1874–1920', *Past and Present* 61 (November 1973): Pat Mitchell's doctoral thesis provides a useful corrective to this view; Patricia Mary Clyne Mitchell, *The Girls' Friendly Society 1870–1900* (Open University, 2003).

22 The best study of the internal operation of the GFS is Mitchell's doctoral thesis.

23 Koven, *Slumming*, p. 11. See, for example, Thomas Wright 'The Journeyman Engineer', in *The Great Unwashed* (London: Tinsley Brothers, 1868), pp. 79–96.

24 Research on hooliganism suggests that many of the same triggers worried those engaged with young working-class men. See G. Stuart Hall, *Adolescent Psychology: Its Relation to Physiology, Anthropology, Sex, Crime, Religion, and Education* (New York: Appleton, 1904); John R. Gillis, *Youth and History: Tradition and Change in European Age Relations 1770–Present* (New York: Academic Press, 1981); John Springhall, *Coming of Age: Adolescence in Britain 1860–1960* (Dublin: Gill & Macmillan, 1986). The founder of the GFS, M. E. Townsend, published *A Word to the Girls about the Girls' Friendly Society* (London, 1875); the Ladies'

Association for the Care of Friendless Girls issued *Friends in Need* (London: Hatchard, 1885).

25 In the GFS, the purity rule was known as 'Rule 3', and provoked vigorous debate in 1879–80. Mitchell, chapter 4.

26 Mrs Papillon, a central member of the GFS, found herself forced out over her stance that 'impurity' in the past should be overlooked as long as members' current lives were sexually respectable during the 1879–80 controversy.

27 Wendy Gamber, 'Antebellum Reform: Salvation, Self-control, and Social Transformation', in Friedman, p. 133.

28 Dorice Williams Elliott, *The Angel Out of the House: Philanthropy and Gender in Nineteenth-century England* (Charlottesville: University Press of Virginia, 2002), p. 6.

29 Edith Picton-Turbervill, *Life is Good* (London: Muller, 1939); Beatrice Webb, *My Apprenticeship* (London: Longmans, 1926).

30 Gillian Kersley, *Darling Madame: Sarah Grand and Devoted Friend* (London: Virago Press, 1983).

31 F. K. Prochaska, *Women and Philanthropy in Nineteenth Century England* (Oxford: Clarendon, 1980).

32 Nancy Marie Robertson, *'Deeper Even than Race': White Women and the Politics of Christian Sisterhood in the Young Women's Christian Association, 1906–1946* (PhD thesis, New York University, 1997).

33 Constructive philanthropy is sometimes known as 'philonthrocapitalism'. It is philanthropy that works within a capitalistic economic system and which stresses assisted self-help.

34 Elliott, *The Angel Out of the House*, p. 4, citing Norris Pope, *Dickens and Charity* (London: Macmillan, 1978), p. 140.

35 See E. P. Thompson, *Customs in Common: Studies in Traditional Popular Culture* (New York: New Press, 1990) for a discussion of time discipline as it related to work.

36 The Waifs and Strays now operates as the Children's Society.

37 This is described as 'good deeds conservatism' in a study of contemporary women's philanthropy: Diana Kendall, *The Power of Good Deeds: Privileged Women and the Social Reproduction of the Upper Class* (Boston: Rowman & Littlefield, 2002). It also accords with the 'benevolence tradition' described by Boylan.

38 See Michael J. D. Roberts, 'Charity Disestablished?' and Humphreys, *Sin, Organized Charity and the Poor Law*.

39 Margaret Preston, *Charitable Words: Women, Philanthropy and the Language of Charity in Nineteenth-Century Dublin* (Westport: Praeger, 2004), p. 52.

40 Of course traditionalists thought most of them required conversion.

41 'Virtuoso religiosity is the polar opposite of charismatic religiosity, in that the charismatic introduces a "new thing" or a distinctive "gift", while the virtuoso is set on a course toward embodying the received traditions of a faith community.' William H. Swatos, *Encyclopedia of Religion and Society* (Walnut Creek: Altimira Press, 1998).

42 YWCA Archive, Modern Record Centre (MRC). Minna Gollick, 'The YWCA and the New Situation', *The News Letter: A Journal for Secretaries and Club Workers*, December (1919), 18–19; 'Report on Biennial Conference, 29 April – 3 May'. *The News Letter: A Journal for Secretaries and Club Workers (1918)*: 25–26; and Snow, Dorothy M., et al., *The Joyous Servant: The Life Story of Laura Anna Barker Snow* (London: Oliphants, 1941).

43 [25] September 1918, MRC MSS 243/14/23/7. The letter was signed by four prominent members, including the editor of a popular magazine linked to the Association (Snow): N. Proctor, Laura Barton Snow, Blanche E. Webster, and Lucy S. Williams.

44 The YWCA archive held at the Modern Record Centre contains the records of dozens of subcommittees including: Employment and Emigration Department, Unemployment Sub-Committee, Industrial Law Committee, Social and Legislation Committee, Hostels and Holidays Committee, and a War Committee.

45 See Koven, *Slumming* and Frank Prochaska, *The Voluntary Impulse: Philanthropy in Modern Britain* (London: Faber & Faber, 1988), pp. 42–52. A 'slummer' was an upper-class individual who visited the slums for thrills rather than to convey assistance. It was a pejorative term coined in the 1880s.

46 Preston, *Charitable Words*, p. 52.

47 Lawrence J. Friedman, 'Philanthropy in America: Historicism and its Discontents', in *Charity, Philanthropy, and Civility in American History* (Cambridge University Press, 2003), pp. 16–17.

48 Prochaska and Harris both make this assumption at times, as does much of the literature from the 1970s and 1980s, and it still appears, eg: Mark Peel, 'Charity, Casework, and the Drama of Class in Melbourne, 1920–40, "Feeling Your Position"', *History Australia* 2005 (2), pp. 83.1–83.15. See Martin for the issue from a philosophical perspective, pp. 128–44.

49 Friedman, p. 11.

50 Koven suggests that empowerment and social control motivations co-existed and fed off each other (*Slumming*, pp. 18, 284–85).

51 M. J. D. Roberts, *Making English Morals: Voluntary Association and Moral Reform in England, 1787–1886* (Cambridge: Cambridge University Press, 2004), p. 294.

52 Elliott, *The Angel out of the House*, p. 1.

53 For example, see Robert Roberts, *The Classic Slum* (Manchester: Manchester University Press, 1971).

54 Carolyn Steedman, *Dust: The Archives and Cultural History* (Rutgers, 2002).

4 Women, religious ministry and female institution-building

Carmen M. Mangion

Nineteenth-century sisterhoods, convents and deaconess institutions were forms of ministry which provided a female-centric focus for the development of religious vocation and allowed the development of women's autonomy and authority. The interplay between gender, religion and cultural change was particularly resonant in these religious ministries as women banded together, undertaking a life of prayer and philanthropic work with a salvific focus. Their efforts were acknowledged by clergy and laity as useful, even essential: they filled church pews, built up church coffers and ministered to men, women and children in a variety of guises. Yet women's ministries remained ancillary and subordinate to men's into the twentieth century and these women-only spaces were an awkward fit within the surrounding culture. Anglican sisterhoods were seen as the enemy within the Church of England, Roman Catholic conventual life was viewed as the foreign 'other', and deaconesses, though generally supported by church authorities, were never enthusiastically embraced. The decision to separate from their natal family, to remain unmarried and celibate and to live within a community of women was contrary to normative cultural understandings and expectations of Victorian femininity. Yet despite considerable public antipathy, these particular religious cultures were attractive alternatives for women seeking something other than marriage or a life dominated by familial responsibilities. Religious congregations and deaconess orders alike offered women a degree of autonomy and power to manage not only their own institutions but also to develop schools, orphanages, reformatories, refuges, hospitals and homes developed to meet religious imperatives. By the twentieth century, as institutional Churches obdurately maintained their stance on the necessary and sacrosanct division between women's and men's ministries, these groups of women, once so counter-cultural, appeared to have accepted their place within clearly demarcated, gendered boundaries of religious ministry.

This chapter seeks to understand these developments by charting, in turn, the formation of Anglican sisterhoods, the re-establishment of Catholic religious life and the 'revival' of the female diaconate in Britain from their nineteenth-century beginnings through to 1930. It then considers public and religious responses to these three forms of sororial cultures. Much of the discussion will engage with the nineteenth century, as these histories have been more extensively developed in the historiography. The seemingly more conservative forms of female institution-building of the early twentieth century will be addressed more briefly and speculatively as this topic has yet to attract the interest of academic scholars.

Women welcomed communal religious ministry and for many these female subcultures were liberating places. Yet, there were still ties that bound, a Rule[1] to be adhered to and authority to obey. These were acceptable constraints for those who found that religious life met their needs for personal faith and Christian service and, for the minority, increased power and authority. These female-governed structures functioned relatively independently although linked with church hierarchies that often attempted to limit their authority and subjugate their governmental structures. Although I address British women's religious ministry very broadly, the scope of the chapter tends towards the active rather than the contemplative religious institutes, English rather than Scottish or Welsh examples and Catholic and Anglican as opposed to Presbyterian and Nonconformist, again reflecting the emphases of the present historiography.

Historiographical considerations

In this historiographical overview, of all three forms of women's religious ministry, we can discern distinct shifts in a corpus of works ranging from those with celebratory and didactive objectives to more nuanced histories providing critical analyses of women's religious cultures. Much of the early historiography of Anglican sisterhoods, for example, consisted of either eulogistic texts on religious institutions or laudatory biographies of their founders. Peter Anson's *The Call of the Cloister: Religious Communities and Kindred Bodies in the Anglican Communion* (1955) and A.M. Allchin's *The Silent Rebellion: Anglican Religious Communities 1845–1900* (1958) chronicled the establishment of Anglican sisterhoods in broad, panegyric terms. T. J. Williams's three publications *The Park Village Sisterhood* (1965), *Priscilla Lydia Sellon: The Restorer after Three Centuries of the Religious Life in the English Church* (1965) and *A Hundred Years of Blessings within an English Community* (1946) were representative of the genre of official hagiography that sought to commemorate individuals who were instrumental in the development of Anglican sisterhoods. These histories provided rich accounts of religious life but with little critical analysis. By the 1970s, however, a new generation of historians had begun to problematise female Anglican religious life. Michael Hill's *The Religious Order: A Study of Virtuoso Religion and its Legitimation in the Nineteenth-Century Church of England* (1973) argued that sisterhoods were legitimated by reference to the Church and their utility as church workers, although he saw in sisterhoods 'something akin to an incipient feminism'.[2] Brian Heeney's *The Woman's Movement in the Church of England 1850–1930* (1988) and Sean Gill's *Women and the Church of England from the Eighteenth Century to the Present* (1994) both noted the rapid development and independence of Anglican sisterhoods; Gill argued that sisterhoods had an import that belied their small numbers.[3] John Shelton Reed's *Glorious Battle: the Cultural Politics of Victorian Anglo-Catholicism* (1996) placed more emphasis on sisterhoods as a countercultural movement, opposed to and disaffected from the dominant values of Victorian England. Next, the historiographical gaze moved from without to within conventual life. Susan Mumm's *Stolen Daughters, Virgin Mothers: Anglican Sisterhoods in Victorian Britain* (1999) brought readers inside the convent, using institutional documents to explore the rich details of women's lives and experiences within these religious communities. Joy Frith's forthcoming monograph, *Anglican Sisterhoods and the Politics of Victorian Identity*, also draws on internal sources but employs the concept of identity politics to explore gender (both femininity and masculinity), sexuality and imperialism.[4] Significantly, these recent texts engage far more with feminist and cultural theory than previous works, examining the discursive and experiential aspects of religious life along the interrelated fault lines of gender, class and ethnicity.

The historiography on Protestant deaconesses is much patchier, consisting of the usual hagiographical accounts of individual deaconesses and the institutions they led. Heeney's and Gill's accounts portray Anglican deaconesses as part of a wider movement of 'church feminism' but as less radical than Anglican sisters because their activities were controlled by clerical and ecclesiastical authorities.[5] Janet Grierson and Catherine Prelinger emphasise the struggle for ministerial equality between the deacon and deaconess.[6] Henrietta Blackmore's dissertation based on institutional sources from various deaconess institutions is the most sustained analytical work on the influences that shaped the ministry of Anglican deaconesses but sadly remains unpublished.[7] Muriel McEwan's dissertation, also unpublished, presents an exploration of Scottish deaconesses, investigating their gender relationships, identities and subordination.[8] Nonconformist deaconesses have been the focal point of Nicola Morris's *Sisters of the People: the Order of Baptist Deaconesses, 1890–1975* (2002), E. Dorothy Graham's *Saved to Serve: The Story of the Wesley Deaconess Order, 1890–1978* (2002) and Laceye C. Warner's unpublished dissertation *Methodist Episcopal and Wesleyan Methodist Deaconess Work in the Late Nineteenth and Early Twentieth Centuries: A Paradigm for Evangelism* (2000). These works point to the significance of women's ministry to the mission of their church, their use of a separate-spheres ideology to support the development of professional identities but also the limits placed on women's authority by church hierarchies. These texts serve to increase our understanding of deaconesses in their specific denominational and cultural contexts.

The scope of the historiography of Catholic women religious is also less robust.[9] Here, too, the early historiography has tended to focus on the great and the good, typically concentrating on the founders or congregation histories. Recently published biographies of congregation leaders such as Cornelia Connelly and Mary Potter as well as histories of individual congregations including Maria McClelland's *The Sisters of Mercy, Popular Politics and the Growth of the Roman Catholic Community in Hull, 1855–1930* (2000) and John Watts's *A Canticle of Love: The Story of the Franciscan Sisters of the Immaculate Conception* (2006) provide more critical and contextual analysis of individual English and Scottish women religious and the communities they led.[10] Publications by Susan O'Brien, Barbara Walsh, Francis J. O'Hagan, Karly Kehoe, as well as my own research, have taken broader, more thematic approaches to women's religious communities that highlight issues of identity, class, education, ethnicity and gender.[11] Much of this more recent work tackles the language of sisterhood itself, by acknowledging the contested nature of women's relationships within institutional spaces while recognising these women's agency through their self-conscious choice of the religious life.

Despite these shifts to a more contextualised, critical analytical approach, these religious ministries continue to be underrepresented in general texts on women's, gender and religious histories.[12] Women's embrace of institutional religious life, their adamant support for the patriarchal church and, as Sue Morgan has argued, the presupposed conservative nature of their beliefs, make them unlikely role models for feminist rehabilitation.[13] And yet, as the following discussion will argue, their nineteenth-century origins point to a type of feminist practice that sat uncomfortably with dominant Victorian ideals, offering alternative ways of being both women and religious.

Public responses to women's religious ministries: Anglican sisterhoods

The Anglican religious life was introduced by the Oxford Movement, founded in 1833 by a group of Oxford academics whose aim was to re-catholicise the Church of England. This brought with it a renewed emphasis on the sacraments, personal prayer, obedience, asceticism and the pursuit of holiness. Many of these reforms were regarded as contentious and derisively labelled 'Romanist', but none were more emotively debated than the Anglican sisterhoods. In May 1841 Marian Hughes (1817–1912) became the first English woman to take religious vows in the Church of England. Due to family responsibilities, it was not until 1851 that she founded the Society of the Holy and Undivided Trinity. By this time five other Anglican sisterhoods had been established. The first of these, the Park Village Sisterhood, formally known as the Sisterhood of the Holy Cross, was formed and financed by a committee of laymen in 1845.[14] Eleven years later, it was absorbed into the Society of the Most Holy Trinity, the second Anglican sisterhood which had been founded by Priscilla Lydia Sellon (1821–76) in 1848 in response to a public plea from the Bishop of Exeter, Henry Phillpotts, to address the 'spiritual destitution' of those living in the slums of Devonport. Sellon's mode of life and philanthropic work drew together a like-minded band of women who nursed in hospitals and during cholera epidemics, taught in day and night schools and industrial schools, and managed homes for orphans and young women.[15] Indeed, most early Anglican sisterhoods were established either as a result of clergy who perceived an acute social need or, more often, by individual women like Hughes and Sellon, who sought a spiritual way of life that combined philanthropy and prayer. Thus, the slow initial growth of Anglican communities was fuelled by the supportiveness of the Anglo-Catholic movement,[16] their commitment to redress the spiritual and physical destitution of Britain's poor and the eagerness of women to explore this alternative way of life.

By the end of the nineteenth century there were over ninety sisterhoods, most of which were located in London or southern England. Nineteenth-century entrants to the Anglican conventual life were typically in their early thirties. They spent approximately six months as postulants on the fringes of religious life engaged in the philanthropic works of the sisters. Those who persevered entered the novitiate for two to four years and became more fully integrated into the congregation and its spiritual life. Thus, after three to four years, an Anglican sister professed the vows of poverty, chastity and obedience and became a full member of a community.[17] Over 10,000 Anglican women experienced sisterhood life in the nineteenth century as postulants and novices but only several thousand were professed.[18] Many candidates, motivated by faith and social conscience, anticipated a productive life ameliorating social ills and saving souls.[19] The high attrition rate of the postulancy period, which Susan Mumm estimates to be 30 to 50 per cent of all entrants, probably reflects the frustrated expectations of those whose idealisation of the religious life was incompatible with its daily reality.[20] Ecclesiastical disapproval was also a factor which will be addressed in the following discussion.

The first generation of Anglican women who joined a sisterhood entered into uncharted and frequently hostile territory. Congregation documents, both published and unpublished, regularly recount the familial opposition that early members faced. Such rejection might have been expected from Evangelical or Broad Church parents whose antipathy towards the Oxford Movement and Anglican sisterhoods was primarily theological, but even Anglo-Catholic parents voiced concerns about 'losing' daughters to Anglican sisterhoods. Caroline Shortt (1839–1922) was perfectly self-assured about her vocation to the All Saints Sisters of the Poor in 1859 but her attraction to the religious life was discouraged by her Anglo-Catholic family. Shortt waited patiently for her parents' approval before formally entering All Saints; she was professed in 1868 at the age of 29.[21] Looking back over forty years, Shortt reflected in her memoirs that 'one grew to know that the Catholic Cause was the persecuted cause – that even a little cross on one's prayer book, or having a "Christian year" in one's possession brought about Protestant sneers'.[22] She recalled that in the early days the habit she wore was 'disliked & scoffed at' and that 'passers by … showed positive hatred of our outside dress – "made faces" at us & called us "Sisters of Misery".' Even one's own relations, she observed, 'pitied us.'[23] Although Shortt's reminiscences were written in 1907, the vitriol of this public loathing was still palpable.

Victorian antipathy towards Anglican sisterhoods was informed by two strands of thought, one religious and the other secular. Anglican sisterhoods embodied the Oxford Movement's call to 'catholicise' the Anglican faithful through their teaching, nursing and parish visiting. Unsurprisingly, the 'catholic' character of their lifestyle was troublesome to some, like the Evangelical vicar George Everard (1828–1901) who argued in 1890 that sisterhoods were 'the hot-beds of out-and-out Romish doctrine. What immense influence, in a quiet way, they are exerting in all parts of the country, it is not easy to overestimate.' Everard believed sisterhoods encouraged a 'mighty current Romewards'[24] and threatened Protestant hegemony. His concern reflected the anti-Catholic rhetoric that, according to Linda Colley, resounded well into the nineteenth century.[25] Visually, Anglican sisters embodied their involvement in religious ministry through the outward symbols of their faith such as the cross referred to on Shortt's prayer book or the distinctive habits that they wore. These physical markers, so similar to those of Roman Catholic sisters, only encouraged further Victorian religious rancour. The secular strand of opposition stressed Anglican sisters' rejection of dominant family discourse which delineated woman's role as wife, mother or daughter as a central aspect of femininity.[26] The Anglican writer Penelope Holland (d. 1873) argued that 'good and able' women 'should know their vocation is the world, and not the convent'.[27] Duty, according to Holland, was first to be found within the family unit. Anglican sisters' lifelong vows of poverty, chastity and obedience were thus profoundly disturbing to Victorians. These vows reflected a primary duty to an institution other than the family and a sexual chastity that was perceived as anti-familial and anti-maternal. In addition, many resented the implication of the religious sister's 'higher calling'.

Although anti-sisterhood narratives remained a constant presence in the press and literary publications, an increasing tolerance was visible by the 1870s. According to Shortt, 'Bit by bit, step by step so far, it [sisterhood life] has broken down protestant prejudice.'[28] Canon Jeffreys speaking at the 1878 Church Congress similarly acknowledged that

> There was no public opinion at all in their favour twenty years ago; they have created public opinions; it has not created them. *The Times* and other leading publications were for a long time not at all favourable to these institutions; they have slowly worked their own way, and now great numbers of people are full of admiration.[29]

Anglican women religious themselves were largely responsible for the shift in public opinion through their demonstrable 'social utility' in managing schools, orphanages, hospitals and refuges in local communities throughout Britain, but also by spreading the Christian mission to outposts of the Empire.[30] Mid-Victorian family ideology had begun to shift as well. Henrietta Blackmore's analysis of the Christian and popular press indicates that even the deep-rooted notion of a daughter's first and most absolute duty owed to her family had begun to fade.[31] By the early twentieth century, there was a marked acceptance of Anglican sisterhoods centring on their 'good works' as well as their religious ministry. This was not an isolated phenomenon; it reflected the changing nature of women's roles. What had once been a novelty had simply become more commonplace and it was accompanied by women's greater access to education, employment opportunities and politicisation.[32]

Public responses to women's religious ministries: deaconesses

The 'revival' of the ancient order of the deaconess occurred twenty years after Marian Hughes became the first Anglican sister and was meant to offer an alternative to the increasingly popular yet troublesome sisterhoods. Elizabeth Catherine Ferard (1825–83), the founder of the English deaconess movement, trained at Theodor Fliedner's Lutheran Deaconess Institute in Kaiserswerth, Germany and was subsequently ordained by the Bishop of London, Archibald Campbell Tait, in 1861.[33] That same year Ferard opened the North London Deaconesses Institution and, by 1863, was leading a team of two deaconesses and six aspirants who visited the sick, managed the Infant School and Girls' School at St Luke's and governed the nursing department of the Great Northern Hospital.[34] Their 'experiment' encouraged nine further foundations of deaconess communities by 1887. Also in 1887, Deaconess Isabella Gilmore (1842–1923) founded the Rochester Diocesan Deaconess Institution which diverged from Ferard's 'sisterhood lines' by providing centralised training for the deaconesses but no community life. Gilmore's 'parochial model' was intended to place the parish not the female community at the centre of the life of the deaconess.[35] Deaconess Institutions introduced by the Scottish Presbyterian Church in 1887, the Methodists and Baptists in 1890 and the Scottish Episcopal Church in 1915 operated mainly as training centres and also followed the parochial model.[36]

After the emotive public responses towards Anglican sisterhoods the public reaction to deaconesses was more muted. Blackmore has argued that attitudes towards deaconesses were certainly less polarised and that the feminist press, especially the *Englishwoman's Review*, was particularly supportive of the professional role of deaconesses in the church.[37] Yet the general public appeared unable to distinguish between an Anglican sister and a deaconess, especially as the first cohort of deaconesses lived together in communities. Anglican bishops and deaconesses, aware of this confusion, were therefore keen to differentiate the two groups of women. Deaconesses dressed in intentionally dark, conservative outfits that were distinctive enough to separate them from other women philanthropists but were not considered as 'outlandish' as the religious habit of the Anglican sister. Churchman John Saul Howson (1816–85), described as the 'foremost advocate of the deaconess cause', published numerous texts explaining and promoting the work of the Anglican deaconess.[38] More importantly, advocates stressed her Protestant and English credentials:

> The Deaconesses of the English Church are, then, it must be remembered, distinctly Anglican; and the strength of the Institutions will surely be found in the steadfast maintenance of Anglican principles as distinct from all extremes either of Ritualism or Puritanism.[39]

Gilmore's parochial system faced additional difficulties. Some deaconesses felt isolated without the support of a community and commented on the loneliness of the life.[40] The general support of the Anglican episcopacy for the deaconesses was widely publicised but also highly problematic as will be discussed later in this chapter. This ambivalent attitude was reflected in the small numbers of women who became deaconesses: 431 Anglican women by 1919, 92 Methodist women by 1901[41] and 124 Scottish Presbyterian women by 1947.[42]

Public responses to women's religious ministries: Catholic convents

Although conventual life had been abolished in Britain after the Reformation, English women's religious communities had survived in exile. To escape the persecution of religious orders during the French Revolution, twenty-four groups of exiled nuns relocated in England between 1792 and 1800.[43] For most of the nineteenth century these contemplative religious orders, enclosed behind convent walls, remained in the shadows of the 'modern orders',[44] congregations of religious sisters who led lives of prayer but worked outside the cloister building, a Catholic infrastructure of schools, hospitals and a wide variety of social welfare institutions. The Faithful Companions of Jesus were the first of the active congregations to settle in England in 1830, followed by the Ursulines of Jesus who founded a convent in Edinburgh in 1834. By 1900, eighty active congregations and thirty-three contemplative orders were residing in England and Wales and managing over 596 convents. It is likely that over 10,000 women became professed religious sisters and nuns by 1900, with possibly a further 10,000 who left after a trial period, having realised 'no vocation' for the religious life.[45] By 1937 an additional seventy congregations were founded in England and Wales; by then there were approximately 950 convents.[46] Scotland by 1914 had twenty-two religious institutes overseeing sixty-five convents.[47]

Nineteenth-century Catholic religious institutes faced similar opprobrium to that of Anglican sisterhoods but Catholic anti-nun literature published in Britain, North America and Australia was unequalled in its vitriol.[48] Genevieve Dupuis, founder of the Sisters of Charity of St Paul the Apostle, sanguinely noted in 1863 that

> In this heretical country they speak against us. They say we do not eat enough or that we sleep on straw; that the Superior kills her Sisters; in fact all sorts of detractions of this kind. Fiat.[49]

The anti-Catholic lecture circuit featured stories of imprisoned nuns, sexual debauchery and unrelenting cruelty.[50] These stories were a call to action to men like Charles Newdegate (1816–87), a Conservative MP from North Warwickshire and unbending advocate of the national church. His efforts to legislate mandatory inspection of convents began in 1852.[51] The Anglican Convent Enquiry Society (CES) was established in 1889 and investigated alleged abuses associated with convents. The CES lobbied persistently (and unsuccessfully) for parliamentary inspection of convents during the 1890s and on into the early years of the twentieth century.[52] The last attempt to legislate convent inspection which failed was in 1912. Walter L. Arnstein has argued that much as the Victorian public and the House of Commons would have liked to inspect and regulate convents in the same way as lunatic asylums, factories and schools, there was never sufficient hard evidence of mistreatment.[53]

Despite fervent opposition to Catholic convents, however, many Protestants acknowledged the merit of the sisters' charitable work. According to the annals of the Faithful Companions of Jesus, the citizens of Middlesbrough mourned the death of Sister M. Lucy Fletcher: 'Her death was no sooner known than a veil of mourning seemed to be thrown over the whole town; Protestants as well as Catholics, all expressed their regret at seeing disappear from their midst one whose devotedness they had learned to appreciate.'[54] Their hard work, usefulness and devotion encouraged public Protestant appreciation for the Catholic sisters of Middlesbrough. Even more telling, perhaps, was the financial assistance of Protestants. The Sisters of Nazareth benefited from the efforts of non-Catholic Sir Squire Bancroft, a 'generous friend' of the sisters whose charity reading brought in £200. A recitation organised at the Albert Hall by Protestants generated a further £1,000.[55] While this shift towards increasing Protestant appreciation should not be overstated, such evidence illustrates that a level of acknowledgement and acceptance did exist.

As expected, Catholic reactions to the arrival of sisters and nuns were more enthusiastic. When the sisters of Notre Dame de Namur arrived in Blackburn in 1850, they were greeted by

> [a] crowd at the station waiting for us, the whole town was agog with excitement. They followed the carriage to the garden gate, which we had to close again at once, to prevent the people from coming into the house, for in their enthusiasm, these good Catholics, nearly all Irish, would have all wanted [sic] to tell us how happy they were to see us come.[56]

The philanthropic work of the sisters was integral to the success of the Roman Catholic Church. They ministered to Catholics, rich and poor, and developed an infrastructure of schools, orphanages, homes and social welfare institutions that developed the faith of the Catholic laity and attended to their material and educative needs. Throughout the nineteenth century, there was more cooperation than competition between Catholic convents. Although rivalry for entrants existed, there was plenty of work to be done, especially in urban conurbations such as London, Liverpool and Manchester. By 1937, the majority of the 956 Catholic convents, 44 per cent, were located in London and the South-East and another 39 per cent were spread in the South-West, the Midlands and the North-West. The remaining convents were spread throughout the North-East, Yorkshire and less populated areas such as East Anglia and Wales.[57]

Anglican and Catholic sisters and deaconesses developed three distinct forms of religious ministry; linking them together was a conviction that they had an important role to play in the evangelisation of the laity. The training for these forms of religious life occurred in women-managed spaces and all of the sisters and many of the deaconesses lived and worked together in homosocial communities. All groups faced some level of opposition from the Protestant majority, but deaconesses were perceived by the general public as more palatable than sisters and nuns. In spite of this, Protestant women interested in religious ministry were drawn to the sisterhoods. With their lifelong vows of poverty, celibacy and obedience lived in women-only spaces, the sisterhoods attracted over 10,000 women, while less than 500 Anglican women were ordained as deaconesses. Catholic sisters and nuns were far more prolific, but religious life had been an accepted part of Catholic culture for a little under two millennia and the convent was considered a laudable choice for Catholic women. By the 1860s, Catholic and Anglican sisters as well as Protestant deaconesses had become a powerful, visible force as evangelists and philanthropists. Public antipathy to these religious ministries may have waned somewhat by the end of the nineteenth century but, as the following discussion illustrates, the tenor of the relationships between these women's ministries and clerical authorities was another matter entirely.

Women's ministries and clerical authority: Anglican sisterhoods

Whether approved by episcopal bodies or not, all three communities of women were established outside of the ecclesiastical structures of the church. Yet each had a distinct relationship with their church hierarchies that both hindered and fostered their autonomy as a corporate body. By asserting their authority to participate in a religious ministry of both words and in deeds, these women re-envisioned the concept of ministry to include visible female roles that implied an official capacity within the church. Tim Jones argues that the ontological positioning of Anglican deaconesses and sisterhoods provided a new spiritual status for Anglican women.[58] Women evangelised and ministered to the physical and spiritual needs of the faithful and the not so faithful, but tensions arose when they transgressed the liminal boundaries of their authority.

Anglican sisterhoods were often led by confident female leaders, mother superiors, who held firm ideas of what constituted religious life and successfully exercised their authority relatively free from male control.[59] Some founders welcomed episcopal approval, believing this would encourage recruitment and financial security. Etheldreda Benett (1824–1913), who founded the Society of the Sisters of Bethany in 1866, operated without episcopal sanction until 1889 when she offered the Bishop of London, Frederick Temple (1821–1902), the office of Visitor.[60] Others, such as Emily Ayckbowm (1836–1900), who established the Sisters of the Church, believed that an episcopal relationship would invite unnecessary interference with community affairs.[61] And some like the Community of All Hallows lost the Bishop of Norwich, Samuel Hinds' support when they opted to become a religious sisterhood despite his disapproval.[62] Thus, many Anglican sisterhoods developed without any prescribed episcopal oversight and were autonomous from the Church of England hierarchy. As Frith demonstrates, such autonomy had a price as it could become more difficult to attract funding and new recruits.[63] Bishops and clergy, for their part, disagreed as to the 'rightful' authority of the Church of England over Anglican sisterhoods; no model of religious life had existed in the Church of England and so there were no canonical guidelines. The resulting stalemate between the bishops and clergy who supported sisterhood autonomy and those who did not manifested itself in the lack of formal church policies regarding Anglican sisterhoods. This left them relatively free to chart their own course but also somewhat isolated from church support.

There were many attempts to develop regulations for managing Anglican sisterhoods. Church conferences and Convocations formally investigated women's religious communities and issued a series of pronouncements regarding matters of episcopal authority. These were very one-sided decrees arrived at with little, if any, dialogue with members of sisterhoods. The 1891 Church Convocation recommended strictures over those who could take vows and suggested episcopal approval for convent foundations, philanthropic work and the rules governing sisterhoods.[64] A special commission formed at the 1897 Lambeth Conference addressed the rights and jurisdictions of bishops regarding liturgical and ritualistic practices, vows and legal matters concerning sisters and deaconesses. Their final report (circulated in 1902 and presented again at the 1908 Lambeth Conference) noted conventual life should recognise the 'authority of the episcopate'. It outlined the responsibilities of the Visitor (either the bishop or his representative) who sanctioned the constitutions of the community and ensured they were followed. It also maintained that sisterhood constitutions should contain the 'distinct recognition of the Doctrine and Discipline of the Church of England as supreme'.[65] The 1920 Lambeth Palace conference report remarked that a 'closer relationship between a community and the Bishop' as well as the 'creation of central advisory bodies' with representatives from the community 'would promote co-ordination and mutual communication'.[66] By the 1930 Lambeth Conference, sisterhoods were reported to have had an 'increased experience of the [sic] problems'[67] and it was noted that

> [the] interrelation between the two should be clarified and strengthened. We believe that the time has now come when the Episcopate ... should be prepared to give formal sanction to approved Communities, and when [sic] the Communities themselves will welcome such sanction.

The recommended duties of the Visitor became increasingly prescriptive in terms of approving the convent rules, the taking and dispensing of permanent vows, expulsion from the Community, elections of community leaders and services in the chapel.[68] What was evident from these incessant and increasingly detailed rulings was that bishops' concerns about their authority over sisterhoods were not being addressed satisfactorily. It is unclear as to how various Anglican sisterhoods responded to these directives. As Convocation and conference decrees were not compulsory, the rulings were unenforceable. The implication derived from the reiteration of these numerous dictates was that some sisterhoods were quite content to operate as autonomous units, respectful of the church hierarchy but not finding it necessary to yield to the pressures of its jurisdiction. Further research into the influence of these pronouncements from the perspective of Anglican sisters is necessary in order to understand more about the power relations between sisterhoods and the Anglican bishops. In the end the Established Church was forced to accept as a *fait accompli* the self-managed administrative structure of the sisterhoods.

Women's ministries and clerical authority: deaconesses

As the ecclesiastically-sanctioned alternative to sisterhoods, deaconesses on the other hand came directly under clerical and episcopal authority: as the Rev. Rich wrote in *The Churchman* in 1907, the deaconess was applauded as 'the servant of the clergy; she does not plan out her own work, but receives it from her rector'.[69] The 1862 Chronicle of Convocation commended the five deaconesses who worked 'under the regulation, discipline, discretion, and control of Mr. Hayne', vicar of Buckland in Plymouth.[70] Yet even this more overt control did not mitigate clerical concerns about deaconesses' responsibilities and authority. Some resented the 'head deaconess' who governed the community with her all-female council, assigned deaconesses to a parish and mediated any tensions between the women and the local clergy. Isabella Gilmore's parochial model, where the deaconess institution acted as a training school, removed this particular layer of female authority and was thus more popular with clergy and bishops. In Gilmore's structure, once assigned to a parish deaconesses came under the authority of the clergy and bishop in just the same way as male deacons. In this approach Gilmore complied with what she believed was the true 'Primitive Model' derived from Scripture. She argued that this model allowed deaconesses

> to be as nearly as possible in the same position as the Deacons ... they were to receive their own stipends and in all ways manage their own affairs; they were to live in their parish, and if a near relation could live with them, so much the better; in any difficulty the matter was to be referred to the bishop.[71]

But Gilmore was not simply acquiescing to patriarchal authority; she was proposing a parity of responsibilities between deacons and deaconesses which conjured up a different set of clerical fears, namely that 'a deaconess may be apt to think of her office more highly than she ought'.[72] The persistent unwillingness of the Anglican Church to formalise the role of the deaconess throughout the nineteenth and early twentieth centuries is indicative of such gendered concerns over authority.

Deaconesses pressed for canonical regularisation of their responsibilities, authority and status, believing this would increase a community's stability, reduce the variability of Episcopal control and generally reduce confusion about their institutional identity. Deaconess institutions comprised various traditions: some were training institutions while others were centres where deaconesses led a community-based life. In some dioceses bishops 'set apart' deaconesses; in others they ordained them. This disparity led to confusion; one churchwoman writing in 1880 noted that 'the clergy of our Church have but a vague idea of what the calling and position of a deaconess means'.[73] Significantly, a newly appointed bishop could alter the structure of the deaconess institution in a diocese. Emma Day (d. 1920), founder of the Deaconess Institution in Canterbury, was trained by Elizabeth Ferard and adopted the sisterhood structure with the approval of Bishop Harold Browne in 1874. Bishop Herbert Ryle, who became Bishop of Winchester in

1903, insisted instead on the parochial model of deaconesses which meant the abandonment of the community life. Day noted:

> We had tried for some years to combine the Sisters' life with the Deaconess office. The double basis appealed strongly to me and to many others, but in practice it was not sound. Bishop Ryle did us the great service of placing the Home on a distinctly Deaconess basis. The result has proved his wisdom: life is simpler, and duty is clearer.[74]

Day's 'spin' on Ryle's alterations concealed the pain and confusion this change had actually caused the deaconesses, who found community life integral to their vocation. Deaconess Dora alluded to the high price of Day's loyalty to her bishop: 'The changes were somewhat dearly purchased, and of course on Mother Emma's head fell much of the adverse criticism of those who did not agree or did not understand.'[75] The absence of canonical regulations could lead to such arbitrary changes in a diocese. Paradoxically, the role, functions and authority of deaconesses in comparison to religious sisterhoods appeared indefinite and variable despite Episcopal control.

In 1899, while addressing deaconesses in Westminster Abbey, the Bishop of Birmingham, Charles Gore (1853–1932) commented that 'Deaconesses were regarded as an Order of the clergy' but that 'it only waits for the church to take more formal action on its behalf'.[76] And wait they did. By the early twentieth century, the questions regarding the role of deaconesses became more persistent and vocal. Was the female diaconate permanent or temporary? Were they equal to the male diaconate or were they paid church workers?[77] Female church workers obtained professional training and began to form women's organisations to press their issues. The Central Committee for Women's Church Work (1908), the Anglican Church League for Women's Suffrage (1912), the inter-denominational Society for the Ministry of Women (1929) and the Anglican Group for the Ordination of Women to the Historic Ministry of the Church (1930) lobbied the church for more formal pronouncements regarding their roles and functions as church workers. These examples of what Brian Heeney calls 'church feminism' included deaconesses who insisted on inclusion in the diaconate at the same level as men. They formed lobbying groups such as the Head Deaconesses' Association (1908) to advance their claims as well as to discuss issues in common.[78]

The 1920 Lambeth Palace Conference report acknowledged that the Church had 'under-valued and neglected the gifts of women and has too thanklessly used their work',[79] but despite this rhetoric the report still held to the 'differences between women and men' and rejected the deaconesses' equivalence with deacons. The conference recognised the diaconate of women as the 'only Order of the Ministry' with Apostolic approval and recommended it be restored formally and canonically. However, some six resolutions that came out of the Conference were nonbinding. The Convocation of Canterbury in 1923 and the Convocation of York in 1925 further defined the status of the deaconess by using the word 'ordained', referring to them as an 'apostolic Order of Ministry in the Church of

God', but not as 'Holy Orders'.[80] The 1930 Lambeth Conference again explicitly rejected any parity with deacons; a deaconess was 'outside the historic Orders of the ministry supplementary and complementary to them'.[81] Although twentieth-century deaconesses were adamant in their demands for recognition and parity with deacons, the church's response became more unequivocal in its rejection of any equality between the male and female diaconate.

Women's ministries and clerical authority: Catholic convents

Unlike Protestant sisterhoods and deaconesses, the roles and functions of Catholic women religious had been evolving since late antiquity. One distinct area of struggle was for an apostolic religious life lived outside the cloister.[82] What had been expressly forbidden by the Roman Catholic Church until the eighteenth century was enthusiastically embraced in the nineteenth century as the Catholic Church recognised the practical, evangelical and catechetical skills of women religious.[83] In Britain, as elsewhere, these congregations proliferated, filling the educative and missionary needs of an immigrant church.[84] The authority over sisterhoods that Anglican bishops coveted was part and parcel of female religious life. Every religious community needed a bishop's permission before opening a convent in his diocese. Local bishops had a right of visitation which included ensuring that the communities' rule and constitutions were being followed and that the material and spiritual needs of all sisters were being addressed.

Administratively, Catholic religious communities were structured under two systems, diocesan and pontifical right. Diocesan communities operated under the authority of bishops and were located typically in their diocese. The vast majority of communities embraced the second structure, pontifical right, encouraged by Rome in its drive to centralise its authority. However, this system also reflected the needs of active congregations at local, national and international levels and signalled women's confidence in their skills as leaders, business managers and missioners. These centralised structures, like many of the Anglican sisterhoods and community-based deaconess institutions, were managed by a female Superior General elected by members of the General Chapter and supported by a Council of Sisters who together directed the efforts of the congregations. While individual convents were under the obedience of a bishop, the ultimate authority came from the rule and constitutions that had been approbated by Rome. These institutional documents were sacrosanct; once approved by the Pope they could not be contravened by the sisters or by the bishops or clergy.

Although in many ways prescribed and limiting, women could use the pontifical authority built into their rules and constitutions to 'manoeuvre' bishops and clergy who wanted to alter a congregation's objectives or circumvent the authority of female congregation leaders. Within larger congregations women religious could redirect unwelcome requests to a higher internal authority. As church workers, sisters were very much in demand and some congregations felt free to leave a particular diocese or locale if the clergy interfered in day-to-day operations. In Glasgow, Father Peter Forbes' dispute with Sister of Mercy Elizabeth Moore

(1806–68) ended with Moore returning to Limerick along with eleven members of the convent; two professed sisters along with two postulants and six novices remained in Glasgow. Forbes' relationship with the Sisters of Mercy remained difficult and the community lost three superiors in two years.[85] While Moore's departure indicated a strong degree of religious agency, as Karly Kehoe points out, much depended on individual congregation leaders. The French Franciscans also had pontifical status, but shortly after arriving in Glasgow in 1847 they separated from their French motherhouse and formed a new congregation. The new rule and constitutions, co-written by the coadjutor Bishop of the Western District of Scotland, Alexander Smith, unsurprisingly gave the ecclesiastical visitor an authoritative role within the congregation.[86]

Using the boundaries and structures created by the church, Catholic women religious created spaces for negotiation, sometimes expanding boundaries and on other occasions retreating back within them. However, circumstances changed with the canonical approval of active women religious in 1900. From the decrees *Conditae a Christo* (1900) and *Normae* (1901) to the codification of Canon Law (1917), came numerous regulations created to monitor and standardise the behaviour of women religious. Tellingly, Mary Ewens describes the early twentieth century as the 'Great Repression'.[87] Liz West argues that

> Feminine social action in the world was to remain troubling to the magesterium [sic] of the church. It was a problem resolved by the 1917 Code of Canon Law, which imposed a modified monastic enclosure upon all women's congregations. Now, the world was 'shut out' and a quasi-monastic state evolved, which was also based upon concepts of moral activity rather that [sic] on the charismatic dimension.[88]

Despite these changes Catholic religious life continued to attract many women; the cohorts who entered in the 1920s and 1930s were the largest in Britain's history. This was a period of great Catholic institution-building. Published congregation histories prior to the 1960s included numerous images of schools, hospitals and the large motherhouses that came to reflect the institutionalisation of religious life.[89]

The attractions of religious life in the nineteenth and early twentieth centuries tell us much about the contemporary culture. Anglican and Catholic religious institutes as female-managed spaces were attractive to women who valued a lifestyle that included 'works of mercy', a well-defined spiritual life and personal stability, despite being accompanied by a strict moral code that today would seem oppressive and highly regulated. Perhaps such moral codes and accompanying regulations were more culturally consonant than is often recognised. Even though most Catholic religious congregations opted for pontifical right, an arrangement that allowed greater flexibility when dealing with the local episcopal authority, there remained a strong patriarchal dimension to their relationship with Rome and the ecclesiastical hierarchy which legitimated their identity and status. Paradoxically, a sense of identity and status were strong within Anglican sisterhoods despite their much looser connections with the established Church and weaker within deaconess institutions, which were more strongly linked to the Church. Thus, Anglican sisterhoods were willing to distance themselves from episcopal sanction while deaconesses sought canonical regulations that they believed would ensure some sort of institutional regularity and status. The diversity of deaconess life was regarded by many as a negative factor that undermined stability and some even saw canonical regulations as a means to obtaining parity with deacons.

Episcopal concerns about these forms of women's religious ministry centred around control and management. The Anglican hierarchy developed a series of regulations that were unenforceable and never universally accepted by all sisterhoods. In the Catholic context, the dynamic growth in numbers of congregations, convents and sisters led to a reassessment of the relationships between women religious and the ecclesiastical establishment and in the early twentieth century, the introduction of a codified canon law encouraged greater uniformity, institutionalisation and a separation from the world that reflected what some saw as a 'cloister in the world'. Many today argue that it also stifled the flexibility of Catholic women's religious institutes.[90]

Concluding observations

The religious historian Michael Hill identified nineteenth-century Anglican sisterhoods as 'the first signs of incipient feminism among women in the middle class'.[91] Whether they were the 'first' is debatable, as many of the chapters in this collection demonstrate, but certainly women's desire for religious ministry on their own terms encouraged them to challenge patriarchal authority. In 1904, Sarah Burstall argued that women's leadership in the church had influenced the 'Women's Movement', citing as evidence

> ... the extraordinary development of sisterhoods ... the growth of deaconesses' institutions ... the work of the Salvation Army [and] ... the enormous multiplication of women missionaries.[92]

Women's sphere of action in these sororial networks included their role not simply as church workers but as church leaders within their own communities. Jane Rendall and Olive Banks have both argued that the prevailing doctrine of female moral superiority limited women's feminist vision, yet scholarship on the sisters and deaconesses reveals a genuine radicalism inherent in their mission.[93] The furore around their efforts in the nineteenth century attests to this. They eschewed the familiar, domestic and traditional paths of spirituality and chose new ways of serving their church. These communities encouraged female autonomy and self-determination without an explicitly feminist discourse. They achieved a form of 'feminist practice' that problematised their relationship with patriarchal religious institutions while evincing great respect for the church.[94] They recognised their distinctive contribution to religious ministry while maintaining a separate-spheres framework that accepted many of the gendered ideals of femininity. Sisters and deaconesses embraced women's 'special' traits; they believed themselves to be more moral, obedient and benevolent. Yet they modified and subverted Victorian gender ideology to suit their needs, rejecting a life controlled by men in favour of a set of behavioural norms developed and administered by women. They challenged the Victorian public to think differently about the capabilities of women creating their own spaces and cultures for the development of feminine Christian spirituality. In so doing, they constructed for themselves a more public and prominent role in religious ministry. By the twentieth century, they were no longer institutionally marginalised but their growth and their more prominent role within the church came at a price. The flexible organisations of the nineteenth century became the hierarchical, unbending institutions of the twentieth century.

Overall, it is important to recognise that women were more attracted to a communal lifestyle with lifelong vows and regulation than to the 'independent' lifestyle of the parochial deaconesses. They were willing to accept the rigours of an authoritative institutional structure under female management in exchange for a 'corporate' identity that both increased their independence and limited their personal freedom. Many women, especially those in leadership roles, had some measure of autonomy, authority and agency. But in choosing a religious life, they were not choosing a life free from the control of others or free from patriarchal ideals; rather they were actively choosing the restrictions they were willing to accept. Indeed, although these three types of religious ministry commanded a collective power that was able to negotiate to some extent with ecclesiastical structures it was that same community-based collective power that most limited women's independence and individual freedom.

These histories, of course, do not end in 1940. After the lull of apparent complacency towards women's inequalities in church structures, a flurry of activity developed throughout the 1960s. For Anglican women, this led finally to an acknowledgement of the equality between deacons and deaconesses in 1978 and of women to the priesthood in 1992. For Catholic sisters, the change was equally striking. Vatican II (1962–65), a council called by Pope John XXIII, encouraged all women and men religious to review their history and their mission in order to meet the needs of a changing world. As a result, many religious congregations abandoned the numerous institutions they managed and developed a social justice ministry that was more flexible, less hierarchical and more responsive to the needs of the individual. Many also dismantled the institutional focus of private life and developed more fluid forms of leadership and living. Some began to question the male prerogative of the priestly function and groups such as the Catholic Ordination of Woman have become an active voice for change. But this return to radicalism has had a price; some conservative Catholics have been rancorous in their criticism and long for the return of the habited nuns teaching and nursing in Catholic institutions. This need to circumscribe women's religious ministry is curiously reminiscent of Victorian attitudes to sisters and deaconesses.

As this chapter has made clear, much about these particular communities and religious ministries still needs explanation. More research is necessary, for example, to uncover their attitudes towards their church's prescriptions, to understand the benefits of the contemplative form of religious life, and to explain the impact of institutionalisation and the other changes that took place in the early twentieth century. Such knowledge is relevant to understanding a world that still seeks to contain women's efforts and limit women's contributions in the name of gendered difference. It is time to rehabilitate these unfashionable pious women and recognise the significance of their ministries to the development of religious cultures in Britain.

Acknowledgments

Many thanks to the editors and Joy Frith for their insights and valuable comments on the early drafts of this essay. Also I wish to acknowledge the many congregations and archivists who welcomed me into their archives, but most especially the Faithful Companions of Jesus Generalate Archives, the Sisters of Charity of St Paul the Apostle Archives, Notre Dame Archives British Province and the Sisters of Nazareth Generalate Archives.

Further reading

Henrietta Blackmore, 'Autonomous Mission and Ecclesiastical Authority: The Revival of the Deaconess Order in the Church of England, 1850–1900' (unpublished doctoral thesis, University of Oxford, 2004).

Henrietta Blackmore (ed.), *The Beginning of Women's Ministry: The Revival of the Deaconesses in 19th Century Church of England* (Suffolk: Boydell & Brewer, 2007).

Joy Frith, *Anglican Sisterhoods and the Politics of Victorian Identity* (Manchester University Press, forthcoming 2010).

Sean Gill, *Women and the Church of England from the Eighteenth Century to the Present* (London: SPCK, 1994).

Janet Grierson, *The Deaconess* (London: CIO Publishing, 1981).

Brian Heeney, *The Woman's Movement in the Church of England 1850–1930* (Oxford: Clarendon Press, 1988).

S. Karly Kehoe, *Creating the Scottish Church: Catholicism, Gender and Ethnicity in Nineteenth-century Scotland* (Manchester: Manchester University Press, forthcoming 2010).

Carmen M. Mangion, *Contested Identities: Catholic Women Religious in Nineteenth-century England and Wales* (Manchester: Manchester University Press, 2008).

Susan Mumm, *Stolen Daughters, Virgin Mothers: Anglican Sisterhoods in Victorian Britain* (London: Leicester University Press, 1998).

Susan Mumm (ed.), *All Saints Sisters of the Poor: An Anglican Sisterhood in the Nineteenth Century* (Suffolk, England: The Boydell Press, 2001).

Susan O'Brien, '"Terra Incognita": The Nun in Nineteenth-Century England', *Past and Present*, 121 (1988), pp. 110–40.

John Shelton Reed, *Glorious Battle: The Cultural Politics of Victorian Anglo-Catholicism* (Nashville: Vanderbilt University Press, 1996).

Notes

1 The 'Rule' along with constitutions were the governing documents that defined the aims and parameters of a religious institution.

2 Michael Hill, *The Religious Order: A Study of Virtuoso Religion and its Legitimization in the Nineteenth-Century Church of England* (London: Heinemann Educational Books, 1973), p. 204.

3 Sean Gill, *Women and the Church of England from the Eighteenth Century to the Present* (London: SPCK, 1994), p. 163.

4 Joy Frith, *Anglican Sisterhoods and the Politics of Victorian Identity* (Manchester University Press, forthcoming 2010).

5 Brian Heeney, *The Woman's Movement in the Church of England 1850–1930* (Oxford: Clarendon Press, 1988), p. 71; Gill, *Women and the Church of England*, p. 167.

6 Janet Grierson, *The Deaconess* (London: CIO Publishing, 1981); Catherine M. Prelinger, 'The Female Diaconate in the Anglican Church: What Kind of Ministry for Women?' in *Religion in the Lives of English Women, 1760–1930* edited by Gail Malmgreen (London: Croom Helm, 1986), pp. 161–92.

7 Henrietta Blackmore, 'Autonomous Mission and Ecclesiastical Authority: The Revival of the Deaconess Order in the Church of England, 1850–1900' (unpublished doctoral thesis, University of Oxford, 2004).

8 Muriel McEwan, 'Ministering in Affliction: the "Brown Deaconesses" of the Church of Scotland 1888–c.1948' (unpublished doctoral thesis, Open University, 2007).

9 Roman Catholic and Anglican religious sisters and nuns are referred to as women religious. The terms sisters and nuns were used interchangeably in the nineteenth and twentieth centuries although with the codification of Roman Catholic Canon Law in 1917, the term sister came to refer to women who took simple vows and worked outside the convent and the term nun came to refer to contemplatives who took solemn vows and lived a life of prayer behind cloister walls.

10 For example, Judith Lancaster, *Cornelia Connelly and her Interpreters* (Oxford: Thex Way, 2004); Elizabeth A. West, *One Woman's Journey: Mary Potter Founder – Little Company of Mary* (Richmond, Victoria, Australia: Spectrum Publications, 2000).

11 See 'Further reading'.

12 Martha Vicinus's, *Independent Women: Work and Community for Single Women, 1850–1920* (London: Virago Press, 1985) remains the most prominent exception. She touts Anglican sisterhoods as being in the 'vanguard of women's single-sex organizations, in both their organizational autonomy and their insistence upon women's right to a separate religious life' (p. 48).

13 Sue Morgan, 'Faith, Sex and Purity: The Religio-Feminist Theory of Ellice Hopkins', *Women's History Review* 9 (2000), pp. 13–34.

14 Susan Mumm, *Stolen Daughters, Virgin Mothers: Anglican Sisterhoods in Victorian Britain* (London: Leicester University Press, 1998), p. 6.

15 See Thomas J. Williams, Priscilla Lydia Sellon: *The Restorer after Three Centuries of the Religious Life in the English Church* (London: SPCK, 1965) and Peter F. Anson, *The Call of the Cloister: Religious Communities and Kindred Bodies in the Anglican Communion* (London: SPCK, 1955).

16 The Anglo-Catholic movement developed from the Oxford Movement.

17 See Mumm, *Stolen Daughters, Virgin Mothers*, pp. 20–30, 42.

18 A.M. Allchin, *The Silent Rebellion: Anglican Religious Communities 1845–1900* (London: SCM Press, 1958), p. 120. The actual numbers of Anglican sisters professed is difficult to quantify given the limited access to convent archives. Susan Mumm has collected approximately 2,200 biographies from the twenty-eight sisterhoods who granted her access to their archives. Mumm, *Stolen Daughters, Virgin Mothers*, pp. xiv, 227.

19 Mumm, *Stolen Daughters, Virgin Mothers*, p. 14.
20 Mumm, *Stolen Daughters, Virgin Mothers*, p. 26. Mumm estimates another one-third to one-half were dismissed during their novitiate.
21 Susan Mumm (ed.), *All Saints Sisters of the Poor: An Anglican Sisterhood in the Nineteenth Century* (Suffolk: Boydell Press, 2001), p. 3.
22 Mumm, *All Saints Sisters of the Poor*, p. 49.
23 Mumm, *All Saints Sisters of the Poor*, p. 52.
24 George Everard, *'Danger and Duty': A Few Words to Fellow Protestants* (London: John Kensit, 1890), pp. 3, 11.
25 Linda Colley, *Britons: Forging the Nation 1707–1837* (London: Yale University Press, 1992), pp. 22–25.
26 Leonore Davidoff and Catherine Hall, *Family Fortunes: Men and Women of the English Middle Class 1780–1850* (London: Routledge & Kegan Paul, 1987), pp. 321–56.
27 Penelope Holland, 'Two Views of the Convent Question', *Macmillan's Magazine* 19 (1869), p. 537.
28 Mumm, *All Saints Sisters of the Poor*, p. 51.
29 *The Chronicle of Convocation* (London: Rivingtons, 1878), pp. 265–66.
30 Eleanor Joy Frith, 'Pseudonuns: Anglican Sisterhoods and the Politics of Victorian Identity' (unpublished doctoral thesis, Queen's University, Canada, 2004), Chapters 6 and 7.
31 Blackmore, 'Autonomous Mission', pp. 71–83.
32 Kathryn Gleadle, *British Women in the Nineteenth Century* (Basingstoke: Palgrave, 2001), p. 188.
33 Prelinger, 'The Female Diaconate', p. 163. Kaiserswerth opened in 1833 and trained over 15,000 deaconesses by the turn of the century.
34 North London Deaconesses' Institution 1863 *Annual Report*, pp. 1–6. It was renamed the London Diocesan Deaconess Institution in 1868 and the Deaconess Community of St Andrew in 1943.
35 Blackmore, 'Autonomous Mission', p. 2.
36 Grierson, *The Deaconess*, p. 37, Prelinger, 'The Female Diaconate', p. 182. The Sisters of the People, founded in 1887, were precursors to the Methodist deaconesses.
37 Blackmore, 'Autonomous Mission', pp. 60–72.
38 He published 'Deaconesses in the Church of England' in the *Quarterly Review* in 1860; it was reissued with additional material as *Deaconesses: The Official Help of Women in Parochial Work and in Charitable Institutions* (1862).
39 Elizabeth M. Sewell, 'Anglican Deaconesses', *Macmillan's Magazine* 28 (Sep 1873), p. 464.
40 Prelinger, 'The Female Diaconate', p. 174.
41 Blackmore, *The Beginning of Women's Ministry*, Appendix 2. E. Dorothy Graham's *Saved to Serve: The Story of the Wesley Deaconess Order, 1890–1978* (Peterborough: Methodist Publishing House, 2002), p. 2.
42 McEwan, 'Ministering in Affliction', p. 1.
43 Carmen Mangion, *Contested Identities: Catholic Women Religious in Nineteenth-Century England and Wales* (Manchester: Manchester University Press, 2008), pp. 34–35. Caroline Bowden and Michael Questier's AHRC-funded project 'Who were the Nuns?' identifies members of the English convents during their period of exile. For more information see http://wwtn.history.qmul.ac.uk/.
44 This is a tentative observation as little comprehensive research has been published on the experiences of nineteenth-century English contemplative nuns.
45 Mangion, *Contested Identities*, p. 37. *The Revival of Conventual Life in Scotland* (Edinburgh: John Chisholm, 1886). Most religious institutes managed multiple convents.

46 Barbara Walsh, *Roman Catholic Nuns in England Wales, 1800–1937: A Social History* (Dublin: Irish Academic Press, 2002), pp. 177

47 Mark Dilworth, 'Religious Orders in Scotland, 1878–1978', *Innes Review* (1978), p. 93.

48 D. G. Paz, *Popular anti-Catholicism in Mid-Victorian England* (Stanford, California: Stanford University Press, 1992).

49 Sisters of Charity of St Paul the Apostle Archives, Birmingham: Box 1, 30, letter dated 19 August 1863 from Geneviève Dupuis to Mère Elie Jarret.

50 Philip Ingram, 'Protestant Patriarchy and the Catholic Priesthood in Nineteenth Century England', *Journal of Social History* 24 (1991), pp. 783–84.

51 Walter L. Arnstein, *Protestant Versus Catholic in Mid-Victorian England: Mr. Newdegate and the Nuns* (London: University of Missouri Press, 1982).

52 René Kollar, 'Magdalenes and Nuns: Convent Laundries in Late Victorian England', *Anglican and Episcopal History* (2004), pp. 321–22.

53 Elizabeth Sloan Chesser, 'Convents in England: A Plea for State Inspection', *The Nineteenth Century and After* 72 (1912), 830–35; Arnstein, *Protestant versus Catholic*, p. 222.

54 Faithful Companions of Jesus, Generalate Archives, Broadstairs, Kent: A656 Middlesbrough, 1874, p. 10.

55 Archives of the Sisters of Nazareth: DD/1/1/2 'Hammersmith History of Foundation, 1891–1907', p. 40 and DD/1/1/1 'History of the Congregation', 1885, p. 186.

56 Notre Dame Archives, British Province, Liverpool: BX PRV/1, Letter from Soeur Clarie (Clarisse Noel) to Mère Constantine dated 8 July 1850.

57 Walsh, *Roman Catholic Nuns*, pp. 178–81.

58 Timothy Willem Jones, 'Sex and Gender in the Church of England, 1857–1957' (unpublished doctoral thesis, The University of Melbourne, 2007), pp. 81–83.

59 Mumm, *Stolen Daughters, Virgin Mothers*, pp. 137–65.

60 *The Society of the Sisters of Bethany: 1866–1966* (Cowley, Oxford: Church Army Press, 1966), p. 9.

61 Susan Mumm, 'A Peril to the Bench of Bishops: Sisterhoods and Episcopal Authority in the Church of England, 1845–1908', *Journal of Ecclesiastical History*, 39 (2008), p. 70.

62 Frith, 'Pseudonuns', pp. 158–59, 216. Frith also recounts the loss of episcopal support for the Society of St Margaret. Also, more famously, Priscilla Lydia Sellon lost the support of the Bishop of Exeter, Henry Phillpotts, for the Society of the Most Holy Trinity. See René Kollar OSB, 'Flowers, Pictures, and Crosses: Criticisms of Priscilla Lydia Sellon's Care of Young Girls', *Anglican Theological Review* 86 (2004), pp. 451–71.

63 Frith, 'Pseudonuns', p. 246. Allchin notes the recruiting difficulties of the Community of St John the Baptist at Clewer and the Community of St Mary the Virgin at Wantage. Allchin, *The Silent Rebellion*, pp. 44–52.

64 *Chronicle of Convocation* (1891), p. 45.

65 Randall T. Davidson (ed.), *The Five Lambeth Conferences* (London: Society for Promoting Christian Knowledge, 1920), pp. 440–44. René Kollar, 'The 1897 Lambeth Conference and the Question of Religious Life in the Anglican Communion', *Cistercian Studies*, XXVI (1991), pp. 319–29, pp 328–29. The Lambeth Conference was a consultative body of bishops that met every ten years. Its resolutions were nonbinding.

66 *The Lambeth Conferences (1867–1930)* (London: SPCK, 1948), p. 92.

67 Strangely, no problems were specifically named.

68 *The Lambeth Conferences (1867–1930)*, p. 270.

69 Rev Lawson Carter Rich, 'The Deaconesses of the Church in Modern Times', *The Churchman* (4 May 1907).

70 *Chronicle of Convocation*, 12 February 1862, pp. 914–15.

71 Lawson Carter Rich, *The Deaconess of the Church in Modern Times* (1907).

72 *Deaconesses in the Church of England* (London: Griffith and Farran, 1880), p. 43

73 *Deaconesses*, p. 11.

74 *Mother Emma: Deaconess and Pioneer: Reminiscences by Some of her Friends* (Winchester: Warren and Son, 1921), p. 9.

75 *Mother Emma*, pp. 14–15.

76 Grierson, *The Deaconess*, p. 37.

77 Heeney, *The Woman's Movement*, p. 131.

78 Grierson, *The Deaconess*, pp. 40–41. After 1918, the Deaconess Chapter continued their work.

79 *Ministrations of Women in the Church* (London: League of the Church Militant, 1920), p. 15.

80 Grierson, *The Deaconess*, p. 51

81 Grierson, *The Deaconess*, p. 133. For an excellent analysis of how sexuality informed the debates on the deaconess see Jones, 'Sex and Gender in the Church of England, 1857–1957', pp. 155–61.

82 Jo Ann Kay McNamara, *Sisters in Arms: Catholic Nuns through Two Millennia* (Cambridge, Mass and London: Harvard University Press, 1996).

83 Bishops and clergy for the most part welcomed the 'works of mercy' of women religious, but the Roman Catholic Church as an institution did not canonically give these women recognition as religious until 1900 and Pope Leo XIII's decree *Conditae a Christo*.

84 Carmen Mangion, 'The "Mixed Life": Balancing the Active with the Contemplative', in Laurence Lux-Sterritt and Carmen Mangion (eds), *Gender, Catholicism and Spirituality: Women and the Roman Catholic Church in Britain and Europe, 1200–1900* (London: Palgrave, 2010).

85 S. Karly Kehoe, 'Nursing the Mission: The Franciscan Sisters of the Immaculate Conception and the Sisters of Mercy in Glasgow 1847–66', *The Innes Review*, 56 (2005), pp. 54–56.

86 S. Karly Kehoe, 'Irish Migrants and the Recruitment of Catholic Sisters in Glasgow, 1847–78', in *Ireland and Scotland in the Nineteenth Century*, ed. Frank Ferguson and James McConnell (Dublin: Four Courts, 2009), pp. 35–47.

87 Mary Ewens, *The Role of the Nun in Nineteenth Century America* (New York: Arno, 1987).

88 West, *One Woman's Journey*, p. 180.

89 Susan O'Brien, 'Religious Life for Women', in V. Alan McClelland and Michael Hodgetts (eds), *From Without the Flaminian Gate: 150 Years of Roman Catholicism in England and Wales 1850–2000* (London: Darton, Longman & Todd, 1999), pp. 108–41, p. 126.

90 For example, Susan O'Brien, 'Religious Life for Women', p. 123 and Margaret MacCurtain, *Ariadne's Thread: Writing Women into Irish History* (Galway: Arlen House, 2008), p. 311.

91 Hill, *The Religious Order*, p. 10.

92 Sarah Annie Burstall, *Christianity and Womanhood* (London: Charles H. Kelly, 1904), p. 17.

93 Olive Banks, *Faces of Feminism: A Study of Feminism as a Social Movement* (Oxford: Martin Robertson, 1981), p. 26; Jane Rendall, *The Origins of Modern Feminism: Women in Britain, France and the United States, 1780–1860* (London: Macmillan, 1985), pp. 106–7.

94 Rendall's definition of feminist practice is 'the association of women together for a feminist purpose'. Rendall, *The Origins of Modern Feminism*, pp. 1–2.

5   'With fear and trembling'

Women, preaching and spiritual authority

Pamela J. Walker

In 1879, Rosina Davies left her Welsh mining village to become a preacher with the Salvation Army. When she announced her intention to her mother she was beaten. 'Mother feared all the excitement and freedom was a stepping stone to a worldly stage of life' reflected Davies in her memoirs. And it probably was. When she preached, she recalled meeting with 'persecution, zealous prejudice and selfish unwillingness that a Girl Evangelist should come into the arena and fight the Good Fight in public'. After all, 'for a woman to take part in any public capacity was unthinkable'[1] for most British people at the time. One minister scoffed that it was only curiosity that brought the crowds in and that he too would attract the same audience if he wore a dress. But Davies persisted, preaching not just across Britain but throughout the United States and Canada for more than sixty years. Her story demonstrates the presence and popularity of women preachers in nineteenth- and twentieth-century Britain, as well as the challenges they faced through transgressing dominant social and cultural expectations for Christian women.

British women filled the churches and chapels throughout the nineteenth and twentieth centuries.[2] They formed the backbone of congregations and sometimes made up more than two thirds of those attending services of worship.[3] They were also active in social welfare, religious education, fund-raising for imperial and home missions, and in writing hymns and religious tracts. Yet the clergy and ecclesiastical governing bodies were monopolised by men, as they had been since the Reformation. It is therefore not surprising that debates about women's place and role can be found in every aspect of British religious life throughout the period. Women's preaching was both a contentious theological question, as well as a practical concern which remained unresolved throughout the twentieth century.

Scripture, of course, was central to Protestantism, and the faithful read the Bible regularly.[4] Sermons began with a biblical text and then explicated its meaning and significance. Preaching was one of the most authoritative and meaningful aspects of Protestant practice. It was central to worship, providing a source of knowledge, meaning and authority through which reprobates might be converted, the cold-hearted renewed, and the faithful refreshed. Preaching instructed individuals in theology and the pressing questions of the day. It was a continuation of the work of the apostles charged by Christ to 'go ye into all the world, and preach the gospel to every creature' (Mark 16:15).

The debates about women's preaching were taken up in very different ways by different denominations and varied by region, social class, and national history. Britain's religious life was distinctive because it consisted of the Anglican Church (a state church with the monarch at its head), many Nonconformist and Dissenting denominations established during the seventeenth century and after, and a number of small but notable Catholic and Jewish communities.[5] During the period under consideration, women's ordination to the priesthood was never a central question for British Catholics. The Roman Catholic clergy's most important work involved the administering of the sacraments, a function from which women in this tradition were, and still are, excluded. The Jewish community expanded greatly after 1880, developing its own institutions and social communities. Many of its women leaders were involved in providing for the needs of new immigrants but the rabbinate was exclusively male. Jewish women did not acquire the education to participate in public religious services although their religious service in domestic and familial life was critical to Jewish practice.[6] Overall, women's preaching was primarily a Protestant issue. This chapter, therefore, focuses mainly on this particular religious tradition, beginning with a broad consideration of the historical and social context of Protestantism and then highlighting the various denominational differences in debates around women's preaching and ordination.

The wider social and historical context

Ever since the Reformation, Protestants had engaged in impassioned debates about how and when an individual might speak and the religious significance of those words. Protestant theologies of preaching varied, and the definition of preaching was always fluid. In some instances it meant a formal, authorised presentation that was part of a worship service. In other instances it was a spontaneous, emotional outpouring that demonstrated the presence of the Holy Spirit in the speaker. In some denominations including Anglicans and many Nonconformists, preaching was a paid, ordained, professional role which required an education and a licence from the governing body. In others such as Quakers and Salvationists, education was regarded as irrelevant and those who preached were not paid. Tradition also played a role in determining who preached and how one preached. For some Protestants, an appeal to the past meant little and could even signal an unwillingness to embrace a fuller and more dynamic understanding of scripture revealed since the Reformation. For others, the clergy were part of a continuous succession dating back to apostolic times. Place and audience influenced perceptions of what was authoritative: preaching commonly referred to a clergyman's sermon delivered from the pulpit whereas very similar words, delivered by a woman to children in a Sunday school, might not constitute preaching at all; thus an individual not officially authorised to preach might speak quite legitimately within that context. A woman like Rosina Davies, speaking out of doors to a gathered crowd, could be described as brazen and disorderly, or be admired for her zeal and righteousness in the service of God. The significant point here is that the audience and setting mattered greatly in the definition of what did, or didn't, constitute preaching. In terms of their own self-justifications, many women, notably Salvation Army women, proclaimed preaching as their right. More typically, women declared that they were not speaking in their own capacity as women but as vessels (or ventriloquisers) of the Holy Spirit.[7] Given this enormous variability with regard to audience, setting and personal vindication of the right to preach, in order to comprehend the forbidding or sanctioning of female preaching it is essential to analyse its denominational specificities.

Women's preaching was also associated with particular longstanding divisions between Protestants concerning the site of spiritual authority. In the Church of England, for example, religious authority was (and is) derived from the institution itself which determined the educational and professional status of its clergy. By contrast, Quakers upheld a more individualistic understanding of religious authority as being empowered by the Holy Spirit. Many Protestants relied on a reading of scripture that restricted women's authority to speak. Two passages were critical to these debates:

> Let your women keep silence in the churches: for it is not permitted unto them to speak; but they are commanded to be under obedience, as also saith the law. And if they will learn any thing, let them ask their husbands at home: for it is a shame for women to speak in the church.
>
> (1 Cor. 14:34–35)

> But I suffer not a woman to teach, nor to usurp authority over the man, but to be in silence. For Adam was first formed, then Eve.
>
> (1 Tim. 2:12–13)

Since the Reformation, these two passages had been used to prohibit women's preaching and leadership functions in religious bodies. But the divisions between men and women, and between speech and silence, were never clear or unequivocal. As a result, the debates over women's preaching were closely bound up with definitions of what constituted preaching and the authoritative status of the preacher.

Many historians of religion have defined a shift in denominational attitudes whereby in their early, charismatic or sectarian phases, religious movements invariably permitted women's preaching and other sensationalist practices such as spontaneous speech from the congregation or physical manifestations of the spirit, but that with increasing institutional stability and growth came the increasing dominance of social convention; thus women were marginalised from anything other than suitably feminine activities such as fund-raising, teaching children or charitable work.[8] Recent historical scholarship, however, has complicated this broad periodisation and argued that women's preaching did not always end with denominational stability. As research develops to include a wider array of denominational histories, more nuanced understandings of women's preaching practices within sectarian movements and more established denominations may be reconsidered.

Historians of women have also raised broader questions surrounding the way in which religious activism intersects with feminism, if at all, and how it might have improved women's social status. Female preaching was always a challenge to established social custom, albeit inadvertently, opening up new areas of work and authority for women. Methodist and Quaker women, for example, were frequently denounced for daring to disrupt the gender order. This suggests that women's preaching may well have contributed to the broader nineteenth-century climate of emancipatory activity around women's roles. Indeed, David Hempton and Myrtle Hill have argued that 'evangelical religion was more important than feminism in enlarging women's sphere of action during the nineteenth century'.[9] Other scholars, including Janice Holmes, have argued that women's preaching and religious activism did not necessarily enhance women's status or authority.[10] It is certainly the case that many women preachers, including some Salvation Army women, affirmed the doctrine of female submission and opposed women's rights activism as a worldly diversion from spiritual matters. Equal rights and status with men was not the primary goal of women preachers. They cared more for spiritual concerns than secular rights and this has problematised the historical relationship between female preachers and feminism. It is clear that even conservative Victorian beliefs about gender could open up ways for women to participate in particular forms of preaching. Victorians frequently described women as receptive, emotional, and gentle and, as part of the wider cultural 'feminisation of religion', women were often regarded as more receptive to the call of the Holy Spirit. The home was the centre of familial and religious life and a Christian mother used prayers and lessons to lead children, servants, and even errant husbands to God. In the same way, women preachers employed maternal imagery and language to justify their leadership. They were 'mothers in Israel', pious women who nurtured and protected their spiritual children.[11] For some women, these conventional gendered ideals paradoxically endorsed their claims on the right to preach.

This is not to say that certain women did not draw explicit connections between spiritual and political liberty, the silencing of women in the Church and in society more widely. Christabel Pankhurst is a well-known example of a woman who moved from suffrage activist to social purity advocate to evangelist and writer preaching the imminent return of Christ.[12] After 1918 several suffragists including Maude Royden sought ordination in the Church or established preaching careers in those denominations that welcomed them. New research may enrich our understanding of how women's preaching intersected and diverged from feminism and how divisions of class, empire and location complicated those alliances.

As noted earlier, debates about preaching divided Protestants long before the nineteenth century and were never peculiar to Britain. Protestant women had preached, with and without sanction, since the Reformation.[13] Yet nineteenth- and twentieth-century British women made their claims to preach in an intellectual and social context that shaped their activities in very distinctive ways. The rise of evangelicalism and revivalism, the growing concern over the feminisation of religion, and the campaigns to enhance women's role in public life informed the ways in which women's preaching was organised and understood. Evangelicalism and revivalism were two influential strains of nineteenth-century Protestant theology and practice. Evangelicalism became a visible and influential force in both Church and Nonconformist communities in the nineteenth century. As David Bebbington has famously formulated, evangelicalism placed conversionism, activism, biblicism and the atoning role of Christ on the cross at the centre of their theology.[14] This opened up opportunities for the laity, especially women, because religious leadership and spiritual experience did not necessarily require ordination or formal education. Evangelicals also placed great emphasis on the word, spoken and written, and the nineteenth century witnessed a number of powerful women orators and writers.[15] The tenets of evangelicalism were taken up in different ways by Anglicans, Methodists or Quakers but its overall effect was widespread and its influence powerful.[16]

Revivalism was a second stream of religious expression that characterised this period. Revivalists argued that to wait upon God to raise up a revival of religion was 'an expression of sloth'.[17] Instead, Christians should and could plan and execute religious revivals using techniques suited to the times. Revivals were a recurring feature of British religious life throughout the nineteenth and twentieth centuries. Newly industrialised urban communities offered especially rich opportunities to reach unregenerate souls, and a trans-Atlantic flow of people, books, and music also fed the revivalist phenomenon. Women were often greater participants in revival events than men. The emotional (sometimes described as hysterical) nature of revivals became associated with feminine vulnerability and receptivity to the Spirit. Thus revivals could exhibit trangressive features as occasions when social conventions were discarded and dreams, visions and ecstatic worship predominated. Women's involvement, whether deplored or celebrated, was a defining feature of revivals.[18]

The conviction that religious adherence was in decline shaped Protestant activity throughout the nineteenth and twentieth centuries. British Protestants were dismayed by the absence of men from the pews as well as the diminished allegiance of working-class men and women, particularly in large cities. Clergy lamented the people's indifference and their own failures. Many Britons believed that because religious adherence had weakened, new techniques were required to rebuild the faith, giving new justification and a sense of urgency in the pioneering of innovative methods of outreach. Places of worship became centres of social service work, leisure and education and revivalists used spectacle, music and street preaching to draw the crowds.[19]

The period also witnessed significant changes in women's education, legal status and professional opportunities. Women founded institutions of higher education, organised for female suffrage and participation in elected government, and sought admission to the professions. As noted before, women's claims to preach could be considered as part of an effort to expand women's rights and a wider shift in women's work and status that characterised the nineteenth and twentieth centuries, although the relationship between preaching and feminism is not a straightforward one.[20] Preaching was one of many professional opportunities undertaken by women, particularly in the later nineteenth century as churches and chapels became centres of social welfare and leisure activity. Women took leading roles in moral reform including the rescue of fallen women and the care of children as well as missions to the 'unsaved'. Debates about women's preaching were frequently part of debates about social reform and for some women, including Maude Royden and many Salvation Army women, preaching was one way for women to further social reform by encouraging individual spiritual renewal and calling for better legislation or improved social institutions. Movements that claimed to improve women's lives, including temperance, social purity and the elevation of the domestic realm, were widely supported by evangelicals and revivalists.

The Church of England

As the largest and most influential denomination in Britain during the period under consideration, the Church of England took a leading national role in education, political representation and numerous social welfare institutions. The Established Church offered particular challenges and opportunities for women's preaching. Its unique origins and duties as a State church coexisting alongside rival Nonconformist denominations that enjoyed greater levels of success in attracting the working classes, in addition to the longstanding hope of some Anglicans for reunion with Rome, made this nineteenth-century religious institution a particularly embattled one on a number of theological and pastoral fronts. Church of England clergy were invariably middle class, well educated, salaried professionals. This posed particular barriers for women, who had very limited access to university education and the professions until well into the twentieth century and were thus unable to gain the necessary credentials. It was also a question of social class because such qualifications were hard for anyone to obtain without status and money.

Women's exclusion from the clergy was a theological as well as social and cultural issue, explained by reference either to the Pauline restrictions on women's speaking cited previously in this chapter, or to the seeming absence of female apostles. It was not until 1994 that women were finally permitted to be ordained in the Anglican Church and were able to officially preach from the pulpit, offer sacraments and fulfil other clerical duties. Yet throughout the nineteenth and early twentieth centuries Anglican women did in fact preach and teach in ways that suggest it was the setting, audience and status attributed to the activity that ultimately delineated what was and was not considered acceptable for women. Anglican churches were centres of religious female activism that included many examples of teaching theology, reflecting on scripture or praying publicly. The distinction between teaching and preaching not infrequently relied on the particular physical space; a woman could deliver to a Sunday school class what would be classified as a sermon if delivered from a pulpit. Similarly, in terms of audience, women were able to speak to other women and children with far less clerical resistance and by 1862, according to Brian Heeney, over 300,000 British women were engaged in teaching Sunday school classes. The Biblewomen were another good historical example of women teachers of religion. The group was founded in 1853 by Ellen Raynard and sent working-class women into their own neighbourhoods to offer spiritual guidance, sell Bibles and instruct the poor on religious questions with a 'motherly and missionary heart'. Until the 1920s, these women worked and ministered largely free of clerical interference or supervision.[21] Neither Sunday school teachers nor Biblewomen were regarded by the Church as preachers, despite their work requiring public addresses on theological questions, a willingness to instruct others, and the requisite biblical knowledge to perform their duties.

Clergy wives, who frequently undertook considerable duties as teachers, home visitors and other parish responsibilities, provide us with another important historical example of sustained religious activism. In the early nineteenth century, clergy wives were depicted as having a lifelong commitment to their husband's vocation. In her book *Women of the Church of England* (1907), Aubrey Richardson referred to them as 'clergywomen' although this was suggestive of an equal role; subordination to their husbands was essential.[22] Although in another context or space they might well have been considered less favourably, the parish work of dutiful Sunday school teachers, Biblewomen and clergy wives was regarded as eminently appropriate by the male clergy. The inconsistency of the principles used to determine women's legitimate roles was not lost on one notable Anglican feminist, Maude Royden, who parodied the distinction drawn between teaching and preaching when she asked, if Christ had observed a congregation rising from the pews and walking to a schoolroom so a woman could preach to them, 'would he have recognised any great principle?'[23] To many women, these distinctions were arbitrary and lacked any spiritual meaning, serving only to exclude women.

Many Anglican women protested their exclusion from the priesthood. Josephine Butler (1828–1906), feminist campaigner against state-regulated prostitution and devout Anglican, called it an 'astonishing and melancholy thing' that the Church had ignored the lessons of the first Pentecost where 'your sons and your daughters shall prophesy' and that Christ's first announcement of the Resurrection was made to a woman.[24] Other Anglican women's rights activists shared her convictions, of whom the most well known was Maude Royden (1876–1956). Royden was the daughter of a Liverpool MP and educated at Lady Margaret Hall, Oxford. She worked in settlement houses, assisted in parish work and religious education and was a prominent activist for women's suffrage. Her political and religious work were always intertwined and reflected her conviction that the women's movement was the 'most profoundly moral movement ... since the foundation of the Christian church'.[25] For Royden, the silencing of women was based on prejudice and could be only overcome by faith and prayer.

In 1916, Royden was invited to join the National Mission of Repentance and Hope by Archbishop Randall Davidson. The group was charged to find new means to revitalise the Church in the midst of the grief and despair wrought by World War I. The Mission included many prominent Anglicans and the more conservative members were dismayed at the presence of women, declaring 'that women should speak in the Church is in direct conflict with Holy Scripture and ... with the common order of the Catholic Church'.[26] While the National Mission effort did not result in any substantive change for women's quest for ordination, it occasioned strong debate on women's roles that was widely reported in the press and amongst Church members.

Royden began her preaching career in 1917 at the Congregationalist City Temple, a well-known London landmark, under the title of 'Pulpit Assistant'. Police were needed to control the crowd that had gathered to hear her first sermon. For many High Church Anglicans, she erred not only in preaching but in doing so in a Nonconformist church which seemed to endorse those who had left the Established Church and so stood in the way of any eventual reunion with Rome. Royden always maintained that her relationship to her own church remained unchanged. The sacraments did not have a central place in Congregationalist services equivalent to that of Anglican practice and, as she never assumed the authority to offer communion, Royden argued that she was not, in fact, performing a clerical role in Anglican terms. Royden concluded her work at the City Temple in 1920 and went on to found the Fellowship Guild, a gathering place for worship and social activities outside of any institutional church that included women preachers and lay participation. She also made regular radio broadcasts that brought her a much wider public audience.[27] Despite her positive reception, women's ordination remained decades away.

In 1935, a report prepared by a committee of the Anglican church on the ministry of women concluded that as 'the consensus of tradition and opinion is based on the will of God', women's ordination should not be contemplated further.[28] Regardless, women continued to press for ordination during the interwar years. For some feminists, the struggle for admission to the priesthood replaced equal suffrage as the focus of their activism. When women were finally ordained in 1994, the key point of contention still remained that of the sacraments rather than preaching. For many, the sacraments represented a more powerful challenge to the established divisions between male and female, clergy and laity. In one instance, a woman priest offered communion to a congregant who declined the wafer and bit her hand. Many congregations simply refused to acknowledge the authority of the sacraments when offered by women.[29] The presence of female clergy remains a point of contention in Britain and among the global Anglican communion.

Methodism and women's preaching

Methodism provides an important denominational example of female preaching in nineteenth- and twentieth-century Britain. Methodists have been the subject of a rich historical scholarship dating back to the earliest years of the movement and there exists a substantial and detailed historiography on women's preaching unmatched by most other denominational histories.[30] The idea of religion as a compensation and distraction from the pains of life or a bulwark against political unrest has provided a starting-point for many debates regarding the influence of

British Methodism. E.P. Thompson, in his immensely influential *The Making of the English Working Class* (1963), argued that Methodism was an important cultural force that instilled a strict work ethic in the British labouring people, offering a 'chiliasm of despair', a place of solace for those whose lives were shattered by industrialisation.[31] Much of this analysis gave scant attention to women. Scholars have noted that Thompson's path-breaking castigation of Methodism and its fostering of passive deference to social order applied only to men.[32] In contrast Methodism offered women enhanced authority in the church as well as at home. If the church did discipline men, it was often received with delight by their wives and many women were active in reform work directly aimed at curbing men's drunkenness and disorderly behaviour. Methodist women could control their own religious lives to a greater degree than women in other denominations and this included assuming positions of leadership and authority.

Methodism began as a movement under the leadership of John Wesley (1703–91) to encourage greater piety within the Church of England. They rejected predestination, a theology endorsed by most eighteenth-century Dissenters, and preached instead that God's grace was available to all. After Wesley's death in 1791, the movement broke from the Established Church and formed a separate denomination.[33] Women formed a majority of worshippers from the earliest years even though Wesley had been reluctant to contemplate seriously women's preaching. Several ardent Methodist women wrote to him, asking for his permission to speak. Mary Bosanquet (1739–1815) suggested that if Paul had instructed women to cover their heads when they spoke (1 Cor. 11:5) then he was surely giving direction on how women should conduct themselves when they preached. Wesley conceded that women were permitted to preach but only when their call came from God. Thus, though women could hold no institutional power, they could possess charismatic authority if their work demonstrated that it was inspired by God.[34] In the late eighteenth century, Methodist women often spoke at class meetings which were small gatherings of the faithful organised to promote spiritual growth. A small number spoke before larger audiences. Methodists appointed clergy but also permitted lay preaching which was often conducted outside the bounds of a regular Sabbath service. This practice allowed men without formal education or ordination to preach.[35] Some women were also able to serve as lay preachers in this capacity. Sarah Crosby, for example, rode 900 miles in 1777 and spoke at over 800 meetings. But these women were relatively few and their work was episodic, unlike the regular, paid employment enjoyed by male clergy. After Wesley's death, the Methodists became divided over governance, forms of worship, clerical authority, and regional differences; women's preaching was one major question of dissent. In 1803, the Wesleyan Methodists voted that women should not preach, a decision which reflected a wider desire for a regular clergy structure that was responsible to the governing body. Other Methodist sects, particularly those established to evangelise, embraced more revivalist methods whereby women's preaching became a part of established practice. Those groups newly established as a result of disputes about local control and lay participation in governance, less frequently permitted women to preach.[36]

In *Prophetic Sons and Daughters* (1985), Deborah Valenze has argued that early-nineteenth-century labourers and villagers responded to the upheavals of industrialisation by creating a unique religious culture. Between 1795 and 1814, Methodists broke away to form the Bible Christians, Primitive Methodists, Independent Methodists, the Methodist New Connexion and other smaller sects. Valenze argues that within these breakaway groups, the labourers, artisans and agricultural workers who made up the majority of the members created a distinctive form of 'cottage religion'. They met in cottages, encouraging a fervent, democratic and enthusiastic religion. Here, women assumed leadership in ways not permitted elsewhere because of their prominence in that cultural setting. According to Valenze:

> Sectarian Methodism aimed to revise contemporary evangelicalism with attitudes and values excluded from institutional religion ... Nowhere did this quarrel with Victorian convention appear more dramatic than in the sectarian camp meetings and female preaching ... [37]

These sectarian meetings actively encouraged female preaching and several influential Methodist leaders wrote tracts in defence of the practice. Elizabeth Smith (1805–36), for example, was born into a labouring family, raised in the Church of England and apprenticed as a dressmaker. Aged twenty, she joined the Primitive Methodists and was sent as a travelling circuit preacher to Wales. Smith gave up the security of paid work in return for the uncertain living she received from her audiences and travelled alone to unfamiliar locations, walking from one place to the next, preaching. Valenze argues that personal misfortune and poverty made women such as Smith immensely self-reliant. Preaching equipped them to withstand criticism and loneliness and provided them with the rebelliousness essential for a female preacher.[38]

The growth of urban centres and accompanying rural depopulation, the decline of a plebeian, cottage-based economy, the centralisation and growth of administration in Methodist sects and the establishment of an educated clergy all brought 'cottage religion' to an end. Valenze argues that female Methodist preachers had lost their base of power and support by the mid-nineteenth century and were rarely heard.[39] Jennifer Lloyd's new study *Women and the Shaping of British Methodism: Persistent Preachers 1897–1907* (2010) contests this picture of decline, however, arguing that women *did* continue to preach into the twentieth century, but in new ways. Serena Thorne (1842–1902), a descendant of the founders of the Bible Christians, had a long and distinguished career as a preacher and evangelist. She began preaching in 1860. Six months later her name was entered on the preaching plan and she began to travel as an itinerant evangelist. In Wales in 1862, over one thousand people gathered to hear her preach on a single occasion. The following year Thorne emigrated to Australia with two brothers and a sister where she worked first for the Primitive Methodists and then the Bible Christians with great success. One local paper reported that she preached 'a really eloquent sermon ... the words flowing from her lips with a marvellous rapidity and precision'.[40] She was successful enough to fully support herself by her preaching. Thorne became engaged to marry a fellow Bible Christian until he admitted that he disapproved of women preaching, at which point she broke off the engagement. He immediately responded that he had had a change of heart and would never 'oppose or hinder' in her work. They married in 1871 and spent the rest of their lives preaching in Australia. Thorne was also a prominent advocate of women's suffrage and temperance.[41] Her long career suggests that women's preaching endured past the early years of sectarian Methodism and could persist into the 1870s with support from the church governing bodies, lay people and sympathetic family.

Some sects, notably the Bible Christians, continued to engage female evangelists in the early twentieth century; Lillie Edwards was one of the last. Although the Bible Christian conference recognised her effectiveness as a preacher, for those congregations in financial distress, her lower salary was a strong inducement to engage her services. Edwards was sent to a number of communities during the 1890s on the recommendation of the central Conference with an accompanying note that she 'worked at low cost'. She was much praised for her ability to re-establish financial order and bring in new converts.[42] After the Bible Christians merged with other small Methodist sects in 1907 to form the United Methodists, Edwards disappears from the records. But her career again points to the continuing work of female evangelists throughout the period.

In the later nineteenth century, women also established institutions that expanded opportunities for religious activity, including preaching. The growth of deaconess institutions allowed women an officially sanctioned role in working with the poor, most often women and children, as well as offering religious teaching and social care. Again, deaconesses' work was not referred to as preaching despite involving public addresses aimed at conversion and the exhortation of the faithful. Some Methodist women undertook formal training as deaconesses and some Anglican deaconesses were ordained by a bishop, but there was never an officially sanctioned form, nor was their status closely defined by any denomination. Some regarded these women as a revival of the apostolic tradition of deaconesses such as Phoebe (Rom.16:1), others looked to the German Lutheran deaconess as their model.[43] One highly regarded Methodist deaconess, Sister Annie, was celebrated for her ability to 'bring down the power of God upon a meeting' when she spoke publicly. She was a working-class woman with little professional training but she was recognised for her service and dedication.[44] Other denominations, often moved by Andrew Mearns' *Bitter Cry of Outcast London* (1883), established similar institutions to address material and spiritual forms of poverty.[45] Many encouraged women to preach, sometimes just to other women, sometimes more formally as evangelists. As one Methodist group declared in 1903, 'Some of the Sisters preach the Gospel ... When the committee found that some Sisters possessed great evangelical gifts, they recognised therein the wisdom and goodness of God.'[46] The Wesleyan Methodist Sister Jeanie Banks preached at over 300 missions in 1901 throughout the British Isles.[47] Again, these women were not numerous but their work persisted into the twentieth century.

Revivalism, evangelism and female preaching

By the mid-nineteenth century, the influence of revivalism had created different opportunities for women as participants in short-lived revivals and as evangelists working to generate a more enthusiastic religious spirit. In the 1860s, female evangelists spoke at large gatherings, in halls or outdoors, with the purpose of drawing in new converts, reaffirming the faith of those who had fallen away and bringing fresh energy to waning congregations.[48] This movement was not confined to one denomination. As one Scottish minister declared in the *Revival* in 1868, evangelists were 'irregulars, freelances, knowing no church, understanding nothing of parochial divisions, subject to no master but Christ'.[49] Women evangelists were thus free of some of the denominational constraints that might have otherwise limited their work, but they lacked institutional support. Mid-century American revival movements, most notably the work and writing of Charles Finney (1792–1875) and James Caughey (1810–91), influenced the revivals in Britain. Revivalism was widespread, flourishing in Belfast in 1859 among the Presbyterians and inspiring the founders of the Salvation Army, William and Catherine Booth, to leave the Methodist New Connexion in 1862 to devote themselves to itinerant evangelism. Another prominent woman was Geraldine Hooper (1841–72) whose preaching career was well known to Anglicans and Nonconformists alike. From 1863 onwards, Hooper preached over 4,000 times to audiences that sometimes numbered in the hundreds. One Exeter newspaper reporting on Hooper's exploits declared, 'We hope soon to hear that this zealous young woman has got a good husband. That is the best cure for teaching propensities.' Hooper did marry, but continued to preach alongside her husband. The couple built a hall in Bath where she spoke in the afternoon and he in the evening. This continued until her death in 1872.[50] Hooper's work was accepted because it was effective in bringing about conversions and refreshing the faith of her audience. Yet it certainly challenged established practice.

The Ulster Revival of 1859 was an influential example of Protestant revivalism and has been described by Janice Holmes as a 'spontaneous outbreak of religious excitement ... which result[ed] in a large number of conversions ... characterized by protracted meetings, lay activity and physical manifestations of conversion'.[51] It involved primarily Presbyterians because they were the majority of Protestants in the region. Women's participation was immediately a cause for alarm. One woman, known only as 'R', began exhorting others to convert immediately after experiencing her own conversion. 'R' told the people to 'arise and follow me', echoing the words of Jesus, and marched from house to house, with a large crowd behind her. A Presbyterian minister asked her to calm herself, lest 'people think she was deranged'. 'R' replied that she must speak. 'Must I not do the will of my heavenly Father? ... I cannot hold my peace. It is not I, but the Spirit of the Lord, that is speaking.'[52] The minister was 'awed into silence' and also followed her procession through the streets. However, her spiritual leadership was brief and 'R' soon ceased to speak publicly. In a brief moment of religious upheaval, her marginalised status as a woman had empowered her; with the return to normal denominational life, the justification for her public speaking passed.

Women were particularly prone to report visions of heaven and hell at revivals and to demonstrating physical bodily signs of spiritual presence like stigmata. Such manifestations, it was believed, provided evidence that women were in direct communication with the spiritual world and had bypassed clerical authority. The Ulster revival was short lived and the community soon returned to its normal denominational structure. Some new initiatives, however, found support. The Belfast Female Mission, for example, was established to send women out to speak to poorer women about their spiritual state. This work was regarded as both useful and 'proper' for women.[53] Janice Holmes argues that the Ulster revival allowed women to exercise an unusual degree of religious leadership, preaching, prophesying and exhorting publicly. The 1859 revival, Holmes argues, did not result in long-term opportunities for women and for many onlookers women's preaching was clear evidence of spiritual excess and chaos. One Belfast newspaper in July 1859 lamented, for example, that admissions to the Lunatic Asylum had risen and clergymen feared the spread of false doctrine from poorly educated laypersons.[54] It was not the only such event. The Welsh Revival of 1904 followed similar lines although its gendered aspects have not yet been subject to any sustained research.[55]

One instance of religious revival leading to a highly successful established denomination was that of the Salvation Army. William (1829–1911) and Catherine (1829–90) Booth believed the Methodists, with their rules and governing bodies, had served only to stifle their ability to save souls. Catherine Booth had begun to preach in her husband's Methodist New Connexion pulpit in 1860 when he fell ill, permitted only as an unusual arrangement. After the Booths broke with the Methodists, they began to preach together. The response was mixed. Many celebrated Catherine's effectiveness. At the same time, she proclaimed women's 'right to preach' in her widely circulated 1859 pamphlet, arguing that men and women had an equal call to preach.[56] This claim was potentially highly disruptive to established practice and her activity certainly did not reflect Victorian feminine modesty and submission. In one newspaper, she told her mother, 'I am represented as having my husband's clothes on!'[57] Catherine drew large crowds and relished the disruption this caused:

> When [the Wesleyans] come to invite Mr. Booth, he will politely tell them that he cannot come if his wife is forbidden to help him! Or else accept their invitation and announce me just as usual as a matter of course, and then what will become of the rules and usages ... Next to the glory of God and the salvation of souls I rejoice to be a thorn in the side of *such* persons.[58]

After several years as itinerant revivalists, the Booths settled in London and established the home mission that would become the Salvation Army in 1879. From its earliest years, the Salvation Army endorsed women's preaching and spiritual authority. By 1884, over one thousand Salvationist women were preaching in towns across Britain and later throughout Europe and the Empire.

Women worked with full denominational authority, preaching, raising funds for the support of their corps (congregation) and, even more radically, offering communion until the practice was discontinued in 1883.[59] Many were young, single women who seized this opportunity for paid work and spiritual authority. Like their Methodist predecessors, many of them were working class and therefore had fewer qualms at being paid for work. Their theology and practice also reflected their class background, borrowing tunes from the music halls and displaying posters promising the preacher was 'A Wonder! Dressed in American costume! With a Turban on her Head! Splendid Singer, Good Talker and Proper Tambourine Player'![60] Salvation Army women felt unconstrained by feminine convention and used sensationalist methods to attract audiences. Eliza Haynes unbraided her hair, put flowing ribbons in it and hung a sign around her neck that read, 'I am Happy Eliza'. She paraded the streets of Marylebone until a crowd gathered and she commenced preaching. The Army's notoriety spread and women officers became stock figures of fun in comic magazines and music hall songs. In one song about Happy Eliza, the singer related, 'They said pray come and join us and I was just in the mood, They're Hallelujah Sisters and they're bound to do me good … Though they're often deep in thought, they don't forget the plate.'[61] Catherine Booth commented in 1886 that women could easily gain attention because 'generations of the suppression of women, and the consequent prejudice and curiosity with respect to her public performances conspire immensely towards attracting people'. When one corps had trouble filling the hall, the chief of staff concluded, 'If there is no other plan for working the place, we had better send lasses'.[62] Rosina Davies' critics recognised that novelty brought an audience. Salvationists warmly agreed and did not hesitate to capitalise on the excitement a woman preacher could create.

The Salvation Army offered women greater authority than virtually any voluntary organisation before World War I. Yet it never sought equality for women. It affirmed wives' duty of obedience to their husbands, usually paid women less than men and rarely appointed women to the highest ranks. The Salvation Army's history after 1918 has yet to receive close scholarly attention and it is not clear yet, therefore, how women's preaching altered as the movement grew larger, established corps in many parts of the British empire, and developed a well-regarded social service wing.[63] But it is clear that women's preaching in the Salvation Army persisted long after the charismatic early years.

The Society of Friends

The Society of Friends, or Quakers, provide us with a very different example of the historical interaction between women, preaching and religious authority. Established in the 1650s in England as one of many movements advocating religious and political change, it was a charismatic sect that condemned the Established Church and social order and proclaimed a new religious vision. In the early years, many Quaker prophets and writers were women as the movement thoroughly endorsed their spiritual authority.[64] The Friends were also significant in early

American history and historians of social movements, including abolition and suffrage, have studied the work of Quaker women.[65] But British nineteenth- and twentieth-century Friends have been much less studied. By the nineteenth century British Quakers had shifted from revivalist street practices to a more 'socially secluded' community with a well-established system of self governance, communal care and social engagement.[66] Its members were mostly middle class, even prosperous. Women continued to speak publicly but in a context particular to the Friends. Quaker ministry was never a paid profession nor was it exclusively the work of one member of a congregation. Rather, any individual could speak at a meeting under the spontaneous prompting of the Holy Spirit, devoid of any personal will. In that sense, it was quite unlike the preaching undertaken by other Protestant denominations; it was not, for example, associated with ordination or any sacramental duties. Yet preaching was similar in that it offered spiritual direction and counsel and women's speaking was at times debated.[67]

For women in other denominations, evangelical theology's stress on conversion and missionary activity opened up new opportunities for preaching. For Quaker women, however, evangelicalism's emphasis upon scriptural authority and salvation marked a decisive shift in direction that was not always welcomed. Some women feared it would undermine support for them speaking. As one Quaker woman in 1834 lamented, if the guidance of the Holy Spirit ceased to be the principal justification for speaking, 'how can we any longer receive the ministry of women?'[68] Despite these concerns, women's ministry in the Friends grew during the nineteenth century. Historians Sandra Stanley Holton and Sheila Wright, who have examined Quaker women in local and national contexts, have suggested several reasons for the persistence and growth of women's ministry. Quakers frequently educated their daughters and sons for leadership. That leadership was exercised in the Women's Meetings which were authorised to accept new members, give permission to marry, discipline female members and correspond with the Men's Meeting. Although they were excluded from national governing bodies, women's authority was therefore sanctioned, albeit separately, within the Friends organisational structure.

Quaker women often regarded their domestic duties as a snare that would distract them from their obedience to God, hence they extended and even challenged the boundaries of the dominant middle-class domestic ideal.[69] Women engaged in a 'travelling ministry' that included addressing meetings and audiences of non-Quakers on spiritual questions and social issues of the day such as slavery. Quaker women embraced this work despite the many disruptions and discomforts it often caused and the sometimes painful self-sacrifice that was required. One woman who had initially resisted the call to ministry recorded that she had fallen ill as a consequence of her spiritual disobedience. On accepting her call to speak she at once recovered her health.[70]

Women did experience opposition from outsiders when they spoke but membership of the Society of Friends had always meant social opposition and even persecution, as with the seventeenth-century Quaker Mary Dyer who was executed for heresy in Massachusetts in 1659.[71] Even in more settled times, persecution for refusing to pay tithes or swear oaths of allegiance still punctuated the lives of Quakers. Indeed, the community felt bound together by a shared culture of opposition. Moreover, the theology of 'inner light' was a vital tenet of the Quaker faith.[72] If preaching did not strictly involve individual will, then gender was no more important than any other worldly distinction. In their adherence to this radical belief and their commitment to education and training for leadership, the Quakers provide an important example of the continuity of female preaching in the face of increased institutionalisation and growth.

Congregationalists and women's preaching

Denominations that have hitherto received less scholarly attention can further complicate our understanding of women's preaching and suggest new directions for research. Congregationalists, like the Quakers, traced their origins back to the Reformation. Like other Dissenters they denounced what they perceived as the corruption of the Established Church. As one Congregationalist declared in 1686, 'the present ministry [in the Church of England] I conceive to be more defiled and polluted ministry not only because they have resisted greater Light. But also because they have protested against a Reformation.'[73] A minister, so Congregationalists taught, must first be called by God; ordination simply recognised that call. Ministry, they insisted, was Christ's appointment which could not include women due to the Pauline injunctions. This said, seventeenth-century Congregationalists did recognise women's prophesying and there is much evidence that women spoke and preached as prophets. Historians have not yet fully analysed the connections between early Congregationalist theology and later nineteenth-century developments. It is interesting to note, however, that the first woman ordained into the Christian ministry was a Congregationalist, Constance Coltman (1889–1969). Coltman entered Mansfield College, Oxford in 1915 where her financial means not only allowed her to pursue an education but later to supplement her earnings in order to support her household. In 1909, the Congregational Union Council had approved women to seek ordination although its minutes also recorded that no woman was actually expected to do so. This 'revolutionary proceeding', as the *Christian World* described it at the time, allowed Coltman to be ordained on 17 September 1917.[74] Coltman married the next day and she and her husband served in joint appointments to many churches during the following decades. She declared women's ordination as 'the crown and culmination' of the women's movement and encouraged other women to follow her.[75] The Congregational theology of ordination, in recognising God's call as paramount, clearly enabled women to claim that God could also call them.

But this particular history raises more questions than it answers. Further research might consider why the Congregational Union Council made this decision when no other denomination of similar theological persuasion did. Why did the Council alter its policy if no woman was expected to follow it? How did Coltman and other women reshape Congregationalist ministry and that of women's public teaching and speaking outside the ordained ministry? In what ways did Coltman's ordination influence other denominations? Further research that compares Congregationalists with other Nonconformists in the early twentieth century could more fully explain the origins and consequences of women's ordination.[76]

Women's roles in Christian Science

The Christian Scientists offer a final example of women's leadership in a new denomination led by a woman. The church was founded in Boston, Massachusetts, by Mary Baker Eddy (1821–1910). Several women trained by Eddy came to Britain in the 1880s and 1890s to establish centres of Christian Science teaching that would grow into established churches.[77] The Christian Science Sunday service did not include preaching as practised in other Protestant churches but it did provide opportunities for women to teach doctrine, speak publicly and address audiences unfamiliar with the teachings of Christian Science. Services consisted of readings from the Bible and Eddy's *Science and Health*, read aloud in turn by First and Second Readers. Reading these texts aimed to put 'worshippers' in continual contact with the sources of spiritual growth and renewal.[78] The office of Reader rotated and was shared equally by men and women. The Readers were elected by the church members, conducted two services weekly, and sat on the church's board of directors with oversight of finances, membership and other church matters.[79] The position of practitioner was also open to both men and women. Practitioners received training in the teachings of Christian Science from teachers endorsed by the church and were to work with individual church members to achieve healing through a 'true understanding of God'.[80] Healing was not only the visible healing of physical malady but a spiritual healing of disease that would dissolve suffering and bring a full appreciation of God's truth. While practitioners were experts in the practice of Christian Science, every individual was expected to engage in extensive, daily reading and study. Practitioners were paid a fee for services but the details of payment varied. In Britain, Christian Science was differentiated from other denominations in that practitioners were overwhelmingly women. The *Christian Science Journal* of March 1903 lists thirty-three women and eight men practising in England; all the practitioners in Ireland, Wales and Scotland were women.[81] The reasons for this are, in part, practical. The church was founded by a woman and opened all offices to men and women equally. But other heterodox religious movements of this period drew a heavily female following and the appeal of these movements merits further study.[82]

The Christian Science practice of healing came under close scrutiny in 1898 when a practitioner, Athelie Mills, was charged with manslaughter after a man she had attended died. The man's female companion, already a student of Christian Science, had summoned Mills when he became dangerously ill. That she charged one guinea a week was widely reported and the court questioned how she could claim the authority to offer Christian doctrine and accept payment. Mills was acquitted but the case occasioned much speculation about Christian Science, and the predominance of women within its ranks was frequently remarked on.[83] One newspaper complained that 'silly women ... who actually believe that people who do a faith cure for money are especially blessed by God' were following this 'fad'.[84] The *Manchester Weekly Times* offered a recipe for 'New Women' that included 'equal portions faith cure, mind cure and Christian Science ... beat well, serve in bloomers, on a bicycle'.[85] These detractors drew a connection between radical religion, radical politics, female hysteria and social subversion that may shed light on the appeal of Christian Science for women. Historical research on Christian Science is limited and, to date, no scholarship on the movement in Britain has been published.[86] But even this brief account raises fascinating questions about the appeal of this egalitarian denomination for its large female following. The practice of Christian Science required diligent study and the opportunity to attain leadership roles within the movement, but also a willingness to embrace an unorthodox faith that attracted ridicule from its many critics. Placing this denomination within the wider context of women's preaching and religious authority would enrich the history of women and spiritual authority enormously. The late nineteenth and early twentieth centuries are associated with religious decline, yet this denomination grew quickly, as did other heterodox movements, and its theology challenged the divisions between faith and science that so characterised the era.[87] Like revivalism and evangelicalism, it was a trans-atlantic movement with a strong appeal to women.

Conclusion

For centuries, Protestants excluded women from preaching and from conducting ritual and sacerdotal roles. But women found ways to preach. This work was often difficult and their anxieties and doubts illustrate the particular challenges nineteenth-century British women preachers faced. Catherine Booth spent years travelling with her husband as an evangelist accompanied by her young children, even continuing to work throughout her pregnancies. Along with such practical difficulties, even prominent women suffered from anxiety and self-doubt. Catherine O'Bryan, a respected Bible Christian, expressed such thoughts in a poem, 'When I with fear and trembling too, the pulpit fill'd my work to do. If all there knew my real state No doubt some pity would create'.[88] Her daughter, Mary, after nearly forty years of preaching, wrote in 1862 of her 'severe mental depression suffering before appearing in public'. In 1870, O'Bryan's granddaughter Serena Thorne was 'ashamed and confounded to see how dull and imperfect I am'.[89] Catherine Booth resisted the call to preach until the devil suggested to her that she would look like a fool. She realised she had never been willing to be a fool for Christ and this compelled her to step forward and preach. But, she told her audience later, she had had no idea of the 'life of trial' it would create.[90]

Nineteenth-century British women employed arguments and practices in defence of preaching that were particular to their widely varying circumstances. Quaker women had a long tradition of preaching and involvement in decision-making bodies and female ministry increased through the nineteenth century.

As Methodism fragmented into breakaway groups and formed new alliances through-out the nineteenth and twentieth centuries, structural changes both constrained and expanded women's preaching opportunities. Whereas Quaker women regar-ded the influence of evangelicalism on women's ministry with suspicion, revivalists saw it as inspiring women's call to preach. Revivalism generated worship styles and religious organisations that included women in new ways. Salvation Army women, for example, pioneered new ways to evangelise, and institutionalised women's preaching as a defining feature of the movement. Even in the Church of England women established new institutions such as deaconess orders that permitted them to speak publicly and gain a measure of formal recognition for their work.

Many questions remain. Little research has been published on Baptists, Con-gregationalists or other Nonconformists. There is no comparative perspective with Methodism, where women were so prominent and active. It is difficult to discern if female preachers worked across denominational lines and whether or not the ordination of the Congregationalist Coltman facilitated other Nonconformist women's claims to preach. The twentieth century is yet to be explored. By the 1950s, Britain's religious diversity was greater than ever before and yet we know little about how that diversity reshaped traditional or new religious cultures of, and attitudes towards, female preaching. By the end of the twentieth century, the majority of Christians lived outside Europe and the complex relations created by imperial missions were being remade. Women's preaching and ordination con-tinues to divide Protestants across nations, theologies, and cultures.[91]

Acknowledgments

Thanks to Paul Dervis, Joy Dixon, Harold Goldman and Ellen Ross for their generous and astute comments on this essay and to the editors for their insightful criticism and guidance. This essay is dedicated to the memory of my mother, Elizabeth Walker, and her sisters Cathy Perron and Margery Sinclair.

Further reading

Olive Anderson, 'Women Preachers in Mid-Victorian Britain: Some Reflections on Feminism, Popular Religion and Social Change', *The Historical Journal* xii 3 (1969): pp. 467–84.

David Hempton and Myrtle Hill, 'Born to Serve: women and evangelical religion', Alan Haynes and Diane Urquhart (eds) *The Irish Women's History Reader* (London: Routledge, 2001).

Janice Holmes, *Religious Revivals in Britain and Ireland, 1859–1905* (Dublin: Irish Academic Press, 2000).

——, 'Women Preachers in the New Order', in Sheridan Gilley and Brian Stanley (eds) *Cambridge History of Christianity* (Cambridge: Cambridge University Press, 2006).

Sandra Stanley Holton, *Quaker Women: Personal Life, Memory and Radicalism in the Lives of Friends, 1780–1930* (London: Routledge, 2007).

Beverly Kienzle and Pamela J. Walker (eds) *Women Preachers and Prophets Through Two Millennia of Christianity* (Berkeley: University of California Press, 1998).

Christine Krueger, *The Reader's Repentance: Women Preachers, Women Writers and Nineteenth Century Social Discourse* (Chicago: University of Chicago Press, 1992).

Jennifer Lloyd, *Women and the Shaping of British Methodism: Persistent Preachers, 1807–1907* (Manchester: Manchester University Press, 2010).

Deborah Valenze, *Prophetic Sons and Daughters* (Princeton: Princeton University Press, 1985).

Pamela J. Walker, *Pulling the Devil's Kingdom Down: The Salvation Army in Victorian Britain* (Berkeley: University of California Press, 2001).

Notes

1 Rosina Davies, *The Story of My Life* (Llandyssul, Wales: Gomerian Press, 1942), pp. 27, 31. Davies does not provide her birth date but she was probably born around 1860.

2 Hugh McLeod, *Class and Religion in the Late Victorian City* (London: Croom Helm, 1974), p. 308.

3 Clive Field, 'Adam and Eve: Gender and the English Church Constituency', *Journal of Ecclesiastical History* 44:1 (January 1993), p. 65.

4 Timothy Larsen, *A People of One Book: The Bible and the Victorians* (Oxford: Oxford University Press, forthcoming).

5 Except in Ireland where Roman Catholics were in a majority.

6 Rickie Burman, 'She Looeth Well to the Ways of Her Household: The Changing Role of Jewish Women in Religious Life, c. 1880–1930', in Gail Malmgreen (ed.), *Religion in the Lives of English Women* (Bloomington: Indiana University Press, 1986) and Jean Spence, 'Working for Jewish Girls: Lily Montagu, Girls' Clubs and Industrial Reform, 1890–1914', *Women's History Review* 13:3 (2004), pp. 491–509.

7 Beverly Kienzle and Pamela J. Walker (eds), *Women Preachers and Prophets Through Two Millennia of Christianity* (Berkeley: University of California Press, 1998).

8 This debate is reviewed by Janice Holmes in 'Women Preachers in the New Order', in Sheridan Gilley and Brian Stanley (eds), *Cambridge History of Christianity: World Christianities c. 1815–1914* (Cambridge: Cambridge University Press, 2006).

9 David Hempton and Myrtle Hill, 'Born to Serve: Women and Evangelical Religion', in Alan Haynes and Diane Urquhart (eds), *The Irish Women's History Reader* (London: Routledge, 2001), p. 119.

10 Janice Holmes, 'Women Preachers in the New Order'.

11 Leonore Davidoff and Catherine Hall, *Family Fortunes* (Chicago: University of Chicago Press, 1987) and Callum Brown, *The Death of Christian Britain* (London: Routledge, 2001).

12 Timothy Larsen, *Christabel Pankhurst: Fundamentalism and Feminism in Coalition* (Rochester: Boydell, 2002).

13 Kienzle and Walker, *Women Preachers*, pp. xii–xxi.

14 David Bebbington, *Evangelicalism in Modern Britain* (London: Allen & Unwin, 1989).

15 Christine Krueger, *The Reader's Repentance: Women Preachers, Women Writers and Nineteenth Century Social Discourse* (Chicago: University of Chicago Press, 1992).

16 Janice Holmes, *Religious Revivals in Britain and Ireland, 1859–1905* (Dublin: Irish Academic Press, 2000), p. xii.

17 John Kent, *Holding the Fort: Studies in Victorian Revivalism* (London: Epworth Press, 1978), p. 18.

18 Richard Carwardine, *Transatlantic Revivalism: Popular Evangelicalism in Britain and America* (London: Greenwood Press, 1978).

19 Jeffrey Cox, *The English Churches in Secular Society* (Oxford: Oxford University Press, 1982) and Hugh McLeod, *Piety and Poverty: Working-Class Religion in Berlin, London and New York* (New York: Holmes & Meier, 1996).

20 Martha Vicinus, *Independent Women* (Chicago: University of Chicago Press, 1985), chap. 2 and 6.

21 Brian Heeney, *The Women's Movement in the Church of England, 1850–1930* (Oxford: Clarendon Press, 1980), pp. 47–49 and Elizabeth Nightengale (ed.), *Mrs. Collier of Birmingham, A Biblewoman's Story*, second edition (London: T. Woolmer, 1885).

22 Heeney, *The Women's Movement*, p. 24.

23 Sheila Fletcher, *Maude Royden: A Life* (Oxford: Basil Blackwell, 1989), p. 132.

24 Ibid., p. 3.

25 Ibid., p. 139.

26 Ibid., p. 147.

27 Ibid., pp. 153–62, 212–26.

28 Fletcher, *Maude Royden*, p. 267 and Heeney, *The Women's Movement*, chapter 6.

29 Robert McClory, 'Women of the Cloth', *Reader* 23:45 (August 12, 1994):14–18.

30 This large historiography includes studies of the whole movement, including Rupert Davies and Gordon Rupp, *A History of the Methodist Church in Great Britain* (London: Epworth, 1965), David Hempton, *Methodism: Empire of the Spirit* (New Haven: Yale University Press, 2005) and Bernard Semmel, *The Methodist Revolution* (New York: Basic Books, 1973) and studies of individual sects including Geoffrey Milburn, *Primitive Methodism* (Peterborough: Epworth Press, 2002) and Thomas Shaw, *The Bible Christians 1815–1907* (London: Epworth Press, 1965).

31 E.P. Thompson, *The Making of the English Working Class* (Harmondsworth: Penguin, 1968, second edition), chapter 11.

32 Jennifer M. Lloyd, *Women and the Shaping of British Methodism: Persistent Preachers, 1807–1907* (Manchester: Manchester University Press, 2010), introduction, I am grateful to Dr Lloyd and Manchester University Press for allowing me to read and cite from the manuscript version of this book.

33 Phyllis Mack, *Heart Religion in the British Enlightenment: Gender and Emotion in Early Methodism* (Cambridge: Cambridge University Press, 2008).

34 Lloyd, chap. 1, ms. pp. 50–51.

35 Lloyd, chap. 1, ms. p. 51.

36 Lloyd, chap.2, ms. p. 110.

37 Deborah Valenze, *Prophetic Sons and Daughters* (Princeton: Princeton University Press, 1985), p. 87.

38 Ibid., pp. 123–32.

39 Ibid., pp. 277–78.

40 Lloyd, chap. 5, ms. p. 256.

41 Lloyd, chap. 5, ms. pp. 253–59. On Methodist women, see also David Shorney, 'Women May Preach But Men Must Govern: Gender Roles in the Growth and Development of the Bible Christian Denomination', *Studies in Church History* 34 (1998): 309–22 and Gareth Lloyd, 'Repression and Resistance: Wesleyan Female Public Ministry in the Generation After 1791', *Wesley Historical Society* 55 (October 2005): 101–14.

42 Lloyd, chap. 7, ms. pp. 408–9.

43 Heeney, *The Women's Movement*, pp. 67–74, Sean Gill, *Women and the Church of England* (London: Society for Promoting Christian Knowledge, 1994), p. 165.

44 Lloyd, chap. 7, ms. p. 372.

45 Alison Bucknall, 'Martha's Work and Mary's Contemplation: The Work of Women in the Mildmay Conference and the Keswick Convention, 1856–1900', *Studies in Church History* 34 (1998): 405–20.

46 Lloyd, chap. 7, ms. p. 392.

47 Lloyd, chap. 7, ms. p. 394.

48 Olive Anderson, 'Women Preachers in Mid-Victorian Britain: Some Reflections on Feminism, Popular Religion and Social Change', *Historical Journal* 12:3 (1969): pp. 457–85.

49 *Revival*, September 10, 1868, quoted in Lloyd, chap. 5, ms. p. 259.

50 Lloyd, chap. 3, ms. pp. 170–72.

51 Holmes, p. xix. See also John T. Carson, *God's River in Spate: The Story of the Religious Awakening in Ulster 1859* (Belfast: Presbyterian Church in Ireland, 1958) which provides some historical background despite its sectarian tone.

52 Holmes, p. 11.

53 J. N. Ian Dickson, 'Evangelical Religion and Victorian Women: The Belfast Female Mission, 1859–1903', *Journal of Ecclesiastical History* 55:4 (October 2004): 700–25.

54 Holmes, p. 12.

55 See John Harvey, 'Revival, Revision, Visions and Visitations: The Resurgence and Imaging of Supernatural Religion', *Welsh Historical Review* 23:2 (2006): 75–98 and John Harvey, 'Spiritual Emblems: The Visions of 1904–5', *LLafur* 6:2 (1993): 75–93.

56 Pamela J. Walker, 'A Chaste and Fervid Eloquence', in Kienzle and Walker, eds, pp. 288–302 and Susan Mumm, 'I Love My Sex: Two Late Victorian Pulpit Women', in Jean Bellamy, Anne Laurence and Gill Perry (eds), *Women, Scholarship and Criticism* (Manchester: Manchester University Press, 2000).

57 Pamela J. Walker, *Pulling the Devil's Kingdom Down: The Salvation Army in Victorian Britain* (Berkeley: University of California Press, 2001), p. 34.

58 Walker, *Pulling the Devils Kingdom* , p. 37.

59 The practice was discontinued for theological reasons. See Walker, pp. 117–20.

60 A.C. Tait Papers, Lambeth Palace Library, London, Salvation Army poster, undated, probably 1882, vol. 285, f.55. Walker, *Pulling the Devils Kingdom*, p. 191.

61 As quoted in Walker, *Pulling the Devils Kingdom*, p. 197.

62 Walker, *Pulling the Devils Kingdom*, p. 198.

63 Janice Holmes, 'Gender, Public Disorder and the Salvation Army in Ireland, 1880–82', in Rosemary Raughter (ed.), *Religious Women and Their History* (Dublin: Irish University Press, 2005), pp. 63–81.

64 Phyllis Mack, *Visionary Women: Ecstatic Prophecy in Seventeenth-Century England* (Berkeley: University of California Press, 1992).

65 Catherine Brekus, *Strangers and Pilgrims: Female Preaching in America* (Chapel Hill: University of North Carolina Press, 1998).

66 Sandra Stanley Holton, *Quaker Women: Personal Life, Memory and Radicalism in the Lives of Friends, 1780–1930* (London: Routledge, 2007). I am grateful to Dr Holton for generously sharing notes from a forthcoming article on Quaker women's ministry.

67 Holton, chap. 1.

68 Sheila Wright, *Friends in York: The Dynamics of Quaker Revival, 1780–1860* (Keele: Keele University Press, 1995), p. 31.

69 Helen Plant, 'Subjective Testimonies: Women Quaker Ministers and Spiritual Authority in England', *Gender and History* 15:2 (August 2003): pp. 305–7.

70 Holton, p. 132.

71 On Mary Dyer, see David D. Hall, *Worlds of Wonder, Days of Judgment* (Cambridge: Harvard University Press, 1989).

72 Wright, p. 40.

73 Geoffrey F. Nuttall, 'The Early Congregational Conception of the Ministry and the Place of Women Within It', *The Congregational Quarterly* 26:2 (1948): p. 158.

74 Elaine Kaye, 'Constance Coltman: A Forgotten Pioneer', *Journal of the United Reformed Church History Society* (1998): pp. 134–46.

75 Kaye, 'Constance Coltman', p. 144.

76 Works on this subject include Neil Dickson, 'Modern Prophetesses: Women Preachers in Nineteenth Century Scottish Brethren', *Records of the Scottish Church History Society* 25:3 (1995): pp. 87–117; Arthur Fawcett, 'Scottish Lay Preachers in the Nineteenth Century', *Records of the Scottish Church History Society* 12:2 (1955): pp. 97–114 and John Briggs, 'She Preachers, Widows and other Women: The Feminine Dimension of Baptist Life Since 1600', *Baptist Quarterly* 31 (1986): pp. 337–52.

77 Gillian Gill, *Mary Baker Eddy* (Reading, MA: Persus Books, 1998) and James Butler, *The Early History of Christian Science in the British Isles* (unpublished typescript, Mary Baker Eddy Library, Boston, MA, 1965). See also Anne Harwood, *An English View of Christian Science* (New York: Fleming Revell, 1898).

78 Stephen Gottschalk, *Rolling Away the Stone: Mary Baker Eddy's Challenge to Materialism* (Bloomington: Indiana University Press, 2000), p. 228.

79 Mary Baker Eddy, *Manual of the Mother Church, The First Church of Christ, Scientist in Boston Massachusetts* (Boston: The Christian Science Board of Directors, 1895) and First Church of Christ Scientist, Edinburgh, *Constitution and Bye-Laws* n.d. (The Mary Baker Eddy Library, Boston).

80 Gottschalk, p. 182.

81 *Christian Science Journal*, March 1903, p. lxxxii. See also March 1898, p. xlviii which lists four practitioners in London, all women.

82 See Joy Dixon in this volume.

83 The case was covered by *The Times* (London) in detail between August and November 1898 and other British newspapers also reported on it. The church reported on these events in *The Christian Science Journal*, December 1898, pp. 622–25.

84 *The Graphic* (London), November 5, 1898, p. 4.

85 May 17, 1895, p. 8.

86 One of the few to address women is Beryl Satter, *Each Mind a Kingdom: American Women, Sexual Purity and the New Thought Movement* (Berkeley: University of California Press, 1999).

87 See Joy Dixon, *The Divine Feminine: Theosophy and Feminism in England* (Baltimore: Johns Hopkins University Press, 2001) on heterodox movements.

88 Lloyd, chap. 3, ms. p. 146.

89 Lloyd, chap. 2, ms. p. 188.

90 Walker, *Pulling the Devils Kingdom*, pp. 38–39.

91 John Wolfe (ed.), *Religion in History: Conflict, Conversion and Coexistence* (Milton Keynes: Open University Press, 2004) and Werner Ustorf, 'A Missiological Postscript', in Hugh McLeod and Werner Ustorf (eds), *The Decline of Christendom in Western Europe, 1750–2000* (Cambridge: Cambridge University Press, 2003).

6 Professionalising their faith
Women, religion and the cultures of mission and empire

Rhonda A. Semple

In 1900, the application of Miss Florence Syrett to join the interdenominational London Missionary Society (LMS) resulted in a flurry of correspondence. After Syrett's father made public his concerns that the LMS had tricked his daughter into a career teaching 'little brown children' and taking her away from her duty as his daughter, additional family members, the directors of the LMS and the general public weighed in on the subject via dozens of letters published in *The Daily Chronicle*. Following this inauspicious start, Syrett went on to a successful career as a missionary – marrying, staying healthy and maintaining ties to her home congregation in North London which supported her overseas work. Like many nineteenth-century women, Syrett served the mission first as an independent professional and later, unpaid, as a wife. In doing so, she was simultaneously empowered by and resistant to the middle-class, liberal Protestant identities that so powerfully defined women's religious experiences in modern Britain. While Syrett's identity as an educated, middle-class English woman positioned her as an ideal mission candidate, she would be obliged to reshape the expectations of '[blessed] respectability' that so strongly delineated the western female ideal. Women such as Syrett contributed to a reconfiguration of British domestic society and of modern religious belief and practice. Although there has been a resurgence of interest in new imperial histories, including the history of missions and women's roles in the British Empire over the past two decades, these fields have yet to be fully integrated. This chapter seeks to do this by exploring four missionary organisations central to Britain's modern imperial identity and focusing on the gendered implications of such work.

Missionaries, gender and empire: religion and the 'new' imperialism

In the 1960s, the 'Miss Syretts' of the British Empire – the everybodies and nobodies – began to elicit historical interest. Critical engagement with these non-elite subjects, and their relations with the formal empire and the cultures with which they interacted, resulted in important new fields of enquiry. These interdisciplinary approaches de-centred extant ideas of metropole and periphery, instead juxtaposing formal and informal structures of power and authority with questions of gender, sexuality, race, ethnicity and social position. These post-colonial analyses have resulted in a complex re-telling, widening the focus from the home country and incorporating a reciprocally influencing web of cultures and individuals in the modern imperial world. This chapter examines the relationship of women and gender in these formations from the early nineteenth century through the interwar period. It focuses on British missions in the tradition of mainstream liberal Protestantism, including the London Missionary Society (LMS, est.1795), the Wesleyan Methodist Missionary Society (WMMS, est.1813), the mission committees in the Church of Scotland (CofS),[1] and the China Inland Mission (CIM, est.1865). The study of female missionaries who occupied a position of gendered subordination inflected by sexual, social and racial privilege can illuminate much about the nature of imperial power. The study of these four missions helps us to understand how theology, class and nationality intersected with gender in the mission field. While British women also joined Catholic overseas missions, their experience of being raised Catholic in a Protestant nation and then being employed in an international religious order requires additional analysis beyond the scope of this study.

Wives, sisters, 'daughters of the regiments', travellers, medical professionals, teachers and mission workers – in short, a myriad of women joined the British empire in the second third of the nineteenth century. Their experiences reflected both their institutional 'place' and individual choice. Missionary women contributed to the informal empire both in Britain as the supporters of missions, abroad as female relatives of male professionals and then as missionaries in their own right. Research to date has focused on the personal and professional opportunities available to women as British imperial influence spread across the globe. In the 1860s significant numbers of women joined missions as professionals themselves.[2] Mid-Victorian advocates for women's increased role in missions argued that only distinctly feminine characteristics could 'save the heathen' – not only spiritually (through evangelism) but also physically (through social welfare).[3] Throughout this period women also became the prime 'objects' of mission work. Wives and mothers were regarded as potent vectors of culture and belief; those same women, once trained, might then evangelise their worlds. This chapter outlines how important it is for historians to analyse the function of religious belief in women's decisions to enter professions in general and overseas missions in particular, and to consider the impact of their religious beliefs on communities around the world.

As with empire studies more broadly, the focus in scholarship on missions has shifted from established western institutions to an exploration of the non-elite: those who were neither male, evangelical, white English, British nor middle class, but who were, nevertheless, active agents in the mission field.[4] This methodological de-centring has resulted in a more complex but richer contribution to our understanding of mission cultures in the British imperial past. In turn, reading 'against the grain' of the primary evidence generated in missions has contributed to linguistic, cultural, and anthropological studies of the various countries in which Christian missionaries were active.[5] Most recently, interest has shifted back to

Western Europe and the North American settler communities that generated missions. This new focus aims to understand the social and religious impulses that generated the Protestant mission movement and explore how those conditions were impacted by mission work and ideology. The consideration of home and field as two interconnected, mutually influencing parts reflects the growing interest in the role played by missions and missionaries in the British Empire,[6] as well as the postcolonial assertion that no metropole could remain uninfluenced by those caught under the 'colonial shawl'.

Negotiating duty: class, kinship and the religious imperative to save

Miss Syrett's example is instructive in this regard, illustrating the exquisite negotiations of change and continuity so familiar to the student of women's lives. Hers was the experience of divided duty – as daughter, believer, female community member. Her father expected her to remain at home and care for him, educated and able, but she felt called to work overseas. Her church had made such a career available to women, and respectable British society agreed that women had the right to make such a choice. Syrett's experiences were part of the radical transformation of British society that resulted from several interconnected global processes. Imperial networks helped to spawn evangelical revivals that spread across Britain, Europe and North America in the late eighteenth and nineteenth centuries, radicalising, reinvigorating and personalising a Protestant theology that demanded its adherents live out the imperative to change their world.[7] This brand of religious 'enthusiasm' which aimed at nothing less than a complete social transformation, translated far beyond direct action, instead shaping the very cultural 'tone' of Britain and the Empire in the modern period.

Links between religious belief, institutional influence and cultural hegemony were central to imperial control. This control was informal, however, and it is the untangling of meanings embedded in these informal tendrils of authority that has proved so fruitful for historians. While British mission organisations were never formally aligned with the institutional apparatus of Empire, both domestic and colonial governments supported religious activity where it buttressed their authority. All too often it did not. Denominational conflict and moves to separate church and state in the nineteenth century frequently mitigated official government positions.[8] Not surprisingly, missionaries courted official support with caution. Imperial authorities were often less than delighted with 'excitable' evangelicals because of their marginal status in Britain and the potentially destabilising effects of evangelism on non-Christian populations. Indeed, in several instances, anti-colonial agitation had its genesis in mission communities.

The central role played by gender in modern missions is becoming clearer. The women who organised, supported and staffed nineteenth-century missions were driven to do so out of a distinctly feminised theology which advanced women as ideally suited to the joint evangelical imperative of faith and good work. In British India the provision of western education and campaigns against child-marriage and *sati* illustrate how religious and moral reform was increasingly measured according to a western definition of women's well-being. Evangelical responses to women's experience in the slave trade were similarly shaped by gendered expectations where literary tracts argued that women's bodies and souls were being destroyed through enforced physical labour, rape and the forcible removal of their children. Evangelical efforts to expose such practices linked the mission movement with broader humanitarian projects in nineteenth-century Britain; the policing of gendered identities was central to that process.[9]

Making faith institutional?

The institutional structures of British Protestant missions were organised in one of three ways: a first group were the separate denominational or non-denominational voluntary societies (like the LMS) whose members helped finance the mission; a second group were the mission committees or voluntary organisations within an existing denominational infrastructure (such as the Foreign Mission Committee of the CofS); and a third group was comprised of a select number of mission societies (like the CIM) whose membership consisted of the mission workers themselves. Each group may only be fully understood by examining both the official and unofficial institutional structures of the organisation. In each case, the function of the central mission committee was that of both organiser and conduit – of information, prayers and funds from various mission stations around the world to the auxiliary societies located along the length and breadth of Britain. The mediation of such far-flung associations caused inevitable tensions but these diverse networks also forged connections between like-minded individuals in Britain committed to the mission enterprise and the transmission of ideas and knowledge between radically different cultures.

The LMS provides us with an example of the non-denominational voluntary society. Although it quickly became primarily Congregational, both its workers and supporters were drawn from British Nonconformist society more broadly. Members of its ladies' committees derived authority from their position relative to men – both their male relatives and the male-dominated authority structure of the Protestant churches on which the mission societies relied. The Ladies' Board of the LMS was established in 1875 to examine and train women candidates and to help place them in missions. It functioned until 1891 when it was replaced by a Ladies' Examination Committee. At this point women also joined men on the Board of Directors. Throughout, neither the Ladies' Board nor the examination committee exercised independent authority to hire and place personnel; their role was to vet and recommend candidates to the male-dominated Board.[10] Any substantial power wielded by women on the LMS was exercised through diffuse fundraising networks and mission auxiliaries – small, congregation-based volunteer groups connected under the umbrella of the mission. A number of examples exist in which the Ladies' Committee struggled to balance the needs of their workers, supporters and the mission society.[11] In the 1870s and 1880s, for example, women on local auxiliaries resisted the efforts of the Board of Directors to control all mission funds as part of the Board's efforts to increase administrative efficiency.

It took the Board nearly twenty years to 'regularise' the dispersal of funds through official LMS networks. That length of time suggests women's fund-raising success granted them real authority within a male-dominated organisation; that the Board found it necessary to treat their grass-roots supporters carefully is underscored by terse letters in which auxiliaries 'suggested' continued Board interference might cause them to reallocate their funds away from mission work. They were apparently a fund-raising force to be reckoned with.

In the second model of missionary organisation, committees were created, staffed and functioned within the institutional framework of an already existing denomination. The various missionary activities of the Scottish Presbyterian churches fall under this category, as does the work of the WMMS.[12] In this model, the work of mission committees, their use of funds and the polity guiding their activities all came under church authority, although the gendered mediation of power and authority within those structures was an evolving process. The administration of missions in the Scottish churches, for example, operated with a surety of purpose underpinned by the financial and theological assurance of the Presbyterian Church. Yet that same strength and surety could be highly gendered and inflexible. Presbyterian polity was based on strong lay participation; yet, while women's right to vote as electors was confirmed in the early eighteenth century, that right was contested throughout the nineteenth century and women's eldership was term-limited rather than life-ordained. Presbyterian church polity also required the equal representation of lay and ordained members in church governance. With women barred from ordination until 1929, this invariably resulted in a male majority on governing bodies. Despite this, women extended their domestic roles into wider church society; as Leslie Orr MacDonald argues, 'the feminization of the Church was notable, measured largely in terms of work done, not status bestowed'.[13] Women's presence was institutionalised by the formation of a Women's Guild 'to unite the women of Scotland ... for worship, fellowship, and service' in 1887.[14] But women commonly worked within the boundaries of a gendered church order which deemed it respectable for women to focus on 'domestic' concerns alone.

These informal, gendered hierarchies reinforced the formal ecclesiastical control of the General Assembly (the highest church court). The various mission-concerned women's committees were in fact 'merely' sub-committees of the Foreign Mission Committee of the General Assembly. The women on the Ladies' Committee were able to raise funds and recommend candidates but not act independently. They were further hampered by the fact that, as the wives, daughters and sisters of prominent Edinburgh ministers and mission supporters, they were inextricably linked to the men's side of mission work. The men held the purse-strings and so women's work remained reliant on men for capital outlay. By 1910, concern over gender relations had combined with issues of race to dominate mission affairs. For the following decade, sustained debates over the nature of women's work in missions and membership of mission councils reflected similar, secular controversies over women's roles. By 1929, the Church came upon a solution: at that time the newly formed Mission Council of the re-united Church of Scotland absorbed the women's committees into its mandate and in so doing included, yet muffled, concerns particular to women.

While the success of Scottish missions stemmed from a solid base of sound finances, a longstanding commitment to education and the weight of an established administrative system, the achievements of the China Inland Mission (CIM) was based on the remarkable personality and administrative capability of a single figure, Hudson Taylor. In part because the CIM was a comparative late-comer to missionary work and because of its exponential growth – it had outgrown all British missions except the Church Missionary Society (CMS) by 1900[15] – the organisation's administrative procedures were forced to develop quickly. Having defined itself against other British missions in terms of its administration in the mission field, by its workers and what it termed its faith-based initiatives (the non-solicitation of funds for work begun with no assurance of support), the CIM produced an operational manual in 1896 entitled 'Principles & Practices'[16] as a rapid codification of its policy and practices. The CIM successfully created its own 'brand' of professional mission, the future of which was ensured through inter-marriage amongst the leadership and the education of the succeeding generation of workers at their school for the children of missionaries at Chefoo. The CIM proffered a distinctive administrative structure. The members of its London Council recommended mission workers only to its central administration, based first in Hangchow, then Yangchow and eventually Shanghai, which was comprised of missionaries rather than the supporters of missions.[17] CIM members were promised no formal wage, relying instead on 'faith' that God would provide. The uniquely gendered feature of Hudson Taylor's mission was his explicit commitment to attracting female mission workers. Single women were hired in greater numbers earlier on than in any other mission; occasionally they were expected to continue working after they had married and had children. The mission's adherence to this practice was sorely tested by criticism from outsiders in addition to the difficulties of hiring single women, but their intentions certainly distinguished them from the practices of other mainline Protestant missions. By the 1880s Taylor's commitment to female mission workers had influenced other missions, which by the end of that decade were hiring the same number of female workers as the CIM.[18]

Membership of the Ladies' Council, formally created in 1889, was limited to women related to men in charge of the CIM. Prior to this, the London Council had dealt with women's applications. This practice came under scrutiny in 1888 over a difference of opinion on a specific candidate. The role of women councillors was then formalised, with women invited to 'inquire into the character of candidates ... test their suitability ... decline such as appear unsuitable, and ... recommend for acceptance by the London Council such as appear suitable'.[19] On subsequent occasions the London Council reminded women that their position was only to provide support and advice.[20] Although in charge of the various small training homes for women, they were further reminded that any decision required the approval of the London Council and Hudson Taylor himself.[21] Thus, even with its overt commitment to women's work, the CIM, like other nineteenth-century missions, defined and controlled women's administrative contributions relative to men. Although the CIM began with a commitment to using women as evangelists, this was quickly curtailed in the interest of effective operation when other missions, the British government, and the wider public putpressure on the mission to conform more closely to contemporary middle-class ideas regarding what was acceptable behaviour for women.[22] Immediately after Taylor's pioneering mission party of 1866, the mission curtailed its hiring of women; although female applicants flooded their offices, the number of women who joined the mission did not rise significantly until the 1880s; by then, as hasbeen suggested above, this pattern was no different from other societies. Thegrumbling against CIM missionaries – in newspapers and in letters from other missionaries and expats – only increased after the events of the Boxer Rebellion.[23]

Women's work in missions in the nineteenth century mirrored women's efforts to create organisations and informal networks outside of specifically religious contexts but, unlike their secular counterparts who enjoyed relative autonomy, women mission workers were hampered by wider church structures.[24] In each of the examples discussed, women's work had the greatest effect when mission structures were less centralised. In each of the missions discussed, a central committee relied heavily on less formal associations of women to raise public awareness and funds and to recruit potential missionaries. Familial and informal church ties often rivalled in importance more formal ecclesiastical structures in determining women's influence.

Becoming professional and shaping the profession

What did mission work look like? Male missionaries were ministers and pastors; they established churches, attracted congregations, preached and proselytised. In each of the missions under consideration, men hired in the early nineteenth century were of artisanal origins and the majority of them were ordained. A successful missionary candidate was willing to undertake any task necessary. Once 'in the field' he might be required to turn his hand to writing, printing and translating both religious and other material. Missionaries were also required to negotiate contracts, build houses and plough fields, or to supervise such work. Scots like Alexander Duff (1806–78; India 1829) created policies that shaped the colonial world. His evangelicalism influenced both missions in India and government education policy that education in the subcontinent – be it in the vernacular language or English – offered the most important opportunity for conversion.[25] Teaching took place in purpose-built schools, unfurnished rooms and out-of-doors. From the 1830s until the education debates of the 1880s, missions built secondary institutions that developed into universities around the world – in India, southern Africa, New Zealand, the eastern USA and Canada.[26] Missionaries also lobbied colonial governments, fed the victims of famine and opened orphanages and refuges. These practices often drew criticisms from evangelicals who worried that such work was too secular in nature.

Although the presence and activity of women is not explicitly outlined in this portrait, they were certainly there. British women joined missions as the relatives of male missionaries. They worked hard as wives and mothers establishing western-style homes in unfamiliar places. Women acted as a moral shield, protecting white men from the indigenous culture. And while they modelled 'the' Christian family, they corresponded with supporters and wrote for the myriad of mission-related magazines published in this period. These same women instigated the mission schools, hospitals and social work passed on to the first wave of women hired in their own right from the 1860s onwards as single mission workers.[27] By the 1890s women in missions, in both formal and informal capacities, as outlined above, outnumbered men globally[28] and, as will be discussed later, locally hired mission workers outnumbered the British mission workers at least ten to one.[29]

Yet even the professional women were not considered equivalent to their male counterparts. Instead single women were assessed according to their 'ladylike qualities'. As recruitment standards changed towards the end of the century, female candidates were expected to demonstrate quantifiable vocational qualifications as well as religious commitment. But this professionalisation of female mission workers was still shaped by the gendered expectations of nineteenth-century middle-class British society, as we saw earlier applied to Florence Syrett. Women were limited by a lack of educational qualifications and work experience and did not fit easily into a male professional model of training, remuneration and professional status. At the same time, women who applied to missions did so on the wider cultural expectation that they, as respectable British women, were 'qualified' to change those colonial cultures currently frustrating conversion efforts.[30] Thus women's roles in missions were based on deep ambiguities around their professional status. In 1899, Miss Syrett was able to graduate with a respectable teaching degree from Homerton College, but she remained a daughter first and, as such, her father expected her to manage his home and obey his wishes. A male became fully professional through training and his status as head of a household; the status of a professionally-trained woman remained ambiguous because of her relatively subordinate position.

Selecting the right girl for the job

The official and unofficial apparatus of Nonconformist churches played a central role in the selection of female candidates. Each organisation relied on official church structures as well as the personal contacts made and maintained within those structures to recruit and assess appropriate candidates. Initially, wives were vetted alongside their husbands by the same committees. Ladies' committees were formed to deal separately with female candidates between the late 1850s and 1880s. In all cases, this gendered division of labour was challenged around the issue of funding control, resulting in frequent reminders of women's position in relation to the main committee.[31] Shortly after the turn of the century, in what is a pattern for each type of mission discussed, the administration of men and women's work was merged and gendered concerns were thus muted.

While sharing many organisational similarities, mission networks also reflected national and denominational differences. As Leslie Orr MacDonald points out, widely shared assumptions existed about what made a good Presbyterian missionary.[32] The letters written by and in support of Scottish Presbyterian candidates suggest that both writers and readers understood this implicitly. In contrast, women applying to the LMS, who were mostly Congregational, felt it necessary to spell out their commitment to chapel and community. For Presbyterians, Kirk membership alone indicated commitment, whereas the LMS required explicit articulations of faith and works. The CIM's support network, at least initially, appears to have been even more subjective, centred as it was around Hudson Taylor and his friends and colleagues. Taylor was forced to rely on recommendation letters solicited from acquaintances, as the working-class backgrounds of male and female candidates made it unlikely they could supply formal school references. Similarly, their wide variety of church backgrounds, or even lack of formal affiliation, eliminated another source of reference. While this would have disadvantaged CIM candidates relative to candidates to other missions, it was not unusual in the CIM, where it was more often women's seeming difficulty with foreign languages and the fear of scandal that shaped a gendered professionalism in that organisation.

Male candidates attended specific training institutions for mission work which makes it possible to analyse their curriculum and studies. Women, by contrast, were taught at varying levels in diverse institutions. Because the professionalisation of 'feminine' occupations lagged behind their masculine equivalents it was difficult to assess the level of training.[33] A Scottish nurse, for example, may have learned nursing at home in a private school or at a nursing school attached to a hospital. By the 1870s she might have applied to a Presbyterian mission after completing either a two- or four-year course. The quality and nature of mission training was not fully regularised in Britain until after the First World War. Some women were hired and sent overseas right away, although the majority spent some time in mission training homes. Methodist women had already gained experience of travelling and preaching informally as part of the general Methodist movement.[34] From the 1860s a variety of missionary training homes were established all over Britain – William Pennefather established the Training Home for Female Missionaries associated with the Mildmay Hospital in East London in 1860. Anglican missions trained women at various locales, including the 'Willows' and the College of the Ascension at Selly Oak, Birmingham. The Church of Scotland created a Women's Training Institute in Edinburgh called St Colm's where trainees took in-house courses and at the University of Edinburgh, gaining practical knowledge through work in local nurseries, hospices and district visiting.

Miss Syrett's education fits somewhere in the centre of this confusing terrain. Homerton College became a women-only institute in the 1890s when it moved to Cambridge, but it retained its connections with the Congregationalism for which the College had trained ministers up until the 1840s. Thus Miss Syrett received solid academic training alongside respectable peers in an institution with long-standing links to her family's denomination. Hers was indeed a privileged educational background and her father was correct when he described her as a valuable asset to the mission.[35]

Spirituality, health and wealth

Due to the variety of training approaches, mission committees invariably applied criteria other than academic excellence to assess female candidates.[36] Women were hired to the various Protestant mission bodies based on three general criteria. The most important criterion was the candidate's evangelical commitment to spiritual and social uplift through mission work. Both in their applications and through letters and reports from the mission field, missionaries described their spiritual state and religious response to their surroundings. A candidate's religious motivation was gleaned from a personal statement and from letters of support. Candidates to the LMS and the Presbyterian societies were expected to be regular church attendees and to produce letters of support from a minister or elder who would attest to the religious background of her family, their support for her mission endeavours and the candidate's own involvement in church activities. Importantly, neither the LMS nor the Scottish missions were interested in hiring workers who wished to escape family responsibilities. This puts Miss Syrett's carefully worded letter of application into context; in it she addressed directly the fact that her father opposed her application to the mission, that she had never disobeyed him previously, and only did so 'out of a strong missionary purpose'.[37] Missionary exceptionalism sanctioned her respectful act of rebellion.

Candidates' papers leave no doubt that gendered ideas were pivotal in the selection of candidates. Middle-class notions of culture and respectability prevailed. The ability to sew, knit, sing and play the piano, have the 'right' accent, know the 'correct' way to use cutlery as well as how to dress – all denoted valuable qualities. Fine manners were considered so important because candidates would be representing Christian belief and the British nation in an imperial setting.

As women moved into secular professions – first as teachers and later as nurses, doctors and administrators – new hiring practices were also adopted for women missionaries. Greater emphasis was placed on formal secular education and experience. Scottish candidates were generally better educated than their LMS colleagues – many had professional work experience as teachers and nurses and some as trained doctors. Working-class candidates who applied to the CIM, on the other hand, came with few credentials. Most had not been church volunteers and possessed no letters of reference from ministers or family members, perhaps because either the mobility of working life or the dramatic nature of their religious conversion had isolated them from their family and church community.[38] Their jobs as seamstresses, clerical workers, governesses and occasionally factory workers were respectable labour, but middle-class concerns regarding single girls' freedom of movement and association lowered the estimation of these workers until the last decade of the century.[39] For the CIM, such concerns were overcome by sufficient religious motivation.

Candidates to missions needed to be healthy and of the 'right' age.[40] In the LMS, these factors were cited most frequently as the reason for rejection and reflected a very real concern given the high rates of illness and death among missionaries. The Free Church of Scotland listed health second only to spirituality and required medical certification of a candidate's fitness for work in tropical climates.[41] The health of LMS wives was rated just as highly.[42] Evidence came from family doctors, ministers, relatives and the candidates themselves. One 1885 recommendation letter commented that 'Dr Miller does not know the patient well enough to give the sort of report that is needed'.[43] By the turn of the century, therefore, the Society's own doctors were providing reports that favoured robust candidates like Myfanwy Wood who could walk 'twenty-seven miles in a day'.[44]

The family histories of candidates could provide valuable health information such as sibling deaths from measles, scarlet fever and other common childhood illnesses. Tuberculosis was reported in family after family, candidates' dental problems were discussed and digestive disorders also caused anxiety. Societies received applications from candidates who had experienced mental instability; the CIM required one male candidate to undergo mental treatment.[45] He was not hired in the end but another candidate with complete hearing loss was.

Married to the mission

Although women were 'married to missions', that designation was complicated.[46] Less than 10 per cent of the workforce was made up of single women prior to the 1850s; thus certain women interested in a life overseas jumped at the opportunity to marry a mission candidate. Although unpaid, wives were also vetted through the candidate process alongside their husbands. As a mission partner the mission societies emphasised a wife's role as representing British culture and modelling Christian behaviour. British records are circumspect in the discussion of male sexuality but it is clear that men living and working alone created a moral quandary for the missions; a British wife might prevent an inappropriate inter-racial liaison.[47] This underscores a functional understanding of men and women's sexuality that is undercut by occasional private correspondence which offers evidence of married couples' healthy sexuality. In private letters we see evidence of the interplay between public expectation and private reality: the presence of 'white' women on the mission field may have stopped inter-racial marriages and acted as public models, but missionary marriages were also life partnerships of love and passion, which is a reality too easily lost in the historical study of missions. Furthermore, married women developed professional practices based on their feminine qualifications which underscored women's position as moral guardians. Mission women were expected to focus their efforts on 'domesticating' female mission adherents. Mission schools, including those established by the LMS in South Africa, the Basel mission in West Africa, the Universities Mission to Central Africa in Tanganyika and the Scottish missions in North India, also acted as veritable factories of 'good', westernised Christian workers who were the potential wives and mothers for the male mission adherents. Thus the model of mission wife was buttressed by the presence of local Christian women and their families. However, faced with more work than they could complete part-time, it was the mission wives who argued for missions to hire the professional single workers of the second half of the nineteenth century.

As recent scholarship shows, the inter-relation between gendered roles and class status in Britain was frequently mirrored in the myriad cultural encounters that comprised the imperial experience.[48] Mission workers not only acted out of an acute fear of the foreign environment's influence on their own children, their own precarious class position left many mission families preoccupied with social status.[49] Many families took advantage of mission society programmes that paid for the sons and sometimes the daughters of missionaries to attend school in Britain. The CIM in particular made the education and upbringing of mission children a central feature of its 'Principles & Practices' guide. However, evidence also reveals the difficulty of maintaining boundaries between mission families and the cultures being evangelised. Mission records are scattered with inter-racial marriages and children brought up alongside close friends from local communities, often feeling more Kikuyu than English and speaking Bengali or Punjabi. Many mission children reported feeling part of a 'third culture'. Although these experiences should not be overstated, those instances where children felt inculturated into local society and quite alienated from their mission organisation should not be ignored.[50] Indeed, this as yet under-researched feature of mission culture indicates that resistance and adaptation to colonial boundaries were the rule rather than the exception.

A woman's role in maintaining cultural difference could lead to misunderstandings and contribute to profound cultural dissonance. The early-nineteenth-century 'Christian family model' often underlined the racial divide in Christian communities since a wife and child required expensive domestic help which an African minister could not afford.[51] As is now well described, missionaries played a central role in the western attempt to reshape societies through the reconstruction of women's roles. In South Asia they contributed to the campaigns against infant marriage and *sati*, in East Asia they agitated against the practice of foot-binding, and throughout the African continent they found fault in indigenous practices of female circumcision, payment of bride wealth, polygamous marriages and female corporal punishment. As Adrian Hastings has observed, 'African women had then, on becoming Christian, to be reshaped as well as re-clothed.'[52] Hastings cautions against a simple interpretation of either non-western practices or the western-Christian response to them, however. He identifies cases where a hard line on monogamy could cause real harm with discarded women left destitute but also notes that missionary teaching helped to dislodge strongly-held beliefs in polygamy in places like Buganda and introduced the possibility of marriage choice for women. According to Hastings, missionaries' attacks on the practice of bride wealth, for example, reflected a misunderstanding of how the gifts worked. Whereas missionaries believed it reinforced a woman's subordination to her family, in fact the money was protection of her continued value in society. Preventing the exchange of bride wealth could therefore actually endanger women. Fascinatingly, some indigenous women openly rejected Christian marriages. In post-World War I Buganda, for example, Igbo women viewed western monogamous marriages as prisons and not nearly as desirable as multiple-partnered marriages which could be mutually supportive and socially satisfying for wives.[53]

So, while a theology of women's mission to other women was central to their work, British women's attempts to act on that imperative had complex outcomes. Concerns about gender were intricately connected with local mission practice but they were also constantly under negotiation. Between the 1830s and the 1880s, missionary organisations debated whether social welfare had any place in the mission endeavour at all, and many expressed concerns about what messages should be imparted through an increasingly professional, specialised, and religiously liberal mission workforce. It is a question that has never been fully resolved.

Doing devotion

As we have seen, in nearly all Protestant missions women worked in a number of capacities, utilising their 'natural' talents as communicators, caregivers and organisers whether formally employed by the mission or 'engaged' to the mission as blood relatives or through marriage. This section offers a case study of the WMMS, whose archived letters from the 1830s reveal a process common to all missionary societies – that wives and female relatives were very often busy in unpaid work and needed support, which led to the hiring of single female workers. In the late 1850s British Methodist women formally organised at home in order to meet the expressed needs of missionary wives, and the trickle of interest, money, and workers continued through the next decades until the 1880s and 1890s when, in response to better organisation, increased financial resources, a larger pool of more knowledgeable, trained and willing candidates and the push of revival, missions joined the 'scramble' of missions in a modern imperial order.

The first single women hired by the WMMS resembled those hired by other mainstream Protestant missions. As elsewhere, many married their male missionary colleagues so quickly that the WMMS women's auxiliary joined other organisations in lamenting the potential loss of female workers, although they also acknowledged that married women would continue to work.[54] Indeed, during the 1860s and 1870s, the majority of 'women's work' was performed by WMMS wives and daughters. Even so, the few women hired by the WMMS outnumber and predate the women hired by the CMS – where the belief was that the need for women's work was being met by smaller specialised societies[55] – and by the LMS, where the single women hired tended to be the widows and daughters of their male missionaries.[56] Although many women were teachers, through the 1870s records indicate frustration with the educational preparation of applicants and with the number and quality of candidates presented. The WMMS women's auxiliary met these challenges in a number of ways. Their fundraising successes allowed them to expand and professionalise the mission institutions they supported, and fund-raising schemes that emphasised connections between British donors and the mission work they supported only increased the collections.[57] They also managed to attract a smattering of professional women with higher formal qualifications to positions in those institutions from the 1880s onwards. These included teachers trained at college and university rather than through ragged schools, and a smattering of medical practitioners.[58] In the 1890s this trend continued as the WMMS hired increasing numbers of female physicians – a valuable commodity in any mission – to staff its expanding hospital services throughout India and contribute to community welfare through dispensaries, travelling clinics and critical famine care. On the home front, the women's auxiliary further expanded and formalised its organisation and fund-raising efforts in support of medical work and the mission schools that were required to meet ever-higher educational requirements from the government in India.[59] As was the case in other missions, certain female workers failed to thrive in the mission environment; some were unable to learn foreign languages, and the occasional worker was sent home with 'mental problems'. Yet, most women worked effectively within the culture of missions, carving out an increasingly varied field of women's work.

By the end of the nineteenth century, the major missionary organisations were grappling with the question of whether or not education, medicine and social services were legitimate means of evangelisation. All three areas were dominated by women numerically if not in terms of authority. This debate reflected the influence of the Holiness movement, a movement in which women could act as lay leaders and in which emotive religious expression was allowed. A second influential strand emerged from the increasing importance being placed on scientific notions of health and education and the significant role of women in raising fit children for the nation. The result of these trends was twofold. In all missions, indirect evangelism through education and healthcare became more important. Admission and administrative procedures became influenced by the secular professions, often emphasising professional qualifications over a candidate's religious qualities. The attraction of 'good works' meant that more lay workers, women included, were hired by mission societies, a fact that began to undermine the dominance of ordained clergy on mission stations.

Dutifully recorded?: the historiographic challenge of gendering missions

Mission personnel sought not only to propagate their faith abroad but to communicate the results of their work to sending societies and individual mission supporters. Their letters and reports are an invaluable resource for the historian interested in the details of their lives and work. Any analysis of the socio-economic position, nationality, educational background and denominational identity of both male and female candidates now builds on significant scholarship based on such records.[60] However, in the mission societies' catalogues, women are often absent from view. It is often difficult to find evidence about women's committees, the work of specific female mission workers or deliberations over gender-specific issues, even when evidence suggests that women were involved. That women's work can only be accessed obliquely contrasts starkly with the many references to the 'main' work of the mission, which was defined by men, performed by men and recorded by men.[61]

Of course women are not entirely invisible in either the official archives or in published mission histories. For example, the most significant history of the WMMS, a five-volume work authored by George Findlay and William Holdsworth, published as a centenary memorial, outlined women's work in the field and at home in various supportive roles.[62] But the authors failed to identify women's contributions as a central analytic and structural feature in the growth and development of the mission. Similarly, in their history of the LMS, Findlay and Holdsworth celebrated the work of the 'ladies': '[F]rom the outset – women have played an indispensable part in the actual service', they wrote. 'Not infrequently they have been the initiators, rather than the auxiliaries, in the mission movements of the Church.'[63] Despite this acknowledgment, the space devoted to women's work was slim – maybe 10 per cent of the volumes – and the few women discussed were, as might be expected, the exceptional ones. Either the 'homely' but able ones like Barbara Heck who 'under God brought into existence American and Canadian Methodism',[64] were highlighted, or those fortunate enough to fulfil the 'true calling' of a missionary woman as a missionary wife '[who] became virtually the pastor of the flock of Christ around her dwelling, seeing to its care in her husband's absence, and thus making him free for wider evangelism'. For Findlay and Holdsworth, 'The greatest help our pioneer missionary women lent to the cause of Christ was found in the exhibition of a Christian domestic life, shedding the light of a pure, gentle and beneficial womanhood amid the loathsomeness of heathen society.'[65] The gendered and racially-inflected nature of such assessments is not hard to miss. Ultimately, they concluded, missionary women left 'public advocacy and administration to the other sex [and] took themselves to the drudgery of charity'.[66] Yet we know from other evidence that women would never have characterised their work as 'drudgery' or of a secondary importance. When one looks hard enough, there is plenty of evidence in the missionary archives about women's lives – their beliefs, educational opportunities, family lives and professional attainments – whether formally recognised or not. Women contributed to mission endeavours as mothers, wives and sisters and as single women in their own right whose entrance onto the mission field is seen, somewhat ironically, as a marker of women's 'arrival'. The story of women missionaries requires both the recovery of their diverse contributions and an analysis of how and why their work was so systematically marginalised.

Throughout the nineteenth century missionaries joined the unofficial apparatus that gave substance to the formal British empire as it expanded its political dominance over one quarter of the globe. They participated in a confident evangelicalism, mobilising popular opinion and influencing policy on matters of social justice and the nature of civil society in Britain. Nineteenth-century, mission-generated literature became an important conduit of cultural knowledge about the empire. As lay women came to outnumber ordained clerics, who had dominated the mission field until the last quarter of the nineteenth century, they expanded the notion of what constituted valid mission labour and in so doing transformed the concept of mission professionalism. Women involved with missionary societies also contributed in significant ways to the emergence of a British imperial confidence. They too promoted the belief that non-Christian, non-western societies needed to be 'civilised' through the teaching, social support and preaching of mission societies delivered throughout the formal and informal cultures of empire. While missionaries often criticised – and in turn were criticised by – civil and military imperial authorities, British imperial expansion enabled missions as varied as the LMS and the CIM to send their workers from the Himalaya to Timbuktu and Shanxi.

Female missionaries contributed to the mission enterprise through their work, but also by their 'modelling' of the values of white, middle-class, respectable femininity against which women in other cultures were measured and found wanting. Their efforts were variously rejected, adapted and adopted by those same communities within an institutional framework built on profound inequities. As Antoinette Burton (see Burton, *Burdens of History*) and others have reminded us, British women's empowerment was shaped through systems of institutional privilege and based on unequal valuations of race and place, despite individual belief and choice of action. While there is no simple way to understand the contribution of women missionaries in the imperial project, gendering the study of missions demands a radical re-conceptualisation of the meaning of religion and spirituality in the modern British world. While faith may have restricted women in some ways, it empowered them in others. The Miss Syretts could be who they were, because their faith propelled them to transcend familial, institutional and societal boundaries.

Further reading

Tony Ballantyne, 'Religion, Difference, and the Limits of British Imperial History', *Victorian Studies*, 47/3 (2005), pp. 427–55.

Robert A. Bickers and Rosemary Seton (eds), *Missionary Encounters: Sources and Issues* (Surrey: Curzon Press, 1996).

Fiona Bowie, Deborah Kirkwood and Shirley Ardener (eds), *Women and Missions Past and Present: Anthropological and Historical Perspectives* (Oxford: Berg, 1993).

Andrew Brown-May and Patricia Grimshaw (eds), *Missionaries, Indigenous Peoples, and Cultural Exchange* (London: Sussex University Press, 2009).

Jeffrey Cox, *The British Missionary Enterprise Since 1700* (New York: Routledge, 2008).

Deborah Gaitskell and Wendy Urban-Mead (eds), 'Transnational Biblewomen: Asian and African Women in Christian Mission', *Women's History Review* 17/4 (2008), pp. 489–500.

Mary Taylor Huber and Nancy Lutkehaus (eds), *Gendered Missions: Women and Men in Missionary Discourse and Practice* (Ann Arbor: University of Michigan Press, 1999).

Philippa Levine (ed.), *Gender and Empire* (New York: University of Oxford Press, 2004).

Andrew Porter (ed.), *The Imperial Horizons of British Protestant Missions, 1880–1914* (Grand Rapids: Eerdmans, 2003).

Elizabeth Prevost, 'Assessing Women, Gender, and Empire in Britain's Nineteenth-Century Protestant Missionary Movement', *History Compass* 7 no. 3 (2009), pp. 765–99.

Dana L. Roberts (ed.), *Converting Colonialism: Visions and Realities in Mission History, 1706–1914* (Grand Rapids: Eerdmans, 2008).

Rosemary Seton, *Western Daughters in Eastern Lands* (Santa Barbara: Praeger Publishing, 2009).

Andrew Walls, *The Missionary Movement in Christian History* (Maryknoll: Orbis Books, 1996).

Notes

1 There is no single date for the founding of this organisation, since regional mission societies existed before central bodies were created. The closest estimate, however, might be 1824.

2 Helen Callaway, *Gender, Culture and Empire: European Women in Colonial Nigeria* (London: University of Illinois Press, 1987); Margaret Strobel, *European Women and the Second British Empire* (Bloomington: Indiana University Press, 1991); Vron Ware, *Beyond the Pale: White Women, Racism and History* (New York: Verso, 1992); Timothy P. Foley (ed.), *Gender and Colonialism* (Galway: Galway University Press, 1995); Clare Midgley (ed.) *Gender and Imperialism* (Manchester: Manchester University Press, 1998).

3 See Antoinette Burton, *Burdens of History: British Feminists, Indian Women and Imperial Culture, 1865–1915* (Chapel Hill and London: University of North Carolina Press, 1994).

4 See, for example Kenneth Scott Latourette, *A History of the Expansion of Christianity to the Nineteenth Century*, 6 vols (London: Eyre & Spottiswoode, 1949); Stephen Neill, *A History of Christianity in India: The Beginning to A.D. 1707* (Harmondsworth: Penguin, 1984); G. A. Oddie, *Social Protest in India: British Protestant Missionaries and Social Reforms 1850–1900* (New Delhi: South Asian Books, 1979); Pat Barr, *To China With Love: The Lives and Times of Protestant Missionaries in China, 1860–1900* (Cambridge: Doubleday, 1972); Jean Comaroff and John Comaroff, *Of Revelation and Revolution: Christianity, Colonialism and Consciousness in South Africa*, vol. 1 and *The Dialectics of Modernity on a South African Frontier*, vol. 2 (Chicago: University of Chicago Press, 1991 and 1997); Klaus Fiedler, *The Story of Faith Missions from Hudson Taylor to the Present Day Africa* (Oxford: Regnum Books International, 1994); Robert A. Bickers and Rosemary Seton (eds), *Missionary Encounters: Sources and Issues* (London: Curzon Press, 1996); Andrew Walls, *The Missionary Movement in Christian History: Studies in the Transmission of Faith* (New York: Orbis Books, 1996).

5 Leslie A. Flemming, 'New Roles for Old: Presbyterian Women Missionaries and Women's Education in North India, 1910–1903', *Indian Christian History Review* xx (1986), pp. 127–42; Daniel H. Bays (ed.), *Christianity in China from the Eighteenth Century to the Present* (Stanford: Stanford University Press, 1996).

6 Brian Stanley, *The Bible and the Flag: Protestant Missions and British Imperialism in the Nineteenth and Twentieth Centuries* (Leicester: Intervarsity Press, 1990); Susan Elizabeth Thorne, *Congregational Missions and the Making of an Imperial Culture in Nineteenth Century England* (Stanford: Stanford University Press, 1999); Andrew N. Porter, 'Margery Perham, Christian Missions and Indirect Rule', *Journal of Imperial and Commonwealth History* xix (1991), pp. 83–99; Andrew N. Porter, 'Religion and Empire: British Expansion in the Long Nineteenth Century, 1780–1914', *Journal of Imperial and Commonwealth History*

xx (1992); Andrew N. Porter, '"Cultural Imperialism" and Protestant Missionary Enterprise, 1780–1914', *Journal of Imperial and Commonwealth History* xxv (3) (1997), pp. 367–91; Jeffrey L. Cox, *Imperial Fault Lines: Christianity and Colonial Power in India, 1818–1940* (Stanford: Stanford University Press, 2002). The Position Papers generated by the North Atlantic Missiology Project (NAMP)/ Currents in World Christianity (CWC) are another important resource for literature on missions. Its series *Studies in the History of Christian Mission* (Curzon/ Eerdmans) continues to be published.

7 Mark Noll, David Bebbington, and George Rawlyk (eds), *Evangelicalism: Comparative Studies of Popular Protestantism in North America, The British Isles, and Beyond, 1700–1990* (Oxford: Oxford University Press, 1994).

8 Andrew Porter, *Religion vs. Empire? British Protestant Missionaries and Overseas Expansion, 1700–1914* (Manchester: University of Manchester Press, 2004), pp. 15–38.

9 The EIC banned evangelical activity in South Asia to avoid disrupting existing social and commercial networks from which it hoped to benefit. See David Ryden Beck, 'Does Decline Make Sense? The West Indian Economy and the Abolition of the Slave Trade', *Journal of Interdisciplinary History*, 31:3 (Winter, 2001), pp. 347–74. Clare Midgley argues that female evangelicals effected public change through domestic action in 'Slave Sugar Boycotts, Female Activism and the Domestic Base of Anti-slavery Culture', *Slavery and Abolition*, 17:3 (1996), pp. 137–62.

10 Jane Hunter, *The Gospel of Gentility: American Women Missionaries in Turn-of-the-Century China* (New Haven and London: Yale University Press, 1984), p. 84; Patricia Grimshaw, *Paths of Duty: American Missionary Wives in Nineteenth-Century Hawaii* (Honolulu: University of Hawaii Press, 1989), p. 5; Ruth Compton Brouwer, *New Women for God: Canadian Presbyterian Women and Indian Missions, 1876–1914* (Toronto: University of Toronto Press, 1990), pp. 35–51; Dana Robert, *American Women in Mission: a Social History of their Thought and Practice* (Macon, Georgia: Mercer University Press, 1997).

11 CWM *CP* 1/37 no. 728 Miss E. Bear, Miss M. Chambers to Miss C. Bennett, 29 April 1881.

12 The Church Missionary Society (CMS, est.1799) and the Church of England Zenana Missionary Society (CEZMS, est.1880) are slightly different in that they were voluntary societies that professed loyalty to the established church. They were predated by the SPCK (1699) and the SPGFP (1701). The mission came to be one of the largest of the Protestant missions and central to the life of the Anglican Church both in Britain and abroad. Kevin Ward and Brian Stanley (eds), *The Church Mission Society and World Christianity, 1799–1999* (Grand Rapids: Eerdmans, 2000), pp. 1–2.

13 Leslie Orr MacDonald, *A Unique and Glorious Mission: Women and Presbyterianism in Scotland, 1830–1930* (Edinburgh: John Donald, 2000); see also Rosalind Mitchison and Leah Leneman, *Sexuality and Social Control: Scotland 1660–1780* (Oxford: Basil Blackwell, 1989).

14 Nigel M. de S Cameron, David F. Wright, David C. Lachman and Donald E. Meek, (eds), *Dictionary of Scottish Church History and Theology* (Edinburgh: T & T Clark, 1993), p. 882. Auxiliaries supported general mission activity from 1821; auxiliaries to support women's work were begun nationwide in 1837; women created organisations to support widows and children of missionaries in the 1840s, and to educate the children of missionaries in 1861.

15 Porter, *Religion vs. Empire?*, p. 194.

16 CIM/CP 74, London 1896.

17 Home Councils were established in England, Scotland, Northern Ireland and Eire, Australia (1890), New Zealand (1894), South Africa (1943), Canada and the United States (North American Council established 1888), and Switzerland (1950).

18 Alvyn Austin, *China's Millions: The china Inland Mission and Late Qing Society, 1832–1905* (Grand Rapids: Eerdmans, 2007), pp. 78–110; Peter Williams, 'The Missing Link: The Recruitment of Women Missionaries in Some English Evangelical Missionary Societies in the Nineteenth Century', in Fiona Bowie, Deborah Kirkwood and Shirley Ardener (eds), *Women and Missions: Past and Present* (Oxford: Berg, 1993), pp. 46–50; Rhonda Semple, *Missionary Women: Gender, Professionalism and the Victorian Idea of Christian Mission* (Woodbridge, Suffolk: Boydell & Brewer, 2003); Jeff Cox analyses the numbers of married and single workers in his *The British Missionary Enterprise Since 1700* (New York: Routledge, 2008), pp. 198–212.

19 CIM/LCM 6, 16 December 1890.

20 CIM/LCM 6, 4 August 1891.

21 CIM/LCM 7, 7 June 1892.

22 LCM records a conversation 'about the uneasy feeling about the mission which appears to prevail throughout the country, rumours of which arrive through one or another from time to time … ' CIM/LCM 7, 1 March 1892. Broomhall also mentions occasions when Taylor was castigated by his own missionaries, and by the European press in China, for the mission's deployment of single women; quoted in: Williams, 'Missing Link', p. 49; also see: Fiedler, *Faith Missions*, pp. 299–303; Austin, *China's Millions*, p. 161; and Robert, *American Women*, pp. 204–5.

23 Semple, *Missionary Women* Ch. 5.

24 Philippa Levine, *Feminist Lives in Victorian England: Private Roles and Public Commitment* (Oxford, 1990), pp. 62–63.

25 Andrew Porter, 'Scottish Missions and Education in Nineteenth-Century India: the Changing Face of "Trusteeship"', *Journal of Imperial and Commonwealth History*, 16:3 (1988), pp. 35–57.

26 David Savage, 'Missionaries and the Development of a Colonial Ideology of Female Education in India', *Gender & History* 9:2 (Aug. 1997), pp. 201–21.

27 Grimshaw, *Paths of Duty*, Jocelyn Murray, 'The Role of Women in the Church Missionary Society, 1799–1917', in Kevin Ward and Brian Stanley (eds), *The Church Mission Society and World Christianity, 1799–1999* (Grand Rapids: Eerdmans, 2000), pp. 66–90. Deborah Kirkwood recounts how the gravestone of Ruth Jones at Hope Fountain Mission, Zimbabwe is half the height of that of her husband Rev. Neville Jones. See Deborah Kirkwood, 'Protestant Missionary Women: Wives and Spinsters', in Fiona Bowie, Deborah Kirkwood and Shirley Ardener (eds), *Women and Missions: Past and Present* (Oxford: Berg, 1993), pp. 23–42, here p. 30; Rosemary Seton, 'Open Doors for Female Labourers: Women Candidates of the London Missionary Society, 1875–1914', in *Missionary Encounters*, p. 51.

28 Williams, 'Missing Link', pp. 335–58.

29 Cox, *Missionary Enterprise*, p. 202.

30 Steven Maughan, 'Civic Culture, Women's Foreign Missions, and the British Imperial Imagination, 1860–1914', in Charles Maiser and Frank Trentman (eds), *Paradoxes of Civil Society: New Perspectives on Modern German and British History* (New York: Berghahn Books, 2000), pp. 199–222.

31 Orr MacDonald *A Unique and Glorious Mission*; Jane Haggis, 'Professional Ladies and Working Wives: Female Missionaries in the London Missionary Society and its South Travancore District, South India in the Nineteenth Century' (University of Manchester Ph.D. dissertation, 1991); Williams, 'Missing Link', p. 65. Canadian Presbyterian women had their wings similarly clipped by their General Assembly; see Brouwer, *New Women*.

32 Orr MacDonald, *A Unique and Glorious Mission*.

33 Elizabeth Friend, 'Professional Women and the British Empire, 1880–1940' (University of Lancaster Ph.D. dissertation, 1998), p. 9; Thorne, *Congregational Missions*, pp. 19–21 and 93.

34 Deborah Valenze, *Prophetic Sons and Daughters: Female Preaching and Popular Religion in Industrial England* (Princeton: Princeton University Press, 1985), pp. 50–73.

35 CWM *CP* 38/4 no.1118 Mr W.S. Syrett to Mr Johnson, 9 August 1900.

36 Jane Haggis, 'A heart that has felt the love of God and longs for others to know it: conventions of gender, tensions of self and constructions of difference in offering to be a lady missionary', *Women's History Review* 7 (1998), pp. 171–93.

37 CWM *CP* 38/4 no.1118 Testimonial of Florence Syrett, 9 September 1900.

38 CIM/LCM 6, 4 January 1888, after the death of a member of the mission named Jessie Murray, a series of letters were exchanged between the LC and her family's solicitor. These detail her estrangement from the family on joining the mission. It took until 22 April 1891 for the CIM to agree to return most of the money Jessie had left to the mission back to her family.

39 Moira Jane McKay, 'Faith and Facts in the History of the China Inland Mission 1832–1905' (University of Aberdeen Ph.D. dissertation, 1981), p. 106; CIM/86 *Register of Missionaries*.

40 For each of the societies, candidates were considered to be in their prime between twenty-one and twenty-eight, although a candidate of almost any age was likely to be hired if self-supporting.

41 Free Church of Scotland, *Free Church Rules for Missionaries 1894* (Edinburgh: Free Church Press, 1894), p. 44.

42 'In the case of ladies it is important to ascertain how far they are likely to prove equal to the demands of the married as well as the single state.' CWM *CP* 1/32 no.1087 Victor Barradale, Medical Report of Miss A. Radbone.

43 CWM *CP* 2/28 no. 842 William George Brockway, 12 December, J. Risdon Bennett commenting on Dr F. Miller's Medical Report for Miss F. Abbey, 15 October 1885.

44 CWM *CP* 43/5 no.1254, Myfanwy Wood Medical Report, 1 November 1906, quoted in Seton, 'Open Doors', pp. 50–69.

45 CIM/LCM 5, 16 March and 20 July 1886.

46 Gaitskell points out that while male missionaries were designated as ordained or lay, women were designated as married or single. Deborah Gaitskell, 'Rethinking Gender Roles: The Field Experience of Women Missionaries in South Africa', in Andrew Porter (ed.), *The Imperial Horizons of British Protestant Missions, 1880–1914* (Grand Rapids: Eerdmans, 2003), p. 134.

47 Grimshaw, *Paths of Duty*; Line Nyhagen-Predelli and Jon Miller, 'Piety and Patriarchy: Contested Gender Regimes in Nineteenth-century Evangelical Missions', in Mary Taylor Huber and Nancy C. Lutkehaus (eds), *Gendered Missions: Women and Men in Missionary Discourse and Practice* (Ann Arbor: University of Michigan Press, 1999), pp. 67–112; Jocelyn Murray, 'The Role of Women in the Church Missionary Society, 1799–1917', in Kevin Ward and Brian Stanley (eds), *The Church Mission Society and World Christianity, 1799–1999* (Grand Rapids: Eerdmans, 2000), p. 69.

48 Harold Perkin, *The Rise of Professional Society* (New York: Routledge, 1990), pp. 107–8; Davidoff, *Worlds Between*, p. 260; Leneman, 'No Unsuitable Match'; Strobel, *European Women*; Ware, *Beyond the Pale*.

49 Patricia Grimshaw, 'Christian Woman, Pious Wife, Faithful Mother, Devoted Missionary: Conflicts in the Roles of American Missionary Women in Nineteenth-Century Hawaii', *Feminist Studies* ix (3) (1983), pp. 489–521.

50 Kirkwood reports that the anthropologist Louis Leakey enjoyed generational and gendered status as Kikuyu as a result of his mission upbringing. Deborah Kirkwood, 'Protestant Missionary Women: Wives and Spinsters', in Fiona Bowie, Deborah Kirkwood and Shirley Ardener (eds), *Women and Missions: Past and Present* (Oxford: Berg, 1993), p. 40.

51 Kirkwood, 'Protestant Missionary Women', pp. 23–42.

52 Adrian Hastings, 'Were Women a Special Case?', in Bowie, Kirkwood and Shirley Ardener (eds), *Women and Missions*, p. 115.

53 Ibid. p. 118. Here Hastings is quoting a 1937 report by Margery Perham.

54 SOAS. WMMS Archives. Or, as Deborah Gaitskell has pointed out in her work on South Africa, women's work may indeed have had more effect when they could work from within the framework of wife and mother.

55 Williams, 'Missing Link', p. 54. The CMS hired their first single female missionaries in 1887 for China, and then an increasing number after that. In a remarkable shift, in the 1890s over half of its hires (388 missionaries) were women.

56 Semple, *Missionary women*, 'Appendix'.

57 Ibid.

58 Agnes Palmer was sent to Madras in 1884. Findlay and Holdsworth, p. 51; SOAS, WMMS (SCRR) MMSL X 56 *Ladies' Reports (1881–90) of the WMMS for the year ending December 31st 1881* reports 13 agents employed by the society in 1881, and 10 more mentioned. This also correlates with other societies – Rhonda Semple, 'Ruth, Miss MacIntosh, and Ada and Rose Marris: Biblewomen and *Zenana* workers in Nineteenth-century British Missions to North India', *Women's History Review* 17:4 (Sept., 2008), pp. 561–75.

59 SOAS. WMMS.NT/61 'Notes on the Development of Women's Work in the Home Church'. The women raised £100,000 in two tiers, created a system of campaign and circuit secretaries and a district council, and a place on Synod.

60 C. P. Williams, 'The Recruitment and Training of Overseas Missionaries in England Between 1850 and 1900, with Special Reference to the Records of the CMS, WMMS, LMS and the CIM' (University of Bristol Ph.D. dissertation, 1976); Sarah Potter, 'The Social Origins and Recruitment of English Protestant Missionaries in the Nineteenth Century' (University of London Ph.D. dissertation, 1976); Stuart F. Piggin, *Making Evangelical Missionaries 1789–1858: The Social Background, Motives and Training of British Missionaries to India* (Abingdon, 1984); Williams, 'Missing Link', pp. 43–69; Seton, 'Open Doors', pp. 50–69.

61 WMMS Archives at SOAS, London.

62 G. G. Findlay and William S. Holdsworth, *The History of the Wesleyan Methodist Missionary Society*, 5 volumes (London: Kessinger, 1921), here vol. IV.

63 Ibid, p. 15.

64 Ibid, p. 15.

65 Ibid, p. 16.

66 Ibid, pp. 16–18.

7 Women, religion and reform

Clare Midgley

Reform was a central feature of British society in the nineteenth century. Historians have adopted the label 'Age of Reform' to describe the period up to the Second Reform Act of 1867 and, as historians of women, we can extend this timeframe to include the feminist campaigns launched in the 1850s and reaching fruition with women's suffrage in 1918/1928. 'Reform' first became a key political slogan in the 1780s, when Christopher Wyvill's Association Movement launched a campaign for parliamentary reform. Thomas Clarkson's 1808 history of the campaign to abolish the slave trade helped to turn that campaign into both a moral inspiration and a practical model for many later reform movements. In the Victorian era 'reform' became, in middle-class circles, a self-congratulatory badge of national identity, a sign of Britons' preference for peaceful progress over violent revolution, and a mark of humanitarian virtue. Liberals' appropriation of the reform label, however, ignored both the involvement of Tory paternalists in factory reform and the radical reform agenda of Chartists. Indeed, in the 1830s working-class activists defined themselves in distinction to the middle class around their opposing views on the 1832 Reform Act, factory reform and reform of the poor laws.[1]

The period between 1795 and 1865 has also been labelled 'The Age of Atonement' to signal the immense impact of evangelical religion on British society during this period.[2] In middle-class circles, reform shaded into secular politics at one end and into evangelical philanthropy at the other. The very notion of 'reform' was rooted in religious tradition: Christians from the time of St Augustine had been exhorted to reform their sinful lives, while the sixteenth-century Reformation was foundational to Protestantism.[3] Religious and political motivations intertwined in many reform movements. In the late eighteenth and early nineteenth centuries, for example, Protestant Dissenters campaigned for reforms which would grant them equal religious and political rights, while Evangelical Anglicans such as Hannah More promoted moral reform as a way to revive religion and restore obedience to established authority among the poor.[4] Later, in the Chartist movement, as Anna Clark has noted, men and women drew on an 'eclectic variety of idioms' from constitutionalism to Scripture to support democratic political reform.[5]

Some twenty years ago Brian Harrison pointed to the significance of religion to understanding the genealogy of reform in modern Britain. He stressed how evangelicalism affected 'the whole mode and climate of nineteenth-century reform, even in its more secular dimension', leading the reformer to 'preference for the moral over the utilitarian argument; his preoccupation with the impact of his cause on religious allegiance; his claim to be collaborating with the divine plan'.[6] While these are valuable pointers to the relationship between religion and reform, they set up the archetypal reformer as the middle-class Protestant evangelical male. What, this chapter asks, was the significance to *women* reformers of what Harrison identifies as the evangelical emphases on 'the divinity latent in every human being', 'the moral evolution of mankind' and 'the supremacy of conscience'? What were the implications for *women* reformers of the tying of 'public agitation with private affection' among Nonconformist sects?[7] How, too, can we broaden Harrison's argument through including a consideration of working-class women activists and female religious reform cultures outwith evangelical Protestantism?

Scholarly debate to date on the role of religion in the lives of women reformers in Britain has focused mainly on the motivations of leading middle-class activists from Protestant backgrounds. Writing in 2000 about the 'exemplary' nineteenth-century women activists Elizabeth Fry, Florence Nightingale and Josephine Butler, Anne Summers set out to rectify what she identified as the hitherto underplayed significance of religion in their reforming lives. She attributed this neglect to a combination of factors: feminist secularism, church historians' disinterest in social activism and the focus by social historians on social control rather than religious commitment.[8] Summers's picture was, I think, a little overdrawn. Some nine years earlier Jane Lewis's important study of women social activists in late Victorian and Edwardian England had included a detailed investigation of their religious motivations. Lewis noted that their call to serve others was rooted in perceptions of womanly duty linked to ideas of Christian obligation, and emphasised that they combined the scientific with the spiritual in their approach to achieving a better society.[9] However, other scholars have certainly been reluctant to acknowledge the importance of religion in motivating female reformers. Sybil Oldfield, in her biographical dictionary of British women activists of 1900–50, acknowledged that most saw themselves as Christians but argued that this did not mean Christianity was the main reason for their activism, 'even if they thought that to be the case'. Rather, she preferred to interpret their Christianity as 'the religious manifestation of their humaneness'.[10]

Oldfield seems cavalier in her dismissal of reformers' own understandings of their motivations: as Frank Prochaska has rightly cautioned, 'reading our secular selves into history, it is questionable whether we can fully understand the motives of the faithful in the past, even when we admire their energy and accomplishments'.[11] Yet there is certainly evidence for a shift in the relationship between religion and reform activity as the Victorian provision of social services through Christian voluntary societies gave way to the twentieth-century emphasis on government responsibility. Just as Olive Banks has identified distinctive generations of feminists, so we might trace a genealogy of middle-class female reformers.[12] The activists whose religious motivation is stressed by Summers were born in 1780

(Fry), 1820 (Nightingale) and 1828 (Butler). Lewis suggests that religious motivations were probably strongest for the earliest activist included in her study, Octavia Hill (b.1838), while members of later generations of activists such as Beatrice Webb (b. 1858) and Mary Ward (b. 1851) 'struggled explicitly to reconcile religion with the doubt inspired by science'. Oldfield's humanitarians were part of the generations of reformers who succeeded Webb and Ward. However, rather than a sharp shift from religious to secular approaches to reform in the late nineteenth century, Lewis suggests that 'moral and spiritual concerns remained long after organized religion relaxed its grip'.[13] As Lewis's statement suggests, such discussion of the place of religion in the lives of middle-class women reformers has tended to elide questions of motivation with questions of approach. One aim of this chapter is thus to try to disentangle the two: religious motivation did not necessarily lead to a 'conversionist' approach to reform. My approach is also influenced by my own research which has convinced me of the importance of understanding nineteenth-century reform movements not only within their specific national contexts but also in their imperial, transatlantic and broader transnational dimensions.[14]

This chapter begins by considering the role of religion both in encouraging women's engagement with reform and in setting gendered limits on female activism. Moving on to the organisation of female reform, it tracks the role of religious networks in facilitating the organisation of reform movements at both national and transnational levels. Shifting focus to the level of the individual reformer, the chapter then investigates the extent to which the roots of individual women's commitment to reform lay in their religious backgrounds and beliefs and experiences of religious conversion. It moves on to examine how women's religious beliefs influenced the nature of their approach to campaigning and contributed to the development of gendered languages of reform. Finally, it explores how women's religious beliefs could give them the inner strength to question, criticise and even defy worldly male authority and gender conventions in their pursuit of reform goals.

Organised religion and female reform

Organised cultures of religious dissent and evangelicalism both encouraged active female participation in reform and sought to set gendered limits on its nature and scope. In the late eighteenth century there was a very close link between religious and political or social dissent. Middle-class women linked to rational dissenting/ Unitarian circles were encouraged to participate in political and religious debate by radical ministers such as the Reverend Richard Price of Newington Green near London. Anna Laetitia Barbauld, a member of Price's circle, wrote an influential pamphlet, *Address to the Opposers of the Repeal of the Corporation and Tests Acts* (1790), asserting dissenters' right to hold civic office.[15] Mary Wollstonecraft, who came from an Anglican background, was radicalised by her friendship with Price and her active engagement in politics as a passionate advocate of the rights of both men and women was accompanied by her shift away from Anglicanism and church attendance to a very personal form of religious belief. This belief deeply informed her calls for women's rights. As Barbara Taylor has pointed out, *A Vindication of the Rights of Woman* (1792) is a call for the spiritual redemption of women for whom earthly emancipation is presented as the route to eternal salvation. Wollstonecraft's argument that women would only achieve self-respect through the cultivation of 'a rational will that only bows to God' was indicative of her debt to the rational dissenting tradition which stressed the importance of reason and emphasised women's intellectual capacities.[16]

Some of the new openings appearing for women were, however, closed down as reaction against the French Revolution set in. In the early nineteenth century Unitarian cultural leadership meant that female Unitarians were part of an intellectually vibrant community, but at the same time women's activism was limited by middle-class notions of social propriety as the group sought to compensate for their religious heterodoxy and political unpopularity.[17] Indeed, the issue of sexual propriety led to a split in Unitarian ranks between the more cautious mainstream and the group that Kathryn Gleadle has labelled the 'radical unitarians', around William Johnson Fox and South Place Chapel in London. In the 1830s and 1840s it was this group that kept alive the radical ideas about women's rights promoted by Wollstonecraft, providing the foundations for the reformist women's movement that emerged in the 1850s.[18]

The Society of Friends was another small religious minority that produced a disproportionate number of leading women reformers. Quaker culture was self-contained and, while influenced by broader social trends in gender relations, continued to stand somewhat apart. The denomination became increasingly reliant on women's ministry in the late eighteenth century and early nineteenth century at a time when ministerial roles for women in other Nonconformist denominations was being outlawed. Quaker emphasis on following the inner voice of conscience over worldly authority was even more marked than among other Nonconformists, a position reflected in the lack of formally trained and ordained ministers and manifested in the refusal of Quaker men to take part in military service. Quakers valued social activism over the acquisition of worldly wealth and status, and members of the Society of Friends played leading roles in both the peace and the anti-slavery movements. All this might suggest that Quakerism would be more encouraging than limiting of female reform activism. Indeed, Judy Walkowitz, noting the preponderance of Quaker women on the executive of Ladies' National Association and among the original signatories to the 1870 Ladies' Protest against the Contagious Diseases Acts, suggests an unproblematic link between women's prominent religious role in Quakerism and the Society of Friends' support for women engaging in controversial public causes. She notes that Josephine Butler, the Anglican leader of the feminist campaign, remarked to an Irish Quaker that she wished she had been a Friend as 'She would have gone out on her mission backed *by* the whole strength of the Society and the world would have recognised the *right* of a Quaker woman to speak in public.'[19]

In fact, however, leading Quaker men were ambivalent about their female relatives campaigning on the issue of prostitution.[20] Recent detailed research into

Quaker women's lives has shown that religious freedoms did not necessarily translate easily into freedom to engage in public reform. On the one hand, Quakers did not adhere to the dominant ideology of 'separate spheres' and this helped smooth women's route from private religious commitment into public reform activism. As Sandra Holton notes, home was seen not as a place of retreat from the outside world but rather 'as a relatively open space where religious and ethical values might be enacted' through linking domestic sociability to involvement in social and moral reform. Places of worship, too, were viewed as spaces 'for the enactment of Christian citizenship for women as well as for men'.[21] On the other hand, although the Society of Friends accepted women's ministry it did not accord women an equal role within its organisational structures.[22] In addition, female ministry did not necessarily translate into acceptance of female public speaking outside the space of the meeting house. These limitations on female reform were manifested in the decision of the Quaker-dominated male leadership of the British and Foreign Anti-Slavery Society to ban American female delegates from full participation in the World Anti-Slavery Convention in 1840.[23] Emphasising her belief in the inconsistency of this position, Anna Marie Priestman wrote privately in 1842: 'still we condemn the American practice of women lecturing in public and I do not see where Friends make the distinction between their *condemned* practice and the *approved* one of our own dear female friends'.[24]

Quaker and Unitarian involvement in reform was not only rooted in their dissenting traditions but also fostered by the impact of evangelicalism on British Protestant religious culture as a whole. Evangelicalism encouraged what William Wilberforce called 'Practical Christianity' and it is thus not surprising to find that evangelicals were in the vanguard of the movement for social and moral reform. As Frank Prochaska notes, 'for the great majority of those who imbibed the social gospel of active religion, belief without active benevolence was inexplicable.'[25] This gave an important opening for women, given that the stress on the urgency of bringing about the moral reform of society was combined with an emphasis on middle-class women's role as guardians of morality. Middle-class evangelical women's attempts to reform the poor by imposing their own ideals of domesticity on labouring women met with resistance, however. Among plebeians, 'cottage religion', located in sects which had split off from the evangelical mainstream and which welcomed female preachers, gave powerful sustenance to very different models of femininity.[26]

The concept of 'women's mission' promoted by prescriptive writers such as Sarah Lewis contained an internal paradox: it presented an exalted vision of middle-class women as the 'instruments (under God) for the regeneration of mankind', and at the same time stressed that they should confine themselves to exerting influence from a domestic base.[27] Many women inspired by this vision found ways around the 'separate-spheres' ideology by extending their work into the wider community as philanthropists and social and moral reformers, particularly through a focus on women's mission to women.[28] The appropriate limits of such activities were a matter of debate, disagreement and negotiation. Take the case of anti-slavery. Its definition as a religious and moral question rather than a political issue opened up the possibility for female involvement, but members of the Evangelical Anglican Clapham Sect, who spearheaded the parliamentary campaign, differed in their views as to the acceptability of women setting up their own anti-slavery societies and campaigning in the public sphere. William Wilberforce evoked the authority of the Bible in expressing his disapproval, writing in January 1826: 'All private exertions for such an object become their character, but for ladies to meet, to publish, to go from house to house stirring up petitions – there appear to me proceedings unsuited to the female character as delineated in Scripture.' Hannah More, however, encouraged evangelical middle-class women to move into organised philanthropy and women reformers succeeded in promoting anti-slavery activism as a religious duty. Keen to gain support from the poor, they mobilised the district visiting method of organising that they had developed in earlier evangelical voluntary associations with overt Christian objectives such as the Bible Society and missionary societies.[29]

Large numbers of women from artisan families were drawn into anti-slavery activism through the efforts of these middle-class evangelical women but also through their own membership of Nonconformist chapels. Increasing persecution of missionaries and slave converts in the West Indies stimulated mass anti-slavery petitioning by Nonconformist congregations from 1830 onwards. Prominent Baptist minister, Edmund Clarke, encouraged female participation, and denominational journals publicised female anti-slavery petitions. Around 100,000 women joined their menfolk in signing Wesleyan Methodist anti-slavery petitions in 1833, representing the majority of female members of the denomination.[30]

Female involvement in the temperance movement was even more strongly impelled by evangelicalism. Susie Steinbach has described temperance as 'perhaps the best illustration of the far-reaching potential of evangelicalism',[31] and an examination of the ways in which women's involvement in temperance was rooted in church, chapel and kirk provides an interesting case study of the distinctive ways in which institutionalised evangelicalism shaped female reform culture within different denominational traditions in different parts of Britain. Lesley Orr MacDonald notes that Scottish women's campaigning for reform was 'conducted in the theological and cultural context of Scottish presbyterianism'; under the impact of evangelicalism in the mid-nineteenth century, temperance activity in Scotland became 'central to the lives of huge numbers of women'. It was encouraged by the all-male church leadership who saw it as a seemly cause through which Christian women could use their moral influence to improve Scottish society. However, church-based organisations kept women's activism under strict male oversight and framed temperance as home mission work, discouraging any link to women's rights or legislative reform.[32]

In Wales, where the temperance movement developed rapidly in the 1890s, Ceridwen Lloyd-Morgan notes that 'it was out of the chapels that the temperance movement grew and flourished'. Middle-class chapel-going women led female involvement; in North Wales the majority of the leaders were Calvinistic Methodists. Chapels became arenas of struggle over female leadership: temperance leader Ceridwen Peris later reminisced that 'chapel elders feared the scowls of other members when announcing that sisters were coming there to talk about Temperance'. Women were often not allowed to speak from the pulpit but some male Nonconformist leaders were supportive, and Peris stressed that women's involvement in temperance helped them achieve a stronger, more public role in the chapels where they gained self-confidence, practice in public speaking and experience of organisational work.[33]

Temperance also provided an opportunity for Irish Catholic women migrants to Britain to become active in reform. While Irish Catholic voluntary organisations tended to be male-dominated, in the 1840s many Irish Catholic women living in Britain were drawn into the total abstinence movement by the charismatic priest Father Theobald Matthew, the 'Apostle of Temperance', after he extended his mission from Ireland to England and Scotland, preaching to hundreds of thousands in Lancashire, Yorkshire, London and Glasgow.[34] Other working-class women were drawn into temperance through organisations outside middle-class-dominated church and chapel hierarchies. The total abstinence movement originated with working-class men, and Chartists promoted temperance as part of their campaign to reform working-class domestic life. Temperance appealed to working-class women, often angered by their husbands' squandering of meagre family incomes in the alehouse or victimised by their drunken abuse, and a number of teetotal Female Chartist Associations were established. While the prime motivation was not a religious one, temperance was linked to the broader development of a distinctive Chartist culture that included the formation of Chartist Sunday schools and chapels and asserted working-class independence in the spheres of religion, education and family life as well as politics.[35]

The double-edged role of religious institutions in both fostering and limiting female reform activity is further illuminated through examining the problems which the feminist-led Ladies' National Association (LNA) encountered when trying to gain wider female support for a cause far more controversial than temperance. Formed to campaign against the Contagious Diseases Acts, by 1884 the LNA had 104 local branches around Britain, and in an article on 'Ladies' Branch Associations', leading Quaker activist Mary Priestman stressed the importance of a religious setting as a reassuring social context within which to recruit middle-class women:

> It had been very useful to hold meetings among the attendees of our places of worship when the minister's wife, or some ladies of the congregation will call them together for explanation of the subject, and for prayer and guidance for such an important matter. The influence of religious fellowship and acquaintance is of great value, in overcoming the natural shirking from a painful subject which cannot but be felt by everyone.[36]

However, the LNA paid a price for recruiting women in this way. Local groups were most comfortable with a religious approach stressing rescue work among 'fallen' women and social purity rather than the feminist and libertarian agenda of legislative change promoted by the national leadership. In addition, the organisation does not seem to have made any attempt to recruit support from working-class women through the means of such chapel connections.[37]

Networks of religion and female reform

While male-dominated church and chapel often inhibited the scope of female reform, informal religious networks, both national and transnational, could provide more sustaining webs of connection for women seeking to create independent or radical reform networks. Here the class divide loomed large: working-class women generally lacked both the time and means to move beyond local community networks. For middle-class women, however, such religious networks provided pools of socially concerned individuals and offered a supportive environment from which they could gain strength and succour. Bristol reformer Mary Carpenter's Unitarian network, which spanned Britain and the United States and included both women and men, is described by Ruth Watts as providing crucial 'material, intellectual and moral support' to Carpenter's development as a social reformer.[38] Prison reformer Elizabeth Fry initially met with Quaker women friends to form the Association for the Improvement of Women Prisoners in Newgate before expanding it into an interdenominational national organisation.[39]

Intertwined transatlantic networks of religion and reform were particularly important in encouraging female reformers to radicalise their approach and challenge conventional gender roles. Links with radical Garrisonian abolitionists in the USA from 1840 into the 1860s were developed and cemented through the strong transatlantic religious networks of Quakers and Unitarians. These networks generated a cosmopolitan outlook and operated at multiple levels: formal organisational links, regular overseas tours by ministers and informal correspondence networks of kin and friends. Links with Quaker and Unitarian supporters of William Lloyd Garrison in America encouraged some British women to question the conservatism of the male national leadership of the British and Foreign Anti-Slavery Society (BFASS). Unitarian activist Mary Estlin of Bristol, and Quakers Anne Knight of Chelmsford, Elizabeth Pease of Darlington and Eliza Wigham of Edinburgh became leading British critics of the BFASS and supporters of Garrison. Inspired by radical American women activists, Anne Knight and her friends began to question women's subordinate role in British anti-slavery organisations and to make links between anti-slavery, peace and Chartism. Such developments alarmed the mainstream evangelicals who dominated the transatlantic anti-slavery movement and who sought to discredit their opponents by branding them religious infidels.[40]

Women's temperance campaigning was also profoundly affected by transatlantic religious networks. In the late nineteenth century, the British movement was transformed through the inspiration of American evangelical women: 'gospel temperance' spread through the country like wildfire. The International Order of Good Templars, introduced into Scotland from America in 1869, was the first temperance organisation to assign an equal role to women, and its female officers, public speakers and participators in parades and mixed social and political events contrasted sharply with the limited roles afforded to women within highly patriarchal Scottish church-based temperance organisations. American women were also responsible for introducing strong, women-only temperance organising to Britain. The year 1874 saw the formation in America of the Women's Christian Temperance Union under the militant leadership of 'Mother' Eliza D. Stewart, leader of the Ohio Whisky War, who held prayer meetings outside taverns to get them closed down. Two years later Stewart toured Britain, stimulating the formation of the British Women's Temperance Association (BWTA) in which Margaret Parker, Margaret Bright Lucas and Clare Lucas Balfour became leading figures. The organisation aimed to promote 'the cause of Temperance in the control and ultimate suppression of the Liquor Traffic and thus the moral and religious elevation of the people', and local meetings included hymn-singing and Scripture reading.[41] Its Scottish branch was particularly active and its non-denominational nature encouraged the participation of women from outside the Presbyterian mainstream including Jewish and Quaker women. Inspired by their American sisters, women broke free of the constraints of male church leaders, engaging in petitioning and direct action, which they described as 'God's way of leading them out, often unwillingly and fearfully into the strife'. By 1908 there were 332 branches and over 80,000 members in Scotland.[42]

These developments were associated with the formation of a global women's temperance association under the umbrella of the Women's World Christian Temperance Union which, as Macdonald notes, drew its strength from 'the spirit of sisterhood engendered by the evangelical women's culture'.[43] Under the dynamic leadership of American campaigner Frances Willard, this organisation linked evangelism to political campaigning in a temperance crusade that became a mass women's movement with close associations with the women's suffrage movement. The British organisation, however, was less dynamic and as a result temperance organisations in Australia, Canada and other parts of the empire looked to the USA and not the 'mother country' for inspiration. Evangelical 'church feminism' never became as strong a movement in Britain as in the USA and, in England at least, many temperance workers refused to link their cause with women's suffrage.[44] A major exception to this religion–feminism divide in Britain, however, were the six religious suffrage leagues, discussed in chapter 9.

Personal links with coreligionists overseas inspired a number of leading female reformers. Elizabeth Fry first visited Newgate prison in London at the urging of American Quaker Stephen Grellet.[45] Mary Carpenter was inspired to work with the urban poor by the leading Boston Unitarian social reformer Josiah Tuckerman. Her move in the 1860s into the promotion of secular girls' education in India was the result of the long-standing links between Bristol Unitarians and members of the Brahmo Samaj, a Bengali movement whose project of religious and social reform placed special emphasis on improving the position of Indian women. Its founder Rammohun Roy had died in Bristol while visiting Unitarians there and his tomb became a place of pilgrimage for successive generations of male leaders of the Brahmo Samaj. It was Carpenter's place at the hub of such Unitarian networks that led her to become an international figure in networks of social and educational reformers in India, the USA and Europe.[46]

Links to Protestant reformers in Europe were also important to British women. Elizabeth Fry's work at Newgate inspired visiting German clergyman Pastor Fliedner, leading him to set up a Prussian prison reform organisation and an institution at Kaiserwerth for training Protestant deaconesses as nurses, and later Fry undertook two extensive tours of north-west Europe, successfully promoting her ideas of prison reform among both men and women.[47] Butler also sought to spread ideas for reform throughout Europe from 1875 through founding an international abolitionist organisation to crusade against the repressive treatment of prostitutes, an association that is still active today. Butler's attempts to achieve this through forging links with fellow Protestants met with mixed success, however. As Anne Summers notes, her approach to reform, with its 'personal fusion of liberalism with Christianity', was not easily reproduced in other countries where cross-denominational alliances among liberal Protestants were weak in comparison to the forces of Catholicism, anti-clericism and an evangelical Protestantism which favoured repressive over rights-based approaches to the reform of laws around prostitution.[48]

Religion and the commitment to reform

Examination of the family backgrounds of leading women reformers helps us to plumb deeper into the religious wellsprings of female commitment to reform. Mary Carpenter and Josephine Butler provide two suggestive examples from contrasting religious backgrounds. Both were strongly influenced by the examples of their fathers for whom commitments to religion and reform were closely intertwined, but both also found ways to forge their own paths as female reformers through drawing strength and inspiration from their own deeply personal religious beliefs.

At the root of Mary Carpenter's devotion to reform lay her Unitarian family upbringing and in particular her close relationship to her father Dr Lant Carpenter, anti-slavery activist, educationalist and minister of Lewin's Mead chapel in Bristol. Dr Carpenter was part of that strand of Unitarianism that shared with evangelicals an adoration of Jesus Christ, an approach to religion informed by intense feeling and a warm concern for humanity, but which also upheld the Unitarian denial of original sin, optimism in the goodness and possibilities of humanity to progress through rational education, belief in educating women to make their own judgments, lack of desire to convert others to their faith and a politically liberal outlook. As well as a minister, Dr Carpenter was a progressive teacher, and Mary had an excellent and wide-ranging academic education in her father's boys' school. However, the roots of her decision to devote her life to social reform can partly be traced to the relatively limited vocational opportunities open to her in comparison to her brothers: she lacked access to higher education which could have led her into a career in science like one of her brothers, and she was excluded from the colleges which trained men like her other brother for the Unitarian ministry. Teaching was thus, as for most middle-class women, one of the only occupational routes open to her that was highly valued by the Unitarians.

Her teaching at the non-denominational Lewin's Mead chapel Sunday schools, set up by her father to draw the poor into involvement with the chapel, influenced her future decision to engage in social reform among the children of the poor.[49]

Carpenter's evangelical Unitarianism took a specifically female form that fuelled her passion for reform. Antoinette Burton describes Carpenter's adherence to 'a mid-Victorian religious ethic that emphasized continuous self-sacrifice as the hallmark of the Christian mission to the secular world' and notes that 'the same ethic encouraged female religious enthusiasm that bordered on the ecstatic'. According to Burton, Carpenter experienced tension between the sense of pleasure and satisfaction she gained from her 'blessed work' in reform and her feeling that such a self-denying Christian mission would be a mark of her true piety. It was a tension that seems to have driven Carpenter into the ascetic lifestyle and punishing work schedule which so alienated Frances Power Cobbe when she spent a period at Red Lodge assisting Carpenter in her work.[50]

Josephine Butler's reform efforts were also shaped by an intense religiosity with its roots in her childhood and adolescence. Her parents, John and Hannah Grey, remained within the Anglican communion but were non-sectarian in outlook, had strong links to nonconformity, and were deeply committed to both religious and political liberalism. Caine notes that 'theirs was a non-sectarian religion concerned rather with states of feeling than with particular doctrine ... Far from being a duty, religious beliefs provided the basis for social action and the language in which affection was expressed.'[51] Family life, religion and commitment to liberal reform causes were tied together in the Grey family, as they were to become in the lives of Josephine and her husband. Butler's ecumenical religious background may also have influenced other aspects of her approach to reform: Walkowitz suggests that the experiences of hearing Methodist preaching in her childhood influenced her public oratory as leader of the women's anti-CD campaign, while Helen Mathers notes that, though influenced by evangelicalism, Butler preferred to describe herself simply as a Protestant rather than as an evangelical Anglican.[52]

As a woman, however, Butler's route from this family background onto the public reform stage was not a straightforward one. Like Mary Carpenter she was devoted to a powerful father whose religious beliefs and public work she strove to extend or complement but, in so doing, Caine notes, 'she had to negotiate with a masculine tradition and to establish that she had been specially chosen to undertake a public role'. Her own intense devotion to personal prayer helped her find a way forward, transforming her passionate desire to fight injustice, particularly towards women, into a powerful sense of her personal God-given responsibility to take action. Looking back on her life in 1900 she suggested that she had been chosen to undertake such public work through a religious crisis at the age of only seventeen:

> A strange intuition was given to me whereby I saw as in a vision, before I had seen any of them with my bodily eyes, some of the saddest miseries of earth, the injustices, the inequalities, the cruelties practised by man on woman ... For one long year of darkness the trouble of heart and brain urged me to lay all this at the door of God, whose name I had learned to love.[53]

While this is a retrospective interpretation of an early religious experience, it gives insight into the way in which Butler herself understood the deeply religious well-springs of her reformist zeal. When approached to lead the agitation against the Contagious Diseases Acts, she had immediately thought this might be 'the very work, the very mission I longed for years ago and saw, coming afar off, like a bright star'.[54]

Women's beliefs and approaches to reform

While both Carpenter and Butler drew inspiration from fathers who linked religious belief with reforming zeal, their approach to social and moral reform was very different, reflecting a wider distinction between the Unitarian tradition, with its emphasis on educating individuals so that they could find their own path to religious truth, and mainstream evangelicalism, with its stress on salvationism and conversion.

Mary Carpenter's work among the poor in Bristol was strongly informed by the distinctive Unitarian approach to social reform developed by Joseph Tuckerman. This was a vision of non-proselytising domestic missions to the urban poor which, as Watts notes, stressed 'respect for the unique capacities, needs and value of every individual'.[55] Carpenter set up a ragged school, an industrial school and a reformatory school for girls, Red Lodge, in Bristol. In these she applied the Unitarian approach of the importance of changing the environment to bring about moral improvement, particularly through a type of education which cultivated rational moral principles rather than inculcating religious doctrine.

Carpenter's work promoting secular girls' education in India can be similarly characterised as a religiously inspired mission of secular social reform characteristic of the Unitarian approach. It was an approach that contrasted with the evangelical mainstream and offered a rather different sense of 'women's mission' which does not fit easily within the interpretive frame of 'missionary imperialism'. Though Antoinette Burton represented Carpenter as the archetypal 'imperial feminist' in her influential study of British feminists and Indian women, a closer look at the background of interfaith cross-cultural interchange with the Brahmo Samaj in which Carpenter's project was rooted suggests the need for a more nuanced characterisation of her engagement with India, something I am in the process of exploring myself in current research.[56]

Another leading female social reformer whose approach to reform work among women was informed by the Unitarian tradition was Octavia Hill (1838–1912). Hill's father, James Hill, was a corn merchant and Owenite utopian socialist, who disappeared from the scene when Octavia was only two. The main influences on her early formation as a reformer were thus her mother Caroline Southwood Hill, a writer and progressive educationalist, and her grandfather Dr Thomas Southwood Smith, a well-known Unitarian health reformer involved in campaigns to outlaw child labour and to improve the housing for the urban poor. At her grandfather's home she met leading reformers, intellectuals and writers from Unitarian and other Nonconformist backgrounds. Octavia's mother left her free to develop her own religious beliefs and, while working with her at a co-operative women's craft workshop in London, she came into contact with the Christian socialist circle around F.D. Maurice, a Broad Churchman who influenced her to join the Church of England in 1857 and engaged her to work as a secretary and then as a teacher of young women at his Working Men's College.[57]

Hill's approach to reform was thus rooted both in her upbringing in Unitarian circles and in her later involvement in Christian socialism. Indeed, her Christian beliefs formed the roots of her commitment to social reform and, in common with both Carpenter and Maurice, she fervently believed that self-sacrifice in the service of others was a religious duty. Discussing her calling as a reformer in a letter of 1888 she stated: 'I think our Father especially speaks to those whom he honours by asking them to make sacrifices. I at least have learnt to thank Him so very much for having called me to this terrible out-of-sight work.'[58] In keeping with her Unitarian background, Hill also continued to regard faith as a personal matter and did not see religious conversion as a part of her project of social reform: when she entered into the housing field she made no attempt to interfere with the religious observances of her Irish Catholic tenants.[59]

Hill's views of the role of women as reformers are more complex, however, for here Unitarian and Christian socialist approaches were less well aligned. On the one hand, Gillian Darley points to Hill's support for feminist causes at a period when the women's movement was emerging under the leadership of Unitarian women: she was passionate about improving women's education and increasing their employment opportunities and actively involved with family friend Barbara Leigh Smith Bodichon in the campaign for married women's property rights.[60] On the other hand Jane Lewis argues that Hill accepted F. D. Maurice's view of innate differences between men and women, his belief that men had a greater capacity for understanding and women for feeling, and his conviction that this should inform their wider social roles. However, while this was at odds with the Unitarian tradition of downplaying innate gender differences and emphasising the equal intellectual capacity of women, Maurice's perspective seems to have been adopted by Hill in a way which empowered her own approach to reform. As Lewis notes, for Hill right action depended on depth of feeling, and individual engagement with the poor was the only lasting way to reform their character: by implication women were thus better placed than men to engage in the work of social reform. Driven by this belief Hill became a key figure in national policy-making on housing despite her opposition to granting parliamentary votes for women.[61]

If Carpenter and Hill shared a Unitarian approach to social reform which combined deep religious motivation with scrupulous non-interference in the religious beliefs of those whose lives they sought to improve, both Elizabeth Fry and Josephine Butler were strongly influenced by the mainstream evangelical approach to social and moral reform: a preoccupation with the sinfulness of humanity and the belief that the only true route to salvation and reformation lay in religious conversion brought about by encouraging the individual sinner to open her or his heart to God. Their approach to reform was, however, far from the hierarchical and socially conservative approach of evangelical Anglicans such as Hannah More. Rather, it was deeply egalitarian and radical. As Summers convincingly argues, Fry and Butler shared a 'theological conviction as to the fundamental individuality and equality of each immortal soul' and their respective approaches to prison reform and to the campaign for the abolition of the Contagious Diseases Acts were expressions of 'an evangelical or salvationist egalitarianism' which took a specifically female form of identification with the souls of women who were social outcasts.[62]

The roots of Fry's egalitarian evangelicalism and feminine identification with oppressed women can be found in her Quaker heritage with its stress on lack of deference to worldly hierarchy, pride in a history of religious and social marginalisation and strong female networks. In the case of Butler it lay in a deep questioning of male religious authority. By the time she took on the leadership of the feminist campaign against the Contagious Diseases Acts she was already articulating a feminist theology. Helen Mathers discusses how she used her introduction to the edited essay collection *Woman's Work and Woman's Culture* (1869) to 'preach her own gospel' in which 'she presented her own reading of Christ's teachings on women' arguing that the Church had misinterpreted these and that Christ himself had treated women as of equal importance and had liberated them. Two of the examples of 'liberated' women that she gives are a woman taken in adultery and a prostitute, both of whom Jesus forgave. Butler herself explicitly identified with Mary Magdalene on a number of occasions: 'Looking my Liberator in the face, can my friends wonder that I have taken my place ... By the side of her, the "woman in the city which was a sinner".' Here we can see how Butler's campaigns on behalf of prostitutes were based on a deep religious identification with them rooted in a feminist reading of the Bible.[63]

For both Fry and Butler, as Summers suggests, the ultimate purpose of their reform efforts was 'the re-Christianisation of society'.[64] However, while Fry's emphasis was on the reform of outcast *women* through their conversion, Butler's was on the reform of a *society* that created outcast women, and in this shift of emphasis she created a specifically feminist approach to reform. Whether we choose to describe Butler as a Christian feminist or a feminist Christian, it is clear that her fervent religious beliefs were inseparable from her shock at the ill-treatment of women. Her thoughts in 1869 when considering whether to take up the call for her to lead the women's campaign against the Contagious Diseases Acts indicate that her initial motivation was that of horror on hearing of the abuse of women under the Acts: 'the thought of this atrocity kills charity and hinders my prayers'. A sense of paralysis as both reformer and devout Christian is replaced by finding 'a way of being angry without sin', which then becomes a resolution to take action. Butler prays to God both to keep alive in her a hatred of worldly injustice – 'give me a deep, well-governed, and lifelong hatred of all such injustice, tyranny and cruelty' – and to give her the inner resources to devote her life to the campaign: 'give me that divine compassion which is willing to live and suffer long for love to souls, or to fling itself into the breach and die at once'.[65]

The above exploration of the approaches to reform of just four leading women activists, all from Protestant backgrounds, already exposes the complexity of the relationship between religion and reform. If we broaden out our perspective to encompass Catholic and Jewish women, an even more varied picture of religion and reform in the lives of women in Britain can be developed. Recent work by Carmen Mangion, for example, has revealed that Catholic women religious made an important contribution to religious activism in nineteenth-century England and Wales, reshaping Catholic culture through a combination of evangelism with practical, increasingly professionalised philanthropic work.[66] Among the Anglo-Jewish elite women were active in philanthropic and reform organisations promoting the social, moral and spiritual welfare of Jewish women immigrants newly arrived from Eastern Europe in the late nineteenth century. This was motivated both by philanthropic concern for their co-religionists and by worries that the lack of respectability of the new immigrants was damaging the reputation of all Jews in Britain. As a result, rather than merging their efforts with Christian and feminist organisations working on the issue of child prostitution, they set up their own Jewish 'rescue' organisation in London in 1885 specifically targeted at combating child prostitution and the 'white slave trade' among migrants. Anglo-Jewish women also fostered links with their female co-religionists overseas through organisations such as the Union for Jewish Women, founded in 1902.[67]

Challenging male authority: the role of religion

Strong religious beliefs not only motivated women into entering reform and shaped their approach to reform; they could also provide them with self-justification and the courage to stand up to male authority in asserting their own perspectives on matters of principle as well as in engaging in public speaking to promote reform.

It was this strength of religious conviction and belief in following the inner voice of conscience that gave Nonconformist, middle-class anti-slavery campaigners the courage to challenge the male leadership of the movement on matters of policy, calling in the 1820s for immediate emancipation for slaves in the face of the official policy of the Anti-Slavery Society of amelioration and gradual emancipation. Sheffield women anti-slavery campaigners, under the leadership of evangelical Independent activist Mary Ann Rawson, argued in 1827 for immediate and not gradual emancipation in these terms: 'We ought to obey God rather than man. Confidence here is not at variance with humility. On principles like these, the simple need not fear to confront the sage; nor a *female* society to take their stand against the united wisdom of this world.'[68] The belief in following the inner voice was shared among Dissenters but was arguably strongest among Quakers, and it is therefore significant that Elizabeth Heyrick, who first put forward this radical challenge in her 1824 pamphlet *Immediate, not Gradual Abolition*, was a woman from a provincial family of Rational Dissenters/Unitarians who had become a Quaker 'by convincement'. Her principled stance, as I have discussed in more detail elsewhere, was rooted in both these religious traditions: her rights-based argument echoed the political radicalism of rational Dissenters of the 1790s while her searing critique of the worldliness of a male reform leadership who had 'converted the great business of emancipation into an object of political calculation' drew inspiration from the actions and rhetoric of women members of the Society of Friends who, at just this period, were drawing on their spiritual authority to challenge the 'worldly spirit' of the male-dominated organisational structures of the Society.[69] Later in the nineteenth century Octavia Hill drew similar strength and authority as a social reformer from her deep personal religious beliefs, in particular what Lewis describes as her 'unswerving belief in a divinely revealed right action' and her belief that God, not man, was the only legitimate judge of her work.[70]

Religiously-motivated passion for reform also pushed some leading women reformers into public speaking. Mary Carpenter first found her public voice in 1857 in the sympathetic liberal environment of the National Association for the Promotion of Social Science, but in 1873 in New York she began to speak from pulpits, moving to a direct assertion of her authority as a social reformer within the male-dominated religious institutions of transatlantic Unitarianism. Josephine Butler went further than either Heyrick or Carpenter in challenging patriarchal forms of Christianity and asserting religiously-inspired female reform leadership. In *Woman's Work and Woman's Culture* (1869) she tackled St Paul's teaching that women should be kept subordinate in the Church, arguing that a full understanding of Christ's views of women needed a female as well as a male perspective.[71] Butler looked to history as well as to the Bible for inspirational models of Christian womanhood as her 1885 biography of the fourteenth-century Roman Catholic Saint, Catherine of Siena, shows.[72] Butler saw the campaign against the Contagious Diseases Acts as a religious crusade in which 'we are ready to meet all the powers of earth and hell combined'.[73] Caine, arguing that Butler saw her primary role in the campaigns as 'that of providing spiritual leadership and inspiration', notes that her addresses to the LNA 'in form and in imagery bear a closer resemblance to a great sermon than they do to a campaign speech'.[74] Indeed, her followers and admirers revered her as a 'Christ-like figure'.[75]

Conclusion

From chapel temperance tea parties to saintly national leadership of a feminist campaign, the range of religiously inspired female reform activities in nineteenth-century Britain was, as this chapter has shown, a very wide one. Female involvement in reform in the 'long' nineteenth century was strongly shaped by gendered religious cultures that, as we have seen, were in themselves highly diverse. It was often grounded in intensely personal religious beliefs as well as influenced by family religious background, denominational tradition and the varied impact of evangelicalism on different denominations. Some female reform movements developed within the gendered spaces and structures of formal religious institutions which both encouraged female reform and set limits on its expression, or were associated with the alternative religious cultures developed by plebeian communities and working-class movements. Others were rooted in women's involvement in inter-denominational philanthropic organisations and in webs of support provided by informal religious networks, both national and transnational. Some women accepted and worked within limits set by male religious leaders and patriarchal church structures, while others challenged the gendered hierarchies embedded in both religious and reform cultures.

For many women reformers, 'religion' was not a discrete part of life, confined to Sunday church attendance; it informed their whole outlook on the world, and was inseparable from their humanitarian ethics, their political perspectives and their views on the social position and roles of women. This did not always mean, however, that their reform work was informed by an evangelistic conversionist agenda. Understanding the place of religion in the lives of these nineteenth-century reformers can, in turn, help us to develop more subtle analyses of the shifting nature of female reform in the early twentieth century. While much further work needs to be undertaken on the relationship between religion and female reform in the 1900–40 period, we might posit the declining influence of evangelical approaches to reform and the rising popularity of the approach to reform pioneered by women like Mary Carpenter. There is evidence that religion continued to be a crucial source of personal motivation and strength, but female reformers' public rhetoric increasingly stressed a social scientific approach. It is also clear that from the 1890s alternative moral discourses such as ethical socialism, often referred to as the 'religion of socialism', helped bridge the move from 'religious' to 'secular' approaches to reform among women.[76]

Further reading

S. Holton, *Quaker Women, Personal Life, Memory and Radicalism in the Lives of Women Friends, 1780–1930* (London: Routledge, 2007).

J. Lewis, *Women and Social Action in Victorian and Edwardian England* (Aldershot: Edward Elgar, 1991).

G. Malmgreen (ed.), *Religion in the Lives of English Women* (London: Croom Helm, 1986).

C. Midgley, *Women against Slavery. The British Campaigns, 1780–1870* (London: Routledge, 1992).

S. Morgan, *Women, Religion and Feminism in Britain, 1750–1900* (Basingstoke: Palgrave Macmillan, 2002).

S. Oldfield, *Women Humanitarians. A Biographical Dictionary of British Women Active between 1900 and 1950* (London: Continuum, 2001).

L. A. Orr MacDonald, *A Unique and Glorious Mission. Women and Presbyterianism in Scotland, 1830–1930* (Edinburgh: John Donald, 2000).

A. Summers, *Female Lives, Moral States* (Newbury: Threshold Press, 2000).

J.R. Walkowitz, *Prostitution and Victorian Society. Women, Class, and the State* (Cambridge: Cambridge University Press, 1980).

R. Watts, *Gender, Power and the Unitarians in England 1760–1860* (London: Longman, 1998).

Notes

1 A.R. Burns and J. Innes (eds), *Rethinking the Age of Reform: Britain, 1780–1850* (Cambridge: Cambridge University Press, 2003); T. Clarkson, *The History of the Rise, Progress and Accomplishment of the Abolition of the African Slave-Trade by the British Parliament,* 2 vols (London: Longman, Hurst, Rees, & Orme, 1808); A. Clark, 'The Rhetoric of Chartist Domesticity: Gender, Language and Class in the 1830s and 1840s', *The Journal of British Studies*, 31, 1 (Jan. 1992), pp. 62–88.

2 B. Hilton, *The Age of Atonement: The Influence of Evangelicalism on Social and Economic Thought 1795–1865* (Oxford: Oxford University Press, 1988).

3 J. Innes, '"Reform" in English Public Life: The Fortunes of a Word' in Burns and Innes (eds), *Rethinking the Age of Reform*, p. 74.

4 A. Stott, 'Patriotism and Providence: the Politics of Hannah More' in K. Gleadle and S. Richardson (eds), *Women in British Politics, 1760–1860. The Power of the Petticoat* (Basingstoke: Macmillan, 2000), pp. 39–55.

5 A. Clark, 'The Rhetoric of Chartist Domesticity', p. 64. See also A. Clark, *The Struggle for the Breeches. Gender and the Making of the British Working Class* (Berkeley: University of California Press, 1995).

6 B. Harrison, 'A Genealogy of Reform in Modern Britain' in C. Bolt and S. Drescher (eds), *Anti-Slavery, Religion and Reform* (Folkestone: Wm. Dawson, 1980), pp. 119–48, quote from p. 134.

7 B. Harrison, 'A Genealogy of Reform', pp. 134–35.

8 A. Summers, *Female Lives, Moral States* (Newbury: Threshold Press, 2000), pp. 29–30.

9 J. Lewis, *Women and Social Action in Victorian and Edwardian England* (Aldershot: Edward Elgar, 1991), see especially p. 5.

10 S. Oldfield, *Women Humanitarians. A Biographical Dictionary of British Women Active between 1900 and 1950* (London: Continuum, 2001), introduction, p. xiv.

11 F. Prochaska, *Christianity and Social Service in Modern Britain. The Disinherited Spirit* (Oxford: Oxford University Press, 2006), p. 2.

12 O. Banks, *Becoming a Feminist. The Social Origins of 'First Wave' Feminism* (Brighton: Wheatsheaf Books, 1986).

13 Lewis, *Women and Social Action*, p. 11.

14 C. Midgley, *Women against Slavery. The British Campaigns, 1780–1870* (London: Routledge, 1992); C. Midgley, *Feminism and Empire. Women Activists in Imperial Britain, 1790–1865* (London: Routledge, 2007).

15 K. Gleadle, 'British Women and Radical Politics in the Late Nonconformist Enlightenment, c. 1780–1830' in A. Vickery (ed.), *Women, Privilege and Power. British Politics, 1750 to the Present* (Stanford: Stanford University Press, 2001), pp. 123–51.

16 B. Taylor, *Mary Wollstonecraft and the Feminist Imagination* (Cambridge: Cambridge University Press, 2003), pp. 93–94ff. The quote from Wollstonecraft is from J. Todd and M. Butler (eds), *The Works of Mary Wollstonecraft* (London: Pickering & Chatto, 1989), Vol 5: *A Vindication of the Rights of Woman*, p. 105.

17 R. Watts, *Gender, Power and the Unitarians in England 1760–1860* (London: Longman, 1998).

18 K. Gleadle, *The Early Feminists. Radical Unitarians and the Emergence of the Women's Rights Movement, 1831–51* (Basingstoke: Macmillan, 1995).

19 J.R. Walkowitz, *Prostitution and Victorian Society. Women, Class, and the State* (Cambridge: Cambridge University Press, 1980), p. 122, quoting letter from Josephine Butler to a 'Friend', 24.121, no. 99, Mary Estlin Collection, Dr Williams' Library, London.

20 Holton, *Quaker Women. Personal Life, Memory and Radicalism in the Lives of Women Friends, 1780–1930* (London, Routledge, 2007), pp. 168–71.

21 Holton, *Quaker Women*, pp. 54, 2.

22 H. Plant, '"Subjective Testimonies": Women Quaker Ministers and Spiritual Authority in England: 1750–1825', *Gender & History*, vol. 15, no. 2 (August 2003), pp. 296–318.

23 Midgley, *Women against Slavery*, pp. 158–67.

24 Holton, *Quaker Women*, p. 118, quoting letter from A.M. Priestman to J. Pease, 13 May 1842, 7 July 1842, Millfield Papers 22/01 (a), Clark Archive, C & J. Clark Ltd, Clark, Street, Somerset (emphasis in original).

25 Prochaska, *Christianity and Social Service*, p. 6.

26 D.M. Valenze, *Prophetic Sons and Daughters* (Princeton: Princeton University Press, 1985).

27 S. Lewis, *Women's Mission*, 2nd edn (London, 1839), p. 12.

28 A. Tyrrell, 'Women's Mission and Pressure Group Politics in Britain, 1825–60', *Bulletin of the John Rylands University Library*, 63 (1980), 194–230.

29 Midgley, *Women against Slavery*, quote from R.I. and S. Wilberforce, *The Correspondence of William Wilberforce*, 5 vols (London: John Murray, 1838), vol. 11, letter dated 31 January 1826. For the rise of organised female philanthropy see F. K. Prochaska, *Women and Philanthropy in 19th Century England* (Oxford: Clarendon Press, 1980).

30 Midgley, *Women against Slavery*, pp. 62–65; 83–86.

31 S. Steinbach, *Women in England 1760–1914. A Social History* (London: Weidenfeld & Nicolson, 2002), p. 140.

32 L.A. Orr MacDonald, *A Unique and Glorious Mission. Women and Presbyterianism in Scotland, 1830–1930* (Edinburgh: John Donald, 2000), quotes from pp. 233–34 and 248.

33 Ceridwen Lloyd-Morgan, 'From Temperance to Suffrage?' in A.V. John (ed.), *Our Mothers' Land. Chapters in Welsh Women's History 1830–1939* (Cardiff: University of Wales Press, 1991), pp. 135–58, quotes from pp. 140, 149, 151; source of Peris quote (original in Welsh, translated in Lloyd-Morgan p. 149): Ceridwen Peris (Alice Gray Jones), *Er Cof a Gwethfawrogiad o Lafur Mrs Mathews* (Liverpool [1931]), p. 14.

34 R. Samuel, 'The Roman Catholic Church and the Irish Poor' in R. Swift and S. Giley (eds), *The Irish in the Victorian City* (London: Croom Helm, 1985), p. 267.

35 Schwartzkopf, *Women in the Chartist Movement*, pp. 195, 197, 257–58, 133.

36 Walkowitz, *Prostitution and Victorian Society*, p. 134, original source of quote: Mary Priestman, 'Ladies' Branch Associations', *National League Journal* (London), 1 December 1881.

37 Walkowitz, *Prostitution and Victorian Society*, p. 134.

38 R. Watts, 'Mary Carpenter: Educator of the Children of the "Perishing and Dangerous Classes"' in M. Hilton and P. Hirsch (eds), *Practical Visionaries. Women, Education and Social Progress 1790–1930* (Harlow: Pearson Education, 2000), pp. 39–51, quote from p. 43.

39 Summers, *Female Lives, Moral States*, p.32.

40 Midgley, *Women against Slavery*, pp. 121–77; K.K. Sklar and J.B. Stewart, *Women's Rights and Transatlantic Antislavery in the Era of Emancipation* (New Haven: Yale University Press, 2007).

41 L.L. Shiman, '"Changes are Dangerous!" Women and Temperance in Victorian England' in G. Malmgreen (ed.), *Religion in the Lives of English Women* (London: Croom Helm, 1986), pp. 193–215, quote from p. 205 (original source: British Women's Temperance Association, minutes of the executive committee meeting, 3 December 1879, in headquarters of the British Women's Total Abstinence Union in London). For Balfour see: Kristin Doern, 'Equal Questions: The "Woman Question" and the "Drink Question" in the Writings of Clara Lucas

Balfour, 1808–78' in S. Morgan (ed.), *Women, Religion and Feminism in Britain, 1750–1900* (Basingstoke: Palgrave Macmillan, 2002), pp. 159–76.

42 MacDonald, *A Unique and Glorious Mission*, p. 257 (original source: *The British Women's Temperance Association – Scottish Christian Union: Its Origins and Progress 1878–1908* [1908], p. 26).

43 Macdonald, *A Unique and Glorious Mission*, p. 256.

44 Ibid., p. 207.

45 Summers, *Female Lives, Moral States*, p. 32.

46 R. Watts, 'Mary Carpenter: Educator of the Children of the "Perishing and Dangerous" Classes' in M. Hilton and P. Hirsch (eds), *Practical Visionaries. Women, Education and Social Progress 1790–1930* (Harlow: Pearson Education, 2000), pp. 39–51; H. W. Schupf, 'Single Women and Social Reform in Mid-nineteenth-century England: the case of Mary Carpenter', *Victorian Studies*, 17, March 1974, pp. 301–17; M. Carpenter, Memoir of Joseph Tuckerman, DD (1849); M. Carpenter, *The Last Days in England of the Rajah Rammohum Roy* (1866).

47 J. Rose, *Elizabeth Fry. A Biography* (London: Macmillan, 1980), chs 9, 10. See also A. van Drenth and F. de Haan, *The Rise of Caring Power: Elizabeth Fry and Josephine Butler in Britain and the Netherlands* (Amsterdam: Amsterdam University Press, 1999).

48 Anne Summers, 'Introduction: the International Abolitionist Federation' in *Women's History Review*, 17:2 (2008), pp. 149–52.

49 Watts, 'Mary Carpenter'; Schupf, 'Single Women'.

50 A. Burton, 'Fearful Bodies into Disciplined Subjects: Pleasure, Romance and the Family Drama of Colonial Reform in Mary Carpenter's "Six Months in India"', *Signs*, 20, 3 (Spring 1995), pp. 545–74, quotes from p. 551.

51 B. Caine, *Victorian Feminists* (Oxford: Oxford University Press, 1992), p. 159.

52 Walkowitz, *Prostitution and Victorian Society*, p. 115; Helen Mathers, 'The Evangelical Spirituality of a Victorian Feminist: Josephine Butler, 1828–1906', *Journal of Ecclesiastical History*, Vol. 52, no. 2 (April 2001), pp. 283–312, especially p. 287.

53 J.E. Butler, *An Autobiographical Memoir*, ed. G. and L. Johnson (Bristol, 1909), pp. 15–16, as quoted in Caine, *Victorian Feminists*, p. 162.

54 Butler, *An Autobiographical Memoir*, p. 91 (quoting diary from Sept 1869), as quoted in Caine, *Victorian Feminists*, p. 163.

55 Watts, 'Mary Carpenter', quote from p. 41.

56 A. Burton, *Burdens of History. British Feminists, Indian Women, and Imperial Culture, 1865–1915* (Chapel Hill: University of North Carolina Press, 1994).

57 G. Darley, *Octavia Hill: a Life* (1990); Lewis, *Women and Social Action*, Ch. 1.

58 O. Hill to S. Cockerell, Jr, 8.10.88, Item 60, D. Misc. 84/2, Octavia Hill Papers, Marylebone Public Library, London, as quoted in Lewis, *Women and Social Action*, p. 28.

59 G. Darley, 'Octavia Hill', *Oxford Dictionary of National Biography* (Oxford: Oxford University Press, 2004–9), online version accessed 17/4/09.

60 Ibid.

61 Lewis, *Women and Social Action*, Ch. 1.

62 Summers, *Female Lives, Moral States*, Ch. 2, quotes from p. 121.

63 Mathers, 'The Evangelical Spirituality of a Victorian Feminist', p. 303; the quote from Butler she cites is from G.W. Johnson and L.A. Johnson, *Josephine Butler: An Autobiographical Memoir* (Bristol, 1913), p. 16.

64 Summers, *Female Lives, Moral States*, p. 124.

65 Mathers, 'The Evangelical Spirituality of a Victorian Feminist', p. 288, reproducing quote in Johnson and Johnson, *Autobiographical Memoir*, p. 91.

66 C. M. Mangion, *Contested Identities. Catholic Women Religious in Nineteenth-century England and Wales* (Manchester: Manchester University Press, 2008)

67 L. Marks, 'Carers and Servers of the Jewish Community: The Marginalized Heritage of Jewish Women in Britain', *Immigrants and Minorities*, 10 (1991), pp. 106–27; L.V. Marks, *Model Mothers: Jewish Mothers and Maternity Provision in East London, 1870–1939* (Oxford: Clarendon, 1994); L.G. Kusmack, *Woman's Cause: The Jewish Woman's Movement in England and the United States, 1881–1933* (Columbus, Ohio: Ohio State University Press, 1990), pp. 48, 53–62, 82; R. Burman, 'Middle-class Anglo-Jewish Lady Philanthropists and Eastern European Women: The First National Conference of Jewish Women, 1902' in J. Grant (ed.), *Women, Migration and Empire* (Stoke on Trent: Trentham Books, 1996), pp. 123–49.

68 *Report of the Sheffield Female Anti-Slavery Society* (1827), p. 10 (emphasis in original).

69 C. Midgley, 'The Dissenting Voice of Elizabeth Coltman Heyrick: An Exploration of the Links between Gender, Religious Dissent and Anti-slavery Radicalism' in E.J. Clapp and J.R. Jeffrey, *Women, Dissent and Anti-Slavery in Britain and America, 1750–1865* (Oxford: Oxford University Press, forthcoming); Midgley, *Women against Slavery*, pp. 103–18; K. Corfield, 'Elizabeth Heyrick: Radical Quaker' in Malmgreen (ed.), *Religion in the Lives of English Women*, pp. 41–67; H. Plant, 'Subjective Testimonies'. Quote is from E. Heyrick, *Immediate, not Gradual Abolition* (London, 1824), p. 18.

70 Caine, *Victorian Feminists*, quote from p. 29.

71 Mathers, 'The Evangelical Spirituality of a Victorian Feminist', p. 304.

72 J.E. Butler, *Catherine of Siena* (4th edn, London, 1885), quote from p. 67; Summers, *Female Lives, Moral States*, ch. 4, pp. 66–77; E.J. Yeo, 'Protestant Feminists and Catholic Saints in Victorian Britain' in E.J. Yeo (ed.), *Radical Femininity. Women's Self-Representation in the Public Sphere* (Manchester: Manchester University Press, 1998), pp. 127–48.

73 Mathers, 'The Evangelical Spirituality of a Victorian Feminist', p. 301, quoting from J.E. Butler, *Recollections of George Butler* (Bristol, 1892), p. 223.

74 Caine, *Victorian Feminists*, p. 152.

75 J. Walkowitz, *Prostitution and Victorian Society*, p. 114, quoting Mary Priestman, n.d., Butler Collection.

76 See for example C. Steedman, *Childhood, Culture and Class in Britain. Margaret McMillan 1860–1931* (London: Virago, 1990), especially pp. 12–13.

8 'The Word made flesh'
Women, religion and sexual cultures

Sue Morgan

In this chapter I want to address a 'double deficiency' of particular pertinence to this volume, namely the absence of any sustained analyses of the contributions made by women or by religion to the history of modern sexuality. It is striking, given the ubiquity of religion and sex on the contemporary British cultural agenda, that the histories of these two phenomena have had so little to say to each other. Despite the importance attached by Foucault to religious and confessional legacies of intimate self-discovery, historians have focused principally on legal and medical-scientific constructions of sexuality in a relatively uncritical recapitulation of modernity as a secular process.[1] This chapter therefore offers an alternative conceptual framework with two interrelated lines of argument which run, *inter alia*, throughout. I show that nineteenth- and early-twentieth-century discourses of sexuality and religion were deeply imbricated in the making of modern British culture. As John Maynard has observed, both discourses reflect 'humans' and societies' need to make some sense out of their greatest experiences' and so 'tend to parallel each other in articulating larger structures of meaning or organisation'.[2] Analyses that depict religion as antithetical to sexuality, therefore, misunderstand their interdependence as modes of truth-telling and self-making. And, following Lesley Hall's assertion of a hitherto neglected but 'substantial and important tradition ... of women writing about female sexuality',[3] I suggest that it was not the clerical elite but the prominent participation of laywomen as orators, writers and activists throughout the period that ensured religion remained an influential arbiter of sexual behaviour well into the twentieth century.

While renowned sexologists such as Havelock Ellis struggled to find publishers for their controversial theories, thousands of marriage and sex advice manuals authored by devout Christian women flooded late Victorian middle- and working-class culture via youth movements, diocesan organisations, philanthropic societies and the armed services. Invariably excluded from ecclesiastical debates on moral issues, women spoke and wrote from the sidelines of institutional power in a process Foucault describes as 'reverse discourses' or 'discourses of resistance'. Although not always as radical as such terminology implies, churchwomen were none the less empowered to communicate more freely and perhaps more compellingly on sexuality by virtue of their gendered occupation of a distinctive space between ordained institutional and lay popular religious cultures.

Anna Clark's definition of sexuality (the one used in this chapter) as 'the desires, relationships, acts and identities concerned with sexual behaviour'[4] indicates the protean nature of the subject. Ranging from the private emotional, psychological and imaginative aspects of individual desire to the wider social and political implications of moral conduct, sexuality functioned as a prism through which women and men constructed a kaleidoscope of ideas and values. As this chapter illustrates, whatever their religious or denominational affiliation, women's ideas on sex invariably formed part of a broader set of political and theological agendas. Through a fervent belief in the sacredness of the human body and its life-giving powers (Christ had, after all, assumed a corporeal form), sexual purity was deemed vital not only to a successful marriage but to the social transformation of the nation itself. Women invariably wrote in non-scientific genres such as prescriptive literature, novels, religious essays and marriage or sex education manuals and this has proved a key factor in their marginalisation from 'official' histories of sexuality.[5] Such a heavily didactic source-base raises interesting theoretical questions concerning the tenuous relationship between fictive ideals and actual sexual practices as well as the inherent class tensions surrounding the impact and reception of such texts. Although we cannot 'know' the intimate behaviour of men and women of the past, we can try to discern the 'contradictory conditions which pushed ... sexuality in different directions'.[6] In this chapter, therefore, I combine insights from gender history and queer theory in order to explore the diverse and often conflicting constructions of hegemonic and dissident sexualities articulated by women of faith and the changing circumstances of their production.

Historiographically, no focused studies of the modern Church and changes in sexual morality exist, except as part of wider treatments of the 'Nonconformist conscience' or Victorian social reform.[7] Kenneth Boyd's *Scottish Church Attitudes to Sex, Marriage and the Family, 1850–1914* (1980) was an early exception but written from an exclusively institutional perspective with no reference to women. Social and cultural historians have certainly referred to religion but overwhelmingly in conjunction with its regulatory role, notably through the late-Victorian campaigns for social purity. Feminist historians have produced contradictory assessments of the impact of religious belief upon nineteenth- and early-twentieth-century sexual politics, acknowledging, on the one hand, the power of faith to mobilise women and provide them with a persuasive language of 'moral outrage' whilst, on the other, critiquing religion's overall tendency to limit the radicalism of feminist ideas.[8] One important area of burgeoning research, however, is on the interconnectivity between religious and sexual dissidence. In a useful overview of recent scholarship, H. G. Cocks has drawn attention to the way in which early scientific discourses on sex such as sexology and psychology were 'intimately linked to non-scientific discourses like spiritualism';[9] leading British sex reformers such as Havelock Ellis and Edward Carpenter, for example, embraced the concepts of a 'higher consciousness' and a 'spiritual-evolutionary understanding of the self'.[10] Conversely, as Joy Dixon has explained, psychics, theosophists and mystics assimilated new sexological and psychoanalytic theories of sexuality through 'an elaborate constellation of spiritual beliefs'.[11] Spiritualism and psychical research were important influences in the history of homosexuality with both Ellis and Carpenter forging strong connections between the 'homosexual temperament and unusual psychic or divinatory powers'.[12] As Hall has also made clear, there were in fact powerful commonalities of approach between sexology, feminism and social purity, not least in challenging the prevailing assumption of male sexual privilege as a 'natural' law.[13] By ignoring this and by overlooking sexual science's debt to the surrounding religious climate of moral agitation at the *fin-de-siècle* historians' understanding of the reciprocity of religious and sexual discourse has been seriously impeded.

   This chapter makes its intervention into these stimulating debates and seeks to remedy the said 'double deficiency' by tracing a genealogy of women's activism and writing around sex, focusing on selected individuals from mainstream Christian affiliations so as to complement existing scholarship on alternative spiritualities.[14] Part One examines the dominant heterosexual culture of marriage and reproduction and the changing constructions of marital female sexuality produced throughout the period. Part Two assesses women's anti-vice work including campaigns around prostitution, male sexuality, sex education and venereal disease, whilst Part Three explores the way in which religion could function as an important legitimating site for the expression of less conventional forms of sexual behaviour such as celibacy and intimate female friendships.

PART ONE

From passionless to passionate: marriage, reproduction and the heterosexual imperative

Heterosexuality was, of course, the dominant sexual culture for women and men, naturalised and normalised in the quotidian experience of married life. Between 1800 and 1940 numerous marriage law reforms undermined theological interpretations of holy matrimony as an indissoluble, divine sacrament, and altered the meanings attributed to the intimate relations between husband and wife. The three stated purposes of matrimony in Anglican liturgy – procreation, the prevention of fornication and mutual pleasure and comfort – were all profoundly sexual. But marriage was also regarded as a primary metaphor for the divine/human encounter. As the Anglo-Catholic spinster Ellice Hopkins wrote in 1899, marriage was the 'very type of the union of the soul with God [and] of Christ with his church'.[15] How then did women of faith respond to the controversies over marriage during the period and what changing constructions of female sexuality did they proffer?

Passionless femininity?

Historians generally acknowledge that the eighteenth and early nineteenth centuries witnessed a radical scientific disaggregation of female and male physiology – what Karen Harvey has described as the birth of 'two modern opposite sexes'.[16]

Coterminous with this, dominant representations of female sexuality shifted from that of lasciviousness to domestic virtue. Hannah More described woman's power as moral rather than sexual in 1799 in her influential *Strictures on the Modern System of Female Education* and, by the mid-1800s, women had been de-eroticised, reimagined as sexually passive and characterised primarily by their maternal qualities. Images of the virtuous, self-sacrificing wife and mother permeated nineteenth-century prescriptive and poetic literature, most famously in the works of Patmore and Ruskin. The venereologist William Acton's oft-quoted dictum in 1857 that 'the majority of women ... are not much troubled with sexual feeling of any kind'[17] was less a pronouncement on the female libido than a reassurance to anxious male newly-weds, but it illustrates the by then hegemonic status of passionless femininity. The contribution of this sexual ideology and the critical role of Evangelical morality to an emergent Victorian middle class has been extensively discussed.[18] To what extent women internalised such cultural expectations is debatable but, as the disastrous Parisian wedding night of Archbishop Benson and his wife Mary indicated, the potential trauma of marital sex for virginal, sexually ignorant brides was considerable.[19]

But the ideological work of sexuality developed unevenly. Nineteenth-century sexual discourse was nothing if not paradoxical – even Hannah More's 'ultra-virtuous' evangelical novel *Coelebs in Search of a Wife* (1809) was not 'completely unerotic'.[20] Religious reflections on marriage frequently emphasised its gratificatory as well as prophylactic functions with Quakers, Congregationalists, Unitarians and mystical sects such as the Swedenborgians promulgating conjugal pleasure as 'natural, legitimate and God-given'.[21] Despite the passionless ideal, pious women were not averse to expressing themselves sensually either. The intimate letters of Methodist Sarah Sugden to her husband in 1851, for example, desired them both 'entwined in each other's embrace'.[22]

By the 1880s campaigns for increased moral education and reform were gaining momentum, giving women increased opportunities to discuss sexual purity and marital relations. Using the language of religious ecstasy to depict the sexual act was a common rhetorical device throughout the period. The celebrated birth control campaigner Marie Stopes described mutual orgasm as 'the apex of rapture'[23] in her best-selling work *Married Love* (1918). What historians have failed to recognise, however, is that this discursive 'spiritualisation of sex' was employed by religious women such as the purity reformer Ellice Hopkins and the Christian physiologist Elizabeth Blackwell almost forty years earlier. Hopkins described conjugal intimacy in a strongly pro-sensual manner as an anticipation of the delights of heaven, where 'the soul surrender[ed] herself ... to the eternal Loveliness, as a bride surrenders herself in unutterable love to her husband'.[24] And in *The Human Element in Sex* (1884) Blackwell's observation that those 'who deny sexual feeling to women ... quite lose sight of ... [the] immense spiritual force of attraction which exists in so very large a proportion in their nature'[25] was an important early acknowledgement of the existence of female sexual desire. But spiritual beliefs shaped women's attitudes to the body and sex in highly contradictory ways. In direct contrast to the pro-sensual rhetoric of Blackwell and

Hopkins, for example, the feminist theosophist Frances Swiney regarded the physicality of sex as crude and degrading to women. Swiney's distinctive gynaecocentric spirituality posited women as more highly developed beings than men and her League of Isis, established in 1907, propounded an anti-corporeal philosophy of astral, 'psychic love', controlled by women.[26]

Late-nineteenth- and early-twentieth-century Britain was witness to a series of wide-ranging critiques of conventional marriage by feminists, sexologists, 'New Women' and Freethinkers. Feminist debates concerning women's right to bodily autonomy within marriage were actively supported by Christian women. Both Hopkins and the evangelical feminist Josephine Butler declared the practice of male 'conjugal rights', non-consensual sex and perpetual enforced motherhood as immoral and detrimental to women's health. The renowned Anglican feminist preacher Maude Royden went so far as to propose to the House of Laity in 1923 that women's vow of obedience be expunged from the marriage service.[27] When Freethinkers denigrated the hypocritical 'phallic ceremonials of Christians'[28] in favour of voluntary unions free from either church or state interference, however, churchwomen rejected such notions outright. It was 'pathetically absurd to see the ... whole noble future of the human race, sacrificed to their unruly wills and affections, their passions and desires',[29] tiraded Hopkins in 1899 against the Freethinker and New Woman writer Mona Caird. As Laura Schwartz has shown, the vitality of an anti-religious, Freethinking strand of female intellectual thought at the *fin-de-siècle* has been badly neglected by historians. Women like Caird, Annie Besant and the lesser known Harriet Law (an ex-Baptist) proffered an alternative model of sexual relations based on individual autonomy without necessarily 'endorsing a cynical amoralism'.[30] For religious feminists, however, 'experimental marriages' not only sanctioned male profligacy and increased women's economic vulnerability, they contradicted the very essence of Christian love – permanency – or, as Royden put it: the 'desire to give and burn one's ships'.[31]

Divorce was similarly regarded as abhorrent because of the indissoluble, sacramental status of marriage. Both the 1888 and 1908 Lambeth Conferences reaffirmed the Established Church's refusal to recognise divorce outside of adultery or permit remarriage in the spouse's lifetime. According to Tim Jones, the Church's belief in a 'one flesh' ideology of marital sex meant that remarriage not only raised the spectre of non-reproductive sexual activity but also incest, as seen in Anglo-Catholic opposition to the Deceased Wife's Sister Act of 1907.[32] The social and familial ruptures caused by the First World War meant that the number of annual divorces increased significantly after 1918. Religious responses became increasingly diffuse, ranging from outright condemnation to a more controversial acceptance of divorce on the grounds of individual conscience, a position not unlike that held by secular sex radicals. At one end of the spectrum, Cordelia Moyse and Caitriona Beaumont have shown how the Mothers' Union (MU), the largest Anglican women's organisation with over 500,000 members by 1939, revised its constitution in 1912 for the purposes of disqualifying divorced women from membership, regardless of their maternal status. At times, the MU's stand against divorce was more uncompromising (and uncomprehending) than that of the Church itself.

The only reason they did not publicly oppose the 1923 Matrimonial Causes Act (which finally remedied women's inequitable position concerning grounds for adultery) appears to have been because of the Archbishop of Canterbury's direct instructions, not because they approved of the legislation itself.[33] Although from the same religious denomination, Maude Royden's attitude to divorce took a very different line. She argued in her landmark work *Sex and Common-Sense* (1921) that Christ's teaching was clear: a husband and wife should experience 'a love so pure, so true and so fine as to be regarded as a gift from God'. That the church should compel those 'between whom there is no real marriage at all' to stay together on the basis of a legally registered contract was the very antithesis of Christ's message. If, after careful thought, both parties were in agreement that their relationship was not all that Christ had intended, wrote, Royden, that was a 'decent and sufficient reason for declaring that the marriage is dissolved'.[34] Christian women's theologies on the sanctity of marriage, it seems, could result in radically conflicting solutions.

Birth control and non-reproductive sexuality

Birth control, perhaps more than anything else, signalled the onset of sexual modernity. Yet for many contraception undermined irretrievably the sanctity of marriage by separating the sexual act from its procreative function. As Eva from Cardiff, who married in 1933, remarked, '[Y]ou were flying in the face of God when you decided you weren't going to have children.'[35] In late-nineteenth- and early-twentieth-century Britain a marked reduction in family size indicated widespread knowledge of basic family limitation techniques. Coded adverts for abortifacients and 'the removal of obstructions' were placed in several Welsh religious papers including the Baptist *Seren Cymru* (Star of Wales) and the Methodist *Y Goleuad* (The Light).[36] The desperate plight of working-class mothers suffering multiple pregnancies was exposed in publications such as *Maternity: Letters from Working Women* (1915), causing, during the 1920s, religious feminists including Royden to support socialist campaigners like Dora Russell in trying to obtain free contraceptive advice for poorer women.[37] But birth control had always been a controversial cause to promote, as the 1877 obscenity trial of the then secularist Annie Besant had demonstrated.[38] In 1908 and again in 1920 the Anglican bishops denounced unequivocally 'deliberate tampering with nascent life'[39] on theological, medical and racial grounds. Evidence heard by the National Birthrate Commission set up in 1916 to examine the declining birthrate, however, showed more varied religious responses. Whereas Catholic and Jewish representatives exhorted the spiritual merits of sexual abstinence and opposed contraception outright, Free Churchmen expressed stronger support for the 'moral independence'[40] of individual choice. As these examples suggest, institutional religious responses to contraception would continue to remain at best obfuscatory throughout the interwar years.

The carnage of the First World War altered discussions on contraception and marital relations dramatically. Stopes's runaway success *Married Love* and its sequel *Wise Parenthood* (1918) presented birth control as a key component of modern companionate marriage and a fulfilling sex life. Her influence can be clearly discerned amongst the miscellany of attitudes to divorce and contraception expressed at the ecumenical Christian Conference on Politics, Economics and Citizenship (COPEC) of 1924.[41] COPEC was a noteworthy but ultimately unsuccessful attempt to initiate a new era of Christian social action led by the then Bishop William Temple. Nevertheless, its Commission on 'The Relations of the Sexes' merits greater consideration by gender and religious historians than so far received. Marcus Collins has described COPEC as a firm endorsement of 'Christian mutualism',[42] an important strand of postwar sexual thought. According to Collins, Christian mutualism sought to replace the outmoded sex antagonism conveyed by the Victorian rhetoric of the separate spheres with an alternative understanding of marriage as a partnership of mutual equality and intimacy. Yet the Commission's conclusions were rather more contradictory than he suggests. There were certainly those who argued (as did Stopes) that the glory of parenthood was best secured through intentional and responsible family planning. But, for many others on the Commission, allowing 'a mechanical contrivance [to] interfere with the most sacred and intimate of human functions' provoked a 'genuine repugnance'.[43]

Stopes's own spirituality was complex. Her mother's dour Scottish Presbyterianism had led her to disassociate herself from formal religion while remaining convinced of her powers of direct communication with God.[44] Judging from the grateful letters in *Mother England* (1929) she successfully revitalised many married couples' sex lives, but her antipathy towards institutional religion could backfire. In 1925 she declared, 'I am out for a much greater thing than birth control. I am out to smash the tradition of organised Christianity.'[45] But Stopes underestimated the moral grip of institutional religion in local communities such as that exercised by the Welsh chapels upon the industrial valleys of South Wales. Twenty years earlier this area had been witness to an extraordinary religious revival. Margaret Douglas recounts how, on a visit to Abertillery to celebrate Britain's first hospital birth control clinic, Stopes sniped at the hypocrisy of local ministers who condemned family limitation techniques in others while practising it themselves. A 'long and vitriolic correspondence' ensued in the *South Wales Gazette* between Stopes and the Rev. Ifor Evans, Abertillery's most charismatic preacher. Evans's appeal to the proud godliness, fecundity and nationalism of Welsh mothers won the day. The clinic was closed in 1926, 'killed by gossip' according to Stopes but by 'the Welsh religious element'[46] according to the clinic's beleaguered nurse, Naomi Jones.

Religious organisations such as the Catholic Women's League (CWL) also vehemently opposed birth control. As Beaumont has explained, the CWL mounted a concerted campaign throughout the 1920s and 1930s, disrupting meetings of birth control campaigners in Bolton and Birmingham and setting fire to one of Stopes's mobile clinics in Bradford.[47] The leading Anglo-Catholic gynaecologist and eugenicist Mary Scharlieb, whose eminent medical career on behalf of the welfare of British and Indian women earned her a CBE in 1917, was also an ardent opponent of birth control. Contraception was emblematic of an egotistical secularism which prioritised possessions over children and regarded marriage as an excuse for 'unlimited sexual gratification',[48] she argued. Scharlieb joined the League of National Life in 1926 (the year she was made a Dame of the British Empire) to help galvanise Anglo-Catholic resistance to birth control but, by 1930, Anglican and Catholic hierarchies had parted company on the issue. Whereas the papal encyclical *Casti Connubii* condemned contraception outright as 'shameful and intrinsically vicious',[49] the 1930 Lambeth Conference took a reluctant but momentous step in accepting that, if 'decided on Christian principles',[50] methods other than abstinence for limiting parenthood might be used. This concession aligned the Church of England more closely with an increasing cultural emphasis on marital sexual compatibility by the 1930s. Whether or not it was quite the triumph for 'Christian mutualism' that Marcus Collins claims is arguable. Clergymen such as the Scottish Presbyterian A. Herbert Gray and the Methodist Leslie Weatherhead had certainly established themselves by this time as proponents of an eroticised theology of marriage, but far more research is required before the impact of this discourse can be adequately assessed.[51]

So what of women's own writings on female sexual pleasure? To what extent was 'passionless femininity' displaced by the 1920s? Stopes's *Married Love*, with its descriptions of female orgasm and 'rhythmic sex-tide', is rightly seen by historians as a defining text of sexual modernity. But, as was suggested in the texts by Blackwell and Hopkins, a genealogy of religious authorship on sexual desire can easily be traced back into the 1870s. Hopkins's refusal to regard human corporeality and marital sex as either sinful or indecent was especially pioneering. Drawing upon an incarnational theology, she argued in 1879 that the body was not the seat of evil but the 'temple of the Holy',[52] and that its life-giving functions were an integral part of human spiritual development. Forty years later, in a significant reversal of the Victorian passionless ideal, Maude Royden, A. Herbert Gray and others brought these anti-Manichaean ideas to completion. The notion that women should be 'indifferent to ... [or] repelled by, the physical side of marriage', argued Royden in her essay on 'Modern Love' (1917), was a 'horrifying superstition'.[53] Indeed, 'sex-love', she argued elsewhere, was 'the most perfect form of union that human beings know'.[54]

Of course, twentieth-century texts on female sensuality utilised a far more varied and explicit sexual vocabulary than the more symbolic spiritual language available to a Victorian generation of writers. Royden frequently combined sexological and psychological theories of heterosexual pleasure with Christian notions of spousal intimacy. Fascinatingly, it was not religion that she paid homage to for liberating women and men from 'the veil' of sexual shame and suppression, but modern psychology: 'If Freud has taken the roof off the stuffy home in which civilised men have lived their sexual life', she wrote, 'he may be said to have taken the roof off the world for women.'[55] Yet if the descriptive categories of sex changed, the gendering of passion remained a constant. From William Acton's work onwards, it seems, the intense, short-lived drama of male sexual energy was everywhere contrasted with women's slower sexual arousal. 'Passion comes to a man with greater violence ... like a storm at sea', wrote Royden in 1921, but 'the depths are not stirred'. By contrast, women's sexual needs were 'less violent, and more persistent ... like that silent, uninterrupted thrust of an arch against the wall [or] ... of a dome on the walls that support it'. Slowly and imperceptibly she explained – in what is an intriguing analogy of the implosion of female sexual frustration with the demise of religion – these pressures would 'thrust outwards till the walls on which they rested gave way and the church was in ruins'.[56]

As defensive of married women's autonomy as Royden and others were, however, sexual compatibility could be a problematic gospel. Lesley Hall has shown, for example, that postwar discussions on enhanced sexual enjoyment generated considerable anxiety in men around pleasuring their wives.[57] In addition women, once constrained by sexual modesty, were now expected to be 'naturally' erotic. Whether passionless or passionate, religious discourses of female sexuality thus remained firmly linked with procreation and the heterosexual imperative still held fast.

PART TWO

'An end to secrecy': moral regulation and the gospel of social purity

It was in the regulation of *extra*-marital sexual activity, primarily through working with prostitutes, that religious women were confronted with more visible public cultures of sex. Under the banner of 'social purity' (a movement promoting higher personal and social standards of sexual morality) thousands of women from Christian and Jewish traditions, along with women from smaller movements such as Theosophy, publicly condemned the iniquities of the sexual double standard. Purity activism extended from the mid-Victorian campaign to repeal the Contagious Diseases (CD) Acts with their controversial regulation and medical examination of prostitutes to the defence of unmarried mothers' rights in the interwar period. As a populist movement it peaked in the 1880s and 1890s, prompted by sensationalist portrayals of urban sexual vice such as Rev. Andrew Mearns's 'The Bitter Cry of Outcast London' (1883) and William Stead's 'Maiden Tribute of Modern Babylon' (1885). Nevertheless, as a largely female-dominated network of rescue and vigilance associations the efforts of purity women were truly herculean. The indomitable Ellice Hopkins, social purity's chief architect and protagonist, published prolifically on sexual purity and undertook tours of major British towns promoting the cause for over a decade. Again, the Congregationalist feminist and editor of the purity periodical *The Vigilance Record*, Laura Ormiston Chant, addressed over 400 meetings in a single year and conducted a well-publicised anti-obscenity campaign against the Empire Theatre in London in 1895.[58] Purity also took on very different national characteristics. The Irish Catholic vigilance associations of the early 1900s, for example, regarded the English presence as a contamination of national morals, as did Welsh claims to 'hen wlad y menyg gwynion',[59] although Chant was still invited to address Aberdare's local purity association. Purity women were simultaneously castigated by clergymen for their scandalous activity and parodied by the national press as 'Prudes on the Prowl'.[60] Yet their militant religious vocabulary dominated late-Victorian sexual politics, with the successful passage of the Criminal Law Amendment Act in 1885 and the repeal of the CD Acts in 1886 marking a severe, albeit temporary, defeat for the medical and political elite.[61]

Historiographically, purity's overwhelmingly religious motivations, unprecedented use of the criminal law to police sexual morality and incongruous relationship with liberal feminist ideology has not endeared it to historians. Despite more nuanced analyses from scholars such as Lesley Hall, Frank Mort, Alan Hunt and Lucy Bland, the depiction of women purity activists as socially discriminatory, morally coercive and sexually prurient persists. Hopkins and colleagues such as the temperance campaigner, Sarah Robinson, have been attributed responsibility by historians for untold psychosexual damage upon an entire generation of Victorian youth although, as we have seen, Hopkins's message was not a strictly anti-sensual one. Contradictory historical readings of social purists as conservative perpetrators of a massive propagandist assault on the sexual habits of the working classes (Judith Walkowitz's classic reading) or radical feminist critics of the sexual double standard (advanced by Sheila Jeffreys) illustrate not only the complexity of the purity movement itself but the difficulties posed by religion as an analytical category for historians.[62] I examine some key aspects of purity reform below in order to unpack these dilemmas further.

Prostitution and the moralising of masculinity

The closure of brothels and the prosecution of male sexual offenders was a primary focus of social purists, many of whom were formerly active in the repeal campaign led by the charismatic Josephine Butler. Rescue work was not for the faint-hearted; Sarah Robinson records being violently sick after brothel-visiting in Aldershot.[63] Nonetheless, inspired by Christ's forgiveness of the fallen Mary Magdalene, religious women such as the Salvationist Florence Soper Booth pioneered some of the 'largest, most effective and ... innovative rescue organizations in Britain'.[64] Throughout the nineteenth century such institutions underwent a broad uneven shift from the larger-scale Catholic and Anglican penitentiaries to smaller less punitive homes developed by women like Soper Booth, Hopkins and the Jewish Association for the Protection of Girls and Women (JAPGW), established in 1885. Prostitution, which functioned more as a term of censure than as an observational category, provoked considerable anxiety concerning the regulation of working-class women's sexual behaviour. Lynda Nead has shown that mid-Victorian iconography of prostitution was dominated by two contradictory images: the pitiful outcast and the polluted instrument of male lust and urban filth.[65] Defenders of the CD Acts drew upon the latter image, presenting the prostitute as a serious danger to military health and public order. As William Acton explained in a purposefully dichotomised construction of pure and impure womanhood, 'we are not legislating for "soiled doves" but for a class of women that we may almost call unsexed'.[66] Religious women themselves were not immune to the fears of cross-class contamination that loomed large in Victorian imaginings of prostitution. Irish Catholic penitentiary discourse frequently contrasted the virginal purity of women religious ('the spotless lily') with that of the diseased prostitute ('the foul-smelling weed'[67]). Even Hopkins's self-description as a rescue worker was, significantly, that of 'a sewer rat'.[68]

Dominant purity readings of the prostitute throughout the period under discussion, however, were those of a tragic victim of male sexual abuse. The narrative of seduction was an effective, persuasive trope which adhered to respectable ideals of female sexual innocence through a familiar religious formula of temptation, fall and salvation, as fictionalised in Elizabeth Gaskell's path-breaking novel *Ruth* (1853). The seduction myth leant itself readily not only to effective critiques of men's behaviour but also to class- and race-based antagonisms. Aristocratic men were frequently targeted by campaigners like Stead, for example, and debates on sexual morality featured heavily in early-twentieth-century anti-alien agitation. As Lara Marks has made clear, although Jewish prostitution in London's East End was relatively small-scale, it frequently elicited wider anti-semitic confrontation. This caused divisions within the Jewish community itself between the established middle-class Anglo-Jewish population and more recent Eastern European immigrants. Events such as the Jack the Ripper murders in 1888 and the 'white slavery' scares of the early 1900s stigmatised Jewish men as seducers and procurers of innocent Anglo-Saxon women. Consequently, Jewish women in philanthropic organisations such as JAPGW took a leading role in opposing the white-slave traffic.[69]

Portraying men as sexual abusers allowed reformers like Butler and Hopkins to espouse a radical feminist theological narrative which subverted the responsibility of Eve/women for the fallen state of human nature. In many ways historians' emphases upon the ideological differences between Butler's liberal individualism and Hopkins's legally-enforced social morality have obscured the very real similarities in the two women's sexual theologies. Butler certainly prioritised the prostitute's sovereignty over her own body more than Hopkins and her suspicion of government interference made her a more direct predecessor of Maude Royden who described prostitution as the ultimate 'exploitation of the individual for the advantage of the State'.[70] As is well known, by the 1890s Butler considered the National Vigilance Association (NVA) as overly coercive and Hopkins's efforts as 'rather mechanical'.[71] Yet despite such differences both were outraged by what they perceived as the Church's cowardly silence on moral issues. It was society at large, they argued, not the prostitute that required redemption: 'It is *we*, not they, who ought to cover our faces and blush as they pass us by; for the sin of society is ours',[72] declared Butler. Both rejected outright W.E.H. Lecky's view of the 'ignoble and degraded' prostitute as the 'most efficient guardian of virtue',[73] preaching instead a message of solidarity with their fallen sisters: 'The degradation for these poor unhappy women is … dishonour done *to me*', wrote Butler, 'it is the shaming of every woman in every country in the world.'[74] Hopkins opposed night-time visits to brothels as if 'these poor girls [we]re a distinct race, not altogether human', and was highly critical of co-workers who accepted the necessity of an outcast class of women: 'Let us prove by our actions that our womanhood is ONE', she urged in *Work in Brighton* (1878), 'that a sin against our lost sisters is a sin against us'.[75] Perhaps most radically, in her poem 'The World's Outcast', Hopkins reconfigures the Holy Trinity as composed of Christ, the prostitute and the slave walking to an undeserved crucifixion.[76] The extent to which such protestations of sisterhood were compromised by what Alan Hunt has described as a condescending, class-inflected 'maternal feminism'[77] has been extensively debated. Purity reformers undoubtedly practised dubious forms of moral surveillance over poorer families; Hopkins thought little of working-class parents' rights when she helped to drive through legislation in 1881 that sanctioned the forcible commitment of children of women suspected of being prostitutes to certified industrial schools. And the seduction motif itself was ultimately flawed as its emphasis upon vulnerability and powerlessness effected a blatant infantilisation of working-class women's sexual and maternal agency.

Yet social purity's critique of male profligacy simultaneously mirrored the radical sexual rhetoric of late-Victorian feminism. The movement's focus on male chastity was arguably Hopkins's greatest weapon in terms of successfully persuading the Anglican ecclesiastical hierarchy to speak out on sexual morality. In a combined effort to re-Christianise masculinity and re-masculinise Christianity she co-founded the ecumenical White Cross Army (WCA) in 1883 with Bishop Lightfoot of Durham and inspired Archbishop Benson to establish the Church of England Purity Society for men in the same year. Three hundred pitmen assembled at the WCA's inaugural meeting in Bishop Auckland, Durham, pledging to 'treat all women with respect' and 'maintain the law of purity as equally binding upon men and women'.[78] Twenty years later overseas demand from the military and support from colonial bishops resulted in the dissemination of millions of White Cross pamphlets throughout the British Empire and the USA with the majority titles written by Hopkins. She conducted a relentless campaign on behalf of the WCA, speaking in numerous cities throughout Britain including Edinburgh, Cardiff, Dublin, Manchester and Cambridge to gatherings of between 800 and 2,000 men; Lightfoot later attributed her with having done 'the work of ten men in ten years'.[79] Such was the delicacy of the subject matter though that, rather than establishing separate associations, White Cross sections were invariably incorporated into existing religious groups. In Scotland, for example, White Cross material was absorbed successfully into the programme and teaching of Young Men's Guilds and the YMCA.[80] In a hard-hitting critique of male promiscuity, Hopkins charged working-, middle- and upper-middle-class men with sexually exploiting women and challenged them to exercise equivalent standards of chastity and self-restraint. It was a message that, delivered by an unmarried woman, should never have succeeded – but it did. It succeeded because of Hopkins's melodramatic, romantic depiction of sexual continence as the pre-eminent battle of the modern heroic knight; because she wooed working men with the suggestion that sexual purity would 'protect their own class from wrong'[81] and form part of their demand for wider political rights, and because she combined an impassioned appeal to the sacred dignity of the male body with a resounding call for British imperial advance. National progress was rooted in the sexual purity and chivalry of its manhood, she argued in *The Power of Womanhood* (1899). It was only those races 'that respect their women ... that are the tough, prolific, ascendant races, the noblest in type ... and the most fruitful in propagating themselves'.[82] At times her discourse slipped into an unreflecting ethnocentrism. In the pamphlet *The British Zulu* (1891), for example, the term 'Zulu' was synonymous with sexual depravity. 'Are you quite sure', she asked her readers, 'that the average English-man has got much beyond the level of the dirty savage?'[83] Intuitively, in an influential, often imperialist reconstruction of Christian masculinity, Hopkins connected the sexual firmly to the gendered ecclesiastical order. In so doing she persuaded the Church to abandon its 'policy of the ostrich' and begin speaking out on sexual issues.

Educating for sex

In the early 1900s social purity entered a different phase, focusing on sexual morality not as an end in itself but as a key determinant of national fitness and racial regeneration. Influenced by emerging eugenic ideas on scientific methods of racial improvement, purity reinvented itself through a new medical-moral discourse of 'social hygiene'. Positive sex education was increasingly prioritised as the route to healthy parenthood and a fitter population. As the purity campaigner Rév. James Marchant wrote in the 1911 *Manifesto of the National Council for Public Morals*, the real solution to national immorality lay not in the law but in educating men and women 'into physiological knowledge and lofty ideals of marriage'.[84] From Elizabeth Blackwell's *Counsel to Parents* (1878) onwards, purity women had produced some of the earliest sex education texts for children as a means of promoting positive sexual awareness. Too many mothers sent their daughters 'like ignorant sheep into a world of wolves', complained Hopkins, 'with all the forces of hell arrayed against us we want robust virtue, not helpless innocence'.[85] But nineteenth-century manuals frequently remained at the level of moral homiletics. Women from both mainstream and alternative religious backgrounds described human reproduction in veiled terms through examples drawn from natural history and the animal kingdom.[86] Not until after the First World War did texts such as Scharlieb's *Youth and Sex* (1919) present detailed physiological discussions of female puberty, menstruation and the function of the ovaries and womb. Two features of purity's commitment to the sex education aspect of social hygiene are worth noting briefly. First was its heavily female, domestic authorship. Whether because of the period's general discrediting of male sexuality or an assumption that women's greater reproductive role gave them a moral authority that fathers lacked, 'the reassignment of sex education to mothers'[87] was, according to Claudia Nelson, a radical rebalancing of male and female power within the family. As one late-Victorian writer for the Social Purity Alliance explained, mothers may be reticent to discuss such matters but 'there is no other to whom she can or ought to transfer her burden of responsibility'.[88] Second, sex education illustrated purity campaigners' willingness to engage with new scientific theories such as evolutionism and eugenics. These appropriations were always complex. Tensions around the relative importance of 'heredity' and 'environment' in shaping human nature, for example, remained permanently unresolved. But social purity's commitment to a more rational scientific approach to reproduction, to the choice of partners based on spiritual and moral purity rather than status or affluence, and to an increased role for women in the selection process, was powerful and broad-based enough to harness the energies of women as spiritually diverse as the High Churchwoman Hopkins and the Theosophist Frances Swiney.[89]

Combating venereal disease

Widespread public anxiety over levels of venereal disease formed a mainstay of early-twentieth-century sex education. Back in 1879 in an essay on *Social Purity*, Josephine Butler had warned readers about upper-class men who brought the 'hideous morbid fruits of ... former impurity'[90] into the marriage bed. In the 1890s 'New Woman' novels such as Sarah Grand's *The Heavenly Twins* (1893) exposed the devastating effects of syphilis on families to a shocked readership. In the early 1900s two texts on venereal disease written by women from very different religious and political perspectives were published: the militant feminist Christabel Pankhurst's *The Great Scourge and How to End It* (1913) and Anglican churchwoman Louise Creighton's *The Social Disease and How to Fight It. A Rejoinder* (1914). Whereas Pankhurst's *The Great Scourge* has become a feminist classic, Creighton's response to it has gone largely unnoticed. Yet *The Social Disease* is another valuable example of churchwomen's determination to engage with public debates on sexuality no matter how controversial the subject. Creighton had gained national prominence on purity issues by the 1890s through her successful presidency of the National Union of Women Workers (NUWW) and her involvement with the London Council for the Promotion of Morality.[91] As widow of the highly respected Bishop of London, Mandell Creighton, she was elected with Mary Scharlieb to serve on the Royal Commission on Venereal Disease (RCVD) in 1914.

According to James Covert, *The Social Disease* – largely informed by her work on the RCVD – established Creighton's credentials as a 'moderate feminist'.[92] Like Pankhurst she demanded an equal standard of chastity for women and men, and saw female suffrage (which she had only supported since 1906) as vital to securing laws for women's protection. In a detailed medical discussion of the symptoms of venereal disease Creighton criticised what she regarded as Pankhurst's sensationalist, unsubstantiated presentation of the facts and somewhat 'morbid absorption in its horrors'.[93] The struggle against sexual diseases could only be won, she wrote, if women approached it in a 'calm and sober spirit'.[94] But the difference between the two women was more than one of presentation.

Politically and theologically Creighton had little patience with the separatist approach of radical feminists: 'I think in all this purity question', she remarked, 'women suffer from looking at it too much from the woman's point of view and not considering the man's side.'[95] In accordance with Christ's teaching on the equal value and dignity of all human beings, urged Creighton, women should endeavour to understand the male as well as female perspective. Ironic then, given such sexual political inclusivity, that the book was condemned by one reviewer as an 'attack on males'.[96]

The Social Disease supported and advocated the RCVD's final recommendations of preventive sex education and a state-funded, nationwide system of confidential medical treatment for sufferers, strategies that were implemented in the Public Health (VD) Act of 1917. According to Lesley Hall, over a million patients were seen in 1919 alone, and by 1924 deaths registered due to syphilis underwent a 'dramatic reduction'.[97] Purity organisations such as the National Campaign for Combating Venereal Disease continued to pursue educational action during the interwar years. Despite the previously discussed anti-divorce, anti-birth-control campaigns of the MU and CWL, however, the campaigning power of social purity declined, although its rhetoric never completely disappeared. As Kath Holden has shown, support for unmarried mothers by the Salvation Army, JAPGW and the Church of England Moral Welfare Council drew upon purity-style discourses of male seduction well into the 1930s, defending single women's rights to keep their babies and 'bring up their illegitimate children as active and useful citizens rather than a source of shame'.[98]

In summary, purity constructions of sexuality were undoubtedly paradoxical, forging at best a creative coalition of feminist demands for the elimination of the sexual double standard and religious expectations of male self-restraint. The feminist dimension was not always uppermost, as Vivienne Richmond's study of the Girls' Friendly Society, a purity organisation for girls in service which held virginity as an absolute criterion of membership until 1936, has shown.[99] Social purity was thus a profoundly ambiguous sexual discourse, potentially transformative and oppressive in equal measure. Yet it proved a powerful vehicle through which women were inspired to challenge institutional religious fears of scandal and take a lead in publicly breaching the silence on sex.

PART THREE

Beyond heteronormativity: single women, celibacy and same-sex desire

In such an uncompromisingly heterosexual culture, celibacy and same-sex desire attracted considerable social ridicule and repulsion from both religious and secular sources. This final section considers the way in which religion could also facilitate emotional, discursive and physical spaces for the expression of these two marginalised sexualities as meaningful ways of life.

Female celibacy

Nothing underlined the heteronormativity of women as wives and mothers more than portrayals of single women as frustrated, unproductive members of society. As the novelist Winifred Holtby asked cryptically in 1934, 'Am I growing embittered, narrow, prudish? ... life seems very pleasant; but I am an uncomplete frustrated virgin woman.The psychologists, lecturers and journalists all tell me so, I live under the shadow of a curse.'[100] The sexual pathologising of female celibacy reached its zenith in the interwar years, but anxieties over the demographically 'redundant' woman stretched back to the 1850s. In Charlotte Yonge's *The Daisy Chain* (1856) a life of abject poverty and selfless service to family was the ultimate aspiration for her spinster heroine, Ethel May. But as the only alternative to marriage sanctioned historically by the Christian tradition and attributed superior spiritual authority within Roman Catholicism, celibacy could be a positive sexual choice rather than a default position. Female religious cultures such as philanthropic networks, sisterhoods and missionary activity enabled many single women to transform their lives into public forms of purposeful spiritual and social service.

Yet celibacy's associations with Roman and Anglo-Catholic practices meant that it became a target of virulent anti-Catholic propaganda during the nineteenth century. In what Ellis Hanson has described as the 'pornography of Puritanism',[101] the sexual dangers of convent life and the challenge to the British Protestant family idyll presented by permanent vows of celibacy and auricular confession were widely debated. Even Bishop Tait, a keen advocate of Anglican sisterhoods, prioritised parental authority over daughters' rights of admission.[102] Celibacy was also widely regarded as an unnatural sexual condition: 'Very clearly has nature marked celibacy with disapproval', wrote Annie Besant in 1889, 'the average life of the unmarried is shorter ... the unmarried have a less vigorous physique, are more withered ... more peevish, more fanciful.'[103] Late-nineteenth- and early-twentieth-century commentators as religiously and politically diverse as Havelock Ellis, Mary Scharlieb, Marie Stopes and Dora and Bertrand Russell emphasised the psychological and physical dangers of sexual abstinence as well as its unpatriotic nature. Indeed, women who sought to avoid motherhood were regarded as a danger to the survival of the race.[104] Female chastity was one thing, female celibacy quite another.

Within this hostile context, religious women's defence of the single life included a powerful reconfiguration of femininity. This included rejecting the heterosexual impulse as the summation of female existence whilst raising important ontological issues concerning the relationship between the spiritual and sexual aspects of identity formation. Central to this was the ability to build a meaningful identity and career outside of marriage. Because a woman does not fulfil her sexual nature, wrote Royden, 'it is a monstrous fallacy to affirm that ... she ceases to have any reason for existence'. '[I]t is not upon marriage that the value of any human soul depends.'[105] Single women, it was claimed, although not biological mothers, exercised vital roles as moral and social mothers of humanity. As Hopkins explained, 'some women are called to be mothers of the race, and to do the social work which is so necessary to our complex civilization'.[106] The Unitarian reformer Mary Carpenter urged women who were 'mothers in heart, though not by God's gift on earth [to] bestow their maternal love [on] wretched moral orphans',[107] and in 1907 Baptist writer Marianne Farningham reminded readers that there were 'hosts of women with unfulfilled hearts and unemployed hands ... who love[d] Christ and wish[ed] to serve him'.[108] Even Mary Scharlieb, who believed that sexual abstinence caused physiological 'atrophy of the organs', argued in *The Bachelor Woman* (1918) that celibacy was a valuable means of spiritual self-development, providing 'unequalled opportunities for the practice of mysticism'.[109]

Without husbands or children, female friendships were critical to the emotional survival of single women. As the Quaker Georgina Kirkby observed in 1853, 'every good woman needs a companion of her own sex'.[110] Women's friendships were encouraged by influential conduct writers including Sarah Stickney Ellis and the Jewish novelist Grace Aguilar as a means of cultivating feminine virtues.[111] Religious cultures and their homosocial networks provided abundant opportunities for deep and long-lasting relationships between women, as Linda Wilson and Sheila Wright have demonstrated for Baptist and Quaker communities respectively.[112] But what happened when the emotional intimacy of those friendships became more significant, and how might a focus on religion help us to understand this?

Women and same-sex desire

In the history of male homosexuality scholars such as David Hilliard, John Shelton Reed, Frederick Roden and Seth Koven have explored in detail the contiguity between Roman and Anglo-Catholic aestheticism and male homoerotic sensibilities.[113] Yet religion has only recently been considered in analyses of love and sexual desire between women. Given the relative paucity of unambiguous evidence, the need to acknowledge the otherness and indeterminacy of historical same-sex desires and their resistance to modern understandings of sexuality is, as Cocks states, 'a far more radical step ... than simply identifying them as homosexual'.[114] Using Martha Vicinus's definition of lesbianism as 'an emotional, erotically charged relationship between two women',[115] I briefly explore here the intimate friendships of Ellice Hopkins, the educationalist Constance Maynard, Mary Benson and the little-known Scottish poet and 'Sappho of Strawberry Bank',[116] Bessie Craigmyle. Men were present in these women's lives as influential fathers and colleagues, rejected suitors and, in Benson's case, as a devoted husband of forty years. Yet these women's primary emotional desire was reserved for other women. Moreover, as I will show, it was the familiar, heartfelt language of spiritual love and divine compassion that was so crucial in helping them to articulate their dissident same-sex subjectivities.

Vicinus's groundbreaking study of Mary Benson's same-sex desire is particularly intriguing given the latter's status as an Archbishop's wife. According to the Bishop of Lincoln's daughter Elizabeth Wordsworth, Benson was '[u]nconventional, rather regardless of externals and proprieties and ... mercilessly argumentative'.[117] After several intimate female friendships, Benson married the ambitious and exacting Edward, a man twelve years her senior who, she later admitted, 'was much stronger, much more passionate and whom I didn't really love'.[118] Her most enduring same-sex relationship was with Lucy Tait (the daughter of Edward's predecessor, Archbishop Tait) which outlived the Bensons' marriage and lasted until Mary's death in 1918. Ellice Hopkins, a contemporary of Benson's, remained heavily dependent upon the reciprocal expression of female affection from family members, friends and co-campaigners. She met Annie Ridley in the 1870s while undertaking rescue work in Brighton. References to their friendship are limited, but the two women provided each other with emotional and spiritual support for nearly thirty years, working and holidaying together. Only ill-health prevented Ridley from writing Hopkins's memoirs after her death in 1904. Like Hopkins, the evangelical Constance Maynard, founder and principal of Westfield College in 1882, developed her intimate friendships with women who shared her social and educational convictions. As Elizabeth Edwards has shown, Maynard lived at the centre of two triangular homoerotic relationships, first with fellow Girton students Louisa Lumsden and Frances Dove, and then with the Quaker Anne Richardson and Frances Ralph Gray at Westfield College.[119] Education also provided the social context for Bessie Craigmyle's female affections. Born into a devout Scottish Presbyterian family, Craigmyle was a talented linguist and, according to Alison McCall, regarded by her contemporaries as 'one of Scotland's most promising writers'.[120] Little is known of her romantic life save for two volumes of poetry which are either dedicated to, or about, Maggie Dale, the enduring yet unrequited love of Craigmyle's life. The women planned to set up a medical practice together and Dale took a teaching post in Argentina in 1885 to help fund her studies while Craigmyle attended the Church of Scotland Teacher Training College in Aberdeen. News of Dale's engagement to be married, followed by her untimely death in 1887, caused Craigmyle to suffer a mental breakdown. Craigmyle never realised her earlier literary potential and died alone in the family home in 1933, two days after marking the forty-sixth anniversary of Dale's death.

Four women over two generations, three single and one married, occupying different professional spaces – all, however, held a deep personal faith that enabled them to live out an unorthodox sexual existence. Religious metaphors and language pervaded accounts of their same-sex affections: 'Never was more far-reaching friendship than yours and mine', wrote Hopkins to Ridley. 'It has gone down to hell, it has ascended to heaven.'[121] Spiritual companionship and mentorship could often be a catalyst for more intimate feelings. Vicinus shows how 'Tan' Mylne, the wife of a theology student, helped Benson recover from a deep emotional depression in the 1870s. Benson described Mylne as 'my Mother in Christ' and thanked God for the time she spent in prayer 'with my darling Tan'.[122] Religious differences also sometimes caused tensions, as shown by Maynard's nightly prayers over the spiritual welfare of her agnostic lover Lumsden.[123] More often than not though, homoerotic love sustained religious belief such was the mutually constitutive nature of women's love for the divine and for other women. When Bessie Craigmyle underwent a crisis of faith, for example, it was her passionate feelings for schoolfriend Maggie Laing that provided critical spiritual reassurance: 'Hearing her voice the daily prayer renew', she wrote in her poem 'The Saint', 'I, sometimes, half-believe its words are true.'[124] Craigmyle remained an agnostic for a further twenty years but her poetry suggests that her lifelong love for Maggie Dale helped to mitigate her own spiritual alienation. After Dale's death Craigmyle taught at an Aberdeen boarding-school run by Episcopalian nuns. She left her Presbyterian upbringing, worshipping at the Convent Chapel, Bethany for the remainder of her life. Perhaps she resolved her doubts in order to 'believe in an afterlife in which she would be reunited with Dale',[125] but it is significant that she found her final religious home in an all-female context.

A regular theme in private letters and diaries was the desire for physical intimacy. After illness had kept them apart for several weeks Hopkins admitted to Ridley: 'To touch your hand and kiss you would be like long years of pain and sorrow effaced and all things made new.'[126] It was difficult for women who loved other women to think outside of heterosexual readings of passion as Craigmyle's heartfelt exclamation 'Were I but a man!'[127] suggests. Her poem, 'In the Morning', a strikingly unambiguous and, more importantly, *public* statement of physical same-sex desire, portrays a woman (presumably Dale) 'shuddering and white' after a heated verbal and possibly physical exchange: 'Wild words passed yesterday "twixt me and you"', wrote Craigmyle. 'My careless hands wrought the deep wrong I rue, You swore I should repent it.' But, she pleads, '[a] lover's quarrel should end in after-bliss: Last night our lips were hungering for a kiss, Give it today!'[128] Benson also enjoyed the physical aspects of same-sex love while struggling to sublimate them to a higher spiritual form. 'Once more and with shame O Lord', Benson wrote in 1876, 'grant that all carnal affections may die in me, and that all things belonging to the spirit may live and grow in me – Lord, look down on Lucy and me, and bring to pass the union we have both ... continually desired.'[129]

The extent to which such feelings and behaviour were regarded at the time as sinful or culturally illicit has been much debated by historians. According to Vicinus, Benson 'never considered her love of women to be adultery',[130] although she certainly experienced spiritual torment over her love for Lucy Tait. The heteronormativity of nineteenth-century British culture discussed in Part One with its assumption of female sexual passivity may well have allowed lesbian-like women relative emotional freedom. If active sexual energy was by definition male and the sexual act exclusively reproductive, then intimate female friendships might remain below the radar of social impropriety. Religious observance would have only enhanced women's respectability; Craigmyle's poems, for example, were recommended reading at Aberdeen High School for Girls.[131] Clark has argued that women's same-sex passions often lead not to fixed sexual identities but to a series of private 'twilight moments'[132] where socially prohibited erotic behaviour could form part of one's ordinary life. Benson's unconventional sexuality certainly shored up her highly respectable marriage. As single women, Hopkins, Maynard and Craigmyle fulfilled the pedagogical roles of moral and social motherhood admirably, with Maynard even adopting a little girl, Effie.[133] Thus female same-sex desire did not necessarily destabilise sexual norms and, as Clark observes, could actually be 'complicit in maintaining dominant power structures'.[134]

Theologically, however, all four women expressed a particular transgressiveness. Both Maynard, who grew up in a strict evangelical household, and the Anglo-Catholic Hopkins, regarded the Spirit alone as eternal and the organised form of Christianity as completely immaterial. Benson believed God should contain both motherhood and fatherhood 'for all to take exactly what they need – from the Deep Well of Eternal Quality'.[135] And Craigmyle's darkest poem, 'Re-Awakening', contains fascinating spiritualist echoes as she describes being haunted by the 'spectral illusion' of Maggie Dale: 'At my side there walks a Presence Cold and chill, And the hands of a dead woman Hold me still.'[136]

The fluidity of nineteenth-century hetero- and homosexual identities and the potentially unproblematic status of intimate female friendships receded as sexological and psychological classifications of sexuality gained precedence. The increasingly pathological construction of homosexual identities meant that by the 1920s even the churches were describing homosexuality as a medical condition as well as an occasion of sin. In 1924 the COPEC Commission asserted, for example, that although the Church might view 'the pervert with deepest sympathy', it should 'regard him or her as a defective whose abnormality must be isolated and submitted to special treatment'.[137] COPEC may well have been the churches' earliest official acknowledgement of the existence of the female homosexual, a not insignificant point given the failure of the 1921 CLA Bill to give female sexual inversion a legal identity.[138]

Any doubts over the extent to which religious motifs survived as a form of lesbian self-expression were answered by Radclyffe Hall's censored novel *The Well of Loneliness* (1928). *The Well*, a decisive historical moment in the public recognition of British lesbian identity, told of a woman, Stephen, who sacrificed her own emotional fulfilment in order that her lover, Mary, might escape the ostracism of lesbian existence. The novel was suffused with Catholic imagery of saints, martyrs and Virgin-inverts. Indeed, Radclyffe Hall's own spirituality is an interesting study in the queering of Christian tropes. She and her partner, Una Troubridge, converted to Roman Catholicism, attracted by its rich aesthetic appeal, and later researched into spiritualism in order to contact Hall's deceased lover. According to Joanne Glasgow, the Catholic Church's acute heterocentrism enabled women like Hall to reconcile their alternative sexuality with its spiritual teachings because lesbian sex simply 'did not exist as a Catholic reality'.[139]

Anglican responses to *The Well* were mixed. Writing to Archbishop Lang in 1929, the Bishop of Southwark described it as 'a pathetic cry for pity', yet 'no more suitable for public consumption than a book describing … some horrific physical disease'.[140] Maude Royden disagreed. She condemned the banning of the novel declaring: 'I wish publicly to state that I honour the woman who wrote it … for her courage and her understanding.'[141] Royden, who elicited a grateful response from Hall, had previously expressed sympathy for homosexuals in *Sex and Common-Sense* as 'the most misunderstood, maltreated and suffering of our race'.[142] To be condemned by society as naturally depraved, as a sinner before committing a single sin, was, she argued, an undeserved 'agony of shame'. This said, she strongly disputed Edward Carpenter's pronouncements on the spiritual and evolutionary superiority of the homosexual. The highest types of humanity were not those who contained 'the temperament of one sex in the body of another' but men and women who displayed the qualities of both sexes in a single hypostatic union, following Christ's supreme example where 'power and tenderness, strength and insight, courage and compassion, were equally present'.[143] Like Carpenter and Radclyffe Hall, Royden demanded greater social compassion for the silent suffering and martyrdom of the invert. But unlike them she retained an understanding of the sex instinct as fundamentally creative (reproductive) and saw God's plan as the transcendence rather than consummation of same-sex love.[144] So what, if anything, had changed? H.G. Cocks and Fred Roden have rightly claimed that nineteenth-century religion was 'culturally queer', enabling the existence of 'a variety of polymorphous and unspecific transgressions of gender and sexuality'.[145] More extensive research is required, though, before we can assess the extent to which the sexual capaciousness of religious language and belief declined during the twentieth century as an effect of increasing scientism and secularisation.

Concluding reflections

This chapter has tried to show that women's belief in an incarnate God inspired them to speak out on numerous occasions about sexual intimacy and desire; in this way the Word was indeed made flesh. From the above discussions it is possible to draw some preliminary conclusions regarding the history of British religion, gender and sexual cultures between 1800 and 1940. Callum Brown, one of the few historians of religion to acknowledge the importance of sexual issues to the churches' wider cultural authority, has recently contended that only in the 1960s did 'the relationship of Christianity to issues of sex, sexual orientation and sexual equality'[146] take on an unprecedented importance. While in many ways affirming Brown's reperiodising of secularisation from the late 1800s to much later in the twentieth century, this chapter nevertheless differs in its claim that an equally significant series of interactions between religion (in this case women's discourses) and sexuality occurred in a number of considerably earlier 'sexual revolutions'. Rapidly changing social attitudes to sex and gender, rather than spelling the deathknell of Christian Britain as Brown argues for the 1960s, actually provided the early-twentieth-century churches with some of their keenest opportunities to demonstrate the relevance of faith to a modernising society. And the enduring involvement of female religious commentators in the making of nineteenth- and early-twentieth-century British sexual culture, not least the fundamentally modernist recognition of the sexualised basis of selfhood, demonstrates that the history of sexuality is *not* analogous to that of secularisation. Accordingly I think that it is time that historians jettison the tired and restrictive binaries of religious/secular, reactionary/progressive and spiritual/scientific, in favour of more equivocal theorisations that take as their starting point the complex spiritual and intellectual spaces inhabited by women of faith. Only then will we appreciate the ethical quandaries they confronted in negotiating the demands of religious belief (often in conflict with their denominational hierarchies) with the rapidly changing sexual landscape around them. If, as Cocks has suggested, it is spirituality that constitutes 'the fundamental otherness of sexual desire and the self even in the immediate past',[147] then it is arguably only in the particularity of such moral dilemmas (and their irresolvable status) we will find new ways to think about narratives of modern religion, gender and sex.

Acknowledgements

My sincere thanks go to Jane Rackstraw, Librarian at the University of Chichester, whose efficiency and enthusiasm in obtaining numerous sources helped facilitate the production of this chapter enormously. Thanks also to Jacqui deVries and Joy Dixon for their invaluable comments on an earlier version of this chapter.

Further reading

Anna Clark, *Desire: A History of European Sexuality* (London: Routledge, 2008).

H.G. Cocks and Matt Houlbrook (eds), *The Modern History of Sexuality* (London: Palgrave, 2006).

Marcus Collins, *Modern Love. An Intimate History of Men and Women in Twentieth-Century Britain* (London: Atlantic Books, 2003).

James Covert (ed.), *Memoir of a Victorian Woman. Reflections of Louise Creighton, 1850–1936* (Bloomington: Indiana University Press, 1994).

Sheila Fletcher, *Maude Royden. A Life* (Oxford: Blackwell, 1989).

Lesley Hall, *Sex, Gender and Social Change in Britain Since 1880* (London: Macmillan, 2000).

——, *Outspoken Women: An Anthology of Women's Writing on Sex, 1870–1969* (London: Routledge, 2005).

Sue Morgan (ed.), *Women, Religion and Feminism in Britain, 1750–1900* (London: Palgrave Macmillan, 2002).

Sue Morgan, *A Passion for Purity. Ellice Hopkins and the Politics of Gender in the Late-Victorian Church* (Bristol: Bristol University Press, 1999).

Frank Mort, *Dangerous Sexualities. Medico-Moral Politics in England Since 1830* (London: Routledge, 2000).

Frederick Roden, *Same-Sex Desire in Victorian Religious Culture* (Basingstoke: Palgrave Macmillan, 2002).

Martha Vicinus, *Intimate Friends: Women Who Loved Other Women, 1778–1928* (Chicago: University of Chicago Press, 2004).

Notes

1 See H. G. Cocks, 'Religion and Spirituality' in H. G. Cocks and Matt Houlbrook (eds), *The Modern History of Sexuality* (Basingstoke: Palgrave Macmillan, 2006),

p. 157. See also Michel Foucault's seminal text *The History of Sexuality Vol. 1. An Introduction* (London: Penguin, 1990), pp. 58–73.

2 John Maynard, *Victorian Discourses on Sexuality and Religion* (Cambridge: Cambridge University Press, 1993), p. 3.

3 Lesley Hall, *Outspoken Women: An Anthology of Women's Writing on Sex, 1870–1969* (London: Routledge, 2005), p. 2.

4 Anna Clark, *Desire: A History of European Sexuality* (London: Routledge, 2008), p. 3.

5 See Hall, *Outspoken Women*, p. 2.

6 John, Tosh, *A Man's Place: Masculinity and the Middle-Class Home in Victorian England* (New Haven: Yale University Press, 1999), p. 59.

7 David Bebbington, *The Nonconformist Conscience: Chapel and Church Politics 1870–1914* (London: Allen & Unwin, 1982); Paul McHugh, *Prostitution and Social Reform* (London: Croom Helm, 1980).

8 See Edward Bristow, *Vice and Vigilance. Purity Movements in Britain Since 1700* (Dublin: Gill & Macmillan Ltd, 1977), Frank Mort, *Dangerous Sexualities. Medico-Moral Politics in England Since 1830* (London: Routledge, 2000), Lucy Bland, *Banishing the Beast: English Feminism and Sexual Morality, 1885–1914* (London: Penguin, 1995), Alan Hunt, *Governing Morals: the Social History of Moral Regulation* (Cambridge: Cambridge University Press, 1999), Judith Walkowitz, *Prostitution and Victorian Society. Women, Class and the State* (Cambridge: Cambridge University Press, 1980) and Sheila Jeffreys, *The Spinster and Her Enemies. Feminism and Sexuality, 1880–1930* (London: Pandora Press, 1985). See Jacqui deVries's chapter in this volume for further analyses of the religion/feminism paradox.

9 Cocks, 'Religion and Spirituality', p. 158.

10 Ibid., p. 172.

11 Joy Dixon, 'Sexology and the Occult: Sexuality and Subjectivity in Theosophy's New Age', *Journal of the History of Sexuality,* Vol. 7, No. 3 (1997), p. 411. See also Joy Dixon, *Divine Feminine: Theosophy and Feminism in England* (Baltimore: Johns Hopkins University Press, 2001).

12 Havelock Ellis cited in Dixon, 'Sexology and the Occult', p. 413.

13 See Lesley Hall, 'Hauling Down the Double Standard: Feminism, Social Purity and Sexual Science in Late Nineteenth-Century Britain', *Gender and History,* Vol.16, no. 1 (2004), pp. 36–56.

14 See for example Alex Owen, *The Darkened Room: Women, Power and Spiritualism in Late Victorian England* (London: Virago, 1989), Marlene Tromp, *Altered States: Sex, Nation, Drugs and Self-Transformation in Victorian Spiritualism* (Albany: State University of New York Press, 2006) and Jenny Hazelgrove, *Spiritualism and British Society Between the Wars* (Manchester: Manchester University Press, 2000).

15 Ellice Hopkins, *The Power of Womanhood; or, Mothers and Sons. A Book for Parents* (London: Wells Gardner, 1899), p. 144.

16 Karen Harvey, 'Gender, Space and Modernity in Eighteenth-Century England: A Place Called Sex', *History Workshop Journal,* no. 51 (Spring, 2001), p. 159.

17 William Acton, *The Functions and Disorders of the Reproductive Organs* (London, 1857), p. 112 cited in Frank Mort, *Dangerous Sexualities*, p. 63.

18 See, for example, Nancy Cott, 'Passionlessness: An Interpretation of Victorian Sexual Ideology', *Signs,* 4 (1978), pp. 19–36, Leonore Davidoff and Catherine Hall, *Family Fortunes. Men and Women of the English Middle Class, 1780–1850* (London: Routledge, 2002) and Catherine Hall, 'The Early Formation of Victorian Domestic Ideology', in Hall (ed.), *White, Male and Middle Class* (Cambridge: Polity Press, 1995), pp. 75–93.

19 Tosh, *A Man's Place*, p. 69.

20 Michael Mason, *The Making of Victorian Sexual Attitudes* (Oxford: Oxford University Press, 1994), p. 77.

21 See Mort, *Dangerous Sexualities*, p. 62 for Nonconformist commentaries on sexual pleasure and Michael Mason, *The Making of Victorian Sexuality* (Oxford: Oxford University Press, 1994) for discussions on the Swedenborgians.

22 John Tosh, 'From Keighley to St-Denis: Separation and Intimacy in Victorian Bourgeois Marriage', *History Workshop Journal*, 40 (1995), pp. 198–99.

23 Marie Stopes, *Married Love* (London: G. P. Putnam's Sons Ltd, 1922 edn), p. 130.

24 Ellice Hopkins, *Christ the Consoler. A Book of Comfort for the Sick* (London, 1879), p. 120 cited in Sue Morgan, *A Passion for Purity. Ellice Hopkins and the Politics of Gender in the Late-Victorian Church* (Bristol, 1999), p. 149.

25 Elizabeth Blackwell, *The Human Element in Sex: Being a Medical Enquiry into the Relation of Sexual Physiology to Christian Morality* (London: J. and A. Churchill, 1884), p. 116. Blackwell came from a Congregationalist background but flirted with Transcendentalism and Unitarianism. See Julia Boyd, *The Excellent Dr Blackwell: The Life of the First Female Physician* (England: Sutton Publishing, 2006).

26 See Dixon, *Divine Feminine* and her chapter in this volume. See also George Robb, 'Eugenics, Spirituality, and Sex Differentiation in Edwardian England: The Case of Frances Swiney', *Journal of Women's History* 10 (1998), pp. 97–117.

27 See the discussion in Sheila Fletcher, *Maude Royden: A Life* (Oxford: Basil Blackwell, 1989), p. 238. Although initially rejected in 1923, the House of Bishops passed the amendment in 1925. The revised prayer book of 1927/28 included the option of equal vows and, although never adopted canonically, was approved for use in churches. See Tim Jones, 'Sex and Gender in the Church of England, 1857–1957' (unpublished PhD thesis, University of Melbourne, 2007), pp. 54–55.

28 Theodore Schroeder, 'Concerning Free Love', *New Freewoman* (1913), cited in George Robb, 'The Way of all Flesh: Degeneration, Eugenics and the Gospel of Free Love', *Journal of the History of Sexuality,* vol. 6 no. 4 (1996), p. 593.

29 Hopkins, *Power of Womanhood*, p. 150

30 Laura Schwartz, 'Freethought, Free Love and Feminism: Secularist Debates on Marriage and Sexual Morality, England c.1850–85', *Women's History Review* (forthcoming 2010).

31 A. Maude Royden, *Sex and Common-Sense* (London: Hurst & Blackett Ltd, 1921), p. 56.

32 Tim Jones, 'Incestuous Sacraments: Anglo-Catholic Sexuality and the Deceased Wife's Sister Act' in Bernard Mees and Samuel Koehne (eds), *Terror, War, Tradition: Studies in European History* (Melbourne: Australian Humanities Press, 2007), p. 11.

33 See Caitriona Beaumont, 'Moral Dilemmas and Women's Rights: The Attitude of the Mothers' Union and Catholic Women's League to Divorce, Birth Control and Abortion in England, 1928–39', *Women's History Review*, Vol. 16, no. 4 (2007), p. 467 and Cordelia Moyse, 'Freemasonry of Motherhood: Inventing the Mothers' Union, 1876–1909', *Humanitas* 3:1 (2001), p. 82.

34 Royden, *Sex and Common-Sense*, pp. 106–7.

35 Eva (bc1#1) cited in Kate Fisher, *Birth Control, Sex and Marriage in Britain 1918–1960* (Oxford: Oxford University Press, 2008), p. 149.

36 Russell Davies, '"In a Broken Dream": Some Aspects of Sexual Behaviour and the Dilemmas of the Unmarried Mother in South West Wales, 1887–1914', *Llafur* 3, 4 (1983), p. 28.

37 See Royden, *Sex and Common-Sense*, p. 192 and Fletcher, *Maude Royden*, p. 235.

38 See Mason, *The Making of Victorian Sexual Attitudes* for discussions of Francis Place, Dale Owen, Charles Bradlaugh and Annie Besant in promoting family limitation practices.

39 Resolution 42, Lambeth Conference 1908, www.lambethconference.org/resolutions/1908 accessed June 21st 2009. See also Tim Jones, 'The Disappearing Empire: Anglican Conversion to Contraception, 1905–30' in Kate Darian-Smith et al. (eds), *Exploring the British World* (Melbourne: RMIT Publishing, 2004), pp. 3–17.

40 See Fisher, *Birth Control, Sex and Marriage*, pp. 150–51.

41 The COPEC Commissioners were unable to reach a consensus on divorce and instead simply listed in the report the range of opinions represented. See COPEC, 'The Relations of the Sexes' Report (London: Longmans, Green and Co., 1924).

42 Marcus Collins, *Modern Love: An Intimate History of Men and Women in Twentieth-Century Britain* (London: Atlantic Books, 2003), pp. 30–46.

43 COPEC, 'Relations of the Sexes', p. 71.

44 See June Rose, *Marie Stopes and the Sexual Revolution* (London: Faber & Faber, 1992), p. 17.

45 *Daily Mirror* (16 March 1925) cited in Margaret Douglas, 'Women, God and Birth Control: The First Hospital Birth Control Clinic, Abertillery 1925', *Llafur*, 6, 4 (1995), p. 115. Stopes's lengthy libel suit against Dr Halliday Sutherland, a Roman Catholic who accused her of experimenting on working-class women, compounded her frustration with organised religion, while gaining her enormous publicity.

46 Douglas, 'Women, God and Birth Control', p. 120.

47 Beaumont, 'Moral Dilemmas', pp. 473–75.

48 Mary Scharlieb, 'Social and Religious Aspects' in James Marchant (ed.), *The Control of Parenthood* (London: G. P. Putnam's Sons, 1920), p. 109.

49 www.vatican/va/holy_father/pius_xi/encyclicals/documents/casticonnubii, para 54. Accessed June 28 2009.

50 Resolution 15, Lambeth Conference Archives 1930, www.lambethconference. org/resolutions/1930/1930–15. Accessed May 12 2009.

51 See Collins, *Modern Love*, p. 42 and Lesley Hall, *Sex, Gender and Social Change in Britain Since 1880* (London: Macmillan Press, 2000), p. 121.

52 Ellice Hopkins, *A Plea for the Wider Action of the Church of England in the Prevention of the Degradation of Women* (London: Hatchards, 1879), p. 13.

53 Maude Royden, 'Modern Love' in Victor Gollancz (ed.), *The Making of Women. Oxford Essays in Feminism* (London: George Allen & Unwin Ltd, 1917), p. 38.

54 Royden, *Sex and Common-Sense*, p. 50.

55 Maude Royden, *Sex and Common-sense* (London: Hurst & Blackett Ltd, 1947 edition), p. 29.

56 Ibid., p. 117.

57 Lesley Hall, *Hidden Anxieties: Male Sexuality, 1900–1950* (Oxford: Blackwell, 1991).

58 See Bristow, *Vice and Vigilance*, p. 111 and Lucy Bland, *Banishing the Beast*, pp. 95–123 for Chant's anti-obscenity campaign.

59 Literally 'the land of white gloves', this phrase was also translated as 'the land of pure morals'. Thanks to Andi Morgan for this information. See also Maria Luddy, *Prostitution and Irish Society, 1800–1940* (Cambridge: Cambridge University Press, 2007), p. 162.

60 *Daily Telegraph*, 'Prudes on the Prowl' series, 1894, cited in Bristow, *Vice and Vigilance*, p. 212.

61 Mort, *Dangerous Sexualities*, p. 83.

62 Bristow's *Vice and Vigilance* is most critical of the social purity legacy. See Judith Walkowitz, *Prostitution and Victorian Society* and Sheila Jeffreys, *The Spinster and Her Enemies* for contrasting readings.

63 See Sarah Robinson, *A Life Record* (London: James Nisbet, 1898), pp. 137–38.

64 Ann Higginbotham, 'Respectable Sinners: Salvation Army Rescue Work with Unmarried Mothers, 1884–1914' in Gail Malmgreen (ed.), *Religion in the Lives of English Women, 1760–1930* (London: Croom Helm, 1986), p. 218.

65 See Lynda Nead, *Myths of Sexuality, Representations of Women in Victorian Britain* (Oxford: Blackwell, 1988).

66 William Acton cited in Judith Walkowitz, *Prostitution and Victorian Society*, p. 87.

67 Luddy, *Prostitution and Irish Society*, p. 110.

68 Ellice Hopkins to Mrs Maclagan, cited in F. D. How, *William Dalrymple Maclagan* (London: Wells Gardner, Darton and Co., 1911), p. 224.

69 See Lara Marks, 'Race, Class and Gender: The Experience of Jewish Prostitutes and Other Jewish Women in the East End of London at the Turn of the Century' in Joan Grant (ed.), *Women, Migration and Empire* (Stoke-on-Trent: Trentham Books, 1996), pp. 31–50.

70 A. Maude Royden, *Women and the Sovereign State* (London: Headley Bros Ltd., 1917), p. 103.

71 Letter from Josephine Butler to Florence Booth (26 March 1885) cited in Jane Jordan and Ingrid Sharp (eds), *Josephine Butler and the Prostitution Campaigns Vol. IV* (London: Routledge, 2003), p. 109.

72 Josephine Butler, cited in Jane Jordan and Ingrid Sharp (eds), *Josephine Butler and the Prostitution Campaigns. Diseases of the Body Politic, Vol. 1* (London: Routledge, 2003), p. 5.

73 Acton, ibid. and W.E.H. Lecky, *History of European Morals, Vol. II* (London: Longmans, Green and Co, 1882 edn), p. 283.

74 Helen Mathers, '"Tis a Dishonor Done to Me": Self-Representation in the Writings of Josephine Butler' in Jenny Daggers and Diana Neal (eds), *Sex, Gender and Religion: Josephine Butler Revisited* (Peter Lang, 2006) p. 48.

75 Ellice Hopkins, *Work in Brighton* (London, 1878), p. 9.

76 Hopkins, 'The World's Outcast', in *Power of Womanhood*, p. 173.

77 Hunt, *Governing Morals*, p. 148.

78 The White Cross pledges are cited in many of Hopkins's pamphlets. See Sue Morgan, 'Knights of God: The White Cross Army, 1883–95' in Robert Swanson (ed.), *Gender and the Christian Religion. Studies in Church History, Vol. 34* (London: Boydell & Brewer, 1997), pp. 431–45.

79 Cited in Morgan, *A Passion for Purity*, p. 118.

80 Kenneth Boyd, *Scottish Church Attitudes to Sex, Marriage and the Family, 1850–1914* (Edinburgh: John Donald, 1980), p. 104.

81 Ellice Hopkins, *Ten Reasons Why I Should Join the White Cross Movement* (London: Hatchards, 1885), p. 12.

82 Hopkins, *The Power of Womanhood*, p. 162.

83 Ellice Hopkins, *The British Zulu* (London: Wells, Gardner, Darton and Co., 1891), p. 5.

84 James Marchant, *Manifesto of National Council for Public Morals* (1911), p. 57.

85 Ellice Hopkins, *On the Early Training of Boys and Girls. An Appeal to Working Women* (London: Hatchards, 1886), p. 48.

86 See Elizabeth Blackwell, *Counsel to Parents on the Moral Education of their Children* (1882), Ellice Hopkins, *The Story of Life: For the Use of Mothers with Boys* (London: Walter Scott, 1902) and Ellis Ethelmer (Elizabeth Wolstenholme Elmy), *The Human Flower* (Congleton, 1894).

87 Claudia Nelson, '"Under the Wise Guidance of a Mother": British Sex Education at the *fin de siècle*', in Nelson and Ann Sumner Holmes (eds), *Maternal Instincts: Visions of Motherhood and Sexuality, 1875–1925* (London: Macmillan, 1997), p. 116.

88 E.C.P., *Schoolboy Morality: An Address to Mothers* (London: Hatchards, 1886), p. 4.

89 Hopkins, *The Power of Womanhood*, p. 28.

90 Josephine Butler, *Social Purity* (1879), p. 9.

91 James Covert (ed.), *Memoir of a Victorian Woman: Reflections of Louise Creighton, 1850–1936* (Bloomington: Indiana University Press, 1994), p. 90.

92 James Covert, *A Victorian Marriage. Mandell and Louise Creighton* (London: Hambledon and London Ltd, 2000), p. 304.

93 Louise Creighton, *The Social Disease and How to Fight It. A Rejoinder* (London: Longmans, Green and Co, 1914), p. 14.

94 Creighton, *The Social Disease*, p. 28.

95 Covert, *Memoir of a Victorian Woman*, p. 115.

96 Covert, *A Victorian Marriage*, p. 305.

97 Hall, *Sex, Gender and Social Change*, p. 104.

98 Katherine Holden, *The Shadow of Marriage: Singleness in England, 1914–1960* (Manchester: Manchester University Press, 2007), p. 124.

99 Vivienne Richmond, '"It is not a Society for Human Beings but for Virgins": The Girls' Friendly Society Membership Eligibility Dispute, 1875–1936', *Journal of Historical Sociology*, Vol. 20, No. 3 (September 2007), pp. 304–27.

100 Winifred Holtby, 'Are Spinsters Frustrated?', *Women and a Changing Civilisation* (1934), cited in Virginia Nicolson, *Singled Out* (London: Penguin, 2007), pp. 32–33.

101 Ellis Hanson, *Decadence and Catholicism* (Harvard University Press, 1997), p. 264.

102 René Kollar, 'A Death in the Family: Bishop Archibald Campbell Tait, the Rights of Parents, and Anglican Sisterhoods in the Diocese of London', *Journal of Religious History*, vol. 27, no. 2 (June 2003), pp. 198–24.

103 Annie Besant, *The Law of Population* (1889), pp. 28–29 cited in Hall, *Outspoken Women*, p. 18.

104 See Holden, *The Shadow of Marriage*, p. 85 for a discussion of these authors' attitudes.

105 Royden, *Sex and Commonsense*, pp. 29–31. See also Fletcher, *Maude Royden*, p. 117.

106 Ellice Hopkins, *The Power of Womanhood*, p. 152.

107 Eileen Janes Yeo, 'Protestant Feminists and Catholic Saints in Victorian Britain' in Yeo (ed.), *Radical Femininity: Women's Self-Representation in the Public Sphere* (Manchester: Manchester University Press, 1998), p.131.

108 Marianne Farningham cited in Linda Wilson, *Constrained by Zeal: Female Spirituality Amongst Nonconformists, 1825–75* (Carlisle: Paternoster Press 2000), pp. 186–87. Wilson was a spinster and a headmistress who also wrote for the influential periodical *The Christian World* for 50 years from 1857.

109 Mary Scharlieb, *The Bachelor Woman and Her Problems* (London: Williams & Norgate Ltd, 1929), p. 116.

110 Sheila Wright, '"Every Good Woman Needs a Companion of her Own Sex": Quaker Women and Spiritual Friendship, 1750–1850' in Sue Morgan (ed.), *Women, Religion and Feminism in Britain, 1750–1900* (London: Macmillan, 2002), p. 89.

111 Sarah Ellis, *The Women of England: Their Social Duties and Domestic Habits* (New York: D. Appleton and Co.,1839) and *The Daughters of England* (1842). Grace Aguilar, *Woman's Friendship: A Story of Domestic Life* (London: Groombridge and Sons, 1850).

112 Wright, 'Every Good Woman', pp. 89–104 and Wilson, *Constrained by Zeal*.

113 See David Hilliard, 'Un-English and Unmanly: Anglo-Catholicism and Homosexuality', *Victorian Studies*, 25, 2 (1982), pp. 181–210, Frederick Roden, *Same-Sex Desire in Victorian Religious Culture* (Basingstoke: Palgrave Macmillan, 2002), John Shelton Reed, *Glorious Battle: The Cultural Politics of Victorian*

Anglo-Catholicism (Nashville: Vanderbilt University Press, 1996) and Seth Koven, *Slumming. Sexual and Social Politics in Victorian London* (Princeton: Princeton University Press, 2006).

114 Cocks, 'Religion and Spirituality', p. 167.

115 Martha Vicinus, *Intimate Friends: Women Who Loved Other Women, 1778–1928* (Chicago: University of Chicago Press, 2004), p.xxiv.

116 See Alison McCall, 'The Poetry and Life of Bessie Craigmyle (1863–1933), The Sappho of Strawberry Bank', *The Aberdeen University Review*, vol. LXI, 2, No 214 (Autumn 2005), pp. 109–22. Alison McCall is a pioneering scholar on Bessie Craigmyle and I am immensely grateful for her generous advice and help with materials, including Bessie's poetry, in writing this section.

117 Elizabeth Wordsworth cited in Georgina Battiscombe, *Reluctant Pioneer: A Life of Elizabeth Wordsworth* (London: Constable, 1978), p. 31.

118 Mary Benson, cited in Martha Vicinus, '"The Gift of Love": Nineteenth-Century Religion and Lesbian Passion', in Morgan (ed.), *Women, Religion and Feminism*, p. 75.

119 Elizabeth Edwards, 'Homerotic Friendships and College Principals, 1880–1960', *Women's History Review*, Vol. 4, No. 2 (1995), p. 157.

120 McCall, 'The Poetry and Life of Bessie Craigmyle', p. 109.

121 Hopkins cited in Rosa M. Barrett, *Ellice Hopkins. A Memoir* (London: Wells Gardner, 1907), p. 225.

122 Vicinus, *Intimate Friends*, p. 93.

123 See Martha Vicinus, *Independent Women. Work and Community for Single Women, 1850–1920* (London: Routledge, 1985), p. 201.

124 Bessie Craigmyle, 'My Saint' (n.d. but written pre 1881) in Craigmyle, *Poems and Translations* (Aberdeen: J. and J. P. Edmond and Spark, 1886), reproduced in Alison T. McCall, *There is Room for Roses in God's World. Selected Poems of Bessie Craigmyle* (Aberdeen: North East Genealogy Services, 2008), p. 7.

125 Email communication with Alison McCall, dated January 31, 2009.

126 Barrett, *Ellice Hopkins. A Memoir*, p. 271.

127 Craigmyle, 'A Pretty Face' (n.d.) in Craigmyle, *A Handful of Pansies* (Aberdeen: Taylor & Henderson, 1888), p. 29 reproduced in McCall, *There Is Room for Roses*, p. 19.

128 Craigmyle, 'In the Morning' (n.d.) in Craigmyle, *Poems and Translations*, reproduced in McCall, *There Is Room for Roses*, p. 21.

129 Vicinus, 'The Gift of Love' in Morgan (ed.), *Women, Religion and Feminism*, p. 82.

130 Vicinus, *Intimate Friends*, p. 96.

131 The *Aberdeen High School Magazine* (June 1886), pp. 21–22 included an enthusiastic review of Craigmyle's *Poems and Translations* which concluded 'Let us all get Miss Craigmyle's book'. Earlier school magazines also carried individual poems by Craigmyle. Thanks to Alison McCall for this information.

132 Anna Clark, 'Twilight Moments', *Journal of the History of Sexuality*, Vol. 14, Nos 1, 2 (2005), pp. 139–58.

133 See Pam Walker, 'Adoption and Victorian Culture', *The History of the Family*, Vol. 11 (2006), pp. 211–21.

134 Clark, 'Twilight Moments', p. 146.

135 Vicinus, 'The Gift of Love' in Morgan (ed.), *Women, Religion and Feminism*, p. 85.

136 Craigmyle, 'Re-Awakening' (1888) in Craigmyle, *A Handful of Pansies*, reproduced in McCall, *There Is Room for Roses*, pp. 32–33.

137 COPEC, 'The Relations of the Sexes', p. 31.

138 See Laura Doan, '"Acts of Female Indecency": Sexology's Intervention in Legislating Lesbianism' in Lucy Bland and Laura Doan (eds), *Sexology in Culture: Labelling Bodies and Desires* (Oxford: Polity, 1995), pp. 199–213.

139 Joanne Glasgow, 'What's a Nice Lesbian Like You Doing in the Church of Torquemada? Radclyffe Hall and Other Catholic Converts' in Karla Jay and Joanne Glasgow (eds), *Lesbian Texts and Contexts: Radical Revisions* (New York: New York University Press, 1990), p. 242.
140 Tim Jones, 'Sex and Gender in the Church of England, 1857–1957' (Unpublished PhD thesis, University of Melbourne, 2007), p. 192. Thanks to Tim Jones for permission to quote from his thesis.
141 Maude Royden, 'Well of Loneliness', *The Guildhouse Monthly*, Vol. 3 No. 26 (April, 1929), cited in Alison Oram and Annmarie Turnbull (eds), *The Lesbian History Sourcebook* (London: Routledge, 2001), p. 193.
142 Royden, *Sex and Common-Sense*, p. 145.
143 Ibid., pp. 141–42.
144 Ibid., p. 195.
145 Cocks, 'Religion and Spirituality', p. 158. Roden, 'Same-Sex Desire in Victorian Religious Culture'.
146 Callum Brown, *Religion and Society in Twentieth-Century Britain* (London: Pearson Education, 2006), p. 240.
147 Cocks, 'Religion and Spirituality', p. 176.

9 More than paradoxes to offer

Feminism, history and religious cultures

Jacqueline deVries

Historical studies of the relationship between feminism and religion typically stumble over a paradox so widely accepted that it has nearly become a truism: religion was both a source of oppressive domestic ideology and a starting point for feminist activism. Like all truisms, this one has been repeated so often that it has almost lost its analytical significance. Paradoxes are familiar to historians of feminism,[1] but this one is particularly complex. A number of interpretive challenges have created layers of obfuscation, hindering historians' ability to understand the dynamic and often unpredictable relationship between feminist activism and religious ideas and institutions. Among these challenges are current definitions of feminism, which have been conceived in primarily secular terms; the historiography of feminism, which has long struggled to take religious belief and religiously motivated activism seriously; the elusive nature of religious experience, the effects of which are notoriously difficult to uncover and characterise; and the popularity among feminists of unorthodox forms of spirituality that defy easy categorisation. This chapter will address each of these interpretive challenges as it attempts to peel away the layers of obfuscation and explore some of the ways in which nineteenth- and twentieth-century British feminists drew upon and benefitted from, as well as refashioned and rejected the religious cultures of which they were a part. The subject is so rich that this chapter could not possibly attempt an exhaustive analysis; instead, it sketches out the major trends, chronological breaks and discursive paradigms at work in this dynamic relationship as it developed between 1800 and 1940.

Feminism's relationships to industrialisation, new class configurations, and the spread of political democracy have already been well chronicled, but our knowledge of feminism's connection to Britain's religious cultures is still uneven. During the period surveyed in this chapter Britain's religious cultures underwent dramatic change. In this chapter we follow the story from the Victorian period, when Christianity saturated everyday life, to the early twentieth century, when religious allegiances were shifting, new denominations were emerging as others lost ground and reworked conceptions of the sacred and the secular challenged public discourse and personal belief systems. Feminism grew in tandem with the rapidly shifting religious landscape in complicated relationships of both cause and effect. Britain's evolving religious ideas and practices not only influenced feminism, feminists also helped to transform Britain's religious cultures and institutions.

The only way to move beyond the interpretive paradox is to acknowledge the richness of Britain's religious cultures and the variability of women's perceptions of both religion and feminism. Any discussion of religion must embrace the heterogeneity of individual experience and the impossibility of separating rhetoric, representation and reality. Furthermore, a degree of uncertainty must be assumed in this endeavour, since religious faith, belief and practice do not lend themselves to easy historical exploration.[2] From the typical records available to the historian it is far easier to construct a picture of outward religious practices – which may or may not have anything to do with faith or belief – than it is to peer into someone's soul or mind. Each woman's experience of religious growth or decline, and her perception of religion as liberating or oppressive, was unique. The usual sociological categories – denomination, location, class, and generation – can help the historian identify common patterns, but one must also seek to understand how intersecting circles of loyalty, identity and personality shaped each individual's spirituality and responses to religion (and feminism for that matter).

Historians must also attempt to understand how religious faith, belief and practices can function – sometimes simultaneously – as both empowering and oppressive. Janaki Nair put it well when she urged historians to explore 'the complex ways in which women are, and have been, subjected to systematic subordination within a framework that simultaneously acknowledges new political possibilities for women, drawing on traditions of dissent or resistance while infusing them with new meanings'.[3] Above all, this chapter argues, we must employ an expansive definition of feminism, as well as a flexible understanding of what constitutes faith and belief, if we are to comprehend the range of encounters women had with religion. In many ways, this topic lends itself well to Hans Kellner's charge to 'get the story crooked'.[4]

Historiographical elisions

To transcend the 'deeply historically bound versions of "the feminist past"' which have led to historical amnesia concerning religion, we must explore the paradigms that have produced our current understanding of feminism and its history.[5]

Getting our terms straight (or crooked!) is the first challenge, for the labels used by nineteenth-century women activists to identify themselves and their interests were never fixed. When women organised around shared interests, they did so as anti-slavery activists or advocates of women's higher education, not as self-identified 'feminists' who adhered to a unified set of principles.[6] Until the term 'feminism' became widely applied in the 1890s, women lacked the linguistic tools to conceptualise their disparate activities as representing a common identity and political position. Even after the term was introduced, no consensus existed on what a feminist ought to do, be or believe, especially regarding religious belief and practice. Some women sent rocks hurtling through shop windows in suffrage protests but never questioned the Church's patriarchal structure; others, like Eliza Lynn Linton, rejected Christianity yet clung to a belief in complementary gender roles. In an attempt to historicise our understanding of feminism, Karen Offen suggests that it is 'a concept that can encompass both an ideology and a movement for socio-political change based on a critical analysis of male privilege and women's subordination within any given society'.[7] This definition proposes that opposition to sex hierarchy and the recognition of gender's social construction are intrinsic characteristics of feminism, and it also acknowledges that feminism can include a range of strategies and sites of resistance. Yet questions arise when we factor in religious faith and belief. For example, can we label as 'feminist' only those who rejected the notion that God ordained women's position, as Nancy Cott seems to insist?[8] Can we apply the term 'feminist' to biblically-based ideas of women's roles, however elevated and empowered? An expansive definition can help us see the range and richness of feminist ideas and activities.

When individuals have attempted to write the history of feminism, they have frequently shaped their narrative around a set of assumptions which downplay the importance of religion to its development. Typically, nineteenth-century feminists believed their movement paralleled other great evolutionary trends in history, and early histories often portrayed feminism as 'a teleological story of cumulative progress toward an ever-elusive goal'.[9] Within this framework, feminism's trajectory seemed to reflect other apparent teleological processes, like the march of democracy and the freeing of society from religious dogma (i.e. secularisation). These assumptions were still firmly in place by the 1960s and 1970s when scholars began to plot a coherent history of feminism, but their search for origin stories and like-minded 'sisters' in the past sometimes led to a-historical reasoning. Many early feminist scholars had themselves rejected religious ideas and allegiances and they approached their subject through the lens of Marxist-materialist feminism. To them, religious systems were a monolithic site of antifeminist resistance and a potent source of patriarchal oppression. In her now classic text *Hidden from History* (1973), for example, Sheila Rowbotham portrays religion as a relic, no longer relevant (or interesting) to modern feminists. Even those scholars who didn't dismiss religion outright saw it as having a negligible influence on feminism's development. In *Faces of Feminism* (1981) Olive Banks began her analysis with a chapter on evangelicalism but concluded that British feminism – unlike its American counterpart – had been shaped in minimal ways by religious-based activism like temperance or philanthropy: 'In England there is little evidence that the early evangelical involvement in moral reform led to the rise of a specifically feminine consciousness.'[10] Her conclusions, based almost entirely on secondary sources, reveal more about the flawed and incomplete historiography available in 1981 than the historical relationship between religion and feminism.

This picture began to change with the pioneering classic, *The Origins of Modern Feminism* (1985), in which Jane Rendall asserted that religion, particularly in the form of evangelicalism, provided both a means and a rationale for women's entrance into public and political activities.[11] While acknowledging evangelicalism's complex and ambiguous effects on the position of women, Rendall insisted that nineteenth-century religious activism offered them 'a limited but positive role' and helped to transform both society's perceptions of women and women's perceptions of themselves. Following in this more positive vein, Barbara Caine, Anne Summers, Eileen Yeo and many others have explored in greater detail the ways in which women's religious commitments could assist them in creating meaningful, productive and independent lives.[12] Historians' efforts to understand the work of religion in creating and sustaining women's cultures in the nineteenth century have revealed religion's radical potential for creating pockets of political and cultural resistance.[13]

Yet despite these notable interventions in the historiography, it is remarkable how many studies of British feminism still ignore religion.[14] Even when it is included as an analytical category, the conclusions often reassert the paradox. For example, it is still common to hear the claim, as Philippa Levine has argued, that religion promoted a political passivity and a concern with otherworldliness among women.[15] Just as common is the assertion that religion was a motivating force, providing women with a sense of vocation and opportunity to engage in social transformation. Part of the problem lies with the analytical method. Social history, which has contributed so much to recovering women's lives and stories, has difficulty engaging the intangible, intuitive and emotional nature of religious faith and taking its meanings seriously. A biographical approach, whether individual or collective, can certainly help the historian explore the faith/feminism dynamic more intimately, but only if the biographer is predisposed to do so.[16] It is not easy to interweave analysis of the personal with the public and political expressions of religious faith and belief. As Ursula King observes, the historical investigation of religion is 'an issue of ... personal and corporate identity', and requires us to explore both collective and individual stories.[17] Our historical methodology must reflect these complexities.

Cultural history provides one possible path through the interpretive dilemmas. Modelled in the work of Joy Dixon, Sue Morgan and Callum Brown, the 'cultural turn' offers hope for more nuanced analyses of religion's influence in feminist history.[18] Brown's emphasis on 'discursive Christianity' provides ways to understand not only how religious ideas were produced and circulated, but also how they were internalised and reworked by individuals.[19] Instead of studying structures and institutions, Brown seeks in his work to 'assembl[e] a collage of the cultural representations and experiences of men and women in the past'.[20] Following in this vein, feminist historians are drawing on a wider array of sources – from autobiographies to novels, sermons and periodical literature – and breaking down the monolithic term 'religion' into the more inclusive and expansive terms of 'faith', 'belief' and 'spirituality'. Acknowledging that women's encounters with religion often lay outside of official theological and institutional structures, historians are examining the intellectual, emotional and interpersonal ways in which women intimated the divine and, ultimately, transformed its image.[21] When approaching feminists' encounters with religion, it is wise to keep in mind the words of Caroline Walker Bynum, whose rich essays on medieval gender and sexuality opened up an unfamiliar and puzzling world: 'women in every age speak in a variety of accents'.[22]

Feminism and Britain's religious cultures

The great variety and constant evolution of religious cultures in Britain poses another challenge to historians of feminism. When the women's movement took shape, Britain was still a deeply rooted Protestant nation-state; a shared Protestantism gave meaning and identity to Britons and offered 'an easily available and deeply felt principle to rally around'.[23] The earliest participants in the women's movement came from the Protestant middle classes and often assumed that Christianity could play a positive role in bringing women's emancipation. For example, Mary Wollstonecraft, who is recognised as a daughter of the Enlightenment and a strong proponent of reason, drew upon her Christian faith to imagine a better world; as Barbara Taylor argues: 'It is impossible to understand her political hopes, including her hopes for women, outside a theistic framework. Her contemporaries knew this – they probably took it for granted – but today it is overlooked by most commentators.'[24] Despite her avowed religiosity, Wollstonecraft's posthumous reputation as a sexual libertine contributed to the perception by contemporary feminists that religious belief and feminism were uncomfortable partners.[25]

Like Wollstonecraft, Victorian women activists largely took for granted a set of cultural assumptions which posited that Christianity, especially in its Protestant forms, could provide women with dignity, freedom, and personal fulfilment through service. To many early feminists, religious beliefs were a source of intellectual and emotional sustenance and 'offered a model of love and friendship, of devotion to a cause'.[26] Of course, some Victorian feminists experienced faith crises, such as Frances Power Cobbe, who rejected the evangelical faith of her Anglo-Irish parents and devoted her life to what historian Michael Bartholomew has called the 'moral critique of Christian orthodoxy'.[27] But Cobbe and her counterparts were exceptional. When Victorian feminists experienced crises of doubt, they often kept it quiet and few completely abandoned religious faith entirely.[28] Even those who became atheists and freethinkers were still 'deeply preoccupied with Scriptural teachings on women', argues Laura Schwartz, giving 'testament to the extent to which the feminism of this period was framed by religion'.[29] Nineteenth-century individuals who questioned Christianity on feminist grounds were forced to confront a web of social and cultural assumptions about Christianity's positive effects, created by such sources as August Bebel's popular *Woman* (1879), in which he argued that Protestant attacks on asceticism in the sixteenth century brought unparalleled benefits to women, or W. E. H. Lecky's influential *History of European Morals* (1869), which insisted that Christianity was a bedrock of a harmonious family, a functioning society, and a high view of women.[30] As Sue Morgan has observed, 'Although definitions of gender and sexuality were increasingly couched in medical scientific terms, religion remained the basic moral framework within which such discourses competed for power.'[31]

While nineteenth-century feminism took shape within the contours of a Christian culture, that culture was never homogeneous. The Anglican Church was established in England and Wales, but it competed with dozens of Dissenting and non-Christian traditions – Methodists, Congregationalists, Baptists, Quakers, Unitarians, Catholics and Jews – each of which offered distinctive doctrines, practices, and cultures.[32] Well into the twentieth century, some denominational communities retained their sense of separateness and exclusivity and provided complete and enclosed social worlds.[33] A middle-class Catholic woman, for example, might be sent to Catholic schools, attend a Catholic church, read Catholic newspapers and magazines, join Catholic societies, and, of course, marry a Catholic man. At the same time, denominations were not isolated cultures, as Keith Robbins observes: 'Churches always exist in ambiguous relationship with the society in which they are set. Their members both reflect and reject the values of the wider community to which they belong.'[34] Any denomination is a fluid creation, adapting its theology, polity, and social teaching to a changing national and local context; therefore, we must nuance our analysis and avoid overly deterministic assessments of denominational influences on feminism.

Nevertheless, denominational sub-cultures clearly shaped women's paths towards different forms of feminism. Disproportionate numbers of England's first organised feminists came from Unitarian and Quaker backgrounds. In her prosopography of 194 Victorian feminists, Philippa Levine found that 9 per cent of her total sample came from Quaker backgrounds and 11 per cent were Unitarian – striking figures given that each denomination made up less than 2 per cent of England and Wales' total population of 18 million in 1851.[35] The explanation for this overrepresentation is not simple. As Kathryn Gleadle has shown, the Unitarians may have emphasised women's equal intellectual capacities and stressed progressive education and political reform, but they also expected their wives and daughters to be dutiful and respectable: 'A vital catalyst in the formation of feminist awareness was that the expectations of personal fulfilment, which the Unitarian movement encouraged in women, were not met. The realities of endless household chores and caring rubbed uneasily alongside a dogma which extolled equality for all, intellectual achievement and public service.'[36] The contradiction between Unitarian teaching and practice on gender issues spurred women first to envision a more emancipated society and then, by the 1850s, to actively work for one. Barbara Leigh Smith and Bessie Rayner Parkes left the denomination but still applied many Unitarian ideas in their work in the Langham Place Circle.[37] Similarly, Quaker women, who came to feminist activism later than the Unitarians, also benefitted from egalitarian theology and progressive female education in addition to strong kinship and friendship networks, which provided scaffolding for their public, philanthropic, and political work.[38]

Britain's distinctive religious geographies also contributed to the varieties of British feminism. Welsh religious culture was dominated in the nineteenth century by a resistance to (English) authority. By 1851, Nonconformist chapels outnumbered Anglican churches by more than two to one, and many fostered a sense of Welsh nationalism.[39] The fusion of language, culture, religion and national identity is neatly summed up by R. Tudur Jones' observation that by 1900 the 'life of the churches' was 'a huge continent of Welshness'.[40] Our knowledge of how these unique dynamics shaped Welsh feminism is still expanding. In her account of Welsh women in the twentieth century, for example, Deirdre Beddoe avoids any sustained discussion of religion, dismissing Nonconformist chapels as rigid, patriarchal institutions.[41] Similarly, Angela John asserts that Welsh 'Nonconformity … reinforced domestic values'.[42] Yet, other evidence suggests alternative readings. Edith Picton-Turbervill, who came from a wealthy Evangelical family in Glamorgan and became a suffragist and eventually an MP, declared, 'My religious experience inspired me to attempt achievements I would never otherwise have dreamed of.'[43] Welsh women could boast of a long tradition of political activity, and they enjoyed more educational opportunities than women in England.[44] The role of Nonconformity in shaping these activities is worth further exploration.

In Scotland, religion was also a potent source of cultural identity and social cohesion, the effects of which were contradictory for women.[45] The Calvinist tradition embedded in the Church of Scotland produced a religiosity that demanded evidence of deeply held faith and propped up church-going rates among both the middle and working classes until well into the twentieth century.[46] But scholars are less certain about how to interpret the effects of this religiosity on the rise of Scottish feminism. Calvinist ideas and practices were often conservative, promoting purity, piety and good order which ultimately contributed to strong patriarchal families. Yet, Scottish churches in the nineteenth century followed the same pattern of feminisation as English churches, creating a female domain which, Callum Brown suggests, calls into question the extent of women's subordination within religious institutions and cultures.[47] Welsh and Scottish feminisms are often perceived as less vibrant than the English versions, but whether evangelical or Calvinist cultures were responsible remains an open question.

While these examples only begin to hint at the ways in which regional and denominational cultures could shape women's propensity to become feminists, they do illustrate the need for carefully calibrated local studies that look deeply into regional variations. Krista Cowman's research on women's politics in Merseyside, for example, begins to reveal how heightened sectarianism between Irish Catholics and Anglicans affected local feminist organisations and perhaps contributed to strong regional branches of the Anglican and Catholic suffrage organisations.[48]

Feminism and evangelicalism

Evangelicalism, which crossed denominational lines and touched the lives of women in all areas of Protestantism, may be the single most important reason for the current interpretive paradox. Simultaneously blamed for perpetuating Victorian domestic ideology and credited for the rise of feminism, evangelicalism's effects on women and gender ideals continue to cause heated debates.[49] It is true that evangelical spokespeople reinforced the notion that women should play different and subordinate social roles, but as David Bebbington has emphasised, 'the picture can be painted in too monochrome a way'.[50] Not all evangelicals harboured a dim view of women's potential, and some of the liveliest supporters of women's suffrage came from evangelical communities. Congregational, Baptist, Methodist and other evangelical churches provided a gathering space for women and gave them opportunities to turn their personal convictions into public action. Across England, Scotland and Wales, women found far more than just polite, part-time outlets for their talents in the mission societies, benevolent reform associations, temperance organisations, Sunday schools and purity groups that drew their time and attention. Evangelicalism provided its adherents with a purpose, a supportive community, and a noble worldview. 'Women pursued religion as an occupation', Harriet Martineau once observed of evangelical circles.[51]

However, it is difficult to understand the causal relationship between women's evangelical activities and their desire for gender emancipation. Many individuals who first joined the late Victorian temperance and purity movements went on to champion women's suffrage and other explicitly woman-centred issues, but they tended to conceptualise their activism as an outgrowth of their Christian ideals. If they desired gender equality it was because they believed God had ordained it. Josephine Butler provides the classic example of this.[52] A champion of women's right to control their own bodies, she couched her work to repeal the Contagious Diseases Acts in evangelical terms, as evident in this 1869 article in *The Shield*: 'The question here raised is no question of what are termed "Women's rights". It is a question of God's law; and when things are done ... which openly violate His laws, women, as well as men, are bound ... to raise their voice against them.'[53] But, despite such language, Butler's version of evangelical Christianity was self-consciously feminist. Helen Mathers reminds us that Butler regarded herself as having been liberated, although not by her own actions, but by Christ.[54]

The impact of women's evangelical activities on their clients is yet another murky area. For working-class women and girls, popular evangelical organisations such as the Girls' Friendly Society, Band of Hope and Girl Guides bestowed social and intellectual empowerment, but scholars have argued they also promoted a reverence for puritanical virtues 'useful to the maintenance of good order in capitalist society, and to the recreation of a sober and industrious labour force'.[55] Temperance activists often reinforced women's domestic roles when they enlisted the help of women and girls to reform their male family members' behaviour. But working-class women were not merely passive recipients of these evangelical campaigns. They 'stood to gain a great deal from a temperance environment', including a more stable home environment and a sense of pride and self-worth.[56] As Eleanor Gordon and Gwyneth Nair have argued in their study of nineteenth-century Glasgow, 'Religious belief could (and did) encourage different and even oppositional ways of thinking which lead to a questioning of separate spheres as formulated in terms of "public" and "private".'[57] Still, the link between evangelicalism and feminist activism, which might have been strong for the rescuers, was most likely weak for those being rescued.

The 'New Woman' and the critique of Christianity

By the century's end, the women's movement may have been experiencing an organisational lull, but feminism was undergoing radical redefinition with the emergence of a new generation who coalesced around the figure of the 'New Woman'. Typically recognised as a figure of sexual transgression, the New Woman also became a symbol of religious unorthodoxy, scepticism, and emergent secularism. Her fictional counterparts deliberately confronted religious authority and helped to construct a new feminist discourse on religion in which individual choice, rational reflection and doubt were central features in the expression of a feminist worldview. Meanwhile, non-fictional New Women were stirring up the status quo and breaching the carefully calibrated Victorian gender system through their presence in debating clubs, settlement houses, suffrage meetings and university halls. The collective effect was to bring under scrutiny the assumed alliance between Christianity and women's emancipation.

Fictional representations are a particularly rich source of insight into these late Victorian cultural shifts. Victorian novelists typically preserved the sacred union between religious orthodoxy and male patriarchy.[58] Victorian female characters appeared as faithful beacons of hope and preservers of piety, who were shielded at all costs from the dangers of the religious doubt expressed by the men around them (e.g. Mrs Humphry Ward's *Robert Elsmere* [1888]). When a female character was permitted to doubt Christian doctrine, she was usually either killed off (e.g. Ward's *Helbeck of Bannisdale* [1898]), or gently guided back into the fold by a concerned parson or male relative (e.g. Charlotte Mary Yonge's *The Clever Woman of the Family* [1865]). By contrast, New Woman novelists challenged both male dominance *and* received Christian truths.

The New Woman's reputation as a sceptic and freethinker stemmed in large part from Olive Schreiner's poignant exploration of faith and its loss in her novel *The Story of an African Farm*, published in 1883, a decade before the actual debut of the 'New Woman'. The book became a classic among succeeding generations of feminists, who sometimes spoke of it as a founding text. Schreiner's rebellious young Lyndall 'helped to establish both the intellectual basis and rhetorical tropes of turn-of-the-century feminism', Sandra Gilbert and Susan Gubar have argued.[59] The novel is rich with interpretive possibilities – critics have read it as a call for women's emancipation, a preliminary statement of socialist virtues, and an early challenge to the exploitative imperial and racist relationship between the English and Schreiner's native South Africans. It is also a powerful testament to her original theological imagination.

In *African Farm*, Schreiner did not offer an explicitly feminist critique of Christianity – as would Mona Caird and her American contemporaries Elizabeth Cady Stanton and Matilda Joslyn Gage a decade later. But she did suggest that the rebellion against patriarchy and the rejection of orthodox Christianity were natural allies.[60] With other freethinkers Schreiner believed that the Christian tenets of original sin, eternal damnation and vicarious atonement were thoroughly immoral. A cruel and savage God, willing to damn people to suffering in all eternity, was not a figure with whom she wished to be associated. By pairing the moral critique of Christianity with a moral critique of prescribed gender roles, Schreiner asserted that male superiority was just as immoral as a vengeful God. 'Christianity', she once wrote, 'with its horrible doctrine of a man as *God*!!! and of vicarious atonement, darkened and embittered my childhood.'[61] After its English publication in 1883, the book sold extremely well and Schreiner quickly gained fame and notoriety. *African Farm* appeared at a critical cultural moment when Christianity was already under assault from the new scientific epistemologies and emerging interest in comparative religions, among other developments. As Carolyn Burdett observes, the 'intimately felt individual experience' in *African Farm* 'reverberated with a wider cultural sense of dissolving Christian authority'.[62]

Schreiner was not the only feminist voice contributing to the New Woman's unorthodox reputation. In a notorious series of essays published between 1888 and 1894, later gathered into a collection entitled *The Morality of Marriage* (1897),[63] Mona Caird launched her own critique of Christianity, exposing its complicity with women's subordination in marriage and motherhood. Whereas Schreiner had only *implied* an alliance between feminism and religious scepticism, Caird insisted upon it. Caird is well known for her scathing attack on the institution of marriage (and the 27,000 letters she received when the *Daily Telegraph* invited responses),[64] but is less recognised for her bold analysis of the historical effects of Christianity on women's roles. In *The Morality of Marriage*, Caird rejected all biologically based arguments for women's oppressed position and argued instead that it was the by-product of social and historical developments and, specifically, Christianity: 'If we could only realize how fundamental, in our traditions, is the patriarchal feeling, we should then more clearly see that marriage, with its one-sided obligations, is not a thought-out rational system of sex relationship, but a lineal descendant of barbarian usages, crude and absurd.'[65] Christianity had not created patriarchy, she admits, but it was to blame for developing and perpetuating it. Christianity's ill effects on women could be seen from the Roman Empire through the Reformation, when the introduction of Protestantism deprived women of what little independence they had (often in nunneries) and relegated them to a life of childbearing.

The power of Caird's argument lay in her assertion that it was not merely a few present-day clerics who were responsible for women's subjection, but rather an entire historic system of belief and practice. Caird knew she was entering a thorny debate which would tap into all sorts of cultural anxieties: 'It is usual to trace all improvements in the position of women to Christianity', she conceded. But Caird took inspiration from Karl Pearson, who saw little but evil in the effects of the Protestant Reformation on social relations: 'Whatever may be thought regarding the ultimate influence of this faith on social relations, its first effect was hostile to female interests.'[66]

Feminist spiritualities

Others soon joined the conversation about what a distinctively feminist – as opposed to feminine – spirituality might look like.[67] The journal *Shafts*, a radical feminist periodical published between 1892 and 1899 by the Theosophist Margaret Shurmer Sibthorpe, frequently featured the work of Caird, along with that of Olive Schreiner, Elizabeth Wolstenholme Elmy, and other figures who regularly weighed in on these controversial issues. *Shafts'* pages were filled with passionate discussions of religion and spirituality, and while there was no unified feminist line, it tended to advance an unorthodox perspective: 'The Church has been built on the necks of women', declared one editorial. 'They are, indeed, the great supporters of the doctrines which degrade them ... Let them study the historic effects of the religion to which they have been attached.'[68] Many *Shafts* articles promoted Theosophy and spiritualism as viable feminist alternatives to patriarchal Christianity.[69]

More debate could be found on the pages of the *Women's Penny Paper (WPP)*, which began publication in 1888 under the direction of Henrietta Müller, a Cambridge-educated school board member who become a Theosophist in 1891. Focused more on rehabilitating Christianity than rejecting it, *WPP* published dozens of feminist and woman-centred critiques of religion. Included were reviews of such books as Sara S. Hennell's 3-volume *Present Religion* ('an attempt to produce a scheme of natural religion expressly from a woman's point of view'), letters on such topics as 'Bible Teaching on the Position of Women' (an effort to reconcile the Bible with women's emancipation), and a regular feature entitled 'Bible Readings' (dedicated to exposing '1900 years of bad translations of the Bible'): 'It is time for women to restore as far as may be the integrity and Truth of the Bible, for they are wrong who silently submit to or acquiesce in robbery which is also sacrilege. We want women to be the interpreters and translators, the expounders and teachers and preachers of the Bible.'[70] Women's ministry was another popular topic, with regular features on Laura Ormiston Chant's vibrant preaching in Unitarian, Congregationalist and Methodist chapels.

Nineteenth-century feminist spirituality had its blind spots, however, inherited from a Victorian imperial context rife with classist and racialised assumptions. Critiques of women's place in Christianity could easily veer towards self-righteous assessments of women's degraded position in non-western religions.[71] Even the new esoteric religions like Theosophy and Spiritualism, which attracted small but not insignificant numbers of progressive women by their eastern forms of religious expression, could not escape racist inflections. Theosophists, Joy Dixon observes, struggled to resist 'easy narratives of progress' and 'the dichotomies between the "modern", emancipated, English woman and her "degraded" Indian counterpart'. These '[d]ebates over the content and implications of a feminist spirituality could reinforce divisions among women and between women and men, but they could also generate new solidarities.'[72]

One of those divisions was increasingly evident right at home. Not all progressive women at the century's end participated in or even supported the quest for a feminist spirituality. Other popular women's (and arguably feminist) journals of the decade – the *Women's Herald* and *Woman's Signal,* for example – still presented religion on their pages with completely uncritical eyes and viewed the Church as an ally of women's emancipation. Conservative feminists resisted the decoupling of women and spiritual superiority. The well-known social purity feminist, Ellice Hopkins, for example, remarked rather curtly in *The Power of Womanhood* (1889) that 'Mrs Mona Caird need [not] be taken too seriously, ... it would be ... pathetically absurd to see the whole upward-striving past, the whole noble future of the human race, sacrificed to their unruly wills and affections, their passions and desires.'[73] But the damage had been done, and henceforth feminists like Hopkins could no longer assume a consensus that Christian ideals promoted women's advancement. Discussions of a feminist position on religion and the Church would continue to reverberate among suffrage activists well into the twentieth century.

Feminist spiritualities and the women's suffrage movement

The interactions between religious ideas and institutions and the British women's suffrage movement, which came to dominate the feminist political agenda in the early twentieth century, is gradually receiving scholarly attention.[74] This genera-tion of activists understood feminism's transformative potential in all areas of life, and they harnessed a distinctive feminist spirituality in their campaign for the vote. Since the earliest days of the movement, suffragists based their arguments on their belief in women's special moral character and potential to elevate British national life, a message that intensified in the new century after the introduction of mili-tancy.[75] The Women's Social and Political Union (WSPU), Martha Vicinus has argued, built upon the foundation of Victorian beliefs about women's spiritual nature and made 'a conscious effort ... to forge a new spirituality, based upon women's traditional idealism and self-sacrifice'.[76] Suffragettes fashioned militancy as a spiritual quest, with the vote merely a tool for the larger goals of securing justice, dismantling patriarchy, strengthening the nation and ensuring human evolution. They claimed their movement was a 'Holy War' against the forces of vice and materialism and vowed to fight with no other weapon than 'The Sword of the Spirit'.[77] The suffragette Annie Kenney later observed, 'For the first few years the Militant Movement was more like a religious revival than a political movement.'[78]

Suffragists and suffragettes co-opted religious language, symbols and ideas to such a degree that it is hard to distinguish between unconscious cultural borrow-ings and self-conscious adaptations. Suffragettes spoke about their cause as a Christian crusade, expressed their political claims in the language of faith, and staged political actions that resembled massive Christian revivals. In response to anti-suffragists who regularly accused the militants of promoting ideas and methods that were illegal, immoral, and un-Christian,[79] suffragettes claimed their goals and methods were firmly based on Christian ideals. They cast their oppo-nents as 'Pharisees', 'Crucifiers' and even 'anti-Christs'. As suffragettes set fire to letter boxes, smashed windows, went to jail and withstood forced-feedings, they described their acts of resistance as recreating the 'spirit of the early Christians'. Suffrage rallies were consciously modelled after the revivalist meetings popularised by Victorian evangelists, the Salvation Army and the Labour Church. By 1913, the suffragettes had brandished their 'sword' against the nation's religious institutions – in retribution, they claimed, for collaborating with Britain's government and failing to recognise their righteous motives. In addition to interrupting religious services with cries of 'Votes for Women', suffragettes launched arson attacks against more than fifty churches, chapels and synagogues by 1914.

The movement's openly religious rhetoric has long puzzled feminist scholars. Margaret Jackson, for example, has proposed that suffrage activists used religious vocabulary because most still subscribed in an uncritical way to Christian beliefs and adopted the language because it 'was the only one available to them'.[80] Similarly, Sheila Jeffreys discounts any connection between the suffrage activists' religious language and their actual beliefs, suggesting that they used religious vocabularies strategically as a form of feminist resistance.[81] But these interpretations fail to appreciate the complexity of feminism's relationship to Christian cultural assumptions and its already well-developed critique of religious patriarchy. They also discount the ways in which suffrage activists were deliberately co-opting and subverting religious orthodoxy. Christian discourses may still have been the common currency of British culture, but suffrage activists were actively forging new conceptions of spirituality and its relationship to the political realm.

Individuals responded to the movement's revivalist atmosphere with a degree of passion and sacrifice that came to resemble a quasi spirituality.[82] Many suffragettes described their socialisation into the WSPU's radical cosmology in terms of a conversion experience.[83] In her *Memories of a Militant*, Annie Kenney recalled her own transformation which came shortly after her imprisonment in 1905 for interrupting a campaign rally:

> I knew *the* change had come into my life. The old life had gone, a new life had come. Had I found on my return that I had taken on a new body, I should not have been in the least surprised. I felt absolutely changed. The past seemed blotted out. I had started a new cycle.[84]

An avid Theosophist in 1924 when she penned her memoir, Kenney thoughtfully explores the relationship between her emerging feminist consciousness and her evolving spirituality, advancing the notion that spirituality was compatible with – indeed almost a prerequisite for – emancipation from class and gender oppression. Such self consciousness was far from unique. The dozens of autobiographies produced by suffrage activists provide glimpses – some fleeting, others sustained – of the ways in which religious beliefs and practices intertwined with their development as feminists. Most common was a journey from orthodoxy to unorthodoxy (although not necessarily belief to unbelief) as they became more ensconced in the movement.

For Welsh evangelical Edith Picton-Turbervill, the suffrage movement 'slowly but surely' began to widen her mind 'with regard to theological beliefs and religious outlook'.[85] Raised in a strict evangelical home with a mother who admired Moody and Sankey, Picton-Turbervill devoted her youth to mission work. She taught Sunday school, conducted a temperance choir and organised a mission to the navvies living in huts near Glamorgan. Even after several years as a YMCA missionary in India, she clung tenaciously to narrow evangelical beliefs. But her experience overseas gently raised her consciousness about women's subordination and after her return to England she joined the suffrage movement. By 1916, she was still an Anglican but had become a fervid advocate for women's ordination to the Anglican priesthood.[86]

Even suffrage activists who left organised religion saw a spiritual quality in the movement. Teresa Billington-Greig, who was repulsed by her mother's incessant prayers and daily church visits, left Catholicism for the Ethical Society, drawn by its emphasis on rational and moral approaches for social change. However, her religious scepticism did not extinguish a belief in the underlying morality of humanity, a conviction she brought to her work in the suffrage movement. Describing her decision to give up teaching for work as a WSPU organiser, she depicts the movement as a spiritual phenomenon, poised to supersede the antiquated practices of Christianity and the unjust system of capitalism:

I threw the whole thing over to devote myself to my own idealistic and rebellious socialist dream, which was compounded largely of ethics [and] humanitarianism, to be fulfilled in a dual society which would destroy masculinism and cast aside all creeds and crutches to rely on reason, love and fair dealing. I was one of the idealists who saw as the hopeful dawn, not the political Labour Party then coming to birth before our eyes, but a great missionary movement for mental and moral uplift based on the solid foundation of an equalitarian economy.[87]

For Billington-Greig, activism on behalf of women and the working classes had become her new cosmology.

The rise of 'denominational feminism'

The suffrage movement not only transformed individual lives, it also affected denominational cultures. In an effort to attract the support of their religious communities, suffrage activists joined with supportive clergy to found six religious suffrage leagues between 1909 and 1912, representing the Anglican, Catholic, Free Church, Presbyterian, Quaker and Jewish faiths. Five were based in England, with branches extending into Wales, Scotland and Ireland. The sixth – the Scottish Churches League for Women's Suffrage – was active solely in Scotland. Members of these religious leagues identified themselves as feminists; many were inspired by suffragette militancy and saw themselves as sharing common goals with the 'fighting women'. All were committed to securing political rights for women on an equal basis with men.[88] Their existence is unique among suffrage movements in Western Europe and the United States and reveals the continuing power of denominational groupings in Britain to determine political alignments. The movement provided suffrage activists with an education about not only fickle political parties and wily politicians, but also the influence of Britain's churches, chapels and synagogues on the political process.

The religious leagues engaged in a complex process of association with and differentiation from both the suffrage movement and their own religious communities. Increasingly violent suffrage protests, for example, forced every group to distinguish their ideas and tactics from those of the militant suffragettes.[89] The (Anglican) Church League for Women's Suffrage (CLWS), which counted more than 500 clergymen as members, addressed suspicions that the CLWS harboured subversive and fundamentally immoral tendencies. In an article for the *Evening Standard* the Bishop of Lincoln attempted to separate the suffrage question from other radical social and political movements:

> The women's vote is not, and ought never to be made, a party question. It belongs to those great social problems that go behind and below all party politics ... And this is why we have formed our Church League for Women's Suffrage. We wish to assert that the exclusion of women from the vote is a social wrong – a piece of deliberate inequality which is a peril to our national well-being. As Christian people we are determined to see this wrong removed ... We hope also by our church league to testify to all good and respectable people ... how sane and orthodox an affair this suffrage movement really is. It has no essential connection with Atheism, or revolution, or Socialism, or the mobbing of Cabinet Ministers, or any other terrible thing. It aims only at doing justice to half the population of our country.[90]

Supportive clergy were not above claiming that God was on the side of the suffragists, as Rev. Lewis Donaldson did in an article entitled 'The Religion of Women's Suffrage': 'Underneath the liberating influence in the centuries, uplifting the life of women, I discern the operations of that Holy Spirit which Christ said He would send upon the earth.'[91] Not surprisingly, such arguments failed to convince unsupportive clergy and lay persons, and some denominations were deeply disrupted over the issue.

The Jewish League for Woman Suffrage (JLWS) faced a particularly tough challenge. Despite a strong tradition of Jewish women's organisations in Britain, the JLWS attracted little more than 300 members by 1914.[92] Undaunted, its leaders eagerly claimed the relevance of their Jewish heritage to the suffrage struggle as well as the value of feminism to modern Judaism. One pamphlet argued that the Jewish ideals of liberty and justice should inevitably lead to support for women's suffrage and claimed that Jewish women had special contributions to make: 'We should serve our country with our spiritual heritage as well as with our material and intellectual endowments.'[93] Other pamphlets depicted the JLWS as an organisation working not only to advance the interests of women but also of all

English Jewry who shared with women the experience of discrimination and subordination. When some Jewish women joined the ranks of the militant suffragettes, however, they faced castigation from all segments of the Jewish community. Leopold Greenburg, editor of the *Jewish Chronicle*, who at first had supported the idea of a Jewish suffrage league as a symbol of equality with the Christian churches, later protested that 'suffragist aims' may 'prejudice', rather than help, Jewish women's status and risked inciting anti-Semitism against the entire Jewish community. He argued that a militant Jewish suffragist

> who splintered that plate glass ... aroused indignation against her, not because she was a woman, but because she was a Jewess. That sentiment, once engendered ... spreads itself ... to all Jewesses, and it is easy to see ... the damage we Jews must suffer.[94]

Anglo-Jewish women faced some particularly challenging paradoxes. As Elizabeth DeBruin claimed in the *Westminster Review*, political emancipation had brought opportunities for Jews in Britain but it had also loosened their communal bonds. Similarly, as Jews adopted more English (i.e. Christian) social customs and became subject to English legal precedents, the Jewish woman's traditional authority within the home had eroded.[95] The solution, she argued, was to assign Jewish women greater roles in communal religious life. By 1913, the JLWS had taken up that very issue, sponsoring a deputation to the Chief Rabbi to ask that Britain's synagogues grant women the vote and place them in positions of leadership.[96]

The religious suffrage leagues provide new perspectives on the cultural frameworks informing feminist ideas and action in the early twentieth century. They also reveal the substantial roles women played in reshaping Britain's religious institutions. As Jewish women gained positions on Jewish communal boards, members of the CLWS organised a campaign for women's ordination, giving shape to what Brian Heeney has called 'church feminism' – that is, the effort to gain a 'reasonable share in Church government, in lay leadership of public worship, and in the charter role of the Church's professional ministry'.[97] The new strands of feminism emerging during and after World War I, represented by such organisations as the Anglican League of the Church Militant and the St Joan's Social and Political Alliance, grew out of and contrasted with the concerns and strategies of pre-war feminists, who tended to fashion their goals to *fit within* those deemed acceptable by their religious traditions. Instead, post-war feminists worked to *transform* their religious traditions – to recast them in terms and practices acceptable to feminists. This meant the drive not only to achieve equal voting rights on church councils and equal opportunities to enter the ministry, but also to reinterpret centuries of male-centred and misogynistic theological teaching. The new 'hyphenated feminisms' in the early twentieth century – e.g. 'socialist-feminist' and 'maternalist-feminist' along with 'Christian-feminist' and 'church-feminist'[98] – suggest a process of social and cultural differentiation that made these terms necessary.

Conclusion: only paradoxes to offer?

And so, in the broadest outlines, the paradox remains – that religion was both liberating and oppressive to women. But when feminist engagements with religious ideas and institutions are examined more closely and with attention to shifting historical contexts, that truism appears glib and unhelpful, for it fails to represent the complexity of Britain's religious landscape as well as the nuances in feminism as an ideology and platform for action. In order to understand the diverse ways in which feminists engaged with religion in the past, we must theorise religion expansively, to allow for nuances in personal experience. Religion must be understood 'on its own terms', Mircea Eliade famously declared, affirming the importance of individual spirituality in the modern age.[99] Furthermore, to focus on the paradox – that is, on what religion *did* to women – fails to acknowledge feminism's transformative power on not only the nation's political and educational institutions, but also its religious traditions. As John Kent has argued, feminism provided the 'most serious critical opposition to Christianity' in the modern world, and must therefore become a 'salient point' in religious history.[100] Feminism was far more than just a struggle for equal rights; it was a rich and disparate project of cultural reconstruction.

Further reading

Callum Brown, 'Religion', in Lynn Abrams, Eleanor Gordon, Deborah Simonton and Eileen Yeo (eds), *Gender in Scottish History since 1700* (Edinburgh: Edinburgh University Press, 2006).

Jacqueline deVries, 'Transforming the Pulpit: Preaching and Prophesying in the British Women's Suffrage Movement', in Beverly Kienzle and Pamela Walker (eds), *Women Preachers and Prophets in Christian Traditions* (Berkeley: University of California, 1998).

——, 'Challenging Traditions: Denominational Feminism in Britain, 1910–20', in Billie Melman (ed.), *Borderlines* (London: Routledge, 1998).

Joy Dixon, *Divine Feminine: Theosophy and Feminism in England* (Baltimore: Johns Hopkins, 2001).

Kathryn Gleadle, *The Early Feminists: Radical Unitarians and the Emergence of the Women's Rights Movement, 1831–51* (New York: St Martin's Press, 1995).

Brian Heeney, *The Women's Movement in the Church of England 1850–1930* (Oxford: Clarendon Press, 1988).

Linda Gordon Kuzmack, *Woman's Cause: The Jewish Woman's Movement in England and the United States* (Columbus: Ohio State University Press, 1988).

Sue Morgan (ed.), *Women, Religion and Feminism in Britain, 1750–1900* (London: Palgrave, 2002).

Jane Rendall, *The Origins of Modern Feminism: Women in Britain, France and the United States, 1780–1860* (Chicago: Lyceum Books, 1985).

——, 'Recovering Lost Political Cultures: British Feminisms, 1860–1900', in Sylvia Paletschek and Bianka Pietrow-Ennker (eds), *Women's Emancipation Movements in the Nineteenth Century* (Stanford: Stanford University Press, 2004).

Martha Vicinus, 'Male Space and Women's Bodies: The Suffragette Movement', in Martha Vicinus, *Independent Women: Work and Community for Single Women, 1850–1920* (Chicago: Chicago University Press, 1985).

Notes

1 Joan Wallach Scott, *Only Paradoxes to Offer* (Cambridge: Harvard UP, 1996).
2 Wilfred Cantwell Smith, a historian of comparative religion, has observed that 'faith' may be a more resonant category than 'belief' in the 20th century, in its emphasis on personal meaning over doctrinal knowledge. He defines 'faith' expansively as the way men and women make meaning of their relationship to the world, and he sees its expression in many forms – ritual, art, communal and social actions, interpersonal relations, and intellectual endeavours. Wilfred Cantwell Smith, *Belief and History* (Charlottesville: University of Virginia Press, 1977), pp. 39, 79.
3 As quoted in Jane Rendall, 'Recovering Lost Political Cultures: British Feminisms, 1860–1900', in *Women's Emancipation Movements in the Nineteenth Century* (ed.) Sylvia Paletschek and Bianka Pietrow-Ennker (Stanford: Stanford University Press, 2004), p. 37.
4 Hans Kellner, 'Language and Historical Representation', in *The Postmodern History Reader* (ed.) Keith Jenkins (London: Routledge, 1997), p. 127.
5 The phrase comes from Antoinette Burton, '"History" is Now: Feminist Theory and the Production of Historical Feminism', *Women's History Review*, 1:1 (1992), pp. 25–39.
6 Gerda Lerner, *The Creation of Feminist Consciousness* (New York and Oxford: Oxford University Press, 1993). Her definition of 'feminist consciousness' is inspired by the Marxist model of class consciousness.
7 Karen Offen, 'Defining Feminism: A Comparative Approach', *Signs* 14:1 (Autumn 1988), pp. 119–57. See also Sue Morgan's insightful discussion in 'Introduction: Women, Religion and Feminism: Past, Present and Future Perspectives', in Sue Morgan (ed.), *Women, Religion and Feminism in Britain, 1750–1900* (London: Palgrave, 2002).
8 Nancy Cott, *The Grounding of Modern Feminism* (New Haven: Yale University Press, 1987), p. 3.
9 Joan Wallach Scott, *Only Paradoxes to Offer*, p. 1.
10 Olive Banks, *Faces of Feminism* (New York: St Martin's Press, 1981), p. 16.
11 Jane Rendall, *The Origins of Modern Feminism: Women in Britain, France and the United States, 1780–1860* (Chicago: Lyceum Books, 1985), ch. 3. See also her sensitive discussion in 'British Feminisms, 1860–1900' in *Women's Emancipation Movements in the Nineteenth Century*, pp. 44–6.
12 For a discussion of this work, see Margaret Allen, Sandra Stanley Holton, and Alison MacKinnon (eds), 'Between Rationality and Revelation: Women, Faith and Public Roles in the Nineteenth and Twentieth Centuries', *Women's History Review*, vol. 7(2) (1998).
13 For a fuller discussion, see Morgan, 'Introduction: Women, Religion and Feminism: Past, Present and Future Perspectives', pp. 10–11.
14 Indeed, scholars sometimes forget that religion was a topic feminists discussed. In her recent document collection, for example, Fiona A. Montgomery includes chapters on law, marriage, education, work, politics, health and sexuality, but not on religion. Fiona A. Montgomery, *Women's Rights: Struggles and Feminism in Britain, c. 1770–1970* (Manchester: Manchester University Press, 2006).
15 Philippa Levine, *Feminist Lives in Victorian England* (Oxford: Basil Blackwell, 1990), pp. 11, 34–36. Levine argues that evangelicalism taught women many important skills and tactics that were useful in the women's movement, but ultimately its teachings 'remained inimical' to Victorian feminism.
16 In her more than 400-page biography of Emmeline Pankhurst, for example, June Purvis includes only several passing references to her struggles with religion. June Purvis, *Emmeline Pankhurst* (London: Routledge, 2004). For a positive

example, see Barbara Caine, *Victorian Feminists* (Oxford: Oxford University Press, 1993).

17 Ursula King, *Religion and Gender* (Oxford: Blackwell, 1995), p. 222.

18 Joy Dixon, *Divine Feminine: Theosophy and Feminism in England* (Baltimore: Johns Hopkins, 2001); Morgan, 'Introduction: Women, Religion and Feminism: Past, Present and Future Perspectives'; and Callum G. Brown, *The Death of Christian Britain* (London: Routledge, 2001).

19 Brown, *Death of Christian Britain*, pp. 11–14.

20 Callum Brown, 'Religion', in Lynn Abrams, Eleanor Gordon, Deborah Simonton and Eileen Yeo (eds), *Gender in Scottish History since 1700* (Edinburgh: Edinburgh University Press, 2006), p. 98.

21 For more examples see Jacqueline deVries, 'Rediscovering Christianity After the Postmodern Turn', *Feminist Studies* 31:1 (Spring 2005): 135–55.

22 Caroline Walker Bynum, *Fragmentation and Redemption* (New York: Zone Books, 1991), p. 19.

23 David Hempton, *Religion and Political Culture in Britain and Ireland* (Cambridge University Press, 1996), p. 147. See also Linda Colley, *Britons* (New Haven: Yale University Press, 1993); Keith Robbins, *History, Religion and Identity in Modern Britain* (London and Rio Grande: Hambledon Press, 1993); and John Wolffe, *God and Greater Britain: Religion and National Life in Great Britain and Ireland, 1843–1945* (London: Routledge, 1994).

24 Barbara Taylor, *Mary Wollstonecraft and the Feminist Imagination* (Cambridge: Cambridge University Press, 2003), p. 4.

25 Taylor, *Mary Wollstonecraft*, p. 9.

26 Levine, *Feminist Lives*, p. 36.

27 Sandra J. Peacock, *The Theological and Ethical Writings of Frances Power Cobbe, 1822–1904* (Lewiston, NY: Edwin Mellen Press, 2002), p. 9.

28 The topic requires further investigation. According to Barbara Caine: 'The example of a religious crisis in the formation of feminist consciousness is particularly useful … because it was a central issue to so many.' See her article, 'Feminist Biography and Feminist History', *Women's History Review*, vol. 3, no. 2 (1994): 256.

29 Laura Schwartz, 'The Bible and the Cause: Freethinking Feminists versus Christianity, England 1870–1900', *Women: A Cultural Review* (forthcoming).

30 W. E. H. Lecky, *A History of European Morals from Augustus to Charlemagne* (New York: D. Applegate and Company, 1873), pp. 111–13.

31 Sue Morgan, *A Passion for Purity: Ellice Hopkins and the Politics of Gender in the Late-Victorian Church* (Bristol: Centre for Comparative Studies in Religion and Gender, 1999), p. 38.

32 For an introduction to the influence of different religious traditions on the local level, see Wolffe, *God and Greater Britain*, ch. 3. Julie Melnyk provides a succinct overview in *Victorian Religion: Faith and Life in Britain* (Westport, CT: Praeger, 2008), ch. 2.

33 See, for example, the poignant although anecdotal essays 'Growing up Catholic' by Mary Chamberlain, and 'Dare to be a Daniel' by Alun Howkins in *Patriotism: The Making and Unmaking of British National Identity, Vol. II: Minorities and Outsiders*, ed. Raphael Samuel (London: Routledge, 1989).

34 Keith Robbins, 'Religion and Community in Scotland and Wales since 1800', in Sheridan Gilley and W. J. Sheils (eds), *A History of Religion in Britain* (Oxford: Basil Blackwell, 1994), p. 363.

35 Philippa Levine, *Feminist Lives in Victorian England: Private Roles and Public Commitment* (Oxford: Basil Blackwell, 1990), pp. 31–33.

36 Kathryn Gleadle, *The Early Feminists: Radical Unitarians and the Emergence of the Women's Rights Movement, 1831–51* (New York: St Martin's Press, 1995),

p. 27; see also Ruth Watts, *Gender, Power and the Unitarians in England, 1760–1860* (New York: Longman, 1998); and Helen Plant, '"Ye are all one in Christ Jesus": Aspects of Unitarianism and Feminism in Birmingham, c. 1869–90', *Women's History Review* 9:4 (2000): 721–41.

37 Gleadle, *The Early Feminists*, pp. 177ff.

38 Sandra Stanley Holton, *Quaker Women: Personal Life, Memory and Radicalism in the Lives of Women Friends, 1780–1930* (London: Routledge, 2007). See also E. A. O'Donnell, '"On Behalf of all Young Women Trying to be Better Than They Are": Feminism and Quakerism in the Nineteenth Century', *Quaker Studies* 6 (2001): 37–58.

39 For a fuller discussion, see Keith Robbins, 'Religion and Community in Scotland and Wales since 1800', in Sheridan Gilley and W. J. Sheils (eds), *A History of Religion in Britain* (Oxford: Basil Blackwell, 1994), pp. 373–80, and John Davies, *A History of Wales* (London: Penguin, 1993), pp. 500–507.

40 As quoted in John Davies, *A History of Wales*, p. 500.

41 Deirdre Beddoe, *Out of the Shadows: A History of Women in Twentieth-Century Wales* (Cardiff: University of Wales Press, 2000), pp. 11, 29.

42 Angela V. John (ed.), *Our Mothers' Land: Chapters in Welsh Women's History, 1830–1939* (Cardiff: University of Wales Press, 1991), pp. 1, 6.

43 Edith Picton-Turbervill, *Life is Good: An Autobiography* (London: Frederick Muller, Ltd, 1939), p. 83.

44 John, *Our Mothers' Land*, p. 9. W. Gareth Evans, *Education and Female Emancipation: The Welsh Experience, 1847–1914* (Cardiff: University of Wales Press, 1990).

45 For a perceptive and succinct summary of these dynamics, see Callum G. Brown, 'Religion', in Lynn Abrams et al., *Gender in Scottish History since 1700* (Edinburgh: Edinburgh University Press, 2006). For a more thorough treatment, see Leslie Orr MacDonald, *A Unique and Glorious Mission: Women and Presbyterianism in Scotland 1830–1930* (Edinburgh: John Donald, 2000).

46 C. G. Brown and J. Stephenson, '"Sprouting Wings"? Women and Religion in Scotland, c. 1890–1950', in *Out of Bounds: Women in Scottish Society, 1800–1945*, ed. E. Breitenbach and E. Gordon (Edinburgh: Edinburgh University Press, 1992).

47 Callum Brown, 'Religion'.

48 Krista Cowman, 'We Intend to Show What Our Lord Has Done for Women: The Liverpool Church League for Women's Suffrage, 1914–18', *Studies in Church History* 34 (1998), pp. 475–86.

49 The literature is vast. See references in Sarah Williams' and Sue Morgan's chapters in this volume.

50 David Bebbington, *The Dominance of Evangelicalism* (Downers Grove, IL: Intervarsity Press, 2005), p. 217.

51 As quoted in Jane Rendall, *The Origins of Modern Feminism*, p. 78.

52 For one consideration, see Helen Mathers, 'Evangelicalism and Feminism. Josephine Butler, 1828–1906', in Sue Morgan (ed.), *Women, Religion and Feminism in Britain, 1750–1900* (London: Palgrave Macmillan, 2002).

53 *The Shield*, No. 175 (August 2, 1873), p. 251.

54 Mathers, 'Evangelicalism and Feminism', pp. 132–33.

55 See for example the discussion of Scottish evangelicalism in Breitenbach and Gordon (eds), *Out of Bounds*, p. 114.

56 Breitenbach and Gordon (eds), *Out of Bounds*, pp. 115–16.

57 Gordon and Nair, *Public Lives*, p. 4.

58 Elisabeth Jay, 'Doubt and the Victorian Woman', in David Jasper and T. R. Wright (eds), *The Critical Spirit and the Will to Believe: Essays in Nineteenth-Century Literature and Religion* (New York: St Martin's Press, 1989), pp. 88–103.

59 Sandra Gilbert and Susan Gubar, *No Man's Land, Volume 2: Sexchanges* (New Haven: Yale University Press, 1989), p. 63.

60 Carolyn Burdett asserts, mistakenly I would argue, that the 'religious and spiritual crises of [Undine's] girlhood ... bear little relation to her plight as a woman'. Carolyn Burdett, *Olive Schreiner and the Progress of Feminism* (Houndmills: Palgrave, 2001), p. 16.

61 As quoted in Karel Schoeman, *Olive Schreiner in South Africa, 1855–1881* (Johannesburg: Jonathan Ball, 1989), p.110.

62 Burdett, *Olive*, p. 18.

63 The essays were originally published in *North American Review*, *Westminister Review*, *Fortnightly Review* and *Nineteenth Century* and have been collected as Mona Caird, *The Morality of Marriage, and other essays on the status and destiny of woman* (London: George Redway, 1897).

64 Shortly after Caird's first essay appeared, the *Daily Telegraph* opened a forum on the question 'Is Marriage a Failure?' and received the now well-known number of 27,000 letters in response. A selection of these can be found in Harry Quilter (ed.), *Is Marriage a Failure?* (London: S. Sonnenschein, 1888).

65 *Morality of Marriage*, p. 57.

66 *Morality of Marriage*, p. 73.

67 For a sensitive discussion of this topic, see Joy Dixon, *Divine Feminine: Theosophy and Feminism in England* (Baltimore: The Johns Hopkins University Press, 2001), esp. ch. 6.

68 J. M. Wheeler (no title), *Shafts* (January 1897), p. 9.

69 Dixon, *Divine Feminine*, pp. 162ff. See also Diana Burfield, 'Theosophy and Feminism: Some Explorations in Nineteenth-Century Biography', in *Women's Religious Experience* (ed.) Pat Holden (London: Croom Helm, 1983), pp. 27–55; and Alex Owen, *The Darkened Room: Women, Power and Spiritualism in Late Victorian England* (Philadelphia: University of Pennsylvania Press, 1990).

70 *Women's Penny Paper*, December 1, 1888; June 29, 1889; August 10, 1889.

71 See, for example, a series of articles published in the *Nineteenth Century*: Annie Reichardt, 'Mohammedan Women', *Nineteenth Century* 29 (June 1891): pp. 941–52; Violet Greville, 'Women and Worship in Burma', *Nineteenth Century* 31 (June 1892): pp. 1001–7; and Lucy M. J. Garnett, 'Women Under Islam: Their Social Status and Legal Rights', *Nineteenth Century* 37 (January 1895): pp. 57–70.

72 Dixon, *Divine Feminine*, pp. 165–66, 175.

73 As quoted in Angelique Richardson, *Love and Eugenics in the Late Nineteenth Century: Rational Reproduction and the New Woman* (Oxford: Oxford University Press, 2003), p. 181.

74 For a start, see Jacqueline deVries, 'Transforming the Pulpit: Preaching and Prophesying in the British Women's Suffrage Movement', in *Women Preachers and Prophets in Christian Traditions* (eds) Beverly Kienzle and Pamela Walker (Berkeley: University of California, 1998).

75 Suffragists also used other lines of argumentation, such as working women's rights to be represented. See discussion in Jane Rendall, 'British Feminisms, 1860–1900', in *Women's Emancipation Movements in the Nineteenth Century*, pp. 39ff.

76 Martha Vicinus, 'Male Space and Women's Bodies: The Suffragette Movement', in *Independent Women: Work and Community for Single Women, 1850–1920* (Chicago: Chicago University Press, 1985), pp. 251–52.

77 Christabel Pankhurst's *The Great Scourge* is perhaps the most blatant example of this type of argumentation. Published in serial form in *The Suffragette* in 1913, the articles were compiled into a book in early 1914.

78 Annie Kenney, *Memories of a Militant* (London: Edward Arnold, 1924), p. 298.

79 Brian Harrison, *Separate Spheres: The Opposition to Women's Suffrage in Britain* (London: Croom Helm, 1978). Harrison examines the other side in his insightful essay 'The Act of Militancy: Violence and the Suffragettes, 1904–14' in *Peaceable Kingdom: Stability and Change in Modern Britain* (Oxford: Clarendon Press, 1982), pp. 26–81; see his discussion of militancy as a form of secular faith, p. 44.

80 Margaret Jackson, *The 'Real' Facts of Life: Feminism and the Politics of Sexuality, c. 1850–1940* (London: Taylor & Francis, 1994), p. 27.

81 Sheila Jeffreys, *The Spinster and Her Enemies: Feminism and Sexuality, 1880–1930* (London: Pandora Press, 1985), esp. ch. 2.

82 In his analysis of similar phenomena among British socialists, Stephen Yeo points out that conversion was only quasi-religious 'if "religious" is a label reserved for particular orthodoxies' ('A New Life: The Religion of Socialism in Britain, 1883–96', *History Workshop Journal* 4 [Autumn 1977], p. 10).

83 See, for example, Kabi Hartman, '"What Made Me a Suffragette": The New Woman and the New (?) Conversion Narrative', *Women's History Review* 12:1 (Spring 2003): 35–50.

84 Annie Kenney, *Memories of a Militant* (London: Edward Arnold, 1924), p. 42.

85 Edith Picton-Turbervill, *Life is Good* (London: Frederick Muller, 1939), p. 112.

86 She authored a series of books and pamphlets on the topic, including *Musings of a Lay Woman on the Life of the Churches* (London: John Murray, 1919) and *Christ and Woman's Power* (London: Morgan & Scott, 1919).

87 Carol McPhee and Ann Fitzgerald (eds), *The Non-Violent Militant: Selected Writings of Teresa Billington-Greig* (London: Routledge & Kegan Paul, 1987), pp. 78, 88–95.

88 Brian Heeney, *The Women's Movement in the Church of England 1850–1930* (Oxford: Clarendon Press, 1988); Francis M. Mason, 'The Newer Eve: The Catholic Women's Suffrage Society in England, 1911–23', *The Catholic Historical Review* 72:4 (October 1976): 620–38; Elaine Clark, 'Catholics and the Campaign for Women's Suffrage in England', *Church History* 73:3 (September 2004): 635–65; Jacqueline deVries, 'Challenging Traditions: Denominational Feminism in Britain, 1910–20', in *Borderlines*, ed. Billie Melman (London: Routledge, 1998); Krista Cowman, '"We Intend to Show What Our Lord has Done for Women": The Liverpool Church League for Women's Suffrage, 1914–18', *Studies in Church History* 34 (1998): 475–86; and Linda Gordon Kuzmack, *Woman's Cause: The Jewish Woman's Movement in England and the United States* (Columbus: Ohio State University Press, 1988).

89 In their bombing campaign, for example, suffragettes targeted more than fifty churches, chapels and synagogues.

90 Dr Edward Lee Hicks, 'Church and Suffrage', *Evening Standard* (October 6, 1911), clipping in the Arncliffe-Sennett Collection, Volume 15, British Library.

91 Rev. F. Lewis Donaldson, 'The Religion of Women's Suffrage', *The Optimist* (1912); reprinted in pamphlet form by the Central Society for Women's Suffrage, 11–12.

92 First Annual Report of the Jewish League for Woman Suffrage, 1913–14 (Fawcett Library, London).

93 'Some Reasons Why You Should Join the JLWS', n.d. (British Library).

94 *Jewish Chronicle* (November 15, 1912), p. 19; Kuzmack, *Woman's Cause*, pp. 140–41.

95 Elizabeth DeBruin, 'Judaism and Womanhood', *Westminster Review* (August 1913), p. 125.

96 Kuzmack, *Woman's Cause*, p. 141.

97 Brian Heeney, *The Women's Movement in the Church of England, 1850–1930* (Oxford, 1988), p. 1.

98 For a discussion of these struggles, see Rosalind Delmar, 'What is Feminism?' in Juliet Mitchell and Ann Oakley (eds), *What is Feminism? A Re-Examination* (New York: Pantheon, 1986), pp. 8–33; and, 'Defining Feminism'.
99 For an introduction to Eliade, see Daniel L. Pals, *Seven Theories of Religion* (New York and Oxford: Oxford University Press, 1996), chapter 5.
100 John Kent, *The Unacceptable Face: The Modern Church in the Eyes of the History* (Minneapolis: Fortress, 1987), p. 131.

10 Modernity, heterodoxy and the transformation of religious cultures

Joy Dixon

Introduction

It is increasingly clear that 'secularisation theory' or at least its core notion of 'religious decline as a prolonged, unilinear and inevitable consequence of modernity'[1] is untenable. Various alternatives have been proposed, from Callum Brown's suggestion that the nineteenth century was actually a period of religious expansion and that the 'death' of Christian Britain came in the 1960s, to what Jeremy Morris describes as 'persistence and transformation' rather than decline, accompanied by the 'cultural displacement' of Christianity and the established Church.[2] Given the importance of these debates, it is useful to return to a period once understood as a turning-point in the history of secularisation: the late nineteenth and early twentieth centuries.

This period has long been synonymous with the late-Victorian 'crisis of faith' even though we have known for some time that both church and chapel experienced significant growth well into the twentieth century.[3] If the churches were not disappearing, however, they were changing. Science had not displaced religion, but it posed important challenges to religious authority. In the last decade there have been numerous studies of the multiple transformations of religious cultures in this critical period; this chapter surveys this new work and delineates new developments in thinking about 'secularisation'.

Whatever the status of Callum Brown's reframing of debates over secularisation in Britain, he correctly suggests the importance of gender to these changes. 'Gender', Brown argues, 'is emerging as possibly the single most important definer of the timing and content of long-term change to the Christian religion of Europe.'[4] At the same time, *how* gender is central is of critical importance. Brown's account places the emergence of a new understanding of religion (the 'privatisation of faith') alongside new gendered ideologies (the 'feminisation of piety').[5] But we should not mistake the historical coincidence of these shifts for an inevitable conflation of 'woman' with private piety. As Brown demonstrates, both the idea of the 'crisis of faith' and the definition of secularisation were products of nineteenth-century understandings of 'religion';[6] the categories which underpin the gendered piety Brown describes are also nineteenth-century creations. As Ann Braude points out for the American case, '[t]he theme of secularization is thus closely related to another narrative fiction – the highly gendered concept of "separate spheres", in which a public/private dichotomy is used to describe the distinctive roles of men and women in society'.[7] We need to find ways to write the history of religion and gender without allowing our analyses to collapse back into the Victorian binary of the 'secular man' and the 'spiritual woman'. As Joan Scott reminds us, we must not 'assume the abiding homogeneous collectivity called "women" upon which measurable experiences are visited'. Instead we need to 'interrogate the production of the category "women" itself as a historical or political event whose circumstances and effects are the object of analysis' and thus to 'problematize and historicize' both the significance of those categories and the categories themselves.[8]

Much of the most productive work in this field emphasises the dynamic relationships between secular and sacred, public and private, masculine and feminine. As Mark Knight and Emma Mason explain, 'To insist on rigid boundaries between the sacred and secular, as many thinkers have done from the eighteenth century onwards, is to demarcate religious space in a narrow and misleading manner … there is a continual slippage between the sacred and the secular.' Drawing on Jacques Derrida's use of the *bricoleur*, Knight and Mason discuss the 'rewriting' of religion by the secular and vice versa, emphasising the fluidity and contingency of the process.[9] Harry Cocks also argues for an approach that 'allows us to reshape the history of modernity not as a simple story of secularization which is shaped by the death of religion, but one that is informed by a dialogue between the secular and the spiritual'.[10] This new emphasis – on fluidity, contingency, rewriting, and dialogue – is a useful framework for rethinking the so-called 'crisis of faith'.

My exploration of the period from the 1880s to the 1930s focuses on only one strand (though an important one) in the relationship between gender, modernity and the transformation of religious cultures. There are many ways to define 'modernity'. As Michael Saler puts it, '"Modernity" is one of the most ambiguous words in the historian's lexicon.' Even so, Saler argues that there has been a consistent emphasis on what we might describe, following Max Weber, as 'disenchantment': 'Weber's memorable phrase ["the disenchantment of the world" from his 1917 lecture "Science as a Vocation"] encapsulated a long-standing critique … of the Enlightenment emphasis on reason and science at the expense of other ways of apprehending and being in the world.'[11] In what follows I trace some of the multiple engagements of 'faith' with reason and science: in liberal theology, in the natural sciences (particularly evolutionary biology), in the social sciences (comparative religions) and in the human sciences (sexology and psychology). In each case I have attended to the slippages – between 'man' and 'woman', secular and spiritual, orthodoxy and heterodoxy – which marked these debates, emphasising the historicity of these processes and the various ways that connections between the spiritual and the feminine were made (and unmade) in particular historical moments.[12] I have also focused on movements and organisations which were, admittedly, marginal to mainstream society. At the same time, that very marginality provides an opportunity to explore both the limits and the possibilities of the categories available in this period, reminding us of the extent to which – however natural they may have appeared from the cultural centre – they remained contested and contingent.

Liberal theology and the higher criticism

Women and men occupied radically different positions in relation to changes in biblical scholarship and theological debate. It was only at the end of the century, as Julie Melnyk notes in this collection, that liberal theology began to have significant influence on women's religious thought. And it is certainly the case that from the early decades of the nineteenth century the majority of commentators assumed, as Barbara Taylor put it in her now classic study of socialism and feminism, *Eve and the New Jerusalem* (1984), 'the identification of womanliness with godliness and both with the private virtues of domestic life'. As Taylor goes on to note, 'a morality more convenient and yet more contradictory would be hard to imagine'.[13] Women were, of course, excluded from virtually all positions of authority within both the established and the nonconformist churches even as they were given enormous symbolic importance as the more 'spiritual' sex. This gendered ideology similarly complicated men's relationship to the religious life. In many ways Christian conversion – with its emphasis on the denial of self, surrender to and dependence on Christ – was a paradigmatically feminine experience.[14] Men were simultaneously central (as clerics, theologians, and lay leaders) and marginal (as the supposedly 'secular sex') to Christianity.

If faith was gendered feminine in the nineteenth century, 'doubt' was clearly masculine. As Elisabeth Jay suggests, doubt was often symbolically represented as estrangement from one's wife; accounts like Samuel Butler's *The Way of All Flesh* (1903) and Edmund Gosse's *Father and Son* (1907) dramatised an explicitly masculine crisis of faith.[15] Indeed, as Joanna Dean writes, the literary theme of the crisis of faith has overwhelmingly been 'a masculine one, tied to the religious maturation and vocational difficulties of young college men … It was not simply that the models were masculine or that the narratives drew upon the male – and upper-class – trajectory of university education and clerical careers, but that the very nature of the crisis was conceived of in ways that conformed to a masculine sense of religious identity.'[16] Insofar as the theological scepticism and rational reflection which led to 'doubt' were perceived as masculine qualities, religious doubt was itself unfeminine. Women writers who dealt explicitly with these themes – like Lily Dougall, the subject of Dean's study, or Mary Ward, the author of the best-selling *Robert Elsmere* – tended to articulate their own religious doubts and questions through the male characters in their novels, confirming the masculine nature of doubt even as their own lives challenged that stereotype.

The impact of the 'higher criticism' on British intellectual and religious life is usually dated from George Eliot's translation into English of David Strauss's *Leben Jesu* (published in German in 1835) in 1846. In 1860 the publication by a group of seven prominent theologians of *Essays and Reviews* disseminated 'higher criticism' to a broad audience and, with its insistence on a historical and critical reading of the Bible, 'elicited a far stronger reaction from [evangelicals] than the publication of Charles Darwin's *The Origin of Species* in 1859'.[17] Even considered on its own, George Eliot's role in the translation of Strauss's work complicates any straightforward gendering of doubt in this period, but there were other important examples of women's participation in 'higher criticism' and the development of a liberal theology, a participation which literary and historical accounts of the masculinity of doubt (including those produced by women themselves) has tended to obscure.[18] Mary Ward, for example, was a prominent figure in public theological debate in her own day. Her novel *Robert Elsmere* (1888) was a run-away bestseller with nearly a million copies sold by 1909. In the novel the Anglican priest Elsmere loses his faith in miracles and in the historical truth of the gospels, resigning his post to become a social worker in the East End of London. Here, Ward conveyed her own 'radical abandonment of Anglican orthodoxy'[19] through a male voice, simultaneously challenging and confirming the contemporary gendering of piety and unbelief.

The embrace of religious modernism could legitimate challenges to gendered expectations around family, intellectual and religious life. Lily Dougall was another novelist and religious writer whose work engaged theological debates, negotiating complex relationships between gender, faith and doubt. Her first major theological work, *Pro Christo et Ecclesia* (1900) – a harsh criticism of the contemporary church – brought her to prominence (though anonymously) as a leading Anglican modernist. According to Joanna Dean, 'liberals like Dougall turned to personal religious experience in response to the collapse of biblical authority. They constructed an experiential theology out of evangelical piety, recovered mystical tradition, idealist philosophy, and the new psychology of religion'. Her work as a novelist and writer also helped to authorise Dougall's move away from her evangelical family in Canada to Oxford where she lived for most of her adult life with her companion Sophie Earp. In her own faith she developed a theology of personal experience of the divine linked to the image of an immanent God working in and through history – what Dean describes as a combination of 'incarnational Anglo-Catholicism, Quaker inner light, and modernist mysticism … [in] a religious outlook that was profoundly spiritual and also fiercely [and] combatively independent and liberal'.[20]

The Anglo-Catholic tradition could also underwrite gender and sexual nonconformity for both men and women. By the end of the nineteenth century Anglo-Catholicism was regularly portrayed by its Protestant critics as a 'feminine' style of religion.[21] The Catholic revival (in both its Anglo-Catholic and Roman forms) 'provided Victorian men and women', as Richard Dellamora puts it, 'with a body-centered, gender-crossing rhetoric of ecstasis and conversion that moved far beyond conventional ideas of gender and sexual roles'.[22] The Anglo-Catholic Christina Rossetti, for example, explored counter-hegemonic forms of religiosity in works such as *Goblin Market* (1859), which Frederick Roden reads as a feminist version of the gospels in which 'the female saviour depicted in th[e] poem resonates of Christ through an erotic, eucharistic feast', characterising Rossetti as a 'queer virgin' who rejected the reproductive imperative implicit in the valorisation of the Virgin Mary and challenged hetero-erotic tropes in her depictions of a non-phallic Christ.[23] She also made major contributions to Christian devotional writing (her six major works of devotional prose totalled more than 2,000 pages). While Rossetti's own gender ideology was relatively conservative, she emphasised the biblical basis for women's spiritual and intellectual equality with men, and created a prophetic voice for herself.[24]

In September 1907, Pope Pius X issued the encyclical against modernism, *Pascendi dominici gregis*, condemning both historical critiques of the Bible and the theological dynamism of Catholic modernism.[25] Even after 1907, however, women within the Roman Catholic tradition remained involved in theological experiment. The lesbian and aunt/niece couple Katherine Bradley and Edith Cooper who were the poet 'Michael Field' converted to Roman Catholicism early in 1907. While the two (led by Edith Cooper) vowed chastity after their conversion, they 'actively used Catholic symbol, sacrament, and story as vehicles for articulating their longing for one another'[26] (and for their dog, Whym Chow, whose death in 1906 played a critical role in their conversions, relationship, and understanding of faith). They experimented with trinitarian imagery, a 'private religious iconography [that] united two feminized roles, the crucified Christ and the Holy Ghost, with an active, masculine, God of passion and power'.[27] The work of the lesbian novelist Radclyffe Hall, who converted to Catholicism in 1912, can similarly be read as a radical re-working of theological tropes. Richard Dellamora describes Hall's notorious lesbian novel, *The Well of Loneliness* (1928), as a 'Christological narrative' and as a 'new Gospel, written … to affirm the saving power of love based in dissident desire'. Crucially, Dellamora characterises Hall's text as 'a testament of both faith and doubt', noting the ways it secularises ('by sexualizing the Catholic discourse within which she writes') and yet 'retains its linkage to the mystery of Christ's saving passion'.[28] Many of the important figures in this tradition were converts, drawn by an incarnational theology which could be used to celebrate 'the sacredness of humanity in all its lusty materiality … to integrate what many expressions of Protestantism tended to polarize: sacred and secular, spirit and flesh, revelation and historicity'.[29] In all of these cases, we can trace multiple slippages – between secular and sacred, between sexual and spiritual, and between masculine and feminine. Doubt is portrayed as part of faith; the bodily and sexual are embedded in, not opposed to, the spiritual. Women's embrace of religious modernism simultaneously marked them as 'masculine' (sceptical, rational, doubting) even as it undermined the purported masculinity of doubt itself.

Evolutionary biology, materialism, and scientific naturalism

The publication of Charles Darwin's *The Origin of Species* in 1859 was an important moment in the nineteenth-century renegotiation of the relationship between religion and science. Darwin's identification of natural selection as the mechanism by which evolution proceeded made it possible to explain the emergence of life, including human life, without recourse to a God or gods. At the same time Darwin's work was not necessarily destructive of religion; evolutionary theory could fit neatly into broader shifts in Victorian theology. As Calvinist atonement theology of the early nineteenth century was, in the second half of the century, displaced by an emphasis on the incarnation as the central Christian theme there was more emphasis on God's immanence in the world and a more optimistic view of both human nature and human progress; a theology based on God's imma- nence within creation could certainly accommodate evolutionary theory.[30] The perceived incompatibility between science and religion in this period was more the result of the spread of materialist philosophy (especially in the form of scientific naturalism as it was promoted by figures like T. H. Huxley) than a reaction to evolutionary theory itself. In any case, it is crucial that we recognise what Jeffrey Cox has described as the 'very interesting and ongoing adaptation of religious forms to the modern world',[31] including to materialism and evolutionary science.

Spiritualism in Britain was both an adoption of and a challenge to the evolu- tionary and materialist ethos. The beginnings of modern spiritualism are usually traced to the 'Hydesville rappings' in America, when in 1848 two young teenaged sisters, Katherine and Margaret Fox, claimed to have communicated with the spirit of a murdered pedlar. In the United States spiritualism became associated with a radically democratic form of spiritual practice and a progressive position on the 'Woman Question'.[32] A somewhat less radical version of spiritualism arrived in Britain in the 1850s and by the 1870s the private and family circles of the previous generation had expanded into a network of local societies and neighbourhood associations. The formation in 1874 of the British National Association of Spiri- tualists, dedicated to 'carrying out and publicising carefully documented scientific research into spiritualist phenomena',[33] marked a new level of public prominence for spiritualists, and the movement – with some setbacks – continued to grow into the early twentieth century. (Spiritualism's relatively informal organisational struc- ture makes membership difficult to estimate, but one early historian has estimated that in the years just after the Great War the British movement attracted close to half a million supporters.[34]) Opposition to materialism was a central concern of spiritualists; as Samuel Carter Hall put it in 1884, '[spiritualism] has mainly but one purpose – TO CONFUTE AND DESTROY MATERIALISM, by supplying sure and certain and *palpable* evidence that to every human God gives a soul which he ordains shall not perish when the body dies'.[35] Opposing 'materialism' with material evidence, spiritualists claimed to provide a material proof of the existence of spirit. Spirit voices, direct writing, knocks and raps, and materialised spirit forms 'crossed and recrossed the boundaries between the spiritual and material world', attempting to meet the materialists on their own ground.[36]

This blurring of the line between the material and the spiritual was most dra- matic in full-form materialisation, which became prominent in spiritualist practice in the 1870s. While spiritualists believed that everyone had the potential to com- municate with the spirits, by this period most mediums were young, female and upper working or middle class. As Alex Owen puts it, they were 'precisely those who most closely identified with the dominant ideal of womanhood'. Since med- iums were the 'linchpin of spiritualist practice', the belief that women were parti- cularly gifted spiritual mediums made them, and their negotiation of Victorian gender ideology, central to the history of the movement.[37] Full-form materialisation mediumship, in which the medium produced not only spirit raps or voices, but also 'phantasmic bodies – literally materialized spirits'[38] – highlighted the complexities of that negotiation. In 1873 the young working-class medium, Florence Cook, produced the first full-form spirit materialisation in Britain, which 'represented for confirmed spiritualists the final empirical evidence for the reality of spirit life and the existence of an unseen world'. Cook's dramatic materialisations of 'Katie King' made her a celebrity even as (thanks to the support of a wealthy patron) she maintained her status as a 'private' and therefore more respectable (because confined to the familial and domestic) medium.[39] With Florence Cook safely secured by sealed ropes in a locked and darkened cabinet, 'Katie King' displayed her body in ways that went well beyond Victorian propriety, exchanged kisses and embraces with both male and female sitters and bantered – often crudely – with members of the séance circle. What Marlene Tromp describes as the 'cascading boundary disruption in Spiritualism' disrupted a linked series of binaries – spirit/matter, spiritual/sexual, body/spirit, man/woman – 'blurring the boundaries between the terms, rather than challenging them more directly'.[40] Many materialisation mediums also had non-white spirit 'controls' – like 'Yolande', the teenaged Arab girl who spoke through Elizabeth d'Esperance – and the slippage between the medium's self and these 'racially other ghosts' functioned as a challenge to late Victorian imperialism as well as 'undermin[ing] rigid notions of gendered identity' even as it insulated white women from criticism for disruptive or unconventional behaviour in the séance room.[41]

Alex Owen nicely captures the contradictions of spiritualism's reworking of the relationship between gender, authority and passivity:

> the Victorian séance room became a battle ground across which the tensions implicit in the acquisition of gendered subjectivity and the assumption of female spiritual power were played out. Renunciation of the conscious personality was the price paid for the authoritative voice. The ultimate irony of spirit mediumship, and the measure of its adherence to prescriptive norms, lay in the fact that it operated around a fundamental power/powerlessness duality.[42]

Spiritualism was therefore very closely tied to specifically nineteenth-century understandings of the relationship between gender, religion and respectability. It did not, however, disappear with the nineteenth century; it continued to be popular in Britain well into the twentieth century, receiving an enormous boost in the aftermath of the Great War and reaching its height in the 1930s. According to Jenny Hazelgrove, 'Spiritualism's power of persuasion', within its primarily working-class constituency in this period, 'was rooted in its ability to elicit and co-ordinate a variety of fugitive and fragmented supernaturalisms buried in modernity'.[43] Hazelgrove links the decline of spiritualism to the reworking of images of womanhood in the years between the wars as mediums were 'stigmatised by association with repellent and devouring maternity ... [and] tainted by the stereotype of the frustrated spinster'.[44] The successes of the feminist movement in the second half of the twentieth century also eroded the equation of femininity with passivity, and therefore undermined the view of womanhood on which the image of the spiritualist medium relied even as it opened up new possibilities for women's spiritual leadership in Wicca and 'New Age' movements.

The popularity of full-form materialisation mediumship brought attention to the spiritualist movement but it also brought notoriety, and by the 1880s many spiritualists had turned to supposedly more sophisticated mental phenomena and to new movements like the Theosophical Society (TS), founded in New York in 1875 by the Russian emigrée Helena Petrovna Blavatsky and the American Henry Steel Olcott. The movement's headquarters was relocated to India in 1879 and settled permanently in 1882 at Adyar, a suburb of what was then Madras. The British Theosophical Society was formally organised in 1878. Women were a minority among the early theosophists, who borrowed much of their style and ritual from the Masonic movement, preserving its elite, male character. Like spiritualism, theosophy claimed to meet science on its own ground; the publication of Blavatsky's *magnum opus*, the massive two-volume *Secret Doctrine* (1888), affirmed theosophy's claim to speak 'scientifically'. The *Secret Doctrine* laid out an emanationist view of the development of the physical universe, a process of ebb and flow in which spirit gradually unfolded itself in matter, attaining consciousness and returning to spirit in a higher and more realised form. As individual sparks of the Divine entered incarnation they began a process of spiritual evolution, moving through a series of 'Root Races' and 'sub-races'. A number of theosophists seized on reincarnation as a way of rethinking essentialist notions of manhood and womanhood within an evolutionary framework. As Susan E. Gay, a former spiritualist with Swedenborgian sympathies, wrote in the theosophical journal *Lucifer* in 1890, for example, a woman was in reality only 'a SOUL temporarily clothed in the garb of womanhood'.[45] The ideal, Gay argued, was a divine androgyny that combined the best of both sexes.

Theosophy, like spiritualism, was remarkably open to women's participation and leadership. Henrietta Müller – one of the first women to attend Girton College, Cambridge and the founder of the feminist weekly *The Women's Penny Paper* in 1888 – made a point of asking Blavatsky directly whether women in the TS enjoyed equal rights with men; Blavatsky responded that the Society made no distinction of sex.[46] The 'First Object' of the TS, and the only one to which new members were required to subscribe, was 'to form a nucleus of the Universal Brotherhood of Humanity, without distinction of race, creed, sex, caste, or color'. The First Object was interpreted in various ways, and Henrietta Müller's brand of equality feminism was not universally welcomed within the TS. Women remained a minority within the Society until the early twentieth century when – especially after Annie Besant became President of the TS in 1907 – they began to constitute the majority of members. The influx of large numbers of women transformed the Society, and was accompanied by a new emphasis on the devotional and emotional aspects of religiosity. At the same time the 'feminisation' of theosophy was by no means a straightforward process. As I have argued elsewhere, theosophy in the twentieth century was characterised by a 'sexual division of spiritual labor that distinguished between feminine modes of mystical experience and a more virile, magico-clerical occult tradition. But because the vision of gender relations on which these divisions were based was itself internally divided, the version of feminine spirituality that emerged was a contradictory one.'[47]

Theosophy was always a minority movement. At its height in the late 1920s (when the movement benefited from widespread disillusionment with both orthodox Christianity and mainstream science in the wake of the First World War) the English section of the society numbered just over 5,000 members.[48] Nonetheless, theosophy held a special appeal for women, especially those in the feminist movement. Late-Victorian and Edwardian feminists were substantially over-represented within the TS and within esoteric religions more broadly; almost 10 per cent of prominent women active in the feminist movement were involved in the Theosophical Society or similar movements.[49] Theosophical themes – especially theosophical race theory and the place of the feminine within it – were taken up by a number of prominent feminists and reworked to rewrite both orthodox Christianity and the claims of evolutionary science. These were not unproblematic reworkings, and racism and imperialism provided the enabling context for much of feminist esotericism as it did for esotericism more broadly.[50]

Frances Swiney's work provides a clear illustration of the power of esoteric readings of scientific themes to fuel a feminist discourse. It also highlights the racist context within which this version of global feminism was developed. Swiney was born into a military family in India in 1847; in 1871 she married a major-general and went on to have six children. In the late-nineteenth and early-twentieth centuries she began an active literary career and became active in the English suffrage movement, in both the National Union of Women's Suffrage Societies and the Women's Social and Political Union. Her first major publication, *The Awakening of Women* (1899), celebrated (Anglo-Saxon) womanhood as the pinnacle of evolution, and her work was dominated by a concern with 'racial' purity and 'racial poisons' (which included sperm alongside tobacco and alcohol). In Swiney's uncompromising celebration of the Divine Feminine the male became a transitional phase between the Eternal Feminine Cause and the Eternal Feminine Effect, a waste product of nature and an imperfect version of woman on both the physical and the spiritual planes.[51] Swiney bolstered her spiritual claims with reference to the latest scientific texts. She quoted the German physiologist Ludwig Büchner to make the case that women's brains were more evolved than men's, and the English sexologist Havelock Ellis to the effect that women's delicate and hairless bodies were more evolved than those of their (ape-like) male counterparts. Swiney, a founding member of the Eugenics Society in 1907, 'reformulated eugenics as a moral and spiritual enterprise as opposed to an essentially physical science'.[52] Far from seeing science and religion as irreconcilable, or from attempting to accommodate her spiritual beliefs to new scientific 'truths', Swiney, like many of her contemporaries, fashioned a creative (if troubling) religio-scientific vision of evolutionary progress.

Comparative religions and the impact of other faiths

Alongside these dialogues between science and religion, we also find various renegotiations of relationships between Christianity and other faiths. Debates over the relative merits of various world religions were, in this period, powerfully shaped by the emergence of the new academic discipline of the comparative study of religions. The 'scientific study of religion' was first defined for an English audience by the philologist Friedrich Max Müller in his *Chips from a German Workshop* (1867).[53] As Jeffrey Franklin argues in his study of Buddhism and Victorian literature, 'comparative religion drew on the historicizing trend that also characterized recent "Higher Criticism" of the Bible and took as its purpose the "scientific" comparative analysis of the origins and evolution of religions'.[54] Max Müller saw his reconstruction of the ancient roots of Hinduism as a corrective to negative portrayals by Christian apologists but even so he – like virtually all scholars in the field at the time – adopted an evolutionary framework, arguing that Christianity corresponded to a higher stage of development than other faiths.[55] As they incorporated the insights drawn from the comparative study of religions into their own versions of 'Eastern' spirituality, British men and women produced new hybrid religions like theosophy or Victorian versions of Buddhism along with a 'partial re-centering of the mythic map of the ancient world from Greece, Palestine, and Rome to India'.[56]

The interest in non-Christian religions ranged widely, from Gnosticism to Egyptology to Kabbalah and Islam (particularly Sufism). Sympathetic British accounts of Islam can be found from the early-nineteenth century, though even its defenders often portrayed it as inferior to Christianity.[57] There were small Muslim communities in Britain from the late-nineteenth century and also a handful of British converts to Islam in the same period, most prominently Abdullah (William H.) Quilliam, a solicitor from the Isle of Man who converted after a visit to Morocco in 1887. Quilliam appears to have been drawn to Islam as a rational (and, by implication, masculine) religion, one that 'harmonised with the emerging values of moderation, balance, self-development, and progress through public service'. Quilliam was ridiculed and vilified, and the mosque he established in Liverpool was the focus of substantial anti-Islamic activity; partly as a result of this hostility the numbers of Muslims, converts or otherwise, remained very low in Britain until after World War II.[58] The impact of Hinduism and Buddhism seems, at least given the current state of the field, to have been much greater. The assimilation of Buddhism and Hinduism into British religious culture was not, however, at all straightforward and the gender dynamics that accompanied that process were equally complex. Theraveda Buddhism, for example, viewed by many late Victorians as a kind of Asiatic Protestantism, was often held up as a manly spirituality, 'a rational tradition that emphasizes self-reliance, tolerance, psychology, and ethics'.[59] Buddhism was also widely believed to be compatible with evolutionary science and the Buddhist concept of Dharma or 'Law' was often linked to scientific law, particularly the laws of evolutionary development.[60] This interpretation of Buddhism was, however, a selective reading of both the historical record and the contemporary situation. The most popular rendering of Buddhism in Britain at this time was Sir Edwin Arnold's *The Light of Asia, Being the Life and Teachings of Gautama, Prince of India and Founder of Buddhism* (1879). Arnold's long poem not only popularised a romanticised Protestant image of the Buddha and an anthropomorphised version of the Dharma but it also made available a version of Buddhism which gave a much more significant place to women and women's concerns than other accounts. Women were given an important role in the Buddha's story, 'not only as comforters and providers but as spiritual guides', while at the same time Arnold 'affirmed certain middle-class values concerning love, domesticity, and mutuality between women and men'.[61] A similar split between a rational, ethical, and somewhat austere version of Buddhism and one that made more concessions to Victorian concerns about immortality and the existence of a loving God can be traced in the work of two of the most prominent Buddhologists of the period, T.W. Rhys Davids and his wife Caroline Rhys Davids. Caroline Rhys Davids, the daughter of an Anglican clergyman, attended University College, London, where she studied psychology and philosophy. She worked in both Sanskrit and Pali, and her earliest scholarship dealt with women in early Buddhism. Where the agnostic T.W. Rhys Davids emphasised the ethical and philosophical dimensions of Buddhism, Caroline Rhys Davids (especially after her husband's death) developed a controversial reading of Buddhism which included a soul, an after-life and a mystical vision of the divine.[62] The assimilation of Buddhism into late-nineteenth- and early-twentieth-century British religious culture, partial and uneven as it was, thus also revealed the historical contingencies which could produce radically different configurations of the relationship between gender and 'other' faiths.

A similar unevenness can be traced in theosophical incorporations of Hinduism. Annie Besant found her way to a kind of Hinduism through theosophy, and a close examination of Besant's case reveals how varied constellations of gender, race and religion were created and naturalised. In 1873, Besant had simultaneously lost her faith in Christianity and left her husband, an Anglican vicar; she joined the National Secular Society in 1874, becoming a prominent speaker for the free-thought movement and, later, a socialist. In 1889 she reviewed Blavatsky's *Secret Doctrine* and underwent a dramatic public conversion to theosophy. Besant linked both her own Irish heritage and her attraction to Indian religions, especially Hinduism, to a racialised understanding of spirituality.[63] From 1893 she spent the bulk of her time and energy in India, claiming it as her true home. Once there she became (in alliance with a conservative Brahman elite) part of the movement for the revival of Hinduism, assimilating herself to Indian culture by wearing a sari, furnishing her home in Indian style and bathing in the Ganges.[64] At the same time she saw the imperial relationship with India in terms of a gendered orientalism, as a kind of marriage in which 'the strong concrete mind of Britain would be permeated and illuminated by the sublime spirituality of India'.[65] She idealised India and claimed literally to embody Indian aspirations, often speaking as an 'Indian' temporarily occupying a western body: 'I went to the West to take up this white body, because it is more useful to India, because it gives me strength to plead, and because it gives more weight to what I say.'[66] Besant used theosophical ideas of reincarnation to affirm and deny her whiteness simultaneously, moving between coloniser and colonised and between masculine/British and feminine/Indian.

Just as the results of the encounter with other faiths were multiple, so too were the gendered ideologies which emerged from these encounters. The theosophist Emily Lutyens, for example, constructed a 'shrine-room' in her home in London where she would sit each morning 'draped in a yellow Indian shawl, burning incense in front of a Crucifix and a statue of the Buddha' before leading her servants and family in more orthodox Anglican prayers.[67] In Lutyens' case, these borrowings were a recognition of the essential oneness of the world's religions (and at the same time an erasure of the important differences between them). An equally complex set of identifications marked Lutyens' feminism which blended eugenic theory with the worship of the 'World Mother' – represented in the past by Isis and Mary and incarnated in the 1920s in the figure of Shrimati Rukmini Devi, the young Brahman wife of the English theosophist George Arundale.[68] Lutyens' encounter with 'eastern religions' – via theosophy, the World Teacher (Krishnamurti) and the World Mother – produced a hybrid spiritual practice which was resolutely, if problematically, feminist.

Spiritual eclecticism could also be used to shore up a renovated Christianity which subsumed and transcended other faiths; it could support an anti-feminist as easily as a feminist attitude. This was the case, for example, in Marie Corelli's idiosyncratic rendering of Christianity, which both incorporated and resisted Buddhist and Hindu concepts alongside occult and scientific ones. Corelli was one of the best-selling authors of her day; her novels sold an average of 100,000 copies a year.[69] Her first novel, *A Romance of Two Worlds* (1886), dealt with the occult; *Ardath* (1889) explored reincarnation; in her trilogy – *Barabbas* (1893), *The Sorrows of Satan* (1895), and *The Master Christian* (1900) – she 'rework[ed] central aspects of the Christian narrative'.[70] Corelli's main targets were materialism, atheism and agnosticism, but she also developed a quasi-scientific religious vocabulary: from 'the electric spirit of Divinity in man' to 'the great Chronometer of the Universe'. At the same time, while insisting that 'my creed has its foundation in Christ alone' and criticising modern spiritualism, occultism and Buddhism as misguided or degenerate, she also rejected that version of Christianity which required 'that God, the Creator of Love and Beauty, could desire a bleeding victim as a sacrifice to appease His anger, and that Victim part of Himself imprisoned in human form'.[71] Corelli's novels were populated with Eastern sages, Arab adepts, and Chaldean scientists; the overall effect, however, was to claim whatever insights emerge from these figures for a renewed Christianity purged of its links to Judaism.[72] Corelli was also an outspoken opponent of the women's suffrage movement and her vision of ideal womanhood – 'exquisite, God-given and sacred' – was profoundly conservative. She provided a provocative re-reading of the story of the Fall in which a self-sacrificing Eve gives Adam 'the juiciest side of the Apple'; women are figured as at once more spiritual than men, primarily responsible for the fall and (through their indulgence of bad male behaviour) the authors of their own social and political marginalisation.[73] The eclectic borrowings which marked this late Victorian religious hybridity produced highly variable results, feminist and anti-feminist as well as colonial and anti-colonial.

The psychology of religions and the new sciences of sexuality

By the early twentieth century scholars in a range of academic disciplines had begun to characterise the religious impulse as a 'perversion' of the sexual impulse. In 1902 the American psychologist of religion, William James, described this as one of the 'many ideas that float in the air of one's time'. James argued, in contrast, that 'few conceptions are less instructive than this re-interpretation of religion as perverted sexuality'.[74] Nevertheless, sexologists and psychologists increasingly took the view that spiritual experience was a form of sexual mania. In *Psychopathia Sexualis*, translated into English in the 1890s, Richard von Krafft-Ebing suggested that the spiritual and the erotic were interchangeable: 'Religious and sexual hyperaesthesia at the zenith of development show the same volume of intensity and the same quality of excitement, and may therefore, under given circumstances, interchange.'[75] In 1899 Havelock Ellis published the first edition of his study of 'auto-erotism' in which he included an exploration of 'The Auto-Erotic Factor in Religion'.[76] Ellis endorsed Krafft-Ebing's findings, and cited recent studies which had reached similar conclusions. Throughout Ellis' work – and the work of other early sexologists – numerous case studies illustrated the 'intimacy' of sexual and religious complexes.

Even though William James rejected the equation of religion with 'perverted sexuality' his own re-formulation of the definition of religion in *The Varieties of Religious Experience* (1902) helped open up this possibility. According to James, religion could be defined as *'the feelings, acts, and experiences of individual men in the solitude, so far as they apprehend themselves to stand in relation to whatever they consider the divine'*.[77] James' definition, as Ann Taves has pointed out, 'constituted "religious experience" in a technical sense as an object of study', abstracting it from particular religious traditions and 'linking these diverse experiences together theoretically by means of the experimental psychology of the subconscious'.[78] By privileging interior states – rather than doctrine, institutional organisation or ritual practice – James contributed not just to the psychology of religion but also to its psychologisation, the ultimate privatisation of piety. One result of that process in the twentieth century has been the flourishing of what Paul Heelas has described as 'Self-spirituality' in new religious movements.[79] This shift could also serve to discourage 'modern mystics': the emphasis on religious psychology provided resources for a more 'scientific' mysticism (by explaining it), but it also threatened the basis of religious experience itself (by explaining it away).

The psychologisation of religion appears to have affected women more than men, in large part because of precisely those long-standing links between femininity, religious mania and hysteria which underpinned sexological and psychological writing on sexuality and religion. Evelyn Underhill was one of those who attempted to use the insights of the psychology of religion to shore up her generation's wavering faith. As a young woman Underhill was hostile to institutional religion; her early religious sympathies were deist rather than Christian. She was at one point a member of the Hermetic Order of the Golden Dawn but was increasingly drawn to Roman Catholicism. The papal denunciation of religious modernism left her in a spiritual quandary: she believed Roman Catholicism to be the true church and yet she felt that she could not convert without betraying her modernist convictions. In 1921 she joined the Anglican Church and placed herself under the spiritual direction of the modernist lay Catholic theologian Friedrich von Hügel.[80] Underhill was one of the most prominent Anglican lay-women of her day – an author, popular spiritual director and a pioneer in the Anglican retreat movement. In her first major work, *Mysticism* (1911), Underhill defined her approach as 'avowedly psychological' and set as her goal the development of 'a definite theory of the nature of man's mystical consciousness'.[81] She wanted to develop a psychology of mysticism which did not reduce 'all the abnormal perceptions of contemplative genius to hysteria or other disease'.[82] In the early 1920s, Underhill experienced her own 'rapture' in which she believed that she had literally heard the voice of God. She was, however, immediately overwhelmed by doubt: '[I have a] terrible overwhelming suspicion that after all my whole "invisible experience" may only be subjective ... *how* am I to know for certain this is not just some psychic mechanism? There are times when I wish I had never heard of psychology.'[83] Underhill turned away from an emphasis on direct spiritual experience and stressed instead the centrality of the institutional church, which, she suggested, 'corrects subjectivism'.[84] In her later works the emphasis on 'experience' was entirely replaced by a focus on ritual, liturgy and institutional religion, precisely the areas of male privilege and power in the church.

This was not an inevitable outcome and the impact of the new psychology was very different within movements such as those discussed in Alex Owen's *The Place of Enchantment: British Occultism and the Culture of the Modern* (2004). In *fin-de-siècle* magic, such as that of the Hermetic Order of the Golden Dawn, we find 'a new spirituality that was instrinsically bound up with the self-conscious exploration of personal interiority and the modern drive towards self-realization'.[85] The Golden Dawn, founded in the late 1880s, was a secret and hierarchical order associated with occult Freemasonry. Initiates 'knew from personal experience that ceremonial ritual, the harmonious combination of sacred words or phrases with secret gestures and commands, could produce an extraordinary inner (psychological, emotional, or spiritual) change in the participant'.[86] The theory of mind developed within the Golden Dawn and similar movements rejected the purely secular understanding of consciousness but remained in dialogue with it: occultists insisted on the significance of the 'irrational' in human consciousness even as they resisted 'the modern association of spirituality with irrationality'.[87] In the Golden Dawn, which was largely though not exclusively male, we find a self-consciously virile sense of subjectivity which reconfigured relationships between secular and sacred, objective and subjective, and masculine and feminine in distinctive ways.

Conclusions

There is much that we still do not know about the transformations of both spiritual and secular cultures in this period. As Jeffrey Cox noted almost a generation ago, we simply do not know enough yet about the history of the relationship between gender and religious belief and practice. The extent of the actual 'feminisation' (whatever that might mean) of either Anglicanism or nonconformity still remains unclear.[88] We thus need much more work in order to establish to what extent the experiences of women like Underhill were 'gendered'; this will also require a more explicit attention to the history of masculinity. In 1886, Frederic Myers, of the Society for Psychical Research, wrote that 'the *emotional* creed of educated men is becoming divorced from their *scientific* creed'.[89] Myers implicitly framed the 'crisis of faith' as a crisis for educated men in particular and while this is much too narrow a frame in which to consider these questions, we do need to be more aware of the role of gender in *men's* experience of both faith and doubt.[90]

The historical literature – with the notable exception of work on spiritualism – also remains dominated by the concerns of educated, middle-class men and women. We need to know more about the ways that working-class people negotiated 'religious' concerns and how these were or were not framed within their communities. This means a refusal of 'the language of conventional church historical analysis'[91] and renewed attention to forms of spiritual practice which may exceed or overlap the categories through which we have been accustomed to view them. We also need to be prepared to abandon our assumptions about chronology and the direction of historical causality. As Richard Dellamora puts it in his discussion of Radclyffe Hall's use of Catholic and sexological imagery, 'This religious discourse of sexual difference stands in complex, ambivalent, often resistant relationship to sexological discourse. Chronologically, it can precede, parallel, dialogue with, and contest the truths of emergent sexology.'[92] The point is to rethink our assumptions about the analytic priority we give to 'secularising' trends and to remain open to less easily summarised trajectories in which 'secular' and 'spiritual' remain in dialogue.

At the very least it is clear that the 'crisis' produced not the collapse but the transformation and ongoing adaptation of faith(s). It also seems clear that the language of 'faith' and 'doubt' – like the vocabulary of 'disenchantment' or 'secularisation' itself – is inadequate to the complexities of the process it seeks to describe. If, as Alex Owen puts it, 'the "new" occultism was one manifestation of a secularizing process', and if that secularising process 'spells neither the inevitable decline nor the irreconcilable loss of significant religious beliefs and behaviors in a modern age' then what does it signify? Owen draws our attention to the parallel process by which there has been, since the 1890s, 'an adjustment to an Enlightenment model of rationality and autonomous rational "man"'. In the later nineteenth century a number of important European figures began to focus their attention on the irrational, on those areas of human life which appeared to defy conscious control. From Marx's exploration of the irrationalities of advanced capitalism to Freud's unravelling of the coherent 'ego' and the critique of rationalism in the work of philosophers like Nietzsche and Bergson, we can trace 'a modern reworking of the Romantic tradition' that 'stood in stark contrast with the presumptions of abstract rationalism and the disillusionment of disenchantment'. As Owen concludes, it is precisely the 'unresolved tension between the spiritual and the secular' which marks this period.[93]

All of the movements I have discussed here were, in some sense, outside the mainstream of late-nineteenth- and early-twentieth-century religious life. They are also precisely those movements which are often characterised as 'secular religions' and so perhaps they might be expected to display precisely these kinds of slippages and boundary-crossings. At the same time, however, the complicated histories of these movements remind us of the contingent nature of what otherwise appear to be the natural and inevitable formations of 'secular man' and 'spiritual woman'. We cannot understand the role of gender in the process of secularisation so long as we assume that we know in advance what 'secularisation' (or, for that matter, 'spirituality') looks like; as Joan Scott has argued, we must 'problematize and historicize the categories (among them "gender") that are our objects of study, as well as those we deploy in our own analyses'.[94] As I have argued elsewhere, 'the links between the private, the spiritual, and the feminine ... were actually historical rather than natural phenomena'.[95] By focusing on the historical processes through which these links were consolidated we can see the extent to which contradictory understandings of each of these domains competed with each other, a process which can be obscured by a too-easy reliance on formulations which naturalise these connections. In the various engagements with modernity traced here we can see the making – and unmaking – of the connections between femininity and various and competing versions of 'religion' and the private.

Further reading

H.G. Cocks, 'Religion and Spirituality', in H. G. Cocks and Matt Houlbrook (eds), *Palgrave Advances in the Modern History of Sexuality* (New York: Palgrave Macmillan, 2006), pp. 157–79.

Joanna Dean, *Religious Experience and the New Woman: The Life of Lily Dougall* (Bloomington and Indianapolis: Indiana University Press, 2007).

Joy Dixon, *Divine Feminine: Theosophy and Feminism in England* (Baltimore: Johns Hopkins University Press, 2001).

J. Jeffrey Franklin, *The Lotus and the Lion: Buddhism and the British Empire* (Ithaca: Cornell University Press, 2008).

Lowell Gallagher, Frederick S. Roden and Patricia Juliana Smith (eds), *Catholic Figures, Queer Narratives* (New York: Palgrave Macmillan, 2007).

Jenny Hazelgrove, *Spiritualism and British Society Between the Wars* (Manchester and New York: Manchester University Press, 2000).

Janet Oppenheim, *The Other World: Spiritualism and Psychical Research in England, 1850–1914* (Cambridge: Cambridge University Press, 1985).

Alex Owen, *The Darkened Room: Women, Power and Spiritualism in Late Victorian England* (London: Virago Press Limited, 1989).

——, *The Place of Enchantment: British Occultism and the Culture of the Modern* (Chicago and London: University of Chicago Press, 2004).

Frederick S. Roden, *Same-Sex Desire in Victorian Religious Culture* (New York: Palgrave Macmillan, 2002).

Marlene Tromp, *Altered States: Sex, Nation, Drugs, and Self-Transformation in Victorian Spiritualism* (Albany: State University of New York Press, 2006).

Notes

1 Callum Brown, *The Death of Christian Britain* (London: Routledge, 2001), p. 11.
2 Callum Brown, 'The Secularisation Decade: What the 1960s have Done to the Study of Religious History', in Hugh McLeod and Werner Ustorf (eds), *The Decline of Christendom in Western Europe, 1750–2000* (Cambridge University Press, 2003), p. 36; Jeremy Morris, 'The Strange Death of Christian Britain: Another Look at the Secularization Debate', *The Historical Journal* 46, 4 (2003), p. 975.
3 See Alan D. Gilbert, *Religion and Society in Industrial England: Church, Chapel and Social Change, 1740–1914* (London and New York: Longman, 1976), pp. 23–48. The most significant declines in church membership occurred in the 1960s and 1970s. Hugh McLeod, *Religion and the People of Western Europe, 1789–1970* (Oxford and New York: Oxford University Press, 1981), pp. 134–43.
4 Brown, 'The Secularisation Decade', p. 39.
5 Brown, *Death*, pp. 9, 35–39, 58–59.
6 Brown, *Death*, pp. 30–31. See also Morris 'Strange Death of Christian Britain', p. 969; Brown, 'The Secularisation Decade', p. 38.
7 Ann Braude, 'Women's History *Is* American Religious History', in Thomas Tweed (ed.), *Retelling US Religious History* (Berkeley and Los Angeles: University of California Press, 1997), p. 96.
8 Joan Scott, *Gender and the Politics of History* (rev. edn; New York: Columbia University Press, 1999), pp. 206–7, 218.
9 Mark Knight and Emma Mason, *Nineteenth-Century Religion and Literature: An Introduction* (Oxford: Oxford University Press, 2006), pp. 3, 179–80.
10 H. G. Cocks, 'Religion and Spirituality', in H. G. Cocks and Matt Houlbrook (eds), *Palgrave Advances in the Modern History of Sexuality* (New York: Palgrave Macmillan, 2006), p. 158.
11 Michael Saler, 'Modernity and Enchantment: A Historiographic Review', *American Historical Review* (June 2006), pp. 694–95.
12 The material covered here ranges widely but the central dialogue was still between various versions of Christianity and their (post-Christian) critics. Religious Britain was, at least until the second half of the twentieth century, still dominated by Christianity and even the emergence of hybrid religions like theosophy was shaped by implicitly post-Christian concerns.
13 Barbara Taylor, *Eve and the New Jerusalem: Socialism and Feminism in the Nineteenth Century* (London: Virago Press Limited, 1983), p. 126.
14 On the complexities of evangelical teachings on manliness (and the extent to which men who were 'serious Christians' could be seen as risking masculine identity) see Leonore Davidoff and Catherine Hall, *Family Fortunes: Men and Women of the English Middle Class, 1780–1850* (London: Hutchinson Education, 1987), pp. 108–13, esp. p. 111.
15 Elisabeth Jay, *Faith and Doubt in Victorian Britain* (London: Macmillan Education Limited, 1986), pp. 113–26.
16 Joanna Dean, *Religious Experience and the New Woman: The Life of Lily Dougall* (Bloomington and Indianapolis: Indiana University Press, 2007), pp. 47–48.
17 Strauss characterised Christ's divinity as a 'myth', arguing that its mythic status did not diminish its significance. See Knight and Mason, pp. 74, 131.

18 As Julie Melnyk notes, religious writing by women in the nineteenth century 'encompasses a wide range of purposes, topics, and genres', much of it not specifically 'theological'. Julie Melnyk, 'Victorian Religious Women Writers and Communal Identities', *Australasian Victorian Studies Journal* 10 (2004), p. 72. For women like Mary Ward and Lily Dougall (see below) their substantive engagements with scholarly literature and debate in theology sets them apart from women religious writers more generally. See Christiana de Groot and Marion Ann Taylor, 'Recovering Women's Voices in the History of Biblical Interpretation', in Christiana de Groot and Marion Ann Taylor (eds), *Recovering Nineteenth-Century Women Interpreters of the Bible* (Atlanta: Society of Biblical Literature, 2007), p. 10.

19 Mark M. Freed, 'The Moral Irrelevance of Dogma: Mary Ward and Critical Theology in England', in Julie Melnyk (ed.), *Women's Theology in Nineteenth-Century Britain: Transfiguring the Faith of Their Fathers* (New York and London: Garland Publishing, Inc., 1998), pp. 133–34, 138–40.

20 Joanna Dean, *Religious Experience and the New Woman*, pp. 3, 7.

21 See Oliver S. Buckton, '"An Unnatural State": Gender, "Perversion", and Newman's "Apologia Pro Vita Sua"', *Victorian Studies* 35, 4 (Summer 1992), pp. 359–83.

22 Richard Dellamora, '*The Well of Loneliness* and the Catholic Rhetoric of Sexual Dissidence', in Lowell Gallagher, Frederick S. Roden and Patricia Juliana Smith (eds), *Catholic Figures, Queer Narratives* (New York: Palgrave Macmillan, 2007), p. 117. Dellamora is summarising Frederick S. Roden's argument in *Same-Sex Desire in Victorian Religious Culture* (New York: Palgrave Macmillan, 2002).

23 Roden, *Same-Sex Desire*, pp. 35, 44, 47, 56. Rossetti characterised 'Goblin Market' as a secular text. See Julie Melnyk, '"Mighty Victims": Women Writers and the Feminization of Christ', *Victorian Literature and Culture* (2003), p. 147.

24 Amanda W. Benckhuysen, 'The Prophetic Voice of Christina Rossetti', in de Groot and Taylor (eds), *Recovering*, pp. 165–80.

25 See Frederick S. Roden, 'Introduction: the Catholic Modernist Crisis, Queer Modern Catholicisms', in Gallagher, Roden and Smith (eds), *Catholic Figures*, p. 1.

26 Roden, *Same-Sex Desire*, p. 198.

27 Martha Vicinus, *Intimate Friends: Women Who Loved Women, 1778–1928* (Chicago and London: University of Chicago Press, 2004), p. 101.

28 Dellamora, '*The Well of Loneliness*', pp. 124, 127–28.

29 Michael E. Schiefelbein, *The Lure of Babylon: Seven Protestant Novelists and Britain's Roman Catholic Revival* (Mercer University Press: 2001), p. 182.

30 This is an over-simplification of a complex literature. For a useful overview, see Knight and Mason, *Nineteenth-Century Religion and Literatures*, pp. 161–62. Some Calvinists did find ways to accommodate evolutionary theory. See David N. Livingstone, 'Darwinism and Calvinism: The Belfast–Princeton Connection', *Isis* 83, 3 (September 1992), pp. 422ff.

31 Jeffrey Cox, *The English Churches in a Secular Society: Lambeth, 1870–1930* (New York: Oxford University Press, 1982), p. 266. Spiritualists tended (not always accurately) to associate modern science with materialism, and both with the denial of 'the assertion that spirit exists and functions in the universe as surely as matter'. See Janet Oppenheim, *The Other World: Spiritualism and Psychical Research in England, 1850–1914* (Cambridge: Cambridge University Press, 1985), p. 2.

32 Ann Braude, *Radical Spirits: Spiritualism and Women's Rights in Nineteenth-Century America* (Boston: Beacon Press, 1989).

33 Alex Owen, *The Darkened Room: Women, Power and Spiritualism in Late Victorian England* (London: Virago Press Limited, 1989), pp. 25, 38–39.

34 Geoffrey K. Nelson, *Spiritualism and Society* (London: Routledge & Kegan Paul Ltd, 1969), p. 259.

35 S. C. Hall, *The Use of Spiritualism?* (London: E. W. Allen, 1884), p. 6; quoted in Oppenheim, *The Othes World*, p. 63.

36 Marlene Tromp, 'Spirited Sexuality: Sex, Marriage, and Victorian Spiritualism', *Victorian Literature and Culture* (2003), p. 67.

37 Owen, *Darkened Room*, pp. 1, 4, 8.

38 Molly McGarry, 'Spectral Sexualities: Nineteenth-Century Spiritualism, Moral Panics, and the Making of U.S. Obscenity Law', *Journal of Women's History* 12, 2 (Summer 2000), p. 14.

39 Owen, *Darkened Room*, pp. 42–52, esp. 48; see also Oppenheim, pp. 16–21.

40 Tromp, 'Spirited Sexuality', pp. 70, 73.

41 Marlene Tromp, *Altered States: Sex, Nation, Drugs, and Self-Transformation in Victorian Spiritualism* (Albany: State University of New York Press, 2006), p. 77.

42 Owen, *Darkened Room*, p. 11.

43 Jenny Hazelgrove, *Spiritualism and British Society Between the Wars* (Manchester and New York: Manchester University Press, 2000), p. 23.

44 Hazelgrove, *Spiritualism and British Society*, pp. 163, 276–77. There has been little research on spiritualism in Britain after World War II. Geoffrey Nelson suggested in 1969 that war conditions, increased police persecution, and the failure of the spirits to predict the course of the war combined to cause the movement's decline. Nelson, *Spiritualism and Society*, pp. 162–67.

45 [Susan E. Gay], 'The Future of Women', *Lucifer* (October 1890), pp. 116–22.

46 Dixon, *Divine Feminine: Theosophy and Feminism in England* (Baltimore: Johns Hopkins University Press, 2001), p. 174.

47 Dixon, *Divine Feminine*, p. xiii.

48 Dixon, *Divine Feminine*, p. 90.

49 Dixon, *Divine Feminine*, pp. 5–6.

50 See for example Gauri Viswanathan's discussion of theosophy and race theory in *Outside the Fold: Conversion, Modernity, and Belief* (Princeton: Princeton University Press, 1998), pp. 177–207.

51 Dixon, *Divine Feminine*, pp. 167–72.

52 George Robb, 'Between Science and Spiritualism: Frances Swiney's Vision of a Sexless Future', *Diogenes* 208 (2005), pp. 163–64, 168.

53 Clinton Bennett, *In Search of the Sacred: Anthropology and the Study of Religions* (New York and London: Cassell, 1996), p. 19.

54 J. Jeffrey Franklin, *The Lotus and the Lion: Buddhism and the British Empire* (Ithaca: Cornell University Press, 2008), p. 27.

55 Bennett, *In Search of the Sacred*, p. 46.

56 Franklin, *The Lotus and the Lion*, p. 87.

57 Thomas Prasch, 'Which God for Africa: The Islamic–Christian Missionary Debate in Late-Victorian England', *Victorian Studies* 33, 1 (Autumn 1989), pp. 55–56.

58 Humayun Ansari, *'The Infidel Within': Muslims in Britain since 1800* (London: Hurst & Company, 2004), pp. 82, 124–25.

59 Thomas A. Tweed, *The American Encounter with Buddhism, 1844–1912: Victorian Culture and the Limits of Dissent* (Bloomington: Indiana University Press, 1992), p. 63. On Buddhism as Asian Protestantism, see Franklin, *The Lotus and the Lion*, p. 20.

60 Franklin, *The Lotus and the Lion*, p. 27.

61 Ibid, pp. 34, 43, 47.

62 Susan Thach Dean, 'Decadence, Evolution, and Will: Caroline Rhys Davids' "Original" Buddhism', in Melnyk (ed.), *Women's Theology*, pp. 209–10, 213–14, 223–25.

63 Dixon, *Divine Feminine*, pp. 45–46, 57–58.

64 Nancy Fix Anderson, 'Bridging Cross-cultural Feminisms: Annie Besant and Women's Rights in England and India, 1874–1933', *Women's History Review* 3, 4 (1994), pp. 567, 571–73.

65 Annie Besant, *Apart or Together?* (Madras: National Home Rule League, n.d.), pp. 5, 7.

66 Annie Besant, *Home Rule and the Empire: New India Political Pamphlets* No. 13 (Adyar: Commonwealth Office, 1917), pp. 15–16.

67 Mary Lutyens, *To Be Young* (London: Rupert Hart-Davis, 1959), p. 16.

68 See Joy Dixon, 'Ancient Wisdom, Modern Motherhood: Theosophy and the Colonial Syncretic', in Antoinette Burton (ed.), *Gender, Sexuality and Colonial Modernities* (London: Routledge, 1999), pp. 193–206.

69 Franklin, *The Lotus and the Lion*, p. 89.

70 Knight and Mason, *Nineteenth Century Religion and Literature*, p. 207.

71 Marie Corelli, 'Introduction to the New Edition', *A Romance of Two Worlds* (1886; 2nd edn; New York and Boston: H. M. Caldwell Company, [1887]), pp. 5, 9, 11–13.

72 Jill Galvan, 'Christians, Infidels, and Women's Channeling in the Writings of Marie Corelli', *Victorian Literature and Culture* (2003), pp. 87–88.

73 Marie Corelli, *Woman, or – Suffragette? A Question of National Choice* (Privately Printed, 1907), pp. 5, 16–17.

74 William James, *The Varieties of Religious Experience* (1902; New York: Macmillan Publishing Company, 1961), p. 28.

75 Richard von Krafft-Ebing, *Psychopathia Sexualis*, trans. Franklin S. Klaf from the 12th German edition (New York: Bell Publishing Company, Inc., 1965), p. 6.

76 Havelock Ellis, 'Appendix C: The Auto-Erotic Factor in Religion', *Auto-Erotism*, in *Studies in the Psychology of Sex* Vol. I, Part I (3rd edn; New York: Random House, 1942), pp. 310–25.

77 James, *Varieties*, p. 42. Emphasis in original.

78 Ann Taves, *Fits, Trances, & Visions: Experiencing Religion and Explaining Experience from Wesley to James* (Princeton: Princeton University Press, 1999), p. 271.

79 Paul Heelas, *The New Age Movement: The Celebration of the Self and the Sacralization of Modernity* (Oxford: Blackwell Publishers Ltd, 1996), p. 2.

80 See Dana Greene, *Evelyn Underhill: Artist of the Infinite Life* (New York: The Crossroad Publishing Company, 1990).

81 Evelyn Underhill, *Mysticism: The Development of Humankind's Spiritual Consciousness* (1911; 12th edn, 1930; London: Bracken Books, 1996), p. xiv.

82 Underhill, *Mysticism*, p. 58.

83 E. Underhill, Report to F. von Hügel, June 1923, Underhill Collection, St Andrews University Special Collections, St. Andrews, Scotland, ms 5552, p. 46.

84 Evelyn Underhill, *The Life of the Spirit and the Life of Today* (1922; Harrisburg, PA: Morehouse Publishing, 1994), p. 125.

85 Alex Owen, *The Place of Enchantment: British Occultism and the Culture of the Modern* (Chicago and London: University of Chicago Press, 2004), p. 13.

86 Owen, *Place of Enchantment*, p. 74.

87 Owen, *Place of Enchantment*, pp. 114, 146.

88 Cox, *English Churches*, pp. 25–27, 35.

89 Frederic W. H. Myers, 'Introduction' to Edmund Gurney, Frederic W. H. Myers, and Frank Podmore, *Phantasms of the Living* (London: Trübner and Co., 1886), p. liv.

90 The flourishing literature on the 'queering' of Roman and Anglo-Catholicism in this period constitutes a significant exception to this general neglect.

91 Morris, *Strange Death of Christian Britain*, p. 967; the comment appears in a discussion of Sarah Williams, *Religious Belief and Popular Culture in Southwark, c. 1880–1939* (Oxford: Oxford University Press, 1999). See Williams' contribution to this volume for a compelling example of this approach.

92 Dellamora, '*The Well of Loneliness*', p. 114.

93 Owen, *Place of Enchantment*, pp. 11, 246–47, 257.

94 Scott, *Gender and the Politics of History*, p. 218.

95 Dixon, *Divine Feminine*, pp. 67–68.

Afterword

Women, gender and the re-imagining of a 'post-Christian' Britain

Sue Morgan and Jacqueline deVries

We began this collection of essays with a number of leading questions. In what ways did women create and develop their own diverse religious cultures? How did Britain's heterogeneous religious cultures shape women's beliefs and practices? To what extent were women's faith and beliefs differentiated by their gender, class, national identity, sexuality and denominational affiliation? And what were women's contributions to the making of modern British cultures of belief? The preceding chapters have evidenced the sheer diversity and richness of the recent 'religious turn' in history and the significance of gender as a methodological tool in eliciting new ways of reading the spiritual and the secular. While this collection has been concerned primarily with nineteenth- and early twentieth-century developments, our questions and approaches also offer a framework for recasting discussions of mid- to late-twentieth-century trends.

The place of religion in Britain's social and cultural landscape after 1940 is emerging as one of the salient historiographical debates of our time. New scholarship on the definitions, timing, meaning and causes of secularisation have challenged old master narratives and overturned assumptions that religion and modernity are fundamentally incompatible.[1] As Jeffrey Cox has recently pointed out, 'religion in general, including Christianity, is now seen as not only compatible with modernity, but as in some contexts a species of modernity'.[2] Evidence for this assertion is not hard to find in Britain's cities, where churches and chapels might be sparsely attended, but mosques, synagogues, home-based congregations, and sectarian alternatives draw in crowds.[3]

Since the late nineteenth century, Britain's status as a 'Protestant nation' has diminished, as Catholic immigrants from Ireland and elsewhere reached parity in numbers to Protestants. By the 1950s, Britain's identity as a 'Christian nation' was also undergoing revision. The post-World War II decades may have appeared as a mono-cultural era of Christian family values (in 1956, British church membership rose to its highest levels ever and thousands flocked to Wembley stadium in 1954–55 to hear the US evangelist Billy Graham), but the increasing presence and growth of Jewish, Muslim, Hindu and other non-Christian sectarian communities challenged any easy assumption that Britain remained a predominantly Christian nation. In the last fifty years, a multiplicity of global political and social shifts – decline of empire, patterns of immigration, changing family and employment trends, consumerism and affluence – have contributed to both new patterns of church-going as well as new ideational frameworks. Yet whether these developments amount to the 'death of God', as Steve Bruce has suggested, is still an open question.[4]

Women, along with their gender identities and sexual lives, have been named as key protagonists in such debates. Now approaching the status of historiographical neo-orthodoxy is Callum Brown's argument that the 1960s were pivotal to the death of Christian Britain. In what some scholars have dubbed the 'Big Bang' account, Brown proposed that during the 1960s discursive constructions of Christianity, as expressed through print, speech and personal morality, 'really quite suddenly' began to rupture. Young women, he argued, were central to this process.[5] As birth control and second-wave feminism offered women the possibility of greater sexual freedom and personal expression, church-going rates – which historically had been propped up by women – plummeted. Hugh McLeod has since countered this argument by asserting that although the 'drive for greater individual freedom' did seem to accelerate during this decade, as did women's interest in breaking free of circumscribed gender roles, 'the religious revolution of the Sixties did not come as a bolt from the blue'.[6] Several chapters in this collection similarly underscore the assertion that changing attitudes towards sex, authority, happiness and the meaning of life were longer-term trends with roots in the late nineteenth century and before.

Whether women have renewed and revivified religion or caused its demise, therefore, remains a contested point. First-wave feminism may well have contributed to the decline of organised religion, as women left conservative churches to join more accommodationist traditions like the Quakers and Unitarians and began to reject centuries of misogynistic religious teaching. Second-wave feminism brought with it a host of new but also familiar trends, as women once again challenged religious traditions that had changed little over the twentieth century.[7] As these chapters have demonstrated, however, women have consistently contributed to the revitalisation and re-imagining of the cultures of faith in which they found themselves, despite confronting a series of breathtaking ideological, theological and practical barriers to equality with men in institutional forms of religion.

The questions posed in this volume focusing on women's historical agency might be fruitfully applied to the rich set of available materials for the post-war period. Women have continued to participate actively in voluntary associations with religious affiliations, for example, throughout the late twentieth century. The Anglican Mothers' Union (1876–present), the League of Jewish Women (1943–present) and the Union of Jewish Women (1902–76) may not have been overtly political organisations but they have certainly contributed to the plurality and breadth of feminist concerns. Similarly, as Jessica Thurlow has argued, the St Joan's Social and Political Alliance (1923–present), successor to the Catholic Women's Suffrage Society, may have espoused a more conservative form of feminism than its Protestant counterparts, yet it continually stressed that equality was intrinsic to Christian thought and brought that message to Catholics around the globe.[8] The degree to which religion continued as a concern within mid-century feminist organisations such as the Six-Point Group and the Women's Freedom League has yet to be examined, as does the question of how non-Judeo-Christian women's groups are shaping their respective traditions.

Women's entrance into religious ministry on equal terms with men is, surprisingly, one of the most underexplored stories of twentieth-century gender and women's history. As Pamela Walker asks in her essay in this collection, how did female preachers like Constance Coltman reshape the nature and perception of ministry? And, conversely, in what ways did the churches' resistance to female leadership shape perceptions about organised religion at a time when public opinion about women's roles was changing dramatically and when women were entering virtually all other educational and professional fields? While the Congregational and United Free Churches ordained women in the 1920s and 1930s, the Anglican Church held out until the 1990s, despite significant pressure to do otherwise. When Ronald O. Hall, Bishop of Hong Kong and South China, ordained Chinese Deaconess Florence Li Tim Oi to the priesthood in January 1944 in response to a severe shortage of male candidates, he faced swift censure.[9] Once the beneficiary of an expansive Broad Church tradition, Anglicanism had begun to appear fairly reactionary by the late 1950s. So, too, did the Church of Scotland, which did not admit women as elders and ministers until 1968, even though its American counterpart, the Presbyterian Church of the United States, began ordaining women a decade and a half earlier.[10]

As women entered ministerial and university posts teaching theology, their voices took on a new authority. In contrast to the tentative and clandestine theological musings chronicled by Julie Melnyk, late-twentieth-century women theologians boldly and publicly built upon and deepened women's earlier critiques of androcentric religious traditions. Since the 1970s, feminist theologians and post-Christian writers like Mary Daly, Rosemary Radford Reuther and Daphne Hampson have contributed to a panoramic array of new ways to imagine the divine.[11] They and others have helped to legitimise feminist goddess spirituality, which celebrates the goodness of the female body and will, and to introduce variants of Christian feminism such as Thealogy, which endeavours 'to begin its reflection in a space beyond patriarchal religion'.[12] From the perspective of orthodox Christianity, feminist theology might appear divisive and secular but, from the standpoint of its adherents, it offers an opportunity to explore spirituality outside the confines of a male-dominated tradition. It is noteworthy that British feminist historiography has yet to fully incorporate women's theological discourses into its canon of constitutive elements of gender formation.

Although this volume has been primarily concerned with the relationship of women, gender, religion and the making of modernity, the rupture of post-modernity brings with it new interpretive challenges. Yet, as the contributors to *Redefining Christian Britain: Post-1945 Perspectives* have forcefully argued, Christianity has neither disappeared nor even declined; rather, it has been 'transmuted' and 'reinvented'.[13] Christianity is a 'liquid religion', they assert, 'shaping itself to fit the society that contained it'.[14] Similar claims might be made about Britain's other religious formations. If we are to fully understand the shifting relationship between religion and (post)modernity in all its diverse forms, we must not only incorporate gender and sexuality as analytical categories, but do so in a way that acknowledges the full array of women's agency and influence – that is, to acknowledge how religion *and* gender have 'been constitutive rather than merely reflective of either continuity or change'.[15]

Notes

1 One of the most sustained analyses can be found in Jane Garnett, Matthew Grimley, Alana Harris, William Whyte and Sarah Williams (eds), *Redefining Christian Britain: Post 1945 Perspectives* (London: SCM, 2006).
2 Jeffrey Cox, 'Provincializing Christendom: The Case of Great Britain', *Church History* 75:1 (March 2006), p. 123.
3 See Nigel Scotland, *Sectarian Religion in Contemporary Britain* (Carlisle: Paternoster Press, 2000). For more analysis of mainstream denominations, see Keith Robbins, *England, Ireland, Scotland, Wales: The Christian Church, 1900–2000* (Oxford: Oxford University Press, 2008). For trends among Catholics, see Alana Harris, 'Gatherings at the Family Table: Transformations in Catholic Christology and Popular Religiosity in Britain, 1945–80', in Patrick Pasture (ed.), *Households of Faith* (University of Leuven, forthcoming 2010).
4 Steve Bruce, *God is Dead: Secularization in the West* (Oxford: Blackwell, 2002).
5 Callum G. Brown, *The Death of Christian Britain* (London: Routledge, 2002).
6 Hugh McLeod, 'The Religious Crisis of the 1960s', *Journal of Modern European History* 3:2 (2005), p. 210. For a fuller account of this argument, see his *The Religious Crisis of the 1960s* (Oxford: Oxford University Press, 2007). Other views include Gerald Parsons, 'How the Times They Were A-changing: Exploring the Context of Religious Transformation in Britain in the 1960s' in John Wolffe (ed.), *Religion in History: Conflict, Conversion and Coexistence* (Manchester: Manchester University Press, 2004), pp. 161–89.
7 For one study see Jenny Daggers, *The British Christian Women's Movement: A Rehabilitation of Eve* (Aldershot, England and Burlington, VT: Ashgate Publishing, 2002).
8 Jessica B. Thurlow, *Continuity and Change in British Feminism, ca. 1940–1960* (unpublished dissertation Ann Arbor: University of Michigan, 2006), p. 445.
9 For some excellent research on this episode, see Thurlow, ch. 7.
10 C. Brown, 'Religion' in *Gender in Scottish History Since 1700* (eds), Lynn Abrams, Eleanor Gordon, Deborah Simonton and Eileen Yeo (Edinburgh: Edinburgh University Press, 2006).
11 Theresa Elwes, *Women's Voices: Essays in Contemporary Feminist Theology* (Basingstoke: Marshall Pickering, 1992).
12 Lisa Isherwood and Elizabeth Stuart, *Introducing Body Theology* (Sheffield: University of Sheffield Press, 1998), p. 79.
13 Garnett et al *Redefining Christian Britain*, p. 289.
14 Garnett et al *Redefining Christian Britain*, p. 291.
15 Alexandra Shepherd and Garthine Walker, 'Gender, Change and Periodisation', *Gender & History* 20:3 (November 2008), p. 457.

Index